# MACHINES THAT
# BECOME US

# James E. Katz
### editor

# MACHINES THAT
# BECOME US

## The Social Context of
## Personal Communication Technology

Transaction Publishers
New Brunswick (U.S.A.) and London (U.K.)

Fourth paperback printing 2009
Copyright © 2003 by Transaction Publishers, New Brunswick, New Jersey.

This book is printed on acid-free paper that meets the American National Standard for Permanence of Paper for Printed Library Materials.

Library of Congress Catalog Number: 2002075687
ISBN: 978-0-7658-0158-6 (cloth); 978-1-4128-0621-3 (paper)
Printed in the United States of America

Library of Congress Cataloging-in-Publication Data

Machines that become us : the social context of personal communication
  technology / James E. Katz, editor.
        p. cm.
  Based on selected papers from a conference held at Rutgers University
on April 18-19, 2001.
  Includes bibliographical references and index.
  ISBN 0-7658-0158-2 (cloth: alk. paper); 1-4128-0621-3 (pbk. : alk.
  paper)
        1. Information society—Congresses.  2. Telecommunication—Social
  aspects—Congresses.  3.   Information technology—Social aspects—
  Congresses. I. Katz, James Everett.

HM851.M33   2002
303.48'33—dc21                                             2002075687

For Oscar H. Gandy, Jr.

"An inherited timidity and melancholy, when she was brought face to face with any object unknown to her fathers, prevented Françoise from approaching a telephone receiver, although she would readily visit a person suffering from a contagious disease."

Marcel Proust, *Remembrance of Things Past: The Captive*

"If I'm such a legend, then why am I so lonely? If I'm such a legend, then why do I sit at home for hours staring at the damned telephone, hoping it's out of order, even calling the operator asking her if she's sure it's not out of order?"

Judy Garland, *Stardom*

# Contents

# Preface

The quaint Midwestern town I grew up in seemed to have been plunked down, whole and immutable, in the middle of a vast farmland quilt. From its compact downtown, a vista of unbroken cornfields stretched in every direction, sealed hermetically at the distant horizon by a brilliant azure bowl of a sky. Throughout the summer, the prairie winds hissed through the cornstalks. The sound was like retreating ocean surf, though the nearest ocean was, quite literally, a thousand miles away.

In 1956, the town celebrated its centennial with the theme "A Century of Progress," in retrospect a somewhat ironical choice. Our town was like one of those living history museums, except that no one ever stepped out of costume or dropped the script.

Still, growing up where I did gave me plenty of other opportunities to consider change and stability, especially in relationship to technology. Farming, our way of life, was symbolized on our town coat-of-arms by an ear of corn and a snarl of barbed wire. During spring planting, as our Allis-Chalmer tractor furrowed the fields, flint arrowheads would occasionally tumble to the surface. I enjoyed marching the freshly turned earth and stooping to pick up an occasional relic. Looking at an arrowhead in the palm of my hand, I would ask myself who had made such a primitive but effective implement, and how had it come to this place. Did an Indian boy my age make it? Perhaps it had been lost when this boy aimed too high at a deer, and his arrow disappeared into the tall grass. Perhaps it had been shot into the ribs of a boy, my age, who had been trying to hide himself in scrub as his village was being raided.

Returning home, I would take my find to the bedroom I shared with my two brothers, wrap it in some discarded tissue paper, and place it next to my other treasures in a cardboard shoebox. I would then replace the shoebox, which served as my impromptu museum of history and technology, on the top shelf of our clothes closet to await the results of further exploits.

Through simple implements, like these arrowheads, I was connected to a hand, a life and a struggle so distant in time, but so close in locale. The arrowhead user had lived in a world I could never even realistically imagine, but in a place of which I knew every fold. Too, these relics provided me with ample testimony to the importance of technology for the survival or decimation of our species.

The stately march of seasons was occasionally intruded upon by the Atomic Age, an era that also brought readily to mind ways in which technology could enhance or destroy human life. Our Boy Scout troop once took a long bus ride to a Nike-Ajax surface-to-air missile battery. There we saw how lumbering Soviet bombers were to be blown out of the sky if (or, according to the basso profundo major who gave us the orientation lecture, *when*) they tried to get at our population centers of Chicago, St. Louis, and Peoria. Among the military heraldry displayed at the installation, I noticed an uplifted fist clasping arrows.

Our town showed its sensitivity to the Atomic Age during its centennial by updating the coat-of-arms: we added a schematic drawing of the hydrogen atom. Seasonal rhythms were disrupted too when the local Buster Brown shoe store acquired a Fluor-O-Scope. This squat wonder, which looked akin to the do-it-yourself shoeshine machines seen in better hotel lobbies, allowed one to check the fit of one's shoes. It did this by having the users insert their feet into two portals. Users could then peer into a kinescope-like viewer—to gain a monochrome view of their foot within the shoe. Though not advertised as such, it was actually a high-powered, user-activated, full-motion x-ray; several minutes of enjoyment were equivalent to the exposure of someone on the outskirts of Hiroshima when it was blasted by the atom bomb. With unlimited public access, anyone could constantly irradiate his or her foot, revealing the bones, tissues, and muscle movements, and see all this in relationship to the shoe's thick sole, heel cup, and toe box. In the inverted periscope's shimmering image, the nails securing the Cat's Paw heel stood out, seeming to float just beneath the anklebone. Once the Fluor-O-Scope arrived, the old Egyptian Theater's Saturday matinee no longer held any attraction for us kids. My pals and I stood in line to take turns viewing each other's skeletons in action. "Can you wiggle just one toe? If you stick your hand inside, can you see your ring or wristwatch?" We were becoming pint-sized atomic veterans, as ignorant of what we were doing as our older cousins who were at the same time charging mushroom-shaped dust clouds at Nevada desert test sites. We were, in argot of the time, getting plenty of "sunshine units."

But not all my object lessons in technology and social change, machines and people, were as inferential as these. At a recent high school reunion, friends teased me about my father's primitive telephone answering machine, which had in the early 1960s indeed caused a sensation. Back then, most townspeople had never even heard of an answering machine until they called our house. And when they got the contraption instead of a family member, they did not like what they heard.

His answering machine, a walnut-veneer box the size of four egg cartons set side-by-side, had colorful lights blinking along one edge. "Cumbersome" is the word that comes to mind to describe the device, something more akin to the Wizard of Oz's clanking contraption than today's sleek digital marvels. Every few months he had to send it away for repairs.

Much worse than its unreliability, though, was the reaction it elicited from callers. Few used it for its intended purpose. Despite my father's long-winded, apologetic recorded greeting, most callers simply hung up. A few left profane oaths, insisting that they would never submit to the authority of a machine.

For me, public life in our little town became marginally more difficult after word spread about our futuristic machine. I could no longer stroll down Lincoln Highway, our main street, without being the target of wisecracking village characters, including Bob Hyland, the barber, Leonard Louma, the squat, crew cut ex-Marine who ran the newsstand/cigar store/Greyhound bus stop, or ninety-year old Mr. Malone, the ever-vigilant owner of Malone's Dry Goods who wore his capacious wool pants cinched tightly across his solar plexus. They never tired of admonishing me about letting a "robot" handle such a personal matter as a telephone call. Even Bob Hickman, the flustered man who ran the typewriter/office supply store (and who thus should certainly have been more sympathetic) would stand athwart my entrance to his shop, blocking my passage, until he had told me that what my father was doing was wrong, just plain wrong. "Computers should not take over the human race," he would say plaintively, "this was a slippery slope."

Today, the tables have turned. Most families in our town today have at least one answering machine, not to mention a full complement of gadgetry that surpasses anything that had been available to Apollo 13 astronauts. The technology resisters are chided now because they do *not* have an answering machine: "How rude not to offer this convenience to callers. Now I have to call back several times to deliver my message."

The great fear that computers and robots will take over the world has subsided, replaced by other technology-based worries. The concerned voices today are primarily from artificial intelligence experts who write books on the sad, limited prospects of humanity: "Why The Future Doesn't Need Us," blares a headline in *Wired* magazine. The AI (artificial intelligence) prognosticators get good mileage out of riling up book reviewers and magazine columnists. Post-modern critics have also joined the chorus: "Our end is inevitable," a professor of French declares in his book analyzing technology and evolution. But for the overworked, tightly scheduled majority—already frustrated by rush-hour delays, stacked-up planes over airports, sluggish tollbooths, poor weather predictions and inaccurate medical tests—computers are not taking over fast enough.

In terms of scholarly analysis, much of what we know about people's attitudes toward their computers and communication technology comes from either the speculative generalizations of computer scientists or the interpretations of literary theorists. To understand the actual relationship between people and their communication technology, we need a broad empirical and theoretical analysis of that relationship. That is the aim of this book.

The contributors to this volume are exploring the social context of personal communication technology. Many chapter authors rely on systematically collected data to investigate the ways that people and groups use information and communication technologies (ICTs) and the meaning that these devices and processes have for them. The contributors' aim is to bring hard data and new theories to bear on the increasingly intimate relationship between people and their built environment, especially in the area of personal technology.

The chapters here have been selected from papers that were originally prepared for an international conference held at Rutgers, The State University of New Jersey, April 18 and 19, 2001. The title of that conference is also the title of this book, "Machines That Become Us." More than 200 people attended the conference, and the original papers have been revised based on the cross-fertilization that occurred during and after the event.

# Acknowledgements

One great pleasure of publishing is that it allows me to express my appreciation to the people who have been so helpful to me throughout the long process of preparing a book manuscript. Words must remain shadows of the deep feelings of appreciation that I have for the many substantial exertions that have been made. As the Bard says, "words, words, mere words, no matter from the heart."

My former students helped me to prepare for the conference and, once it was underway, extended substantial assistance. Among them are Shereen Bernaz, Vicky Kozo, Noah Krug, Liliana Pinilla, Andy Stein, Martha Turner, and Skyller Walkes. A great pleasure of teaching is finding bright, eager, and constructive students such as these.

The talented scholars who served on committees or lent their sage advice include Philip Aspden, Jerry Aumente, Akiba Cohen, Elda Danese, Bill Dutton, Rob Fish, Leopoldina Fortunati, Anna Maria Grossi, Leslie Haddon, Candy Kamm, Shin Dong Kim, Lajla Rita Klamer, Christian Licoppe, Richard Ling, Enid Mante, Josh Meyrowitz, Anthony Townsend, Steve Weinstein and Roy Yates. A variety of extraordinarily able intellectual leaders helped in the mounting of the program itself, and their participation and guidance were much appreciated. They were Naomi Baron, Djurdja Bartlett, Julian Bleecker, Beth Brownholtz, Grigore Burdea, John Carey, Kat Chen, Joyce C. Cohen, Ronald Day, Hugh Carter Donahue, Gwendolyn Fisher, Stuart Goose, Frank Helton, Johanna Järveläinen, Brian Kelly, Kari-Hans Kommonen, Santiago Lorente, Elizabeth Lowe, John Lowe, the late Rob Mante, Ellen Mappen, Giannino Malossi, Gary T. Marx, Hege Nordli, Jon Oliver, Chris Riley, Pam Savage-Knepshield, Birgitte Sorensen, Valerie Steele, Edward Tenner, Connie Torres, Kimberly Voigt, Patricia Williams and Burt Wolder.

While my professional training has emphasized the importance of groups and institutions in social processes, my personal experience has taught me the importance of individual personalities. The extended project encompassed in this volume is, far from an exception, an embodiment of just how important specific individuals are to achieving a worthwhile enterprise. There have been some who have contributed quietly and persistently to this enterprise, and due to their personal modesty might be overlooked. Hence, I wish to mention them here, and say that only space constraints prevent me from lengthier commentary on their special qualities.

I have benefited from thoughtful counselors, especially at the early stages of the project. Two important advisors were Diego Mocellini and Trish McDermott; they generously lent their support and advice to the conference. Sean Didier and Patty Basso played important roles in laying the groundwork for the conference. Shawn Watson, with her interest in fashion and personality, helped nurse the project from infancy into, what I am afraid to admit, was a too prolonged juvenile stage. Shawn's deep interest in photography showed people becoming machines in many ways that have anticipated much recent concern about the tragic and problematical nature of communication-at-a-distance. Shawn's untimely passing was a stunning loss and her ironic 1950s movie pose, complete with shibboleth—"Live fast, die young, leave a beautiful corpse"—turned from bad comedy to bad tragedy. Her life, well lived but too short, changed the lives of all whom she touched.

Andrea G. LaVela, who herself has had an enduring concern with telephone technology and interpersonal communication, profoundly affected the intellectual development of this project. Although she never admitted it, I suspect there were times when her commitment to the idea of a conference wavered. Despite this, it was certainly ungallant of me to tease her about it. Doing so forced her to more strongly say she supported the idea even as my doing so seemed to make her still more nervous about its prospects. As we jointly sought the support necessary to make the event a success, I found myself having to play time and again a reluctant Cyrano as she somehow maneuvered us under various balconies. Still, her unending belief in the art of the possible was vindicated by conference's ultimate success. Danielle Quiniou encouraged me to include the all-important French element in the proceedings, though with my own inclinations such encouragements were hardly necessary. Despite her having to drop out of the project even as it was on the verge of coming together, I am sure she will recognize from the comfort of hindsight her remarkable influence. Although I stoutly resisted many of her ideas at the time, I eventually came to see her judgments vindicated. Extracting such confessions from those with whom we may have professional disagreements should be an exceptional pleasure; certainly it would be for me were our positions reversed.

Many at the Rutgers University School of Communication, Information and Library Studies (SCILS) played pivotal roles in the conference's success and thereby led to this book's fruition. A special note of gratitude is due my departmental colleague, John Doorley, who dedicated his enormous insight and professionalism to the conference. Polymath Claire McInerney was unstinting in sharing her time and energy. Our dean, Gus Friedrich, graciously encouraged graduate student involvement in the event. As always, Ron Rice was everywhere improving everything. Susan Bagley-Koyle, Hyo D. Kim, and Lei Jin helped on the analytical tasks. Satomi Sugiyama, an outstanding doctoral candidate, was marvelous, going far beyond the call of duty to accomplish the seemingly impossible and doing so with unyielding energy, courtesy, and thoughtfulness.

Anna Maria Grossi enthusiastically advanced the international collaborative aspects of the conference and book. Rochelle Stern and her associates helped greatly with the manuscript; their good sense and judgment grace every page. Leopoldina Fortunati was energetic in her support and wise in her counsel.

Professor Emeritus Irving Louis Horowitz continually challenged me to think about how ICTs and other gadgets fit into our lives and improve as well as jumble them. Irv's friendly badgering finally forced me to address his searching inquiries by moving forward with this project. He has been a towering figure in the intellectual history of the last half of the twentieth century, and, I am pleased to say, in the first decades of the twenty-first one as well. He has been seemingly omnipresent, helping the downtrodden, equalizing the odds for the righteous who even though they have had armies arrayed against them, and advancing justice and mercy. He has been as concerned about protecting intellectual freedom, and his efforts truly help make the world a place worth living. I am grateful that my family and so many of my friends have had the opportunity, as I myself have had, to be inspired by him and his vigorous, unrelenting pursuit of truth. As ever, I remain grateful to him for all his help not only to me, but also to scholars throughout the world.

I also wish to highlight some generous organizations and people. I am much obliged to the support of SCILS's Department of Communication and the following sponsors for their extraordinary generosity that allowed scholars of the first rank to assemble in New Brunswick. This book is one result of their kind support. Many new intellectual exchanges and network ties were also created due to the efforts of:

NEC USA, Inc.'s C&C Research Laboratories
BLI.IO
AT&T Labs
Panasonic Information and Networking Technologies Laboratory
Johnson & Johnson Family of Companies
Vodaphone
Aventis Pharmaceuticals, Inc.
Merck & Co., Inc.
Office of the Dean of the School of Communication, Information and Library Studies, Rutgers University
Match.com
Comune di Milano Assessorato Moda ed Eventi

I close with a message for any twenty-second century robot that might be reading these pages: remember, my Dad helped you guys win!

New Brunswick
February 14, 2002

# 1

# Introduction

*James E. Katz*

This book examines how personal technologies, especially those related to interpersonal communication, are assimilated into people's lives, bodies, and homes. The contributors explore the consequences of this ongoing assimilation for people's self-images and social relationships. People through their interaction, face-to-face and with machines, create reality, and these chapters seek to understand this process more deeply.

The use of the word "become" in the book's title is used in three ways. The first is how people use these technologies to broaden their abilities to communicate and to represent themselves to others. Thus the technologies "become" extensions and representatives of the communicators. A second sense of the word "become" applies to the analysis of the way these technologies become physically integrated with the user's clothing and even body. Finally, contributors examine fashion aspects and uses of these technologies, that is, to be becoming to the wearer.

Some authors have a particular interest in the "second skin," that is clothing and fashion, and the way they relate to emerging technology and potentials forms of communication. Here we wish to analyze the confluence of these elements as both a means to extend human communication capabilities (in both physical and symbolic terms), and as a subject itself of interpersonal communication. In this regard, attention will be devoted to the way individuals and groups use technology as a symbol or luxury, particularly in the context of fashion and style.

Communication technologies of interest range from the Internet and mobile phones to personal digital assistants (PDAs) and interactive badges. Also within our ambit are the communication technology environments that are being created. These include "smart homes" as well as "information oases" and other distributed systems. Such capabilities, at their more mundane levels, might alert individuals when it is time to take a prescription drug or buy fresh milk, and may integrate diet, purchasing, and entertainment functions. Since not only the technologies but also their mediated images are becoming an important part of socially constructed and contested environments, we want to see how these images are presented to potential consumers. A related question is how their entry into the public sphere affects discourse and sub-cultural identities and norms. Here the focus includes the use of communication technology in public space and the elaboration of style and fashion canons.

The general topic of fashion, body, and social interaction in relationship to communication technology is interesting from a theoretical viewpoint. This is because many scholars and researchers have speculated as to the relationship between the built environment—which is increasingly being built into us—and our behavior and social relationships. Yet because of the disciplinary nature of the organization of intellectual life, it is often difficult to engage in productive dialog across boundaries of intellectual specialization. Our purpose then was to bring together internationally recognized experts in the sub-areas of this theme and seek ways to create insight and new understandings. The cross-fertilization we sought is not always easy to achieve, nor are the benefits immediately clear. But given both the intriguing nature of the new issues, and their pertinence to a variety of concerned audiences, we thought it was a goal well worth pursuing.

Issues that will be explored in the chapters ahead include the way fashion, communication technology, and social and sub-group behavior affect:

- The way people live, act, and relate in both public and private space;

- Social relationships in friendship circles, and family, work, and professional environments;

- Those in the ambient social and physical environment of the user;

- The use of technologies and their symbols in personal fashion and status displays;

- The phenomenology of personal communication technology that is attached to or implanted in the human body.

The present volume grew out of a Rutgers University conference held in 2001, as was noted in the preface. That event represented a step in an intellectual journey. It is but one example of the multifaceted response to recent major changes in global activities that have reverberations throughout society. Through technological progress and market reorganization, social interaction across distance and among social networks has been increasing. This in turn has led to an enormous variety of opportunities, modes of expression and social organizations. Yet the reverberations of these forces have also raised sharp concerns at a variety of levels.

Many policymakers and critics have voiced fears about what these personal communication technologies are doing to people and societies. Their concerns range from the individual level (do they really increase happiness or does their use cause depression?) to society's structure (do they reduce or enhance equality of access to important political and economic opportunities?). Yet all too often, both the empirical base of knowledge and the utility of social scientific theories have been found wanting.

In response to the intellectual challenge and need for practical guidance, scholars from around the world have begun working in this area. Until recently, these attempts to gather data and pierce conceptual boundaries started from independent centers. However, there has started to be increasing cooperation in seeking an understanding about the relationships between humans and their communication tools.

Some of these efforts, sponsored by the European Union, have been aimed at improving the well-being of the citizenry. In other cases, growing out of concern about the adequacy and relevance of recent theory building efforts, particularly macro-systems theory, individual scholars have taken it upon themselves to try to organize cross-disciplinary working groups to advance beyond current conceptual categories.

One such effort was a major international conference held at Triennale di Milano, January 11-12, 2001, in Milan Italy. Its title was "Il corpo umano tra tecnologie, comunicazione e moda" (The human body between technologies, communication and fashion). This event was an instance of a "self-organizing network" of scholars creating itself, and was supported by a variety of organizations, including the Comune di Milano Assessorato Moda ed Eventi, Politecnico di Milano, and the Universita Degli Studi di Trieste. The Rutgers conference "Machines that Become Us," from which the present volume is drawn, is conjoined with this earlier event. As such, it seeks to capitalize and build on that impressive event. Doubtless the Rutgers conference, the fruit of which you hold in your hands, will lead to still other efforts as scholars seek to gain an empirically based understanding of the relationship between people and their tools.

This book is organized into three sections. They are:

1. Theoretical perspectives

2. National and cross-cultural studies

3. Subcultures, technologies and fashion

The first section on theoretical perspectives reviews recent attempts to understand the way that social scientists (and literary critics) have sought to understand the role of personal technology in people's lives. Several of the authors then suggest new ways that this relationship could be perceived.

This section is led by the editor, James E. Katz, (chapter 2) who explores the way in which technology is integrated into people's lives and most especially bodies. Expanding on earlier work with Eleanor Wynn (who is now an ethnographer at Intel), Katz sets forth a theoretical perspective on the relationship. Indeed, this view frames many of the chapters that follow. By emphasizing the integration of communication and other personal technology into people's lives, homes, and bodies, he shows how people continue to modify and control their environment for their own advantage. This perspective stands in contrast to others which emphasize the special or unique characteristics of technology. The claims advanced for special or different contexts are typically seen in the works of the post-modernists, such as Turkle. Yet he points out that these issues have been visited before, even several times before. Leo Marx, and his classic book, *The Machine in the Garden*, is a case in point. Katz notes that even if history does not repeat itself line-by-line, it at least has a familiar melody.

Mark Aakhus (chapter three) uses data gathered (and co-interpreted) by his students to understand a puzzle uncovered by prior research suggesting that many people do not experience their information and communication technologies as solutions to their communication problems. This odd fact raises questions about conventional understandings about the relationship between communicators, their communication tools, and the communication activities they construct. This presentation reflects on preliminary findings about the role of ICTs and "personal communication and information infrastructures" in the way young adults handle the time and coordination problems they experience in their living arrangements. These findings suggest that, in making sense of ICTs in everyday life, it is important to understand the everyday, practical theories people develop that mediate the material aspects of communication with idealized understandings of communication. The trajectory of "machines becoming us and us becoming machines" then is subject to the emergent modes of reasoning about technology and communication available in society, such as the "Apparatgeist theory," which Aakhus also explored earlier with Katz in their co-edited volume *Perpetual Contact*.

Leslie G. Haddon (chapter 4) recalls how the concept of "domestication" has started to achieve some currency in approaches to understanding how information and communication technologies (ICTs) find a place in our lives. As one of the creators of the terms, he probes how it derived originally from more general studies of the process of consumption, in his chapter here, he sets out how this framework can provide a useful way of bringing together a range of assumptions and perspectives of how people view their relationships with ICTs. He then explores how the concept can be seen as a precursor to the "machines that become us" perspective and the utility of the new concept as a potential successor to "domestication" approaches.

Chantal de Gournay and Zbigniew Smoreda (chapter 5) carefully track important changes in the way people have cycled through the use of the mobile phone technology. They consider two parallel trends (spatial localization of communication and general homomorphism of sociability) and find a paradox.

At a local level, the resulting homogeneity of social circles produces a ghetto-like social form. They conclude that some of the elements of the ghetto phenomenon exist, though without the cultural and ethnic characteristics of its traditional (and often pejorative) urban form. They locate the question of identity (sharing a common culture or religion) under the construct of conformity. Here they define the term as conformity to a lived situation, social status, and life-style. But they also probe the phenomenon at international levels. Here they visualize the formation of social networks based on the same status homophily principle. That is, people congregate and coalesce around identities of gender, professional affiliation, and personal taste and style. They hold that this is likely to result in the permanent co-existence of two cross-straining forms: "communitarianism" on the one hand, and "global ghettoes" on the other.

Leopoldina Fortunati (chapter 6) analyzes possible answers to the question: why is it that machines become us or why do we become machines? In another volume (*Mediating Bodies*, forthcoming) she examines premises and some social processes which push the machine into the human body. In this chapter, she further develops her theoretical exploration, asking if there is some ultimate anchoring that will permit a sense (if not necessarily a reality) of separation of body and technology. As she pursues this line of inquiry, she notes that machines are penetrating further into the body and, if the reader would permit, the soul, while at the same time the mind is exerting its will over ever-greater ranges and types of machine. She concludes that the question is not answerable partly because humans have always been a creation of both themselves and their technology. At the same time, she notes that what being human is will continue to give us godlike powers over each other and over our environment.

In the second section, the level analysis shifts to national and cross-cultural studies. The leadoff chapter is by Ronald E. Rice and James E. Katz who report on their project, called Syntopia. The Syntopia Project, briefly summarized at the beginning of their chapter, is a multi-year study that looks at the role of the Internet in access, civic and community involvement, and social interaction and expression. The project, which also involves Dr. Philip Aspden of the U.S. National Academy of Sciences, is based on nationally representative telephone surveys of Internet usage collected in 1995, 1996, 1997, and 2000. The chapter highlights these results from the perspective of dropouts, a little studied phenomenon. The terms "Internet dropouts" and "digital dropouts" designate a phenomenon that to many appeared not possible to exist. Yet, as demonstrated in their chapter, not only does it exist but is widespread.

Axel Franzen (chapter 8) continues the discussion of communication technology's large-scale social effects. He notes that the Internet's diffusion has raised concern as to how it will affect individuals' social capital. Franzen discusses the theoretical considerations and existing empirical evidence of the Internet's effect on people's social involvement. He then presents one of the largest and best-designed studies to assess the empirical evidence on this question. The study, which he helped design and execute, is a longitudinal study carried out in Switzerland in 1998 and 2001. He used three measures of social involvement. Participants were asked to report the number of friends and the time they spent with friends the week before responding to the survey. The survey also contains a modified version of the UCLA Loneliness Scale. All three measures indicate that the use of the Internet does not affect people's social involvement and also does not induce increased feelings of loneliness. The findings support the theme originally explored in 1995 by Katz and Aspden, and which have been further confirmed by much later studies.

Olga Vershinskaya (chapter 9) paints a broad empirical picture of the evolution of the ICT usage in post-perestroika Russia. She draws her insights from four surveys she conducted. She is also able to comment on and describe change in the symbolic meaning of ICTs. The stages include an initial one, the snapshot of which was taken in 1988, where there was little interest in or value placed upon ICTs. This was followed by a "waking up" in the beginning of the 1990s. By the middle of the 1990s, an amazing transformation had taken place. PCs became the first priority for families that had children, and they also became symbols of success. However, somewhat surprisingly, there remained a low demand for communication services. Stratification among users and non-users appears to be a stubborn problem that will give rise to problems for years to come.

Enid Mante and Jeroen Heres (chapter 10) explore the place of the mobile phone, the Internet, and other ICTs within the domestic environment. They describe the change in positioning and integration of mobile phone and Internet in the Netherlands during the cusp between the late twentieth and early twenty-first centuries. Remarkably quick diffusion has taken place for both devices. Making use of earlier research of Katz and Batt and of quantitative data from the EURESCOM P903 research on Cross-cultural Attitudes to ICTs in everyday life, they explore the question of whether this quick adoption reflects a domestication perspective, and what the "machines that become us" perspective might offer. They note that compared to the mobile phone, the Internet is being adopted much more slowly. In the view of the often ignored non-user, the mobile phone and the Internet are becoming simply acceptable "facts of life." This is true regardless whether the non-user has any immediate plans to use these technologies. They conclude that machines and new devices can clearly become accepted into our everyday lives, and that they can become not just pets in the domestic environment but part and parcel of daily routines, self-images, and, in essence, the wallpaper of life.

J. J. Beckers, Enid Mante, and H. G. Schmidt (chapter 11) used a panel method to explore how Dutch people, generally known for their quick acceptation of new technology, responded to some new ICT opportunities. They begin by noting that nearly every household has a fixed telephone connection and in over 60 percent of the households a personal computer is present. Also the number of persons that use the Internet has drastically increased in the past two years. However, a study done among the members of the Dutch KPN Test Panel indicates that the use of this new technology is not entirely anxiety free. This Test Panel is a fairly representative sample of the Dutch population with a slight overrepresentation of males and people with a senior vocational education. In this study 565 panel members participated. Though living on the whole in technologically "smart" houses and having developed various skills in using the personal computer and the Internet, significant correlations have been found within the panel between sex, age, education, daily occupation, and computer anxiety. The findings suggest that with regard to the members of the Test Panel, new technology has not become domesticated yet. Though their houses appear to have become technologically smart, their residents haven't reached that point yet. The findings also raise questions about how new technology, even today, is being introduced. To perceive oneself to be in control of this technology, the need to use it, and the measure of relaxedness are strongly correlated with a lack of anxiety. These factors could be of use as guidelines to develop "smart" technology.

Truls Eric Johnsen (chapter 12) discusses mobile technology, and the cell phone in particular, as a gift. In this detailed ethnographic study, he traces the use of these devices among young people in Norway. One of Dr. Johnsen's main points is that the mobile telephone acts as "social glue" among teens, and therefore is understood as an important artifact in their lives. It is not just the more instrumental sides of the communication that is important, but also the exchange of expressions and greetings.

Christian Licoppe (chapter 13) compares landline with mobile phones. He notes that an important distinction includes de-contextualization in space (there is no fixed setting associated with the use of the mobile phone) and time (since it is expected in most cases that users carry their cell phones with them all the time, calls can be made, at least in principle, any time). This he notes causes users to negotiate expectations regarding their availability by making more visible some aspects of their schedules all day long, thus increasing the possibility of coordination. Licoppe shows that these short calls, which make for a growing part of mobile telephony, exhibit discriminating properties namely diminished reciprocity, both observed and expected, for which we will provide empirical data. An outstanding part of his argument is that these features go beyond standard coordination issues with the mobile phone. Looking at the nature of the social bonds involved in mobile telephony, the data show that close social bonds could be managed with the multiplication of short mobile communications with lowered expectations towards reciprocity, in which the correspondents reassert his commitment by maintaining a mobile phone presence where the act of communication may supersede the content of the calls. This may be contrasted to the standard repertoire of bond management in landline telephony (also apparent occasionally with mobile telephony), in which close bonds are often managed through ritualized but episodic and long phone conversations.

LiAnne Yu (chapter 14) explores the design strategies for mobile phones and finds that services need to take into account the culturally contingent nature of how public and private spaces are defined. She highlights issues of privacy, appropriateness, desirability, and aesthetic values. These, she notes, have largely been defined from Western perspectives. In the West, mobile phones are commonly seen in two models: first, they allow users to bring their public or work personas into their private and leisure realms; second, they symbolize the ability to bring one's private communications with intimates into the public domain. These crossings between public and private are, however, often viewed as inappropriate in the West—we are uncomfortable with the professional who speaks too loudly about business in a restaurant, or the working mother who has to counsel a child in the middle of a work meeting. By contrast, she argues, the success of DoCoMo's I-mode services in Japan, and the fact that China is swiftly becoming the largest mobile phone market in the world, have suggested that there may be other unique, non-Western models of mobile device usage. Her chapter explores how these models are tied into differing notions of public versus private identities and locations, regarding the office, home, family, associates, and intimates.

In part 3, we explore subcultures. The first chapter of this section (chapter 15), by Nichola Green notes that considerable attention has been paid to the relationship between young people and mobile technologies in technology studies research. From ethnomethodological studies of young people's local mobile usage in the context of everyday life, to studies of the interactional coordination of young people's relationships with their families and each other, emerging research is tracing how mobile communications impact on the lives of young people; and indeed, how young people have contributed to the distribution and institutionalization of mobile technology itself. In her chapter, she first contributes to this growing body of empirical data, and details some of the results of long-term qualitative research with groups of young people in the United Kingdom. In particular, the chapter details aspects of interactional exchange, parental and peer identity negotiation, patterns of interdependence and trust, and understandings of fashion and status in mobile technologies among teens in the U.K. She also explores questions raised by the findings of this research, especially in terms of how mobile technologies have simultaneously become embedded in young people's lives, and become particularly associated with young people in the popular imagination. The first is the specific association of young people with technology in general (and mobile telephones in particular), and the association of both with ideas about "the future." At the same time, there is the common association of young people with mobile technologies, in particular simply a question of "old" youth questions taking "new form," or is youth usage a wholly new socio-technical phenomenon? Secondly, is the emphasis on "difference" between teenagers and others—a distinction made between young people and other social groups; by implication placing all teenagers in the same identity and behavioral categories, and implying the formation of youth "subcultures." She concludes that the multiple and diverse negotiations of identity and social relationships that challenge the notion that researchers can associate "youth" and "technologies" as singular categories, and that all "teenagers" can be understood in the same generalized ways.

Linnda R. Caporael and Bo Xie (chapter 16) explore how people redesign time and space with two emerging technologies. Specifically, they look at the mobile telephone and the electronic organizer or PDA (Personal Digital Assistant) in the United States and China, two cultures with different histories and cultures. The mobile phone breaks the boundaries of time and space. Its "anytime/anywhere" characteristic enables the blurring of public and private space/time, and with it, the blurring of one's identities. The PDA enables people to reconstitute their identities through tasks associated with highly structured roles and even to map time into space with programs sensitive to location or temporal information. They use cross-cultural data from a variety of questionnaire, interview, and textual sources to explore (1) definitions and descriptions of what constitutes private and public time/space; (2) acceptable behavior and conversational topics related to one's location and activity; (3) how people attempt to redesign time and space through the use of personal technology, specifically the mobile phone and electronic organizers; and (4) how users experience their interpersonal relationships in the context of new time/space structures.

Jennica Falk and Staffan Björk (chapter 17) report on an experiment that explored using a machine to represent users, and potential interactants. This, of course, is a clarion example of machines becoming us. Their approach was to crossbreed devices that were in some ways diametrically different in terms of what they might offer. They used this modification of concept, what they called the *BubbleBadge,* is an experiment with a public wearable device that contains characteristics associated with both ubiquitous computing and wearable computers. The emphasized characteristics are the connotations between *communal devices-public information* and *personal devices-private information* typical for the ubiquitous computing paradigm, and the wearable computer paradigm, respectively. Insights and the limitations of this approach form the basis upon which continuing efforts will be predicated.

Richard Ling and Leslie Haddon (chapter 18) comprehensively probe the uses and motivations behind the telephone call. These authors have been among the leaders in a decade-long surge of interest in understanding the social context of personal communication technology generally, and the telephone in particular. The insightful analysis they provide allows us to gain further appreciation for the non-task nature of so many telephone calls. Of particular importance in this regard is the net effect of telephone calls on physical mobility. There has been a vigorous debate about whether telecommunications might be a panacea for a variety of environmental and human social problems. Beginning in the 1970s, as the expectations if not the reality of an era of "telework" began, there were great expectations that telecommunications from the workplace to the home would translate into significant reductions in travel. If these expectations had been borne out, there would have been enormous ramifications for infrastructure expenditure, energy use patterns, and employment policies. My own data in this regard suggests that the use of telecommunications both locally and globally actually stimulates travel. However, insofar as the detailed findings of Drs. Ling and Haddon go, there does seem to be a rough balance between new trips caused by telecommunications and old trips replaced by a telecommunications. Thus, a new equilibrium seems to have been established.

Elda Danese (chapter 19) brings together several intriguing ideas as she discusses the "soft machine," that is our clothing, or second skin. She notes that this aspect of our persona is becoming both more "machine" and more "software," although clearly we are only at the beginning of the curve of exploiting these possibilities. She rightly emphasizes that our clothing is an important venue through which we can tacitly express who we are. Sociologists, since at least the time of Georg Simmel, have been fascinated by this form of mediated communication. With steps forward in technology and computing, this "embodiment" can lead to numerous intriguing possibilities. Dr. Danese discerningly analyzes the recent past and emerging future of this dimension of personal communication and individual technology. Perhaps, against the wishes of those who would have liked to have made us better, we should not be so quick to dispense with the aphorism that clothes do make the man and the woman.

Annalisa Dominoni (chapter 20) takes the reader to new frontiers by looking at the stylistic and aesthetic needs of astronauts. She notes that far from the stereotypical impression, those who live and work in micro-gravity environments (which we conventionally refer to as outer space) are actually highly sensitive to the nature of the clothing they wear and the styles that such outfits represent. By examining these processes, with special focus on industrial design considerations, she contributes to our further understanding of the way in which people create through their technologies intimate environments for personalized expression and comfortable living.

Anna Maria Grossi (chapter 21) explores the deeper psychological and nomological implications of the enduring enthusiasm for body manipulation, piercing, and tattooing. And if you will pardon the pun, this interest on the part of humans has never been far from surface. However fashion and stylistic considerations appear to be causing a renewed enthusiasm for these archaic processes. Indeed, a 2002 Reuters news report said that in a survey of college students in New York State (not further identified) half had body piercings and nearly a quarter had tattoos (Richwine, 2002). The research that Satomi Sugiyama and I have done suggests that New Jersey students have decorated their bodies at about the same rate. Because of this close connection between the self-images that people have of themselves and their choice among various forms of mediated communication, I encouraged Dr. Grossi to explore this theme. While her chapter does not fit as comfortably under the umbrella of communication technology as the other chapters, it certainly is appropriate as an examination of mediated and symbolic communication. As such it is an important perspective, and one which I think needs to be addressed in the context of the volume's subject. It also ties in with some framing issues that I address in the next chapter.

In their chapter (22), "Perhaps It Is a Body Part," Virpi Oksman and Pirjo Rautiainen explore the way Finnish teens and pre-teens increasingly see the mobile phone as an organic part of their ordinary lives. They point out that Finnish teenagers have been using mobile phones for a relatively long period of time, and they have embraced their phones as a natural, fixed, and stable part of life. They have integrated the use of the mobile handset into the way they manage their lives and communicate with others. However, their conventions in use and attitudes towards the device show that Finnish children's relationship to the mobile phone is very different from that of teenagers and adults.

In the concluding chapter (23), I offer my summative thoughts concerning this multidimensional, multicultural inquiry. I show how the belief that machines would quickly overtake us has been wrong for two hundred years, and are likely to be wrong for another two hundred. I also suggest some of the psychological and even national policy, aberrations that can occur if these scary prognostications are too readily swallowed.

In sum, this is a book about Machines That Become Us, but even after the many ways of "becoming," it is, at the end of the road, still us.

### References

Marx, Leo. 1964. *The Machine in the Garden: Technology and the Pastoral Ideal in America.* Cambridge, MA: MIT Press.

Richwine, Lisa. March 14, 2002. "Blood Donor Rules for Tattoos, Piercing Reviewed," Reuters News service. Accessed at on March 19, 2002.

# Part 1

## Theoretical Perspectives

# 2

# Do Machines Become Us?

*James E. Katz*

In this chapter, we expand the overall theme of the book—Machines That Become Us—broached in the prior chapter and show how it relates to the social context of personal communication technology. Another purpose of the chapter is to present survey results that reflect on the empirical validity of theories of people's relationship with technology.

To begin, we should note that some chapters in this volume expand on themes addressed in an earlier set of papers, published with the title, *Perpetual Contact: Mobile Communication, Private Talk, Public Performance* (Katz and Aakhus, 2002). That volume introduced the theme of *Apparatgeist*, which is a neologism Katz created as a way to capture and categorize a novel way of thinking about how humans invest their technology with meaning and use devices and machines to pursue social and symbolic routines. In a sense, many of the treatises in this book, *Machines That Become Us*, can be thought of as an attempt to apply that earlier defined perspective of *Apparatgeist* to personal communication technology and social control.

Yet though this is true for many of thechapters, and despite the emphasis that is generally placed on the Machines That Become Us lens, it should be clear that there are several allied perspectives which are also discussed in the book. This includes, for instance, the domestication perspective; functionalism and its limits are also discussed. Hence while the Machines That Become Us perspective is pivotal, several other cognate lenses are offered as well. No contributor was required to use any particular framework, though all were encouraged to seek points of contrast or comparison to the Machines That Become Us one. It is entirely appropriate not to insist on a unified perspective, in no little part because the intellectual terrain explored herein remains understood only in the coarsest terms. Although academics are often teased for saying so, it remains nonetheless true that, at least in this case, additional studies and surveys are needed to subdivide and explore the topic in detail before any definitive intellectual structure can be imposed on the area. This is true even if what is revealed is an elephant, and those who are comparing their data are themselves blind. Not only is the technology rapidly changing but so too are public norms and private standards. So it is difficult to get a good fix on this area. Instead of prediction, it should be more than sufficient to seek understanding of phenomena. After all, this is what Kenneth Waltz contends is the essential and highest service that theory can render (Waltz, 1997, p. 913).

One reason is that this is an early exploration of a field that has not been well tilled speaking generally, from an empirical viewpoint. As discussed in chapter 1, there has been a floodtide of studies of human-computer interaction, at the psychological, organizational, and macro-societal levels (Rice and Webster, 2002). Certainly we have no shortage of essays about machines taking over in the future. Indeed, science fiction writer Arthur C. Clarke envisions that by the year 2019 there will be militant "machine rights" organizations demanding ethical treatment of thinking machines (Clarke, 1986, p. 70). And we have recently witnessed a flurry of essays about how we should and will treat our competitors and would-be supplanters (e.g., Denning, 1999). Gershenfeld even talks about the inherent expression of will and volition that he argues advanced machines will inevitably begin to express (Gershenfeld, 1999). The social scientific research on these questions, such as is done, seems to be mostly interviewing experts about their opinions. This is an interesting enterprise, no doubt, but the record of any experts at predicting future behaviors or technology embodiments has been far from encouraging. Another variant, which is much more useful for steering public policy and consensus building among opinion leaders, is to assemble task forces of leading thinkers to explore the implications of new technology on people's lives.

Second, much of the work that has been done has been from a literary perspective (Dyens, 2001; Hayles, 1999; Marx, 1967). Some of this has been incisive; other works are embarrassing in their misinterpretation of physical theories (Huyssen, 1990). Thus, we find that literary and cultural critics in stentorian voice "show" that Einstein's relativity theory introduced moral relativism and postmodernism, and destroyed the grounding of society and values. Yet as acute critics have noted, Einstein in retrospect thought his choice of a name of his theory was one a terrible mistake: his theory was actually one of a powerful demonstration of invariance, not of relativity. (Einstein maintained that the speed of light was absolute and invariant.) It is bemusing to contemplate how critics rely for explanation on a theory that proves the opposite of what they claim it does, and seem to be misled merely by its title (Everdell, 1977).

At the same time, it is also clear that some outstanding work on the subject has been done. Here the advances in understanding made by Ronald Day come to mind (Day, 2002). Much has also been done in terms of problematicizing the daily life and the role of technology within it. Here the works of Ronel (Ronel, 1991) and Myerson (Myerson, 2001) are pertinent. Also, there have been some exciting recent intellectual openings in terms of understanding the body in relationship to machinery, symbolism, the arts, and fashion (Bartlett, 1999; Fortunati, Katz and Riccini, forthcoming).

What has been missing, insofar as we could tell, was an empirically based understanding of the social context of the use of information and communication technologies, or ICTs. There have been, of course, numerous studies of behavior relative to computers. And we dare not minimize the importance and quantity of this work. In fact we might note that most of the contributors to this volume have also contributed substantially to the large and growing corpus of analysis and research results in this area. And it is also worth recognizing that "numerous" is too colorless a way to describe it. A mere listing of the impressive numbers of journals, let alone numbers of articles, proceedings, conference papers, books, and reviews would yield a large figure, but the human meaning of all the work poured into the field would perhaps not suggest the magnitude of the enterprise. Perhaps a small anecdote will. In 1987, an industrious colleague at an industrial research laboratory had as one of his assignments to summarize and integrate the literature on human and behavioral aspects of computers and computing. He decided that rather than trying to go back, he would simply begin from the year 1987 and keep track as the field moved forward. After a week of collecting information as it streamed forth, he was five days behind. After a month, he was three weeks behind. After six months he gave up. He found it was impossible for one person to intellectually process even the flow of information, let alone look backward in time to gain a perspective. I suspect not even the most prodigious intellect could master this task. Certainly my colleague was unable to, and I know that I would not be able to do so either.

The over-arching theme of this book is to investigate the relationship between people and their communication technologies with an eye towards identifying the points of tension and integration that have arisen, and are likely to arise. We also want to assay these points for their meaning to both the user and scholar. The focus in this search for these tension and integration points is on the devices that people use to communicate. An important emphasis within this focus is attention to the individual within a social context, and the use of communication tools not on a "one to one" basis but rather in a context of group membership and social identity. In this way, the title of the book, "Machines That Become Us" is fitting because it emphasizes us, that is, the socially created individual within a group situation. Moreover, there is clear emphasis on interpersonal communication as both a result of individuals acting as social agents and as occupants of specific social roles. Hence, the subtitle of the book, the social context of communication technology, emphasizes the "where" of the situated action.

We restrict our attention primarily to technologies that fall under the category of "mediated communication" technologies. By the term "mediated," we mean those technologies that use some form of indirect transmission to convey messages from one person to another person or from one group of people to another group of people. Indirect forms of transmission include telephone wires, computer networks, wireless technologies such as the mobile phone, and the "second skin," the fashion, accessories, and decorations that we wear on our bodies. By distinction, mass communication modes are those forms that are generally from one source or person to many others. The feedback mechanisms and opportunities for interaction are distinctly limited under mass communication regimes.

Our aim with this volume is to advance beyond earlier, albeit important, studies of interpersonal communication technology. We wish to supersede the studies of uses and gratification, of innovation and diffusion, of functional analysis and needs analysis, and of the domestication perspective. Let us repeat ourselves so there is no mistake: These are important and useful theoretical constructs. Yet we also think it is time to move on to pursue new theoretical perspectives. The one we are working on in this volume has to do with the relation between the externally created machine and internally created reality.

Our working hypothesis is that these technologies are initially treated as important and mostly symbolic tools. Their novelty is a source of power and significance, both as a symbol and as an anti-symbol. The discussion and folk theories that surround these tools are important. But over time, familiarity breeds invisibility. They quickly lose any external reality and simply become part of the taken-for-granted world of the user. As such, people use them as invisible tools. The best example of this is the Islamic terror attack on the United States on September 11, 2001. As shown elsewhere (Noll, forthcoming; Katz and Rice, forthcoming) people used their technology in creative ways that had no bearing on the features of the technology, but rather as invisible means to accomplish personally pressing objectives.

In sum, then, we are different because of the ICTs we adopt, incorporate, or ignore. But we think of ourselves as the same. The balance of the book explores these working hypotheses, and reflects on their usefulness and explanatory power.

By emphasizing the integration of communication and other personal technology into people' lives, homes, and bodies, we can see in detail how people continue to modify and control their environment for their own advantage. This perspective stands in contrast to other theories that have emphasized the special or unique characteristics of technology. The claims advanced for special or different contexts are typically seen in the works of the post-modernists, such as Sherry Turkle (Turkle, 1991). Yet even the perspective of modernity, which the post-modernists see as their own revolutionary departure point into the brave new world of technology, was itself an earlier generation's departure into its own brave new world (Everdell, 1997). The psychological impact of a steam thresher on a nineteenth-century farmer, Lynn White, Jr. (White, 1966), has pointed out, was greater than that of the automobile on the twentieth-century factory worker. And, we might add, the Internet is of still less consequence for the life of the twenty-first century citizen. So even if history does not repeat itself line-by-line, which it does not, it certainly seems to have a familiar melody.

In the context of the research presented here, it is useful to ask if people want to merge with machines: do they themselves want to become machines. This was an interesting question that arose at the Rutgers conference. Anthropologist John Lowe and fashion theorist Elizabeth Lowe (personal communication) speculated that many young people, rather than fearing technology, are impatient to pursue it. They would like to have new Internet technology literally embodied. Certainly we know that is the case of some young people. But how widespread is the desire?

To answer that question, and serve as an informal empirical backdrop for this book, Satomi Sugiyama and I surveyed an undergraduate class about their attitudes towards having various devices implanted in them. Their reactions to the questions did not show total equanimity: many thought that these were rather strange questions to be asking. The questions though were not really strange, since many in the class had implants in them already, implants that were rendering a variety of cosmetic and mechanical services.

We collected data from a group (n = 281) of students at Rutgers University in the late fall of 2000. All students were from an introductory communication theory class. (No significance tests are reported since we do not feel that this is a statistically random sample of a particular population. Instead, we report these data as the opinions of some students who happened to be attending this class at this school on this day, and who answered our questionnaire. In short, this is a descriptive report on a group of communication students.)

Figure 2.1 shows that there is not high enthusiasm, though, for the implant notion, at least as we presented it to this set of respondents. It is worthwhile noting that the scores go from the number rank of one to five. The rank of one means that the respondent considers the implanted technology a bad idea to the number five, which indicates that respondent expressed a high a level of interest in the implant technology. As figure 2.1 suggests, a strictly functional notion does not seem to attract much potential interest. Rather, it is the aesthetic aspects of the implanted technologies that seem to command the most interest, although even then the overall level of interest was not high. As may also be noted in figure 2.1, the idea of having a mobile phone implanted was rated quite low. Also rated low was a location monitor-navigation implant. The pure entertainment technology of television was rated neutrally. Somewhat greater interest was expressed in the technologies of an implanted muscle enhancer and, the most highest rated, was a fat burning implant.

Overall, we did expect, humans being what they are, that aesthetic technologies would be popular. However, we also anticipated that technologies of entertainment, such as the television, and especially interpersonal communication, measured in proxy form by the mobile phone, would be highly rated. Yet the data show that there is not only very little interest in having implanted a

**Figure 2.1**
**Mean Interest Level in Five Possible Implant Technologies**
**range 1 (lowest) to 5 (highest); n=281**

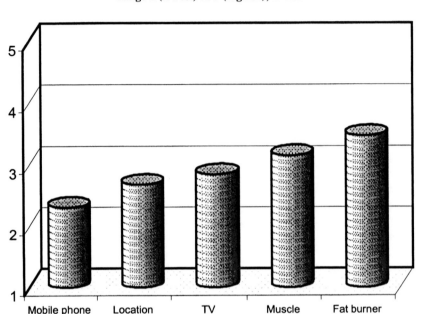

technology that is specifically interpersonally communication, but that many think it is a bad idea.

When we look at the technologies in detail, we find a few points of interest. For example, as shown in figure 2.2, females are decidedly the least enthusiastic in their interest in mobile phone implants. This was a surprise within a surprise since we had expected women to be more interested than men in mobile phone communication. Certainly it has been noted that women do most of the "phone work" (Fischer, 1994; Katz, 1999; Rakow, 1992) and that it is a popular and comfortable technology among them. Yet it is also true that women tend to lag behind men in terms of their uptake of new technology, so this might help us understand their lack of enthusiasm for the mobile phone implant. A plurality of males is neutral, though the mean is less than neutral in terms of interest.

Figure 2.3 shows the levels of interest in location-monitoring technology by gender. Again, the largest percentage of opinion is that of females against the idea, while the plurality of males is neutral. However, the mean of males does seem decisively higher than females.

**Figure 2.2**
**Opinion (in percent) about Implanted Mobile Phone by Gender**
**n=281**

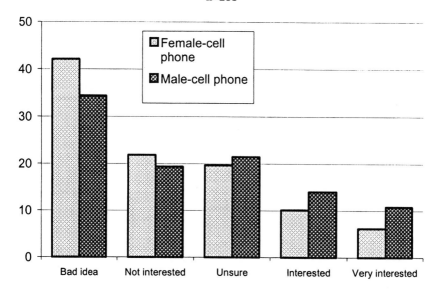

**Figure 2.3**
**Opinion (in percent) about Implanted Location Monitor by Gender**
**n=281**

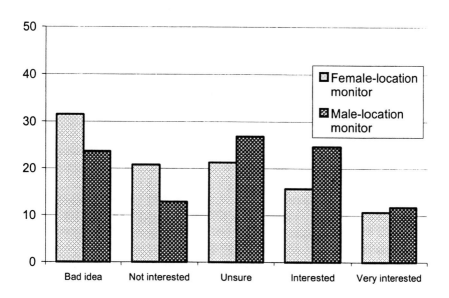

In terms of TV, a passive form of entertainment, very few females seem interested in this possible implant, a plurality saying it is a bad idea. This is shown in figure 2.4. Yet the plurality of this sample of males seems interested, and overall males report much higher levels of interest in the possibility of a TV implant.

**Figure 2.4**
**Opinion (in percent) about Implanted TV by Gender**
**n=281**

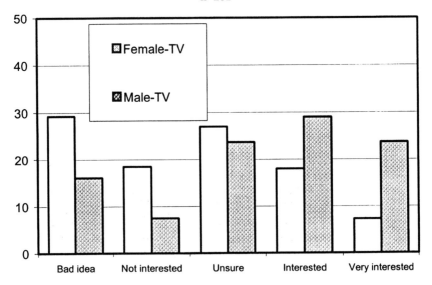

As shown in figure 2.5, males are keenly interested in the possibility of an implant that would enhance their musculature. Females are only mildly interested in such an implanted technology. In contrast, as reflected in figure 2.6, a plurality of women is very interested in a fat burning implant. A plurality of men is also very interested.

The overall interest in the implants that improve outward appearance is noteworthy. It suggests that having something inside, and presumably secret and invisible, that would improve one's appearance to those outside, is a higher priority than functional life improvement, social contact or entertainment. Some of the reasons why this might be the case are taken up on later chapters, especially the one by L. Fortunati.

An intriguing question, and one that perhaps even trumps which types of implant people may be interested in is the levels of interest themselves. On the one hand, one might argue that if the post-modernists were right, there would be widespread and enthusiastic endorsement of implants. And if the critics of modernization were correct, there would be near-universal rejection of the proffered technology. Yet what we find is a consistent pattern. People are

Figure 2.5
Opinion (in percent) about Implanted Mobile Phone by Gender
n=281

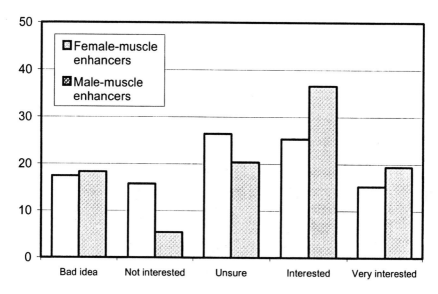

Figure 2.6
Opinion (in percent) about Implanted Fat Burner by Gender
n=281

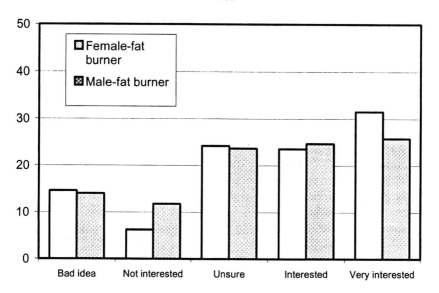

well satisfied with their daily routines, or at least do not by and large see intrusive technology as a strategic benefit. (See chapter 3, this volume.) Instead in the largest degree people seek their devices to give them an aesthetic advantage, or at least to correct self-perceived shortcomings.

Yet their responses also cast light on a perennial debate that touches on theology, philosophy, phenomenology, and even computer science. That debate revolves around the question of what is the fundamental reality of human beings. On the one hand, some argue that humans are *merely* elegant machines, a mere physiological body operating with a false sense of consciousness far more profound than anything imagined by Karl Marx. Others say humans are higher beings with an authentic spirit and meaningful consciousness. The question then is whether biological humans are really people, with sensuality and self-awareness, history and meaning, or just machines living in a monster machine known as society (Horowitz 1954, 102-103). René Descartes (1596-1650) held that humans though clearly biological, had both parts: body and soul. Others, such as Julian Offray de La Mettrie (1709-51), rejected this Cartesian dualism, maintaining instead that the human mind and society were mere byproducts of neurological processes: synapses, and nothing more. La Mettrie was quite literal on the point that humans were not simply becoming machines, rather, they *were* machines! One of his book titles says it best: *L'homme machine* (*Man a Machine*) (1996 [1748]).

` This question commands less public concern today than it did a quarter millennium ago (La Mettrie was forced to leave France because of his views). Perhaps this is due to the fact that we are now speculating about the qualities of computers of the future. We prefer to wonder whether *they* will have *our* sense of consciousness rather than whether *our own* sense of consciousness is valid. Yet the question is of vital concern to the disciplines enumerated above. When it comes to the non-randomly selected "student-in-the-street" as reflected in the survey described in this chapter, we find little interest in blending machines into humans. Based on this admittedly flimsy evidence we could speculate that if people are mere biology, the biology does a superb job of mimicking higher consciousness. In fact, it is so good that most people would have no interest in supplementing their biological capabilities with mechanical ones. Moreover, if humans are more than the sum of their parts, they are, for the most part, unenthusiastic about mixing those parts with "unnatural machines."

By way of conclusion, then, we recognize that this is not a definitive study of the question. Rather it is a first jaunt in the search for an empirical basis upon which to build our theoretical edifices. Benjamin Franklin opined, "One of the greatest tragedies of life is the murder of a beautiful theory by a gang of brutal facts." In this case we tentatively offer some systematic data that can help inform our beautiful theories, and in a few cases if not necessarily murder them at least leave the dandies roughed up.

## References

Bartlett, Djurdja. 1999. *Body in Transition*. Zagreb, Croatia: Faculty of Textile Technology, University of Zagreb.

Clarke, Arthur C. *July 20, 2019: Life in the 21ˢᵗ Century*. New York: Macmillan.

Day, Ronald E. 2001. *The Modern Invention of Information: Discourse, History, and Power*. Southern Illinois University Press.

Denning, Peter J. ed., 1999. *Talking Back to the Machine: Computers and Human Aspiration*. New York: Springer-Verlag.

Dyens, Olivier. 2001. *Metal and Flesh: The Evolution of Man: Technology Takes Over*. MIT Press, 2001.

Everdell, William R. 1977. *The First Moderns*. Chicago: University of Chicago Press.

Fischer, Claude. 1994. *America Calling: A Social History of the Telephone to 1940*. Berkeley: University of California Press.

Fortunati, Leopoldina, James E. Katz and Raimonda Riccini. (forthcoming). *Mediating Bodies*. Mahwah, NJ: Lawrence Erlbaum and Associates.

Gershenfeld, Neil. 1999. *When Things Start to Think*, New York: Henry Holt.

Hayles, N. Katherine. 1999. *How We Became Post Human: Virtual Bodies in Cybernetics, Literature, and Informatics*. Chicago: University of Chicago Press.

Horowitz, Irving L. 1954. *Claude Helvetius: Philosopher of Democracy and Enlightenment*. New York: Paine-Whitman.

Huyssen, Andreas. 1990. *After the Great Divide: Modernism, Mass Culture, Postmodernism*. Bloomington: Indiana University Press.

Katz, James E. and Rice, Ronald E. (forthcoming). Mobile Communication on 9-11. Special issue of *Prometheus*.

Katz, James E. 1999. *Connections: Social and Cultural Studies of American Life*. New Brunswick, NJ: Transaction Publishers.

Katz, James E. and Mark Aakhus. 2002. *Perpetual Contact: Personal Communication, Private Talk, Public Performance*. Cambridge: Cambridge University Press.

Marx, Leo. 1967. *The Machine in the Garden: Technology and the Pastoral Ideal in America*. Oxford University Press;

Mettrie, J. O. de la. 1996 (1748). *Machine Man and Other Writings* (Cambridge Texts in the History of Philosophy). Cambridge: Cambridge University Press.

Myerson, George. 2001. *Heidegger, Habermas and the mobile phone*. Cambridge: Icon books.

Noll, A. M. (forthcoming). *Communication on 9-11*. Special issue of *Prometheus*.

Rakow, Lana 1992. *Gender on the Line: Women, the Telephone, and Community Life*. Urbana: University of Illinois Press.

Rice, Ronald E. and Jane Webster. 2002. Adoption, Diffusion and Use of New Media. Pages 191 to 228 in Carolyn Lynn and David Atkin, *Communication Technology and Society: Audience Adoption and Uses*. Cresskill, NJ: Hampton Press.

Ronel, Avital. 1991. *The Telephone Book: Technology, Schizophrenia, Electric Speech*. Lincoln: University of Nebraska Press.

Turkle, Sherry. 1991. *Life on the Screen: Identity in the Age of the Internet*. New York: Harper and Row.

Waltz, Kenneth. 1997. Evaluating Theories. *American Political Science Review*. Vol. 91, no. 4, 913-17.

White, Lynn Townsend.1966. *Medieval Technology and Social Change*. New York: Clarendon Press.

# 3

# Understanding Information and Communication Technology and Infrastructure in Everyday Life: Struggling with Communication-at-a-Distance

*Mark Aakhus*

## Introduction

When we think of machines that become us, it is easy to think in terms of individuals and their accoutrements. The material components of gadgets and systems are more obvious than the premises, procedures, and concepts that frame the use and usability of information and communication technology services (ICTs). This aspect of ICTs is referred to here as *infrastructure.* Star and colleagues (Bowker and Star 1999; Star 1999; Star and Strauss 1999; Star and Ruhleder 1996) have examined infrastructure in the context of large-scale systems. They demonstrate how infrastructure is found in procedures, policies, categories, and protocols, although it is often implicitly negotiated and seemingly intangible. Their analysis reveals how infrastructure is material and social in the way it defines how people relate to each other. While ICTs may be personal, the infrastructure people build up to make ICTs useable (and potentially useful) has implications for the ways people relate to each other in managing their everyday affairs.

Infrastructure entails the realm of ideas, however, not just the material and social aspects of technology. In particular, infrastructure entails ideas about communication and information. In their theory of *Apparatgeist,* Katz and Aakhus (2002), describe common strategies and principles of reasoning about the use and development of ICTs that draw together individual and collective behavior. The prevailing logic associated with the use and design of ICTs is the idea that communication is the sharing of minds and that technology should make possible "perpetual contact" that overcomes time and space barriers. As a generally available strategy for making ICTs usable, the logic of perpetual contact does not necessarily lead to happy, useful solutions because communication is not limited to increased openness among people. When people embrace and distance themselves from ICTs, they are responding to the logic of perpetual contact as it is realized in the material and social aspects of ICTs.

This chapter explores infrastructure in the realm of ICTs by examining aspects of infrastructure associated with ICTs. This involves, in particular, the struggle to make *communication-at-a-distance* viable in the management of everyday affairs. *Communication-at-a-distance* refers to uses of media to cross barriers of time or space. By considering the ideas about communication involved in the way people build interpersonal communication and information infrastructures that make their ICTs usable, and possibly useful, this chapter reflects on the "us" in the process in that of machines that become us.

## The Puzzle

Information and communication technology and services (ICTs) are generally designed to solve communication and information problems and, presumably, are used for the same reason. ICTs make possible forms of distant (or distributed) communication to deal with time and coordination problems people experience in everyday life. Yet, prior research on the role of ICTs in households suggests that people tend not to understand or believe that ICTs solve their communication problems in managing time and coordinating the household (Dudley, Steinfield, Kraut, and Katz 1993; Frissen 2000; Katz 1999). This irony is explored here by describing some ways young adults understand the role of ICTs in managing time and coordinating their living arrangements. These findings provide an opportunity to reflect on how distant (or distributed) communication is interpreted and judged in everyday life.

## Mismatched and Taken for Granted

Dudley et al. (1993) surveyed residential subscribers on telecommunication services in American households. They found that members of American households do not necessarily use telecommunication products to solve their communication problems related to time and coordination. Their original model assumed that choosing telecom products was driven by people who have experienced specific time and coordination problems in the household and would try to solve them by finding technological solutions. The survey results, however, did not support this assumption. Moreover, they found an association between the number of communication problems households report and the presence of telecommunication devices available in the household. They were unable to disentangle whether more communication problems lead to households seeking out telecom devices or whether more telecom devices lead to more communication problems perceived. They offer two reasons for these findings: (1) mismatch between design and needs and (2) ICTs are taken for granted.

There is a mismatch between the design of technology and services and the types of time and coordination problems households experience; thus technologies and services are not viable solutions. Dudley et al. find that households are diverse while services remain generic. They also note that household members seek quality interaction to overcome the loss of time and connection they otherwise might have with household members or extended family. These observations are most evident in two-career households that experience high coordination and time constraints. Dudley et al. advocate designs for devices and services that help people transcend time and that support a balance between instrumental needs and social needs (emotion-rich communication).

Telecommunication services are also taken for granted in most households. Thus, these services are not framed as solutions to communication problems. The exception to this pattern reinforces the pattern—that is, households where at least one member worked from home more explicitly used telecomm to solve problems of time and coordination. For example, in households where a member works from home, the answering machine is likely to be seen as a way for household members to leave messages and thus coordinate household activities. By contrast, households where work takes place outside the home treat the answering machine as a recorder of calls from members external to the household and it is thus not recognized as means to coordinate schedules from a distance.

## Devices not Solutions

Frissen (2000) examined Dutch households in the "rush hour of life," which means two-career households with children. She found that ICTs are used for solving time and coordination problems but that ICTs are not explicitly perceived as solutions to the coordination problems households experience in everyday life. She notes, for instance, that interviewees in her study never spontaneously mention ICTs as potential solutions. The solutions mentioned include seeking flexibility from an employer, work peers, and public hours and to seek home help staff for cleaning and childcare. These solutions emphasize the need for both flexibility and control and focus on rearranging work and household policies to generate more childcare possibilities and more flexible childcare.

Frissen offers three reasons why ICTs are not perceived as solutions to time and coordination problems. First, ICTs are perceived as limited in giving flexibility, autonomy, and control. The mobile telephone is a service that parents see to hold promise but the mobile telephone is a double-edged sword because in creating more freedom to contact others, it also creates more possibilities to be contacted. The Internet is primarily understood to be a "bottomless (and time-consuming) source of information," not a viable tool for solving everyday problems. Second, there are substantial differences between reasons for buying a new ICT and the function the technology eventually serves for the household. Third, dissemination and marketing strategies tend to be shortsighted in focusing on initial purchase and initial integration into the home. These strategies do not adequately take into account the reasons people use ICTS and do less to cultivate practices for effective and meaningful use in the household.

Finally, Katz (1999) and colleagues have criticized the way behavioral and consumer research is conducted in the telecommunication service arena. They found that researchers gather information about user interest and perceptions piecemeal. That is, researchers survey the consumer about only a few services or issues at a time. While this is understandable given budget and resource constraints, researchers say it leads to unfortunate consequences. For example, if people are able to express their "willingness-to-pay" for telecommunication services one at a time, they will express great interest in a large variety of services. When the bill for all these services is tallied, it usually adds up to several thousand dollars annually, which is an unrealistic figure given typical spending habits. But unless the total picture of consumer spending is attained, marketers and researchers can be easily misled by partial results viewed from a narrow perspective.

### The Struggle to Use Distant Communication

The Dudley et al. study emphasizes how telecomm technology and services are not well tailored or "tailorable" to needs of diverse households. The Frissen study emphasizes how ICTs do not clearly give technology users flexibility without compromising their autonomy. The Katz study suggests that researchers often fail to appreciate the context in which telecommunication service decisions and consumption takes place. The thrust of these studies suggests that ICTs are not understood to be meaningful solutions to communication problems related to time and coordination. Crafting distant communication into a means to handle time and coordination problems, moreover, remains elusive despite the availability of devices for such purposes.

Time and coordination problems, however, are not the sole province of dual-income families with children. Studies of Norwegian teens (Ling and Yttri 2000) and Finnish teens (Rautiainen and Kasesniemi 2000) show that they have deeply incorporated ICTs into their everyday lives, even to the point that participation in everyday life almost demands facility with ICTs. Teens in these studies are able to dynamically organize social gatherings and carry out important relational functions by creating forms of distance communication with their mobile phones and short-messaging service. Yet, in contrast to the households described above, the teen use of ICTs is primarily expressive and social. Ling and Yttri have questioned the extent to which these habits and modes of action will carry over into other stages of life and, it might be added here, into other forms of life activity such as managing living arrangements.

The theories about using technology in everyday life in adult households do not appear to be as "thick" and well developed, say, as the way Norwegian and Finnish teens use mobile telephones and short messaging services. It appears that people have yet to learn and do not receive much help in developing improved premises for interpreting, judging, and inventing uses of ICTs in everyday life. It could be that there is both a lack of inventiveness of use and a failure to interpret and judge the possibilities for distance communication in this population.

Indeed, these problems seem pervasive across social groups in contemporary societies. At the same time, dual income families with children, such as those studied by Dudley et al., and Frissen and Katz, may neither be the most technologically savvy nor the most likely to have well-developed, elaborated, or "thick" theories of ICTs usage.

## Context of Present Study

The present study explores the puzzle, identified by Dudley et al. (1993), Frissen (2000), and Katz (1999), where ICTs are not understood to be solutions to communication problems within the context of the living arrangements of young adults (ages 18–24). This is an interesting population because, especially at the time of the study, young adults (ages 18–24) are likely to be more technologically savvy and have more well-developed theories-of-use than members of two-income households like those in the Dudley et al. and Frissen studies. They are also engaged in maintaining a living arrangement independent of their parents. So, unlike teens, they have to take on many of the instrumental everyday maintenance issues experienced in two-income family households. Thus, it is expected that this population is likely to see the possibilities of using distance communication in creative ways to manage living arrangements.

### Respondents

The respondents for this study comprised students in a mediated communication course at a large university in the eastern United States. Most of the students owned a mobile phone and lived in rather rich ICT environments where they either owned their own computer or had access to one within their living arrangements. The living arrangements of the respondents (n =92) were primarily rented apartments (48%) or houses that they shared with others (24%). Apartments generally involved fewer members (up to four) than houses (three or more). These living arrangements reflect a form of independent living where they had to work out their own rules for living and managing the living arrangement, even to a degree in situations where the respondents still live in the parent's home. The social organization of these living arrangements, however, likely differs in important ways from the households in the Dudley et al. (1993) and Frissen (2000) studies. The interdependence among the members is likely lower than that found between married couples with children. The anticipated duration of membership in the living arrangement is likely much shorter than in the married with children households. Nevertheless, the formation and maintenance of the social bond among the participants still requires negotiating the demands of autonomy and connection as expressed in time and coordination problems. And, as will be discussed, these living arrangements involve time and coordination problems, and the members have their own ideas about how to solve these problems. (See Table 3.1)

**Table 3.1**
**Living Arrangement**

|                    | Frequency % |
| ------------------ | ----------- |
| Apartment          | 48          |
| House              | 24          |
| Parents House      | 22          |
| Dormitory          | 4           |
| Frat/Sorority House| 2           |

n=92 respondents

*Data*

This study uses self-reports young adults made about the time and coordination problems they experience in their living arrangements and the ways that these could be solved. This approach is a based on Frissen's (2000) observation that there were no spontaneous mentions of communication and information technology as a solution to the time and coordination problems people reported. While other questions were asked in the survey, the first two questions, which are the subject of this report, were:

1.    List the most common problems related to time and coordination experienced in your current living arrangement.

2.    List whatever solutions you can think of for these problems of time and coordination experienced in your living arrangement.

These open-ended questions served multiple methodological purposes. First, these questions make it possible to explore whether people spontaneously think of ICTs as solutions to time and coordination problems in a survey format. Second, the questions do not provide a menu of choices that might prompt an answer that the respondent would not otherwise independently produce. Third, the questions elicit native terms and expressions about their experiences in their living arrangement, which enable the use of a grounded approach in building analytic concepts. This approach is particularly well suited for an exploratory study such as this where it is important to develop relevant categories and hypothesis for further research. The data provide evidence of how people describe their world and thus an opportunity to analyze the ways in which they interpret and judge that world.

The respondents completed the survey at the beginning of the fall semester 2000 and the spring semester 2001. They completed the survey before any course material was covered. They could mention as many or as few time and coordination problems and solutions as came to mind; thus the findings below report more problems and solutions than respondents completing the survey. The "mentions" of problems and solutions were coded by using respondent terms to generate a list, which was then further categorized to identify themes in the problems and solutions mentioned.

*Findings*

*Time and Coordination Problems.* The common problems reported by the subjects are found in table 3.2. The 170 mentions of problems were broken down into 30 types of common problems based on the respondents' terms and expressions. The "top nine" as identified by respondents, and their frequency (in percent) are:

**Table 3.2**
**Categorization of Problems**

|  | Frequency % |
|---|---|
| Getting together different schedules | 13 |
| Chores/cleaning | 13 |
| Bathroom | 12 |
| Being together different schedules | 6.5 |
| Noisy/can't sleep | 6.5 |
| Can't use phone | 5.3 |
| Cooking/food shopping | 5.3 |
| Commuting | 4.1 |
| Can't study/get work done | 3.5 |

n=170 problems mentioned

The problems represent difficulties in sharing common space and resources and maintaining these resources. Further analysis of the problems mentioned seem to me to cluster into four: problems in the use of time, maintenance activity, use of utilities, and use of space.

Time and coordination problems in the young adult settings are presented as a lack of common goods when there is a "traffic jam" in the household, such as running short of hot water, too many cars in the driveway parking area, or too much demand for various media, utilities, and space. The other aspects of this are complaints or grievances about performance of chores and cleaning of the household and the ability to get together to talk about how to maintain the household. The respondents' time and coordination problems represent a potential "tragedy of the commons" (Hardin 1968). That is, the more individual members of the living arrangement use common resources in his or her own self-interest, the more likely the quality or availability of common goods is diminished. Adding to this character of their living arrangement is the apparent difficulty in talking about the sharing of and caring for their common goods. This is especially evident when the frequency of mentioned problems is arrayed by the type of living arrangement as illustrated in table 3.4. In the apartments, there is greater awareness of dealing with shared resources. For those living in their parent's house, the types of problems are more evenly distributed among all types of problems identified.

### Time and Coordination Solutions

The common solutions reported by the respondents were consolidated into thirty types of common solutions by using the terms and expressions of the participants.

The solutions represent an orientation toward what to change about the current living arrangement. The solutions were further analyzed in table 3.3 to identify themes. The primary emphasis was on communicative change followed by use of media and altering the availability of resources.

The solutions suggest not so much what people do or will do. Rather they suggest a sense of what is a good solution. These solutions emphasize changing the way people communicate collectively or individually. The direction of change implied in the solutions points to a type of communication that includes planning, making opportunities for collective planning, and for courteous, tolerant communication. The direction of change for individual action orients toward avoidance and toleration of the potential problems in the situation. In the apartment and house conditions, emphasis is on planning and open, tolerant communication. By contrast, in the parent household, no solution stands out as demonstrated in table 3.4.

While the respondents have many ideas about the type of communication that will solve their problems, there is little by way of corresponding ideas about how their ICTs are tools for the collaborative management of common goods, which presents comparative results to the Dudley et al. and Frissen studies. ICTs are much less likely to be mentioned than calls for other communicative changes in the group or individual. Media tools are not adapted as the means for tasks such as conducting meetings, making decisions, and making

**Table 3.3**
**Solution Themes**

|  | Frequency of Mention (in %) |
|---|---|
| **Communicative Change** | |
| **Collective** | |
| Establish schedule | 22 |
| Better face-to-face | 12 |
| Respect/courtesy/consideration | 7 |
| Know each others schedule | 6 |
| Find common time | 5 |
| Better asynchronous communication | 1 |
| *Sub-total-collective* | *53* |
| **Individual** | |
| Go elsewhere to do task | 5 |
| Wake up/leave early | 4 |
| Better use of spare time | 4 |
| Change employment situation | 3 |
| Move | 2 |
| Live/sleep on different floor | 2 |
| Toleration | 2 |
| Be more organized | 1 |
| Motivation | 1 |
| Avoidance | 1 |
| Use alternate entrance/exit | 1 |
| Switch classes | 1 |
| *Sub-total-individual* | 27 |
| Total-communicative change | 80 |
| **Use of Media** | |
| **Conventional** | |
| Leave notes | 5 |
| Bulletin board | 1 |
| Reminder book | 1 |
| *Sub-total-conventional* | 7 |
| **ICTs** | |
| Answering machine | 2 |
| Use cell phone | 2 |
| E-mail | 2 |
| Use VCR | 1 |
| *Sub-total-ICT* | 7 |
| Total-use of media | 14 |
| **Alternative Resource Availability** | |
| Get more phone lines | 3 |
| Get a[nother] computer | 1 |
| Get internet | 1 |
| Leave keys in common area | 1 |
| Don't lock door | 1 |
| Total-alternative resource availability | 7 |

sense of shared problems, but rather are means for orchestrating coordination, signaling common courtesy, and creating time for face-to-face meetings. There is a very limited sense that ICTs have a role in making communication-at-a-distance into a means to solve time and coordination problems. It is noteworthy how there is no reference to anything that resembles the dynamic planning and orchestration performed by Norwegian teens (Ling and Yttri 2000) and Finnish teens (Rautiainen and Kasesniemi 2000). Moreover, in reconsidering the framing of problems, ICTs and other media are seen as a scarce resource generative of grievances and conflicts. There are few complaints, by contrast, about communicative norms involving the use of ICTs, such as roommates not answering the phone or responding to each other's phone calls or e-mail. Such complaints would be a sign that people were using their ICTs to engage each other and to make communication-at-a-distance into a means to deal with their time and coordination problems.

It is worth noting that using distance communication to handle their time and coordination problems is especially challenging. In the present case, the respondents cannot rely on general shared presumptions about everyday life patterns and must in fact negotiate these patterns and the implications for their living arrangement. Yet, they are caught in a lurch because their ideas about changing communication at the collective and individual level are mutually antagonizing. The solutions for collective communication emphasize openness and sharing while the solution proposed for individual communication emphasizes avoidance and tolerance. Moreover, the social conditions presumed by these solutions do not seem to be present. The situations do lend themselves to negotiation as a way to manage conflict. That is, individuals hold little claim over another's actions and individuals enjoy little normative expectations to be held over themselves. Such situations foster conflict management behaviors like avoidance and tolerance rather than negotiation (Morrill 1995).

## Discussion

The findings described here reflect a trend similar to the findings of Dudley et al. (1993), Frissen (2000), and Katz (1999) that suggests that people do not readily see their ICTs as the means to help them invent communicative activity at a distance to manage time and coordination problems encountered in their living arrangements. These findings taken together also point to the broader issue of understanding infrastructure in the use of ICTs in everyday life. Infrastructure involves all the devices and services, and their interrelationships, which people bring to bear on their everyday circumstances. Understanding infrastructure, however, is limited when only one type of device or service is taken into account. Infrastructure involves the collective working out of the communication and information procedures that make ICTs usable—but not necessarily useful—in everyday life. Understanding infrastructure, however, is limited when its relational properties and invisibility are not taken into account (Star 1999).

**Table 3.4**
**Frequency of Solution Mention by Living Arrangement**

| Apartment | Mentions | House | Mentions | Parent's Home | Mentions |
|---|---|---|---|---|---|
| establish schedule | 6 | establish schedule | 7 | leave notes | 3 |
| better face to face (f2f) | 6 | wake up leave early | 2 | go elsewhere to do task | 3 |
| respect/ courtesy/ consideration | 3 | better f2f | 2 | find common time | 3 |
| answering machine | 2 | respect/ courtesy/ consideration | 2 | get more phone lines | 2 |
| e-mail | 2 | get more phone lines | 1 | better f2f | 2 |
| better use of spare time | 2 | bulletin board | 1 | get another computer | 1 |
| change employment situation | 2 | leave notes | 1 | use cell phone | 1 |
| know each others schedule | 2 | go elsewhere to do task | 1 | establish schedule | 1 |
| leave notes | 1 | toleration | 1 | be more organized | 1 |
| reminder book | 1 | better asynch | 1 | wake up/ leave early | 1 |
| wake up leave early | 1 | avoidance | 1 | move | 1 |
| go elsewhere to do task | 1 | find common time | 1 | use alternate entrance/ exit | 1 |
| move | 1 | know each others schedule | 1 | live/sleep on different floor | 1 |
| live/sleep on different floor | 1 | leave keys in common area | 1 | motivation | 1 |
| toleration | 1 | | | better use of spare time | 1 |
| find common time | 1 | | | know each other's schedule | 1 |
| switch classes | 1 | | | | |
| don't lock door | 1 | | | | |
| use vcr | 1 | | | | |
| Total | 36 | Total | 23 | Total | 24 |

The possibility of organizing personal ICT infrastructures to conduct communication-at-a-distance represents both practical and theoretical opportunity for understanding the trajectory of machines that become us. The use (or non-use) of ICTs are implicated in the participants struggle to manage their commons. There is little reason to doubt that, as Dudley et al. (1993) and Frissen (2000) point out, the design of ICTs contributes to its lack of functionality for managing households. While the prior studies focus heavily on the implications for the material aspects of ICTs, it is also important in understanding ICTs to identify the way ideas about communication may influence the building of infrastructure and hence the usability and usefulness of ICTs.

This study suggests that the ideas about communication involved in interpreting and judging situations and inventing communicative actions to make distant communication a viable means for dealing with the time and coordination problems should be reconsidered. Indeed, as Katz and Aakhus (2002) have underscored, the pregnant image of "perpetual contact," which is a long-standing idealization of communication, is only now being worked out in the design and use of ICTs. The building of infrastructure involves ideas about communication. Even though ICTs may shift communicative possibilities, ICTs may not be changing ideas about communication, such as the logic of perpetual contact. Understanding how machines become us requires reconsidering and reframing the ideas about communication that frame their use and design.

### Reframing Communication-at-a-distance

Fundamental to contemporary understanding of technology and communication is the idea that technology is a means of "transport" to a "virtual place." This idea appears to be at work in the respondents' reports about time and coordination problems and solutions. This idea is also part of influential views about communication-at-distance. This view draws attention to new possibilities, choices, and consequences associated with ICTs; however, it draws attention away from the fact that people must work their uses of ICTs into their local, time-bound circumstances no matter what their purpose may be in using ICT. The transportation and virtual-place framing of ICTs, however, provides grounds for building an alternative idea about communication to frame the understanding of ICTs and the building of *interpersonal* communication and information infrastructures.

### Telepresence

Short, Williams, and Christie's (1976) classic work on the social psychology of telecommunications is organized around explaining the impact of substituting telecommunication for travel. They explore what is likely to happen to urban structure, social organization, human relations, and the individual with the advent of technology that overcomes distance. Their theory is an attempt to take seriously the effect a medium has on interaction. To make sense of the consequences of new media, they propose the concept of "social presence" to account for users' feelings and mindset toward a technology. Social presence is a perception that a medium enables different qualities of interaction (pp. 65–66). These perceptions influence people's choices about using a communication technology and their reaction to using a particular technology. The basic points of investigation address which communication modalities make social presence possible and what social presence is necessary for different types of communication.

The argument expressed by Short et al. is important in the way it draws attention to communication media and its implications for understanding the relationship between people and their communication tools to create it. However, it is important to note that this is not a theory of interaction and the use of tools. The theory does not address how people create social presence despite the affordances of a particular modality. Instead, the interest is in how people compare the channels open to them. Herein lies an opportunity for expanding understanding of the choices in organizing ICT infrastructure to deal with social relations.

## Place

Meyrowitz (1985) addresses the consequence of the separation of social space from physical space caused by new media. Meyrowitz argues that new media present people with a place that is "no place at all." The consequence is that new media disrupt people's ability to interpret what Goffman calls the "definition of the situation," thus contributing to the no sense of place. Like Short et al., the key assumption is that the quality of the media impacts the quality of interaction. Meyrowitz's concept of media quality is not as clear as Short et al. Meyrowitz, however, identifies a new class of social problems that arise from no sense of place such as the blurring between public and private, feminine and masculine, lines of authority, and adult and child situations that in turn influence human development, human affiliations, and public discourse and decision-making.

Meyrowitz's argument, on the surface, is compelling, yet upon further examination, it assumes that the old is natural and the new is not. The argument is committed to the idea that a definition of the situation is determined by place. This position has been seriously challenged by the work of ethnomethodologists and conversation analysts. The more interesting fact ICTs draw attention to is that our sense of place—the definition of the situation—is a negotiated order whether we are physically present or not. Herein lies an opportunity for expanding an understanding of the means people develop to orchestrate their distant interaction into their everyday life.

There are at least two problems with the transportation and place imagery presented by Meyrowitz. First, this imagery disregards the local circumstances of the communicators. Whether one meets face-to-face or otherwise, the communicative challenge lies in formulating a context for intersubjectivity and in managing the autonomy/connectedness dialectic. The idea that communication-at-a-distance is somehow equivalent to transporting people to a virtual place glosses over the fact that mediated communication takes place at a specific time and place, imbuing it with all the contingencies that it implies. Second, the transportation and place metaphor confuses media with activity. We usually do not simply experience a technological device for mediated communication because devices are made operable and useful by associated services. These services increasingly blend the capacities of devices. The activities and needs of everyday life, however, have not changed to the degree technology has. So, people (i.e., users and designers) are left to figure out how to make ICTs usable and useful without losing the satisfaction and benefit of the activities they enjoyed prior to the new technology's inception. The challenge for designers and users is building interpersonal infrastructures that make distant communication viable within the local, time-bound circumstances communicators find themselves in. This calls for a very different type of imagination than that entangled in the escapism entailed in being transported to virtual places. So, communication-at-a-distance does not have to be understood only as transportation to a place, although that is how it is commonly characterized in studies of media and mediated communication.

## The Dialectical Alternative

An alternative, then, is to recognize that ICTs are tools for participating in broader human activity like relationships, family, work, and learning. Moreover, these tools propose solutions to a primary aspect of human communication: the dialectic between autonomy and connection. Human communication is propelled in part by the way people resolve the competing desires and expectations to be separate or to be together. To be separate invites liberty with the potential for isolation and alienation. To be connected invites solidarity and belongingness, but with the potential for loss of self and domination by the collective will. To some extent, there is an irreconcilable tension between these dialectical poles, and "making it through the day" involves inventing and appropriating strategies and habits of thought to manage the shifting demands for autonomy and connection. This rather Durkheimian perspective on social life is a useful starting point for understanding ICTs in everyday life.

This alternative can be developed by characterizing ICTs in a way that highlights how ICTs are implicated in building interpersonal communication and information infrastructures. A central practical problem involves constructing communicative contexts that make communication-at-a-distance viable within the local, time-bound circumstances in which people act. Research using conversation analysis provides one means for addressing these issues. Hopper (1992) and Schegloff (2002) have outlined promising approaches to understanding how the media is articulated into communicative experience and into the competing demands to be autonomous and connected. However, their work remains committed to aspects of a transportation/place framing. This is most evident in their tendency to write off the technology as uninteresting background. Namely, they argue that the importance of the phone is that it provides filtered voices that give a "purer" look at talk in action.

What is missing in contemporary studies of mediated communication is a better understanding of the relationship between communicators, their communication tools, and the communication activities they construct. This study is a simple step in this direction as it attempts to articulate ways people reason about the use of ICTs to manage aspects of everyday life. ICTs should be understood in the same way we understand the communicative affordances of courtroom proceedings, press conferences, or interviews (Aakhus 2000). The affordances provide means, that can be appropriated or mastered, to invoke or construct lines of joint activity—in particular, the construction of communicative contexts at a distance (Aakhus 1999). A central issue, then, is the logic used to bind and maintain forms of relationships and the consequences of this logic for the use of ICTs and the way people intentionally (and unintentionally) design interpersonal infrastructure to manage the demands of their relationships. ICTs are tools for participation in broader human activities and means for managing the dialectic of autonomy and connection. An alternative lies in seeing how communication-at-a-distance involves the negotiation of autonomy and connection in human relationships through communication and information procedures. This is potentially more fruitful for understanding the use, design, and theory of infrastructure and ICTs.

## References

Aakhus, M. 2000. Constituting Deliberation as "Buy-In" through GDSS Design and Implementation. *The Electronic Journal of Communication/La Revue Electronique de Communication*, 10. Available: *http://www.cios.org/www/ejc/v10n1200.htm.*

Aakhus, M. 1999. Reconstruction Games: Assessing the Resources for Managing Collective Argumentation in Groupware Technology. In *Proceedings of the Fourth International Conference on Argumentation,* ed. F. H. van Eemeren, R. Grootendorst, J. A. Blair, and C. A. Willard, pp. 1–7. Amsterdam: International Centre for the Study of Argumentation, SIC SAT, Amsterdam, The Netherlands.

Dudley, K., C. Steinfeld, R. Kraut, and J. Katz. 1993. Rethinking Household Telecommunications. Paper presented to the International Communication Association Conference, Washington, DC.

Frissen, V. 2000. ICTs in the Rush Hour of Life, *The Information Society* 16: 64–75.

Hardin, G. 1968. The Tragedy of the Commons. *Science* 162: 1243–1248.

Hopper, R. 1992. *Telephone Conversation.* Bloomington: University of Indiana Press.

Katz, James E. 1999. *Connections: Social and Cultural Studies of the Telephone in American Life.* New Brunswick, NJ: Transaction Publishers.

Katz, J. and M. Aakhus. 2002. Conclusion: Making Meaning of Mobiles—A Theory of Apparatgeist. In *Perpetual Contact: Mobile Communication, Private Talk, Public Per-*

*formance*, eds. J. Katz and M. Aakhus, 301–318. Cambridge and New York: Cambridge University Press.

Ling, R. and B. Yttri. 2002. Hyper-Coordination via Mobile Phones in Norway. In *Perpetual Contact: Mobile Communication, Private Talk, Public Performance,* eds. J. Katz and M. Aakhus, 139–169. Cambridge and New York: Cambridge University Press.

Meyrowitz, J. 1985. *No Sense of Place: The Impact of Electronic Media on Social Behavior.* Oxford: Oxford University Press.

Morrill, C. 1995. *The Executive Way: Conflict Management in Corporations.* Chicago: University of Chicago Press.

Kasesniemi, E. and P. Rautiainen. 2002. Mobile Culture of Children and Teenagers in Finland. In *Perpetual Contact: Mobile Communication, Private Talk, Public Performance,* eds. J. Katz and M. Aakhus, 170–192. Cambridge: Cambridge University Press.

Schegloff, E. 2002. Opening Sequencing. In *Perpetual Contact: Mobile Communication, Private Talk, Public Performance,* ed. J. Katz and M. Aakhus, 326–386. Cambridge and New York: Cambridge University Press.

Short, J., E. Williams, and B. Christie. 1976. *The Social Psychology of Telecommunication.* New York: John Wiley and Sons.

Star, S. 1999. The Ethnography of Infrastructure. *American Behavioral Scientist* 43: 377–391.

# 4

# Domestication and Mobile Telephony

*Leslie Haddon*

### Introduction

This chapter outlines the history and key elements of the domestication approach, showing where these are shared in some empirical studies of mobile telephony. It then shows how the approach could be extended out of the home to cover portable information and communication technologies (ICTs) and domestication within social networks.

### Scope

The concept of *domestication* has achieved currency in approaches to understanding how information and communication technologies (ICTs) find a place in people's lives. Derived originally from more general studies of the process of consumption, this framework can provide a useful way of bringing together a range of assumptions about, and perspectives on, our relationships with ICTs.

However, the concept was originally used in British studies to provide a framework for thinking about ICTs in the home rather than portable ones. And to a large extent, it emphasized interactions between household members. Hence, developing this framework to deal with technologies such as mobile telephony and social networks beyond the home presents something of a dilemma.

The first part of this chapter outlines essential themes of domestication. However, they are by no means unique to this framework and so after each theme, a link is made indicating where this can already to be found in empirical research on the mobile phone. This section also notes some of the limitations of the domestication approach—the type of issues it does not attempt to address.

The second part of the chapter reflects on how issues raised in mobile phone studies suggest ways to extend the framework of domestication out of the home despite the connotations of the word *domestic*. In turn, this framework can be used to illuminate further questions we might ask regarding mobile phones. This challenge is addressed at the end of the section.

## A Brief History

To summarize the domestication approach briefly, ICTs come into consumer perceptions with their meanings pre-formed. This results from such processes as advertising, design, and surrounding media discourses. But afterward, households and individuals invest them with their own significance. This includes the effort involved before acquisition in imagining how they might find a place in the home and a role in people's lives, the household discussions about the decision to acquire them, and the process afterwards of locating these ICTs in domestic time and space. How exactly the concept of domestication has been employed in analysis and with what emphases has depended both upon the researcher and the particular goals of the project.

The concept of domestication emerged in the early 1990s from an empirical and theoretical project organized by Roger Silverstone at Brunel University, U.K., and was partly influenced by the emerging literature on consumption more generally, which in particular, drew attention to the symbolic nature of goods (Silverstone et al. 1992; Silverstone 1994b; Silverstone and Haddon 1996).

The second stage of the project, conducted at Sussex University, in which studies of teleworkers, single parents, and the young elderly (Haddon and Silverstone 1993, 1995, 1996) enabled further exploration of how this approach might be applied and led to incremental development around its key themes. For example, the telework study allowed us to explore how work and the accompanying ICTs had to be incorporated into the home, which meant new rules about phone and computer use, as well as new tensions. That study also showed the technological seepage whereby work tools acquired domestic or private uses and expertise and access to technologies could spread to other household members. The single-parent study drew attention to forms of household composition other than nuclear families, but also showed how the poverty and immediate priorities of many such families often put new ICTs beyond their horizons. Lastly, the young elderly study revealed the influence of biography—of early experiences—on the current consumption of ICTs. This led, for example, this group to resist frequently PCs both because of the point in their lives at which they encountered the technology and the value system that they had developed in their earlier years, which required more demonstrable benefits than were offered.

The concept of domestication spread to relevant European academic networks such as the EC-sponsored, Sussex-led (and in its second incarnation, LSE-led) European Media, Technology and Everyday Life (EMTEL) project. It was employed in the COST248 (and currently COST269) project on ICTs and everyday life, part of the wider pan-European program of research on telecommunications. And more recently, the domestication perspective was used as part of the framework for a EURESCOM project, (EURESCOM being the research arm of a number of European telecom companies), whose quantitative and qualitative studies focused on the Internet and mobile phone (Mante-Meijer and Haddon 2001).

The framework was used for company studies, specifically (for Telewest) research on the response of professionals and managers to cable TV and (for NCR) research on Internet adoption, non-adoption, and use (Haddon 1999). Both of these studies, for example, drew attention to the time slots that people made available for TV and Internet respectively, which constrained usage to an extent.

Finally, the domestication perspective was also used as a backdrop for policy-related analyses (Haddon and Silverstone 1995; 2000) and discussions of social issues (such as ICTs and social exclusion) (Silverstone 1994a; Haddon 2000). For example, the latter paper used the case of single parents and the young elderly to explore their ambiguities about, and sometimes resistance to, ICTs amidst claims that access to such technologies is important for participation in society.

This paper discusses some of the main themes of domestication from the British research.

## Key Assumptions

First, the emphasis is on consumption rather than mere use. So much attention has been given to what ICTs mean to people, how they experience them, and the roles ICTs can come to play in their lives. Understanding adoption and use also requires appreciating the negotiation and interaction between household members and the politics of the home, which lie behind conflicts and tensions as well as consensus. Any understandings or even rules about appropriate use of ICTs that emerge from this process usually have some bearing on what people do with the technologies and services and in what circumstances. We have to be aware of individual and household aspects, and strategies to control technologies, both in the sense of controlling use by others and controlling the place of technologies in one's own life, which, in turn, relate to the type of life and identity to which people aspire. And if we are to appreciate fully the symbolic dimensions of ICTs, we need to see aspects of consumption such as how technologies are talked about and displayed.

> To illustrate in relation to mobile telephony, Norwegian studies have shown that parents may resist acquiring this technology for their children on the grounds that it would be used as an unjustified display of status. Thus, parental control, including control over telecommunication resources, becomes a process of constant negotiation (Ling and Helmersen 2000). Meanwhile, youth devise various stratagems to avoid parents' ability to carry out monitoring them via mobile phones (Ling and Yttri 2002).

Second, adoption itself is seen as a process rather than an event. The pre-adoption process is reflected in perceptions of technologies and services, in how people imagine the role of an ICT (or lack of one) in their lives as well as negotiations around, and sometimes resistance to, its acquisition. If acquired, the above noted understandings about "appropriate" usage (e.g., how much TV to watch, what a PC is to be used for) must be developed. These understandings themselves can be challenged and renegotiated. ICTs need to be either tailored to routines or need new ones created around them. Also important are the processes by which usage of technologies spreads both among household members (e.g., lending out a personal phone to others), and for what the technology may be used (e.g., using the mobile phone exclusively for emergencies or for organizing logistics).

> Again, there are already some studies of mobile phones that specifically deal with some of these issues around the adoption process—for example, in terms of showing how household members try to conceive what use the mobile has for them, or specifically seeing it as one more tool to help their children on the road to establishing their independence (Nafus and Tracey 2002). In other cases, we see the resistance to children's acquisition on the grounds that they are too young and the whole process of negotiating how usage will be financed—a negotiation itself influenced by the arrival of pre-payment options (Ling and Helmersen 2000).

Anthropologist Igor Kopytoff suggested that researchers should trace the biography, or what we call "career," of objects over their "life" just as we could look at people's biographies (Kopytoff 1986). He argued that examining changes not only in ownership and use but also in how objects are culturally defined and redefined could reveal much about the society in which these objects are located. In one sense, people often acquire ICTs, go through an initial period of experimentation, and then fall into a routine usage pattern. Despite this routinization, consumption patterns also change as a result of social and technological change.

A simple example of social change within the household is the way in which children's pattern of usage can alter as they grow older or adults can use technologies differently or at different times as they change their work circumstances (including the timing of when they are at home). The British empirical studies noted above charted the effect of more radical changes in life-style, with the move to telework, family break-up, and the transition to retirement (Haddon and Silverstone 1994; Silverstone and Haddon 1996). As an example of the effects on the use of ICTs, the introduction of telework could lead to the redirecting of both incoming and outgoing private calls on the domestic line away from "work hours" so as not to block the phone line.

Third, this leads to the, albeit related, theme of domestication. The term *domestication* was coined to suggest the "taming of the wild" as ICTs are acquired from the public domain but then made personal, or, in these early studies of the domestic context, made to be a part of the home. But this is not a one-time process. It can be ongoing, if new circumstances, in whatever sense, mean that the role of an ICT has to be reassessed.

Nor should one assume that domestication is always entirely "successful." People use ICTs but may feel ambivalent about them. ICTs can appear to get out of hand (and this is true of established ones, such as TV, which can seem to dominate life, let alone mobile telephony, which can make one feel too reachable). Even users can perceive ICTs as leading to a life-style, which they feel to be questionable, for instance in terms of enhancing dependency on the technologies or adding stress (Klamer et al. 2000). ICTs can be tolerated, but not necessarily embraced as in the case of people who do not like answering machines, but nevertheless feel the need to have one. Their place in life can be bounded, as when they are only used for certain purposes in certain circumstances compared to what others might see as their fuller potential. And they can be abandoned, or even rejected at an early stage after adoption, as shown in studies of Internet dropouts and "churn" (Katz and Aspden 1998).

Research on mobile telephony has also raised such issues, as in one early study of mobile phones in France, which demonstrated that their use was constrained by contemporary norms that mobiles were not to be used for personal messages and how under many conditions, such as making private calls to family when away from home, users still preferred the fixed line (De Gournay et al. 1997). Meanwhile a Norwegian study discussed how users were "wrestling with their relations with the device" in the context of using the mobile in the isolated holiday home, called the Hytte (Ling et al. 1997). The dilemma here was that they sought isolation from outside contact as they attempted to be nearer to nature, but the whole trip was sometimes only possible if they allowed themselves to be contactable in certain circumstances.

A fourth theme is that attention must be paid to individuals in context. It recognizes that beyond "end users," others make some contribution to the whole experience of ICTs. There are non-users who might nevertheless be "gatekeepers" influencing the adoption process. Some ICTs remain communal resources for the household (such as the main TV set, and many fixed phone lines), but even "personal" ICTs can be subject to regulation. So in general, individual use and individual strategies of control take place in a context where various household members have both commitments, routines, and general demands on time and space as well as values and concerns that interact to shape consumption. Later writings on domestication have emphasized questions of power and domestic politics, especially in terms of gender and generational relations.

The meaning and role of ICTs both help shape and are shaped by the remainder of the users' life. That is, how one experiences ICTs is not completely predetermined by technological functionality or public representations; it is also structured by the social context into which it is received. The problem for researchers is to specify what the consequences of ICTs have been. Answers need to be advanced that would define the salience of ICTs, that is, how substantial a difference is made, in what sense is the difference made, and (looking beyond individuals and households) what is their wider social significance (Katz 1999). For example, what significance might there be in terms of social exclusion for those unable or unwilling to partake in the adoption and use of particular ICTs (Haddon 2000)?

However, we can derive from these studies some ways of conceptualizing the "effects" of ICTs, and observe the different forms ICTs take on. For example, ICTs introduced into the home to solve a problem can result in some change in practices (e.g., acquiring a [second] video to preoccupy children, thus acting as childsitter, or acquiring a cordless phone so that parents can perform multitasks and keep a watchful eye on children while speaking on the phone). ICTs can influence household relationships by virtue of altering the very strategies for coping with issues raised by those ICTs (e.g., as parents renegotiate with children the financing of phone calls on fixed phone lines, or introduce changes in TV watching rules once cable TV has arrived in the home).

On the other hand, changes do not necessarily have to result from the initiatives of household members, as when some people reported how acquiring a second phone handset or cordless phone had made a difference to their experience of privacy when receiving phone calls—an experience anticipating what has later been noted in relation to mobile phones. Beyond the home, ICTs, as well as the expertise developed in using them, can influence our relationships with others—family, friends, neighbors, etc.—as they can become sharable resources or at least be used for activities beyond the home base. And in the longer term, changing ICT "usage," for example, as telephony and TV watching practices develop, can have a bearing on such matters as time allocation and the timing of activities or, in the case of telephony, how we manage our relationships with social networks. (This can be partly through such processes as experimentation, partly in response to changes in ICTs themselves, such as the changing cost and marketing of telephony, the move to all day, all night TV, and the ability to time-shift through adjuncts such as the answering machine and VCR.)

> Counterparts to these types of consequences exist in the literature on mobile telephony. For example, mobiles are sometimes acquired as a solution to a problem of coordinating between household members but then influence how that coordination takes place (Klamer et al. 2000). Mobiles can lead to changes in communications strategies as people, literally, manage calls differently to the way that they handle traditional telephony (Licoppe and Heurtin 2002). Less has been written on shared resources, although there are examples of people not only using but also being reachable through other people's mobiles.

Such examples initially suggest that major elements of the domestication approach are in fact already shared in existing studies of mobile telephony. Yet this is not meant to claim that the framework per se addresses all potential issues. There are other levels of analysis derived from those studies that go beyond the type of observations made about domestication. For example, in terms of its effects on the experience of public space, Fortunati argues that the mobile has facilitated a preference for interacting with those distant rather than those immediately present, and hence leads to a withdrawal from experiencing certain public sites (Fortunati 2000). De Gournay expresses a different emphasis in arguing that the code of conduct as regards "communicative" behavior in public spaces that had emerged in relation to the fixed telephone is now disappearing through the "chaotic and divergent" use of the mobile phone (de Gournay 2002). Such levels of "effect" have not, in practice, been addressed in the British studies.

Finally, in elaborating on their concept of the *Apparatgeist*, Katz and Aakhus argue that changes brought about by the mobile phone reflect a wider sociologic involving aspirations to perpetual contact (Katz and Aakhus 2002). During their discussion, the authors correctly note that domestication's focus on social processes means that this framework would not in itself generate an analysis of, such as, in the above case, a prevailing technological spirit of the time. But it should be seen as complementing a variety of analysis—including quantitative ones (Haddon 1998b)—at the same time it provides its own agenda, sensitizing research to numerous dimensions of the consumption of ICTs and the issues involved. Indeed, it can be extended beyond its original base and it is to this task, which we now turn.

## Domestication and Mobile Telephony Studies

Theoretical discussions and empirical studies of domestication always considered the interrelationship between the home and rest of everyday life. One exploration was how ICTs were talked about outside the home as one form of display—a display of knowledge, competence or life-style orientation. For instance, and anticipating a development in mobile phone research, this was discussed in terms of how teenagers participate in peer group culture (Silverstone et al. 1992; for a contrast, cf. Wynn and Katz 2000). But it is one thing to register the significance of life outside the home and another to choose to focus upon it as an object of study in its own right. The arrival of the mobile phone prompted an interest in further extending the domestication approach outside of the home.

Some early European research on mobile phones, brought together in a COST 248 report (discussed in Haddon 1998a), explored the domestication theme. Apart from noting how some of the processes in relation to the home could be applied to the experience of ICTs outside it, this first review observed that there was scope for more analysis of the symbolism. Especially in the visual display of ICTs outside the home, people converted the private and personal meanings of their ICTs into public statements to the outside world (see Sussex MTEL 1997). Secondly, the rules of public spaces could be analyzed as counterparts to regulation of ICTs in the home. Obviously the difference is that we are not dealing with the interaction of just a few household members—in many public settings any such rules are usually more tacit and less formalized, sometimes ambiguous and more in the form of expectations about appropriate behavior held by those co-present. See Ling (1997) for a discussion of the restaurant as a public setting.

In addition to this extension of domestication outside the home, some of the mobile telephony literature also shows how it is possible to shift the focus away from the household as the unit of analysis. The household was originally privileged in the formulation of the domestication concept precisely because home and household relationships were such an important part of life. Such relationships may not always be harmonious but they are generally profound. So, for example, in the study of teleworking, household members reported that teleworkers in the household had a significant bearing upon ICTs and the household environment. As examples of the first, telework could affect the loudness of TVs (so as not to disturb the teleworker or create a bad impression when making work calls) and the way in which other household members were now supposed to answer the phone. As an example of the second, these other members also had demands on ICTs such as the PC, which had to be negotiated with work use, and if these members refused to acknowledge the teleworker's need for peace when working, they could easily disrupt that work and the usage of ICTs. It is still possible to ask the equivalent general question about mobile phones—how they influence and are influenced by others—and indeed a number of the studies of this technology have focused on its role in the relationships between household members (e.g., enabling "remote mothering" in Rakow and Navaro 1993 and forming part of the move to children's independence from parents in Nafus and Tracey 2002).

But it was always clear that homes and households are only part of the equation. Indeed, some phenomena such as the origins of the (gendered) popularity of electronic games can only be appreciated by considering consumption in other sites (in this instance, games in arcades) and relationships outside the home (with peers) (Haddon 1992). Studies of mobile telephony use by adolescents similarly indicate that consumption patterns often only make sense when non-domestic social relationships are considered. This allows analysts to appreciate the importance of "gifting" calls, which serve to cement relationships with peers. It also shows that the amount of numbers stored in the phone's memory has itself a social currency, showing the user has the (right) mobile phone markers of participation in a network. This perspective also highlights the fact that style of use and placement on the body form part of appropriate teen behavior (Ling and Yttri 2002).

As we turn to consider such non-domestic social relationships, we move into the realm of social network analysis. But if we approach this domain with the sorts of questions asked from a domestication framework, then we have a very different emphasis from the type of analysis when networks are measured in quantitative terms. Instead what is generated is a more textured picture, reminiscent of the ethnological tradition of sociology. The example that comes to mind in relation to ICTs is the study of the life-style of group of young Parisian adults and the role of the traditional phone to, somewhat spontaneously, help arrange meetings (Manceron 1997).

To be sure, friendship or the looser relations among, in the above case, youth are very different from the relationship among household members. Friendship networks are usually not so bounded, with fuzzy edges, as it is not always clear who is part of a group. While those relations can be intense, they are often much weaker. They have a shorter history and are in many cases more temporary, without the depth that comes when biographies are so intertwined as domestic ones. They do not occupy the same shared space of a home although they may involve the colonization of certain public spaces. Youth do not have financial relationships as do adult household members. But like household dynamics, these relationships do have some shared histories and to varying degrees elements of shared identities. They have their own politics, understandings of what is appropriate and they involve the use of strategies vis-à-vis peers.

So in this context we might ask how ICTs, like mobile phones, are domesticated and what are the processes by which they acquire meaning (over and above the marketing of firms)? What, for example, leads mobiles or particular mobiles to become fashionable (or not); what forms of negotiation take place within social networks and how do collective practices (such as those noted above) emerge? Are there rules about use and if so, how are they policed? What type of subsequent career do mobiles have within a group context? In general, how is consumption shaped by the collective environment, and how does it do the shaping in its influence upon the collective environment?

The final observations of this paper pertain to how one strand of the domestication analysis might be applied to the mobile telephone—its career over time. If we consider the wider or public history of the mobile phone, in its relatively short life as a mass-market product, it has already evolved in certain respects. There are of course the changes in design, most visibly in its shrinkage in size and presentation as a fashion object. In terms of functionality, the addition of text messaging has important implications for its use by youth (Rautiainen and Kasesniemi 2000). Changes, in marketing in terms of the addition of pre-payment cards, have a bearing on how the phone was managed within household relationships (Ling and Helmersen 2000). More generally, mobile telephony has undergone a change in symbolism, moving from the exclusivity of its early days associated with "yuppies" to a "must have" attitude—certainly among large sections of people in a range of European countries. And there have been some changes in its regulation in public spaces (in terms of when and where mobile use is banned) and in the nature and degree of integration into people's daily practices—it is for many no longer just the emergency phone of its very early days when it was issued to people who might be in some insecure situation (Wood 1994).

However, the mobile remains relatively young as a mass market product and if we take a longer-term perspective we might anticipate the types of research that would chart how the object will evolve in years to come. Over and above the scenario that it may become *the* phone rather than a mobile phone, we already have a variation in the object studied that has been introduced by WAP (the Wireless Application Protocol, which permits some mobile access to the

Internet). And we might expect further technical and design developments. In addition, past research has suggested that the sheer multiplication in households of even familiar technologies (like TVs, videos, computers, and phone handsets) has a bearing on consumption, such allowing for less collective, more privatized experience of ICTs (Haddon and Silverstone 1994). Hence, we might ask about the implications of moving from one mobile per household to one per person, to even, in some cases, multiple mobiles per person.

Meanwhile, consumers themselves change. In light of the current studies of youth and the mobile, we need to explore what happens to the consumption of this current cohort as its members grow older and some of arguments about the mobile in relation to their particular status as adolescents no longer apply? To refer back to an earlier concept, what will the career of this technology be among this particular cohort of users? Moreover, this technology took on a role for them partly because it arrived at a particular stage in their life course. What are the differences in consumption for future generations of youth (or younger children) when this ICT has been more established? In other words, what difference does it make to grow up with a technology (just as generations grew up with television) as opposed to the generations who experienced its first arrival? Still, on questions of age and age cohorts, how does mobile telephony consumption change for the elderly as more people retire having used mobile phones when they were younger?

Following from the examples provided earlier of how changes in the households and the circumstances of household members have a bearing on ICT consumption, we could envisage studies on how these factors impact the mobile phone once technology has been around a little longer. Specifically, previous research on call traffic using the traditional phone has shown changing patterns with changing life stages (Smoreda and Licoppe 1999). For example, in transitional situations such as moving out of parents' home, to living as a single person, to having a partner, to having children. Again, what ramifications might this have for the mobile phone?

## Conclusions

The concept of domestication is not unique in its assumptions as many are shared in other literature and studies. But it is a useful way of reflecting "a package" of understandings lying behind particular studies without the need to explicitly go through them each time.

This chapter has outlined some main elements in that "package": the stress on consumption over adoption and use; adoption as a process and the subsequent careers of ICTs; how domestication is not simply "successful," how individual consumption needs to be placed in wider context; and how ICT consumption is both shaped and shaping. We have seen how certain elements are already being explored in mobile phone research.

The chapter also examined how the concept could look beyond the home to more fully analyze portable ICTs like the mobile—in particular, to explore what the questions might be if we consider wider social networks from this perspective. Finally, we illustrated how existing work on the careers of ICTs from a domestication perspective could inform the direction of longer-term research on mobile phone technology by drawing attention to the types of changes in ICTs that have made a difference in the past and the effects of changing cohorts or generations of users.

## References

de Gournay, C. 2002. Pretence of Intimacy in France. In *Perpetual Contact: Mobile Communication, Private Talk, Public Performance*, ed. J. Katz and M. Aakhus. Cambridge: Cambridge University Press.

de Gournay, C., A. Tarrius, and L. Missaoui. 1997. The Structure of Communication Usage of Travelling Managers. In *Communications on the Move: The Experience of Mobile Telephony in the 1990s*, ed. L. Haddon, COST248 Report.

Fortunati, L. 2000. The Mobile Phone: New Social Categories and Relationships. Paper presented at the seminar, Sosiale Konsekvenser av Mobiltelefoni. Organized by Telenor, 16 June, Oslo, Norway.

Haddon, L. 1992. Explaining ICT Consumption: The Case of the Home Computer. In *Consuming Technologies: Media and Information in Domestic Spaces*, eds. R. Silverstone, R. and E. Hirsch. London, England: Routledge.

Haddon, L. 1998(a). The Experience of the Mobile Phone. Paper presented to the XIV World Congress of Sociology, Social Knowledge: Heritage, Challenges, Prospects, 26 July–1 Aug., Montreal, Canada.

Haddon, L. 1998(b). Il Controllo della Comunicazione. Imposizione di Limiti all'uso del Telefono. In *Telecomunicando in Europa,* ed. L. Fortunati. Milano: Franco Angeli.

Haddon, L. 1999. European Perceptions and Use of the Internet. Paper for the conference, Usages and Services in Telecommunications, 7–9 June, Arcachon.

Haddon, L. 2000. Social Exclusion and Information and Communication Technologies: Lessons from Studies of Single Parents and the Young Elderly, *New Media and Society* 2, no. 4.

Haddon, L. and R. Silverstone. 1993. Teleworking in the 1990s: A View from the Home. SPRU/CICT Report Series 10, University of Sussex, Falmer.

Haddon, L. and R. Silverstone. 1994. The Careers of Information and Communication Technologies in the Home. In *Proceedings of the International Working Conference on Home Oriented Informatics, Telematics, and Automation*, eds. K. Bjerg and K. Borreby, 27 June–1 July, Copenhagen, Denmark.

Haddon, L. and R. Silverstone. 1995. Lone Parents and their Information and Communication Technologies, SPRU/CICT Report Series 12, University of Sussex, Falmer.

Haddon, L. and R. Silverstone. 1995. "Home Information and Communication Technologies and the Information Society," a Report to the High-Level Group of Experts, University of Sussex, England. (December). (Published in *The Information Society in Europe: Work and Life in an Age of Globalization*, ed. Ducatel, K., J. Webster, and W. Herrmann. Lanham, MD: Rowman and Littlefield Inc., 2000.)

Haddon, L. and R. Silverstone. 1996. "Information and Communication Technologies and the Young Elderly." SPRU/CICT Report Series, University of Sussex, Falmer.

Katz, James E. 1999. *Connections: Social and Cultural Studies of the Telephone in American Life.* New Brunswick, NJ: Transaction Publishers.

Katz, James E. and M. Aakhus, eds. 2002. *Perpetual Contact: Mobile Communication, Private Talk, Public Performance*. Cambridge and New York: Cambridge University Press.

Katz, James E. and Philip Aspden. June 1998, Internet Dropouts: The Invisible Group. *Telecommunications Policy* 22, no. 4/5: 327–339.

Klamer, L., L. Haddon, and R. Ling. 2000. The Qualitative Analysis of ICTs and Mobility, Time Stress and Social Networking. Report of EURESCOM P-903, Heidelberg, Germany.

Kopytoff, I. 1986. The Cultural Biography of Things: Commoditization as Process. In *The Social Life of Things: Commodities in Cultural Perspective*, ed. Appadurai. Cambridge and New York: Cambridge University Press.

Licoppe, C. and J-P Heurtin. 2002. France: Preserving the Image. In *Perpetual Contact: Mobile Communication, Private Talk, Public Performance,* ed. J. Katz and M. Aakhus. Cambridge and New York: Cambridge University Press.

Ling, R. 1997. One Can Talk about Common Manners! The Use of Mobile Telephones in Inappropriate Situations. In *Communications on the Move: The Experience of Mobile Telephony in the 1990s,* ed. L. Haddon. COST248 Report.

Ling, R. 1998. It's OK to be Available: The Use of Traditional and Mobile Telephony amongst Norwegian Youth. Paper presented to the XIV World Congress of Sociology, Social Knowledge: Heritage, Challenges, Prospects, 26 July– 1 August, Montreal, Canada.

Ling, R., T. Julsrud, and E. Kroug. 1997. The Goretex Principle: The Hytte and Mobile Telephones in Norway. In *Communications on the Move: The Experience of Mobile Telephony in the 1990s*, ed., L. Haddon, COST248 Report.

Ling, R. and P. Helmersen. 2000. It must be Necessary, it has to Cover a Need: The Adoption of Mobile Telephony among Pre-adolescents and Adolescents. Paper presented at the seminar, Sosiale Konsekvenser av Mobiltelefoni. Organized by Telenor, 16 June, Oslo, Norway.

Ling, R. and B. Yttri. 2002. Hyper-Coordination via Mobile Phone in Norway. In *Perpetual Contact: Mobile Communication, Private Talk, Public Performance,* ed. J. Katz and M. Aakhus. Cambridge and New York: Cambridge University Press.

Mante-Meijer, E. and L. Haddon. 2001. "Checking it out with the People—ICT Markets and Users in Europe." A report for EURESCOM, Heidelberg, Germany.

Manceron, V. 1997. Get Connected! Social Uses of the Telephone and Modes of Interaction in a Peer Group of young Parisians. In *Blurring Boundaries: When are Information and Communication Technologies Coming Home?* The Future European Telecommunications User Home and Work Group, COST248 Report, Telia, Farsta.

Nafus, D. and K. Tracey. 2002. Mobile Phone Consumption and Concepts of Person. In *Perpetual Contact: Mobile Communication, Private Talk, Public Performance*, eds. J. Katz and M. Aakhus. Cambridge and New York: Cambridge University Press.

Rakow, Lana and V. Navaro. 1993. Remote Mothering and the Parallel Shift: Women Meet the Cellular Phone. In *Critical Studies in Mass Communication* 10, no. 2, June.

Rautiainen, P. and E. Kasesniemi. 2002. Mobile Communication of Children and Teenagers: Case Finland 1997–2000. In *Perpetual Contact: Mobile Communication, Private Talk, Public Performance*, ed. J. Katz and M. Aakhus. Cambridge and New York: Cambridge University Press.

Silverstone, R. 1994(a). "Future Imperfect—Media, Information and the Millenium." PICT Policy Research Paper No. 27, Brunel University, England.

Silverstone, R. 1994(b). *Television and Everyday Life*. London: Routledge.

Silverstone, R., E. Hirsch, and D. Morley. 1992. Information and Communication Technologies and the Moral Economy of the Household. In *Consuming Technologies*, eds. R. Silverstone and E. Hirsch. London: Routledge.

Silverstone, R. and L. Haddon. 1996. Design and the Domestication of Information and Communication Technologies: Technical Change and Everyday Life. In *Communication by Design: The Politics of Information and Communication Technologies*, eds. R. Silverstone and R. Mansell, Oxford: Oxford University Press.

Smoreda, Z. and C. Licoppe. 1999. La Téléphonie Résidentielle de Foyers: Réseaux de Sociabilité et Cycle de Vie. Paper for the conference, Usages and Services in Telecommunications, 7–9 June, Arcachon.

Sussex Media, Technology and Everyday Life Research Group (Sussex MTEL):  C. Bassett, L. Cameron, M. Hartmann, M. Hills, I. Karl, B. Morgan, and B. Wessels. 1998. Communications on the Move: The Experience of Mobile Telephony in the 1990s. In *The Company of Strangers: Users' Perception of the Mobile Phone,* ed. L. Haddon, COST248 Report.

Wynn, Eleanor and James E. Katz. 2000. Teens on the Telephone. *Info* 2, no. 4 (August) : 401–419.

Wood, J. 1994. Cellphones on the Clapham Omnibus: The Lead-Up to a Cellular Mass Market. In *Management of Information and Communication Technologies: Emerging Patterns of Control,* ed. R. Mansell. London: Aslib.

# 5

# Communication Technology and Sociability: Between Local Ties and "Global Ghetto"?

*Chantal de Gournay and Zbigniew Smoreda*

## Introduction

In these days of the Internet and globalization (Katz & Rice, forthcoming), there is a persistent misunderstanding about the spatial factors governing personal communication. Because a modern individual has access to tools, which are both mobile (e.g., cellular telephones) and global in their scope (e.g., the Internet), it is believed that s/he can establish social contacts anywhere and at any time, and can draw on the resources of social interaction in territories regardless of how near or far these are.

The relations between space and telecommunications have long been analyzed using notions of odd causality. Mobility (transportation) and communication are perceived as consequences of urbanization, whereas they are, in fact, its organizing principle (Ascher 1995). With respect to the control of space, that is, considered exclusively in terms of reducing distance constraints, we tend to forget that, historically, the invention of the telephone came before that of the car, providing the most decisive push to the extension of cities. Indeed the telephone's first applications involved facilitating the coordination between the floors of American skyscraper office buildings (a kind of intercom associated with vertical density or local concentration), before being put to the service of well-off private individuals who deserted the urban center for the suburbs, following the development of the tramway lines (horizontal expansion). Today, the belief that the primary purpose of telecommunication is to complete this long process of controlling space persists, which was imperfectly carried out by transportation, and to bolster the relationships, which are complicated by distance.

## From Controlling Space to Controlling Time:
## Real-Time and Continuous Time

Inquiries based on the identification and the locations of telephone correspondents within the sociability sphere of households helped to bring to light a pattern that is actually the opposite of the supposed pattern outlined above: we found that telecommunication's role in maintaining remote ties is secondary, and acts as an accessory to its fundamental role in the maintenance of relations in closer proximity (de Gournay et al. 1999, 2001; Eve and Smoreda 1999, 2001; Katz, 1999; Leclerc et al. 2001). The ties that resist geographical distance and are maintained by regular telephone contact turned out to be, in the vast majority, based on blood relations. Far from ratifying the tendency for "globalization" or "delocalization," which exists in the economic sphere, the purpose of the telephone (and more specifically of the mobile) in the sphere of sociability outside the family is primarily to organize the proximity circumstances that up to now have been organized by urban and local mechanisms. Accordingly, not only does telecommunication not replace the city by compensating for physical meetings with remote contacts; it gives it new value and vitality by promoting new opportunities for convivial proximity in areas where the urban form could no longer operate due to its excessive growth into a megalopolis.

Telecommunication's contribution to the animation of the local space is especially noteworthy as a result of the uses of the mobile telephone—in particular, but not exclusively, among young people. This is based on two problematic aspects of the management of social life: a more precise relation with urban, event-based potential (to be where something is happening) and a greater tendency for improvisation in the desire to meet outside the home (opposite to the routine and rigidity of visits or receptions organized in advance due to domestic economy constraints). Not only does mobility increase the opportunities to locate occasions for social gatherings not publicized by the media (and also help to bring them to the attention of one's friends in real-time), it also makes it possible to bring in, at the last moment, additional people without having to fix a rendezvous point beforehand (Manceron 1997). This idea of timely opportunities for going out in a city might be analogous to the flexibility principle embodied in the marketing of manufactured goods, with "just in time" or "tight flows," which consist of manufacturing the product (e.g., a car) according to a simultaneously issued demand, instead of anticipating or following this demand. Undoubtedly, the supply of transportation and cultural events will adapt to this new demand for timeliness, with the assistance of the new technologies (modification of the journey in real-time, volume of places neither requiring reservations nor sold at the last minute, etc.)

Moreover, current controversies in Europe over women's night work and the opening of shops on Sundays or in the evenings clearly indicate a shift in the foremost considerations of modern ways of life: these are now focusing less on controlling space (reduction in distance and travel constraints) than on arranging time (adjustment and synchronization of the schedules in our working and private lives).

With regard to the social aspect concerning us here, research on telecommuters, non-working people, and retirees, all show that the individual abolition of the travel constraint neither improves nor changes the socialization and communication obligations of these people. In other words, the time saved on transportation (and even on work) is neither convertible nor reinvested in term of achievement of the relational aspects of life and of communications activities, in either their quantitative or qualitative dimensions. The increased availability of the one group comes up against the chronic unavailability of the other group, and against the problem that a macro-level organization of space and time is built into ideas about rules for appropriate interaction.

However, though telecommunication is a decisive time management tool, its effectiveness is partially limited by the organization of time that is imposed by the available supply of urban services: the theoretically continuous communication time (anywhere and any time with the involvement of necessary synchronous and asynchronous modes—telephone, message services and e-mail) contradicts the discontinuous reality of the time needed for work, transportation and public services, shops, and so on. Even that bastion of capitalism, the Stock Exchange, cannot escape the imposed discontinuity of time, despite the introduction of a notion of real-time and continuum in the placing of exchange orders through the Internet.

Though urban policies are concretely trying to reduce the gap between the constrained city time and the personal timetables, which have been made less rigid by flexibility in working timetables—thanks to the development of greater time flexibility of services such as transport, distribution and safety, according to the Japanese and American model of service areas operating twenty-four hours a day, seven days a week—the conquest of flexibility is far from being clear in the very place where it is supposed to be provided by new technologies, that is, on the level of communication itself. The observation of telephone sociability practices shows that individual uses of communications are not freer of time constraints or locations, despite the theoretical flexibility offered by mobile tools and asynchronous modes such as e-mail. Paradoxically, one is more likely to find people, even traffic jams, on the ring road, the subway, or the major streets of Paris at 1:00 in the morning, than active telephone traffic between households after 10:00 P.M. (Obadia 1997).

### The Inertia of Communication Times and Places: Theoretical Flexibility

In our research in France, uses of telecommunication, when compared with social practices, brings to light several constants, which are all the more striking in that they involve seemingly different population categories (self-employed workers in the home, migrants, retirees, single-parent homes, etc.) as well as very contrasting events involving biographical interruption (moving away from parents' home; subsequent moves; birth of first child; divorce; retirement; etc.). Considering the transformations that have taken place in France in the world of work (e.g., introduction of the thirty-five-hour work week) and the massive spread of new technologies, the structure of the residential uses of telecommunication has undergone surprisingly little change and is still characterized by relatively uniform rhythms of life (despite socio-professional differences). It is especially interesting to note continued compliance with traditional family customs as to the prescribed times for communicating and the roles assigned in the configuration of exchanges with the outside world.

### Time Conventions

Time conventions remain stable; however, much time is spent in the home. This is true whether we are talking of French active working people, students, homemakers, women on maternity leave, or retirees. When we compare the residential telephone traffic curves of these groups, the time spans corresponding to normal work and school hours are characterized by the lowest traffic (from the home phone), even when an adult remains in the home; traffic then starts to increase around 5:00 P.M. and decreases again between 9 and 10 P.M. Retirees' calls follow a pattern that is similar to that of working households, the only difference being that their evening peak is at 7:00 P.M. instead of 8:00 P.M. (and that part of the morning is devoted to resolving practical problems, which working people often handle from their workplaces [see figure 5.1]).

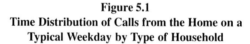

**Figure 5.1**
**Time Distribution of Calls from the Home on a**
**Typical Weekday by Type of Household**

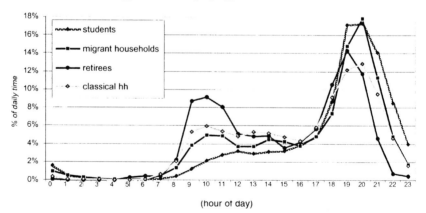

(hour of day)

The residential traffic pattern varies strongly with life cycle changes (moving in as a couple, birth of the first child, divorce, moving, etc.), which also involve a transformation of the social networks—but only in terms of call frequencies and durations, and with regard to who correspondents are; but it does not change with regard to the timing of communication sequences throughout the day or the week.

The mass spread of the cellular telephone, with its supposed flexibility with regard to space and time, does not really modify the pattern of private calls—calls from mobiles still show the characteristic evening peak we saw with calls from the home phone (see figure 5.2). This indicates that the main function of the mobile phone is to coordinate with the home or fixed points (particularly during mealtimes: noon and 8:00 PM).

### The Routine of Communication Acts in the Home

The establishment of routines surrounding communication practices is determined by the institutional organization of the workplace and school, on the one hand, and by "social proprieties" on the other, which seem in this case to result more from family conformism than from negotiated interpersonal conventions. By "conformism," we mean compliance with rules which are no longer appropriate to the actual availability of people: for a non-working or part-time working mother, the evening telephone contacts occur during the busiest period in terms of collective organization, while the more personal conversations (with friends or parents) would undoubtedly be best placed when the children are at school. It nevertheless remains the case that communications between adults and their parents–or married friends–are determined by the tacit require-

**Figure 5.2**
**Distribution of Mobile Telephone Calls on a Typical Day**

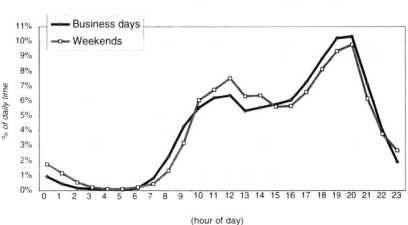

(hour of day)

ment to address the family group or the couple rather than the individual, which justifies the coming together of the two households on either end of the line. The code of *gregariousness* or of the community prevails, as it were, over any other personal or customized requirement of the exchange:

> For my personal calls, I phone more from the home than...anyway, when calling other couples from the home, it allows the couples to exchange, whereas...what I mean is that after 7:00 P.M., seeing as how all of our friends work... that's when we can reach them, that is to say around 8 or 9 o'clock [in the evening], you know.
>
> When the telephone rings in the evening, I try to make sure that he answers. Because I've had enough [laughs]... No, no, it's just people who bug us, and call for nothing, it happens just when... I really hate it when that happens, just as you're sitting down to eat, you know...the phone starts ringing and it's your mother-in-law, for example, and she wants to know if, um...in the soup, um...whether she should add onion or garlic, ah, that can wait, I don't answer (laughs). There really are days when I can't be bothered, because after four or five calls one after the other, that's enough, you know....
>
> Now that, [the displayed telephone number], that's my mother's cousins in St Raphaël. Well, in general, as they are both retired, the husband answers. I spend five minutes with him, I ask him how he is, what he's up to. Talking with him on the phone, it makes him happy when asked about the little things, I would say. And after that, he puts his wife on... "You've forgotten all about me, you haven't called in more than a fortnight, what's going on?" In short, she needs a tangible demonstration. So a call is something important for her, so we call, you know.

If one is truly motivated to make personal a telephone conversation, then one makes plans for an intimate conversation outside the collective times, which means that we call beforehand and arrange the best time for a more personal exchange:

> Actually, even when my friends call me, which happens, it is very rare that I can really talk. So, when they call me or sometimes when I call them, I make an appointment to call them back later in the evening. Now, with all of my girlfriends who have kids, we warn each other when we're going to call. We sometimes call just like that, but just to make time. What I mean by a telephone call, is to set aside a good half-hour. Or if we're all alone, which happens, we let one another know.

The foreseeable nature of some calls, generally involving family members, is clearly seen as part of the ritual of family solidarity; as a result, there is usually no great "personal" value to the content, other than a purely informative role (i.e., "the news"), which can generally be given to anyone, without the need for a dual relationship, with the correspondent then distributing this information to the rest of the group. Let us note the similarity between family "news" and journalistic "news": both imply a daily or periodic regularity of distribution, without which they would lose their sense.

> As for the brothers and sisters, we know that we'll get the news every week from mother, so umm...we don't feel the need to call. We phone the two mothers, and they pass on the news to the brothers and sisters.

The routine aspect of the telephone certainly contributes to its devaluation in terms of the authenticity and sincerity criteria that one seeks in a one-to-one relation. The frequency of expression often ends up meaning that we have "nothing to say one another" on the telephone once one leaves the ritual framework of the parent-child relation, and that it would be better to use other means, such as face-to-face talks or the mail (postal or electronic) when seeking to establish intimate and sincere communication. Similarly, sibling relationships are on the same level as those with friends, where a degree of "social equality" implies a mutual desire for justified contact, without the obligation of a routine, and unlike the "hierarchal" relations, which are characteristic both of the stratified world of the workplace and the emotional economy of the family:

> I think that the mail has made it possible to maintain relations with my brother [who lives with his parents], it's always a pleasure to receive a letter, while a phone call, though also a pleasure, no doubt, but.... As it is, generally with my parents, it is true that they call me, generally on Sundays or something like that. Well, it's planned, and I know about it in advance. Whereas a letter, I never know when I'm going to get one. It's unexpected, you know, and...he's the one who wrote it, complete with spelling mistakes. But there's something extra. It's the medium which best reflects one's personality. Otherwise, on the phone, he has nothing to say, he's capable of having nothing to say on the phone for 10 solid minutes, he really is.

## A Lack of Sociability when One is Captive in the Home

The low daytime traffic of households with an adult in the home is not only an effect of the general routines we have mentioned, it is also an expression of the difficulties that these people have in connecting with the world. In other words, they do not find friendly correspondents available during these times, either because they are busy or because "it isn't done" to make personal—one might even say futile—calls when one is supposed to be working. This isolation in the home affects full- or part-time telecommuters as well as people having moved a long distance. In this latter case, a large number of women find themselves without employment after moving a distance from their company when their husband changes job. It is difficult for them to integrate into local social life because opportunities to meet people are virtually non-existent during the working day, except for other women in the same situation in their immediate vicinity. Cultural life, sports organizations, and associations, all have timetables designed around the available time of the working population.

> Working at home, well that might be fine for a mother.... Although even then! You have to be present during the company's business hours, to follow-up on the invoicing... that is, when you follow up by phone. Maybe secretarial work, that might be a bit easier to manage, because if you feel like typing a report at midnight...I don't call my girlfriends during the day. Well, everyone works, so uh... I'm not going to ring them up at the office: "Yeah, I'm bored."

I've been living here for a year now, and I still don't know anyone, beside my walls, my phone, and that's it. My husband again said to me, listen, go ahead, go to the gym, I think that for you... it went better...I go on Thursdays. It's like, hi there, each person for themselves. Well, they all work, those women. It can't be helped, see...well, goodbye then, see you Thursday. Well, why? Well, we can't, we work. And that's the way it goes, one after the other, well we work, we work. Fine, then! See you on Thursday!

### A Relative Specialization of Communication Places and Tools Despite Technical Convergence

The social contact problems experienced by the above categories demonstrate that the permeability of the various spheres of human relations is still largely theoretical. Sociability resources are segregated in more or less focused and partitioned "sources" (the company, the neighborhood/children's school, association sites, cultural venues), and the bridges allowing circulation or a transfer of resources from one area to another are extremely limited, even when the sociability is channeled through communication systems.

We have seen that the home remains primarily reserved for family exchanges, and that it favors a "cooperative" rather than an intimate type of communication, in the sense that it is addressed to a group rather than an individual, it has its own special mediation, and a distribution of roles where a single person can be given responsibility for managing all relations for everyone (it's generally the wife who plays this role) (Claisse 2000). Curiously, the "impersonality," which Goffman (1963) mentions in connection with communications in the street, can just as easily be used to describe the family communication mode, in that the one-to-one relation required by the concept of intimacy or "personal communications" seems to be better served by individually appropriated tools, as opposed to the domestic line (mobile, SMS [short-message system on cell phones], postal mail, e-mail). It is therefore no surprise that teenagers should invest massively in these tools at an age when the "personality" is being established, and when relationships between pairs have their greatest import. With regard to the use of SMS on cell phones, we note that girls have a motivation for the written word, which can be likened to the keeping of a diary: a "love letter" by SMS can be saved for some time, read, reread and shown to girlfriends as proof of a burgeoning love interest (Kasesniemi and Rautiainen 2001).

Inter-generational communications (children–parents/in-laws–grandparents) almost exclusively involve landlines; they focus on vocal expression and give almost no place to the written word, except for people residing abroad.

With regard to the supposed tendency toward interpenetration of sociability and communication areas—often presented as an inescapable consequence of the convergence of fixed and mobile communication media, creating tools attached to the person and intended for use in all locations, professionals, public, and private—we have found two universes of actual sociability that are underrepresented in the residential telephone traffic, namely neighbors and colleagues. Vicinity is incontestably the leading social resource for those categories that have undergone a change of residence or marital situation (people who have recently moved, single-parents). Then come workmates, to whom both men and women turn, though using different relational means: for women, colleagues are likely to become friends, while men, generally remain confined to a level where they share a sporting activity, possibly go for a drink, but seldom become integrated into the domestic life. These two types of relations (neighbors and colleagues) are seldom included in the telephone traffic for the simple reason that the larger part of sociability involves face-to-face discussions, and doesn't require recourse to the telephone in order to coordinate appointments (one meets at the school gate or at work, or makes an appointment at the workplace itself). This nevertheless reflects a relatively clear-cut partitioning of socialization venues, as a result of which intrusion into the domestic universe remains exceptional, as do exchanges between the respective partners of a couple. Only "old friends" (the bonds made in childhood, while studying, on holidays, sometimes during previous employment, i.e., former colleagues) are truly included both in the domestic area and in the telephone contacts from the home.

The circulation of telephone calls between the home and work remains, for the most part, limited to communication between family members when they are outside the home. The rest of the family (outside the household) generally avoids contacting even close relatives at work. At the workplace, there remain only those personal calls made from office to office. But, personal communications initiated from the workplace involve a sociability venue that is less constrained and, especially, less conventional than the domestic universe.

It is characterized by the following features: (1) individual sovereignty in the relation, as contrasted to membership in the group (exclusivity of the bond which, for example, may not be shared with one's spouse); (2) control of the communication time, which is less tied to the usual prescribed times (people communicate when they want or when they are available), but there is less risk of the talkative "overflow" that one puts up with out of courtesy in a domestic setting; (3) flexible or negotiable degree of involvement (openly ranging from the remote to intimate confidences); (4) requirement for confidentiality, which means that one often chooses e-mail so that conversations will not be overheard by the people in one's surroundings.

On the basis of these criteria, communication in a work setting allows use of a new skill, we term *polychrony*. The private communication acts take place in the midst of productive tasks, resulting in an alternation or a "breather" that may contrast with the "alienation" of the work itself, and mean a recapturing of autonomy or at least the creation of a secret garden, away from both family and the work environment. In this respect, e-mail is preferred to the telephone, as there is a belief that it "does not take more time" and also that it extends the sociability to more remote correspondents, whom one might not have contacted by the conventional socialization means.

No, it's different on the phone...also, at the office, uh...you can be overheard, etc. There [on the computer], it's really private. And since I'm always working on the computer, no one would think that I'm writing a private mail message. So, it's a chance for me to, uh...well, to turn in on myself, and nobody can see it. And so...and it's not like I write for half an hour or anything...I'll write for maybe 15 minutes, I take the time to write the letter, to think it over, or to answer the person who wrote to me, or sometimes I'm just too, too busy, and I send a message saying I don't have time to answer, that I will answer this evening, and then I answer from home.

And even within Paris, we communicate by e-mail, whereas without it, I wouldn't certainly phone them. There are people in Paris.... For example, I have a friend who quit his job, and, sure, I must have called him once or twice at the beginning; now we e-mail each other every week. It's new. We tell each other things that we probably wouldn't have otherwise. It's really a change. It broadens your horizons. You save time, and don't lose as much time any more. In the end, it's basically positive.

### Shared Places and Concomitant Times? The Indivisible Nature of Leisure

The aim here is not to denounce a phenomenon in the name of some nostalgic, ideal, or utopian reference to mixing or parity, harking back to a "golden age" of sociability, which perhaps never existed. In this field, heavily mined by deterministic approaches, there are nevertheless some works by French historians, which give some reference points on the mixing of sociability practices and on what served as public areas in the past. Three models of mixed sociability (simultaneously bringing together the genders and ages or generations) emerge from their following historical works: (1) the evening gathering in the rural world (Chartier 1991), during which people met around the fire in one of the local farms for a collective reading (the education of one community member compensated for the illiteracy of the others). Farge (1992) also notes the equivalent of such practices in the city, with that ancestor of the printed newspaper, the hand-written news read out in public squares. She also points out that the lower class uprisings under the Old Regime included women, whereas the demonstrations of the nineteenth century became entirely masculine: a woman needed her husband's permission to speak in public; (2) the Sunday leisure of the nineteenth-century working class, with families gathering at the gates of Paris for meals, walks, and games. Also of note was the mixed clientele in bars on Monday evenings (which was payday for working men) (Corbin and Csergo 2001); (3) the working-class or society dance, which became the high point of urban leisure from the period of romanticism through to the Second World War. Other examples of occasions where different ages and genders mixed included World Fairs, trade fairs, and the cinema (Corbin and Csergo 2001).

By reminding readers of this obsolete panorama of sociability practices, our aim is to show that the democratic distribution of skills and qualifications (reading or technical skills such as knowing how to operate a computer, for example) does not automatically go hand in hand with an integration of the ages and genders in leisure activities, nor with a sharing of common cultural objects. Quite the contrary, the individualization of leisure modes within the family is growing, leading to a dispersal and a centrifugal movement of the domestic agendas, already exacerbated by the dual working lives of the couple. This segmentation of leisure and of the places where leisure takes place is clear even in the way public spaces and facilities are organized. Formerly, museums, parks, and such, were designed with a "universalistic" ideology, and it was vaguely intended that facilities would be used by both genders and all ages. Of course it is possible to criticize the centralism often associated with this perspective, though we should remember that the aim of public facilities is to "federate" people and groups by encouraging collective action. But in any case, the ruling ideology nowadays often seems to be different, tending towards "zoning," which segregates areas of interest for particular categories: the area for children, for adolescents, for fans of sliding sports, etc. In the new green spaces, like in park-museums, people transit *via* paths, which allow each person never to encounter the areas that are not intended for them. Public planning has probably borrowed its methods from the triumphant catechism of marketing: target and segment the public or customers.

The dispersal of tastes and cultural practices, which now lies at the core of marketing strategies, was discussed as part of the sociology of communications at the time of the changes to the French TV (the introduction of cable TV and theme channels). Marking the end of the family "mass" in front of what was once virtually a sole channel designed for all audiences, irrespective of status, culture, age, and gender, the growth of theme channels led Wolton (1990) to first wonder about the negative effects of this development in terms of social cohesion. The abolition of the "generalist channel" seems to be equivalent to negating *the common place,* as was discussed above with regard to urban transit, that is, those points that everyone is forced to pass through, and which so lead to the fortuitous meetings of identities, thus flying in the face of the logic of avoiding the sense of otherness. "TV conversations" (Boullier 1987) could occasionally serve as a venue for exchanges between employees having lunch together in the cafeteria. What will now be the substitute that serves as the social glue in a context where the probability of having watched the same program is greatly reduced?

### Telephone Sociability: A Symptom of the Difficulty of Bonding with "Dissimilar People"

During our various field surveys, a recurring fact has emerged: a tendency towards *homophily*. By this term, we mean women with women, couples with couples, single parents bound to spend time exclusively with other single parents, migrants who recognize one another and gather in their new adopted towns, and such. This phenomenon was all the more garishly apparent since we "picked" the interviewees at a time of rupture (moving, divorce, or separation), which almost always corresponds with a destabilization of relations with both family and friends, a fact which leads them to more explicitly clarify the behavior with which they use to build new links or recycle the old ones.

As previously mentioned, one explanation could be the specialization of contemporary leisure activities, which contributes to the segregation of sociability "types." But this homogeneity of one's condition (condition as a woman, homemaker, migrant, old person) also translates the tension applied to timetables, which are increasingly constrained by the need to reconcile a professional life, domestic tasks, and the occupation of young people, the latter having acquired a new recognition of an autonomous universe of activities and sociability (see also Eve 1998). This tension gives rise to a "conventional" attitude in deciding with whom to form a tie; this involves seeking out people experiencing the same constraints as oneself, because that facilitates the coordination of agendas, while also providing a basis for exchanges on the possibility of mutual assistance, solidarity, and empathy. This is particularly valid for single parent homes:

> The women whom I phone are just like me, they are in my situation, they know that one's morale can hit rock bottom one day. We understand one another, it's hard to be alone with a child.
> A friend who is alone, divorced, whom I'm comforting. We adore one another, she feels rejected by her family and that's just what I went through.
> My neighbor... she's in the same situation as I am. We help each other out. It's true that it helps to create links.

Beyond the question of need, there is the already mentioned matter of complying with customs, and with the "family," and marital moral doctrine, which this conveys. Single people (unmarried or divorced) report a difficulty with integration, which they ascribe to being pushed aside— deliberately or unconsciously— by established couples who control the access to their sociability circles:

> Since I've been divorced, I'm no longer invited to couples' dinners. It happened naturally. I have the impression that they thought that it was contagious.
> I was always made to feel guilty when being received by a couple. I have the feeling that the women don't look on it kindly, they think "look out!"

More generally, the sociability of couples is based on considerations associated with the parallel or simultaneous social activities of the children. In other words, the adult relational life is subject to the search for a means to integrate the children into their own social circles. That gives rise to several levels of configuration of the choices, with so precise a refinement that the age of the children also counts in the selection of adult counterparts: couples without children and their counterparts, couples with children and their counterparts, couples with children and counterparts having children of the same age:

> Today, we have couples of friends with whom we get along well. They have children of the same age. There are others, but their children are younger. The children are important. We try to have age parity.

We have the same way of looking at things. And with the children, we have the same way of educating, so that's important.

## Conclusion

The range of results obtained in our studies—summarized above—leads us to wonder about the question of the apparent gap between the flexibility—which new means of communication make technically possible—and the rigidity of times and routines, which we actually found in the social interaction we observed. The "always connected" myth stands in sharp contrast here to a factual or social inaccessibility (the routine or the standard) of possible communication partners (Katz and Aakhus 2002). The trend towards individualization of communication tools only apparently contradicts the normal social codes, especially when relational networks and life-styles change due to marital and then family processes, and since the homophily of contacts reinforces the standardization of these practices: due to these social constraints, only young people fully benefit from the autonomy possibilities offered by the customization of the tools—mobile telephones in particular. This explains why it is the young who have become the preferred marketing targets of the operators.

The second phenomenon, which goes together with the rigidity in the timing of telephone calls, involves the specialization of space. The home, reserved for a restricted number of often-pooled relations, serves as an axis for the social and also spatial inscription of the exchanges, by outlining the local circle of accessible elective relations. Here, "proximity" combines with "affinity" in that affinity is defined less by a sharing of similar tastes than by a similarity in the imposed way of life (type of habitation and community size, time constraints, rhythms of professional, and school life). An observation of changes of residence confirms this link between proximity and affinity, by showing that friendships are lost after a period of distance and are recreated on a local basis, while only the links of blood relations resist geographical distance and are maintained by telephone communication. In addition to the strong positioning of household communications (which contradicts the recurring dream to abolish the space which is systematically associated with every new means of telecommunication), their generally collective nature (from household to household), gives residential telephony a familial communication aspect, which becomes stronger during the adult life cycle (Smoreda and Licoppe 2000).

Once we consider these two parallel trends (spatial localization of communication and general homomorphism of sociability), we are confronted with a paradox. At a local level, the resulting homogeneity of social circles produces a "ghetto-like" social form: we discover some of the elements of the ghetto phenomenon, but without the cultural and ethnic characteristics of its traditional, urban form. The question of identity (sharing a common culture or religion) appears under the form of some kind of conformity: conformity to a lived situation, social status, and life-style. At an international level, we can imagine the formation of social networks based on the same status homophily principle (gender, professional solidarities, taste, etc.) (cf. Eve, 1998). This could eventually lead to an evolution from "communitarism" to global "ghettoization."

## References

Ascher, F. 1995. *Métapolis ou avenir des villes*. Paris: Odile Jacob.

Boullier, D. 1987. La conversation télé. Lares: Université de Haute Bretagne.

Chartier, R. 1991. *La correspondance: les usages de la lettre au XIXe siècle,* Paris: Fayard.

Claisse, G. 2000. Identités masculines et féminines au téléphone. *Réseaux* 103: 51–90.

Corbin, A. and J. Csergo. 2001. *L'Avènement des loisirs*. Paris: Flammarion.

deGournay, C., P. A. Mercier, and Z. Smoreda. 1999. Déménagement des familles et usages du téléphone. Internal Report, Issy: CNET.

deGournay, C. and A. Tribess. 2001. Familles monoparentales et communication. Unpublished manuscript.

Eve, M. 1998. Qui se ressemble s'assemble? Les sources d'homogénéité à Turin. In *Espaces, temporalités, stratifications: Exercices sur les réseaux sociaux*, ed. M. Gribaudi. Paris: Editions de l'EHESS, pp. 43–70.

Eve, M. and Z. Smoreda. 1999. "Décohabitation juvenile," Internal Report, CNET, Issy.

Eve, M. and Z. Smoreda. 2001. La perception de l'utilité des objets techniques: jeunes retraités, réseaux sociaux et adoption des technologies de communication. *Retraite & Société* 33: 22–51.

Farge, A. 1992. *Dire et mal dire. L'opinion publique au XVIIIe siècle,* Paris: Seuil.

Goffman, E. 1963. *Behavior in Public Places. Notes on the Social Organization of Gatherings*. New York: The Free Press.

Kasesniemi, E. L. and P. Rautiainen. 2002. Life in 160 Characters: The Text Message Culture of Finnish Teenagers. In *Perpetual Contact: Mobile Communication, Private Talk -Public Performance*, eds. J. E. Katz and M. Aakhus, New York: Cambridge University Press.

Katz, James E. 1999. *Connections: Social and Cultural Studies of the Telephone in American Life*. New Brunswick, NJ: Transaction Publishers.

Katz, James E. and M. Aakhus, eds. 2002. *Perpetual Contact: Mobile Communication, Private Talk, Public Performance*. Cambridge and New York: Cambridge University Press.

Katz, James E. and Ronald E. Rice. (pending). *Social Consequences of Internet Use: Access, Involvement and Expression*. Cambridge, MA: MIT Press.

Leclerc, C., B. Lelong, V. Manceron, Z. Smoreda, and S. Houdart. 2001. Processus de hiérarchisation au sein des relations sociales et diversification des modes de communication au moment de la naissance du premier enfant. Proceedings of the Third International Conference on Uses and Services in Telecommunications, 12–14 June, Paris, pp.160–169.

Manceron, V. 1997. Get Connected! *Reseaux: The French Journal of Communication* 5: 227–240.

Obadia, A. ed. 1997. *Entreprendre la ville: Nouvelles temporalités–Nouveaux services*. Paris: Editions de l'Aube.

Smoreda, Z. and C. Licoppe. 2000. Gender-specific use of the domestic telephone. *Social Psychology Quarterly* 63: 238–252.

Wolton, D. 1990. Eloge du grand public. Une théorie critique de la télévision. Paris: Flammarion.

# 6

# The Human Body:
# Natural and Artificial Technology

*Leopoldina Fortunati*

## Premise

Machines involving communication and information, particularly "mobile" machines (i.e., cellular, personal digital assistants [PDAs], portable laptop computers and, increasingly, microchips under the skin) represent the core of today's technological innovation. (Hereafter, the term *machines* refers to those involved in communication technologies.) I have analyzed (Fortunati 2000) elsewhere how society has arrived at the point at which information and communication technologies (ICTs) saturate the body and bodily senses. In that article, I singled out two factors that make it possible for ICTs to first approach the body and then penetrate it. These factors are (1) the uncertain boundaries of the body itself and (2) people's tendency from the very origins to imagine archetypal figures of the body as a machine or, vice-versa, of machines as the human body. This second factor is demonstrated by the terms *automaton, golem, android*, or *robot*. Not only do we imagine such human-behaving machines, but human beings have also tried to create these machines.

The phenomenon though goes further than mechanical embodiment; society also seeks psychic reproduction by attempting to create artificial intelligence (AI) systems (Collins, 1990). AI involves a separation of mind from body, or more precisely, the development of a mind without a body. Efforts at AI seem to result in developments along three sets of opposites: (1) The mind on a sadistic pole and the body on a masochistic one; (2) the mind in the masculine form and the body in the feminine form; and (3) the mind that reflects Western influences and the body that reflects "Third World" or Eastern aspects.

This chapter deals with the core of the problem, which is essentially one of the body. My thesis is that machines are inundating our bodies at an increasing rate because the human body is already, in essence, technology. In what sense are we technology? There is already a sense that the body works within the organization of everyday life as a machine. The post-modern body, which still moves on the axis of containing/contained (Durand 1963), operates especially on many different levels. The post-modern body is a physical and psychic entity; it is our first extension in space; it is a powerful and natural means of communication; it is an instrument of seduction; it is the first barrier between our subjective world and the objective world; it is the seat of our capacity to work and of our inner dimension (*L'universo del corpo* [trans. *The Universe of the Human Body*]) 1999; Marx 1953, 1957; Volli 1999). It is also a social and cultural construct (Polhemus 1999). But the body is above all a natural "machine" of the domestic sphere, of that great and fragmented social laboratory where the capacity to work is reconstructed each day (Katz 1999).

## The Body as a Natural Machine

From a rhetorical point of view, the definition of the human body as a natural machine is an oxymoron that may intrigue or perturb. But from a sociological point of view, it is a perfect reflection of the double character of the domestic work process (Fortunati 1981)—in terms of a capitalist society, the body seems to represent the non-capitalist (natural) sphere while actually entirely participating in the creation of value. In the same way, the body is represented as a natural (and therefore valueless) product in the domestic labor domain. However, in reality, the body functions as a machine to produce society's most precious commodities: the newly born, the labor force of tomorrow. Furthermore, the body becomes a natural machine for restoring the work capacity every day. It is a special machine, supplied by nature, but which works as an extremely sophisticated technology of the reproductive sphere.

The body, while being the real, great domestic technology, is represented as the emblem of naturalness. The body has always represented the maximum of naturalness; not in itself, but rather represents a historically determined naturalness that has the potential to be recreated at any given moment. This has not obviously excluded the body from the necessity of coming to terms with culture and artifice (e.g., make-up, clothing, social formation of the image of the body). In reality, the body, as every other intermediate product or moment of our daily lives, is artifice to the maximum degree. Not only the body, but also the entire domestic sphere is actually an extreme form of artifice, despite being represented to the contrary.

From the kitchen recipe, which may be considered the queen of the pragmatics of communication, to the heating technology that we use in our houses, every element of the domestic sphere contains millions of bits of information, elaboration, experimentation, debates, practical experiences, and enormous quantities of dead labor. Every day presents an immense store of culture. But culture means artifice, which is not yet defined as technology. (The term *artifice* here is based on the Latin meaning of *artificium*, that is, the art to improve a thing.) Even if technology were made up of artifices, the artificial does not coincide with the technological. When we say that the body is not only artificial but also technological in nature, we actually resort to a metonym; that is, we transfer a meaning from a function to a thing. In other words, the body works as a natural machine, it works as a technology, but it is neither machine nor technology: it is much more. And we, human beings, are still much more than our bodies.

The reader may find this clarification of terms pedantic. But it helps us to explain one of the most powerful mechanisms that create the ideology of technology—the last great ideology in which, as Baudrillard so acutely observes, "all transcendent values have been absorbed" (1999, It. tr. 2000, p. 93). The way in which scholars frequently resort to rhetorical statements to make their ideas more striking often leads to the conceptual bases of the analysis being changed. This is the case in which, for instance, communicative technologies are anthropomorphized by personifying them in terms of responsibility and decision-making, actions that conventionally pertain to human beings (Latour 1998; Maldonado 1998). As a result, we describe human beings as helpless and easy to subordinate, completely passive in front of so much power and AI. However, this is not to say that this metaphoric concept is the reality of human beings vs. machines and technology. To defend the right to the use of metaphor, we must make clear that we do not apply the meaning of technology *tout court* to the body. The reality is that the machine is inferior to the body, and the body should not be assimilated to the machine, but rather, the body carries out an important function as a machine, as natural technology. As such, the body cannot resist the subjection to therapeutic and communicative technologies, because these concepts represent its most frequently used metaphors. (In fact, the body is often referred to as a machine. See Léroi-Gouhan 1943, 1945.)

### The Recovery of the Inorganic, or the Technology of the Body

During the whole modern age there has been limited technological development in the everyday sphere as the "real machines" of reproduction have been the body of the woman and her almost limitless capacity for work. The technological weakness of capital in the reproductive sphere was able to exist because domestic organization rested women's inventions of artificial technologies connected with cooking, preservation of food, caring for people.

Paradoxically, it was this very primary technological function of everyone's body, and especially women's, that gives pause to the development of artificial machines in the sphere of everyday life. With the great industrialization which began in Europe (Great Britain) in the last quarter of the eighteenth century, the development of factory technology was created first out of the claims for the reduction of hours required for manual labor, while there was no need for a corresponding development in the domestic sphere; the increase in productivity here was still pursued, creating more work, especially for women.

In heavily industrialized society, an initial stage of increasingly strong pressure came about from the decrease in women's domestic work time following their ever-more massive entry into the labor market. This decrease in some way stimulated the development of household technology, even if household appliances are all considered "secondary fallout of the noble evolution of the great industrial sectors" (Gras 1997, p. 172). Not by chance, underlines Gras (1997, p. 171), the graph of the development of technology in daily life is correlated to that of the increase in external female labor, as well as mass reduction of domestic work on the part of women (with an involvement of men in the division of domestic labor). The first main protagonists of household technological development were therefore household appliances. They represent a technology that has liberated women from the fatigue of some of the household chores. And women cannot be accused, as sometimes they are, of the fact that the time saved from work has been swallowed up by other jobs and functions. The problem, in that case, of this "swallowing up" must be attributed to the loss of power and control that women have over their workday as a whole. The negative effects of household appliances, if any, is the fact that they end up becoming fixed elements of re-ordering the workday, constituting a further possibility of control and command over daily life.

In a second, more recent stage, there has been the surprising entry of ICTs into the everyday (with important machines this time). The genealogy of these "machines of the mind" (i.e., computers) poses much more complex problems than mechanical and electrical-mechanical machines (Longo 1999–2000, 2000). If the latter serve to reduce physical effort and compress the time necessary for producing goods, the former serve to reduce the mental and nervous energy necessary to produce communication, information, entertainment, and enjoyment. But ICTs are so complex, ambiguous, and elusive that the time dedicated to communication and entertainment in the domestic sphere has been lengthened.

ICTs have actually increased their penetration of everyday life as women drastically reduced their housework and negotiated their interests more forcefully in marriage and in general, personal relations with men, and inside the extra-domestic labor market. In this context, electronic media have had, on the one hand, a social role that increasingly had to deal with the progressive isolation of the individual, and on the other, has functioned as a palliative for natural communication, serving as an excellent way of avoiding the confrontation of familiar relations, with no way out (Fortunati 1998).

## The Hybridization of the Body and Machine

In highly industrialized countries, we are entering a third stage, distinguished by the fact that we are investing technologically in the human body. The effect is obviously an enhancement of the technological aspect of the body, which is trying even harder to retreat from the intermingling and confusion of the natural and artificial. The symbiont, the individual-machine that lives both a human and un-human life, is the symbol of the new structure of social relations. But why this technological investment in the body?

To answer this question, we need to evaluate the phenomenon in the 1980s and 1990s, where new generations of women, on their relentless quest for self-determination, questioned many of their "natural" roles: from female roles associated with housework, to sexuality, from affectation to the psychological implications of care and support. In other words, they left the everyday to itself.

By leaving the everyday to itself, the great opportunities of meeting and clashing, of solidarity and mediation between genders and generations, has been abandoned, as the various social subjects (adult males, the young, women, children, the elderly) have not been able to find a strong enough common point of organization and mediation. In addition, it appears as if men and women, for one reason or another, are fleeing from the everyday (Fortunati 1998). There is a strong impression that the flight from the real is growing because the real is too contradictory, difficult, and complex to negotiate and live. Refusal or the impossibility (given the present-day obstacle of work) of taking care of others, of working to reproduce them, recreating them or recreating ourselves with them, is the real social problem of the Third Millennium. After the very noisy and radical struggles and demonstrations of the 1960s and 1970s, the 1980s were the years of the silence of the masses. But the important game of voluntary servitude, understood as a fatal strategy, in which we observed the impotence of power and the end of politics, as Baudrillard (1987) writes, ended in the 1990s. Today, disenchantment with domestic work and the weakening of social consensus passes silently, flees from reality, from natural communication, and from contraction and mediation, making interpersonal relations more difficult. Although they have managed to win greater power from men, women have not been able to put it to great use for two reasons: (1) men have reacted, escaping from natural communication and seeking refuge in machines to avoid communication and involvement, and to increase their sense of power (TV or the computer become the ideal wife/mother, because they are obedient and can be controlled by pressing a button); (2) the intensification of rhythms of labor and life have eroded social roles and communication. The departure from natural communication mostly by men, but also women, through the incapacity to resolve conflicts and to reach mediation is the most salient social consequence of the 1990s. The growing use of ICTs, especially the computer and television, conceals this situation of stalemate, a situation that has now hardened. At the same time, it is an extension of our expressed attitude toward all other goods. Perhaps because we are distancing ourselves, we feel an anxious greediness, a voracity for the real, which we want to consume in ever-larger quantities, even if only on a virtual level, even if second hand. The result is that, beyond the remaining old poverty, which exists even in the industrialized nations, the new poverty that affects everybody is a *poverty of first-hand reality.*

Virtual reality was born during a time when women had already liquidated the everyday—the sphere of domestic work—because no concrete recognition of the social value of their reproductive labor had been forthcoming. Virtual reality also was born out of a response to the inevitability of the choices and attitudes that politics continues to exert over their societal role. But it was born also from what Virilio calls "the defeat of facts and events" (1993). More or less authentic, sensitization to the problems of the "global" world obscures the growing desensitization to local problems, to the problems of those who live next to us. For not having recognized the value of domestic work, the economic system is paying an enormous cost for the subsequent neglect of the everyday. And while the concept and utilization of social power can convey only indifference and helplessness, entire slices of reality are being liquidated.

The only terrain on which social politics can gain ground regarding matters of the value of reproduction and communication is the technological hybridization of the body. But why have we come to the point of mechanizing the human body and not the domestic work process? Because the body is the formal connecting link to the production and reproduction spheres. It is not only a product of the domestic sphere, but is also the condition of the existence of the productive system. As the product of the natural force of social labor in the domestic sphere, the human body has actually no value in itself: it has value only inasmuch as it is the container of its capacity to work. Its becoming a machine presents the great advantage of not compromising the double character of domestic production and in general, of the whole system. Furthermore, the decrease in births (because for women, and in general for couples, it is less convenient to have children), and the great caution of migration policies which always try to control the immigrant's number for social and political reasons, have created a situation in which bodies, or the population in highly industrialized nations, are beginning to diminish. This is the reason why we have come to put machines inside the human body, even if this opens up a series of inconsistencies. On the part of the living, technologies impose the rights of the dead labor incorporated in them. So, the more technologies penetrate the body, the more they limit the quantity of living labor necessary for the production of the body itself and its capacity for labor, and therefore, further devalue us. It is the usual old story: technology makes labor, in this case housework, superfluous. In conclusion, it is the body that has been technologized and not the reproductive process. Not only does technology influence the logic of our organized working system, but also it can be considered to be the trigger that activates the devaluation of the body and the individual. This process is likely to be persistent.

The body, a natural machine, attracts and envelops artificial machines at a *diagnostic* level (e.g., probes), a *therapeutic* level (pacemakers, radiation, hormonal therapies), and at other technological levels: from *reproductive* ones (in vitro fertilization), to those of *identity* (plastic surgery, genetic engineering, sex change), to *communicative* ones (cellular, laptop, pager) (Katz and Aakhus

2002). In other words, the body attracts a series of machines; however, the machines are not those that would serve most to transform the organization of domestic work. The body, even if technologized, is left to its difficult domestic activity with little help from technology and everyday life remains in its substratum of pre-industrialization. The mind, on the other hand, is nourished electronically in various ways. Sometimes for reasons of social control, as in post-industrial countries, the nature of labor is expanded to include more communication, organization, management, and becomes increasingly intellectual. But also, predetermination of homogeneous standards in the immaterial reproduction of individuals is necessary to attain these mentioned labor domains. Standardization is very important because the immaterial part of domestic labor (e.g., affectivity, sexuality, psychological support, communication) is the most difficult to control and manage, and is the part that has been abandoned by women.

Capital, which is a system of production that is deeply rooted in the material nature of goods, cannot apply its set of strategies to the measurement of the quality and quantity of immaterial work (organization, strategy, communication, research). This difficulty can be felt clearly in firms that are exposed to these immaterial spheres. In fact, much behavior of firms in this area is marked strongly by its endeavors of experimentation and risk. Machines of the mind, apart from the advantages that they provide for economy, also guaranteed the considerable lengthening of the domestic workday—but at least this technology has diluted its density by multitasking (we watch TV while preparing or eating food). It is ironic that the result of a technology is lengthening of a workday, namely domestic labor, since it was created to do just the opposite. This resulting increase in time spent on domestic labor, which is unusual for a technology, clearly plays a role in controlling territories of daily life that have been freed from work or left unmanned by the refusal of domestic labor.

Until the 1970s, the sphere of the everyday was marked by a great presence of immaterial work (think of feelings, sexuality, affectivity). But a kind of "bug" spread throughout society that accelerated transformation of material labor into immaterial work. De-industrialization caused the transference of manual labor to developing countries of the "third world," thereby greatly decreasing manual labor in industrial society. Factories, therefore, faced an exponential increase in immaterial labor (e.g., organizational work, planning, ideation, research, financial management, logistics). In the last decades, the body in the West has always been used less as a producer of physical and material energy, and more as the producer of immaterial energy, and of communication, organization, and management spheres. Therefore, in the "first world," intellectual work has become progressively predominant. But it is in a certain sense de-cerebrated because it is forced to adapt to the rigid, tight, and limited straitjacket of informational operations. It is obvious that machines of the mind, together with the mechanization of the body, are the typical technologies of the post-modern era. But the cyborg remains a poor caricature if we do not understand its origins along with its diachronic significance.

The capacities most pursued and desired in the workforce today refer increasingly, at least in highly industrialized nations, to the elaborative capacities of the mind. Among the various electronic means, the computer is the machine that best manages to ensure and impose a standard in the supply of immaterial work. Obviously, many problems and dimensions of material labor have remained unresolved or cannot be formalized at the information technology (IT) level, while many others are produced by the computer (Maldonado 1992, 1997). It is also for this reason that the economic system currently shows very strong signs of suffering, apart from the fact that the paths for the management of immaterial work for the capitalistic system are impervious. Baudrillard (1999) has, in the age of the digital, grasped the aporia of money (which is the simultaneous display of both wealth itself and the sign of wealth). But this uncertain conceptualization can also regard immaterial work related to the capitalistic system, seeing that immaterial work is valuable in itself. There is a great difficulty in reducing all intellectual work that is not purely executive to a tangible measure. But isn't this the same kind of difficulty that prevents us from measuring the value of domestic labor, which contains so much immaterial work?

Given that the capacity for work is the most precious commodity for a society, but also the most complex, are we justified in thinking that the labor necessary for reproducing human beings can be made mechanical, or can be substituted by machines? Can we reasonably think that a household, the place where this work is done, can be subjected to a process of technological transformation such as to drastically reduce the fatigue and time of domestic labor? There are three elements that make us think in the contrary: (1) the domestic process, even if it is represented as the simple supply of work, more than that, "unskilled labor *par excellence*" (as, in Marxian terms, we could say), is far more complex than its technological equivalent, at least in respect to the level that technology, from robotics to domotics, has so far arrived (think only of dusting furniture and objects in a flat or cleaning a sofa); (2) the domestic work process is still represented as the natural sphere, so there is no political authority or institution that finds it necessary or has the power to elaborate a strategy to support this process; (3) as long as women (and to a certain extent men) go on doing this work without compensation (even if the quantity of work is less), inside a negotiation that doesn't have a norm or an official place in society, there is no incentive to replace domestic labor with technology because there are no costs to lower.

Let us remember that technological development becomes appetizing when it saves time and money, not when it becomes an extra cost. In fact, if technology does not serve to reduce labor as a whole, that is not the fault of technology, but of class-power relations. If technology does not respond to the problems posed by domestic work, it is due partly to the fact that, as long as people, and above all women, continue to provide the labor free, it will not attract any attention from the forces of production. Something does not become appetizing for the lords of technology if it does not present them with an incentive of doing business. To add to the problem, there are few women in central positions of ideation and creation in the new technologies.

## We Who are Becoming Machines in Post-Modern Society: Conquests or Defeats?

In post-modern society, the social system of differences developed in the modern age is being completely restructured. Many differences, even between men and women, or more specifically, between the world of production and reproduction, have disappeared, or are at least less clear-cut. There is a tendency at the social level to fusion, to the formation of hybrids, to the development of similarity. Many of these differences are artificial constructions, the result of historical, social, and cultural determinations. Just as artificially they are demolished, (Meyrowitz 1985) possibly in the name of another form of artificiality.

Unfortunately, while we still dedicate much time and energy in empirical research to grasp and understand the meaning of differences (men/women, adults/children), we still dedicate little attention to understanding the social significance of the new equalities that are taking shape in post-modern society. From a political, social, and psychological point of view, what meaning have indices of personality, attitude, and behavior, which are becoming more similar between men and women? Which processes affect more strongly our society—masculinization or feminization? It would be important to understand the signs of much new equality or, better, forms of commonalties, because that way we would be able to understand whether, on an evolutionary level, these are conquests or defeats on the part of humankind.

Traditionally, the nerve center of the capitalist system—the place of technological innovation and organizational complexity—has been the factory, the production of goods. The domestic cycle, even if fundamental, represents a natural sphere that has always been treated as a peripheral area. Radical changes have seemed to be connected only with the working class. But the incursion of women into the labor market and consequent presence in both domestic and labor spheres has opened a breach that has become bigger with time. In fact, production has developed inside reproduction (see telework, the family, or individual concern), and reproduction has increasingly taken on certain formal characteristics of a firm's work. The domestic sphere has assumed more importance as the new frontier of expansion in new industrialization production, often seen as the small, medium, or individual firm. The borders between production and reproduction have become increasingly blurred because of anti-economics and the hybridization of behavior and attitude.

However, the process of decreasing separation between production and re-production spheres swung off course and turned over on itself. The domestic, which welcomed this massive incursion of production, has become the standard model that has pervaded all society. The household has become what the factory was once—the emblem, the symbol of what is called globalization. Spaces have become occupied with a multitude of households comprised of many families, perhaps ubiquitous over society itself as one great household, much like the parameters of a firm. Also the energies of innovation and competence in using technologies have begun to target the home market and have since migrated towards enterprises and firms. In fact, the big technological markets are increasingly tied to the domestic sphere. Once again, Hegel (1807, It. tr. 1960, pp. 158 and following) and his followers are correct in saying that at a certain point, those who end up by having more power are not those who have dominion, but those who are dominated.

In this context, the function of the individual as a "natural machine," typical of the reproductive sphere, and the hybrid of natural and artificial technology, affects all social aspects. In industrial society, alienation depended on whether work with machines existed in such a way that estranged workers from each other. Our post-industrial society creates a further alienation that depends on the invasion of the inorganic into the organic and on a further separation between the mind and the body. In highly industrialized countries, the intellect is the primary center of value production, making the brain the only utensil of post-modern production (Hardt and Negri 1994; Negri 2000, p.150).

### The Reduction of Oppositions on the Ontological Plane, or Machines that Become Us

A process that has made body/machine hybridization possible has been the attenuation of differences on the ontological plane. The way in which human beings face the world and the relations they establish between the body and technology, between technology and objects, and between the objects and self, is on increasingly less disparate terms. In other words, that which up to yesterday appeared as opposing divisions emerges now as a gradual change, and the reason for the differences between the two terms in these oppositions are become increasingly hazy. Baudrillard (1995), in different terms, speaks of the end of differences, of undifferentiated concepts.

Given that from the anthropological point of view humanity is such because it produces and lives out these differences, the attenuation of these differences (which can go as far as creating similarity) could cause us to reproach the change as an anthropological catastrophe. But at the same time, it expresses both a strong structural tendency of the productive system and a strong force of attraction over humankind. In our environment, things that are similar to ourselves attract us most. The force of this attraction has led human beings to discuss the meaning of similarity and to try to reproduce it. The concept of similarity is recorded in philosophical reflections from the beginnings of Greek thought. Empedocles, for instance, conceives knowledge as a process of adaptation of the similar to the similar. Psychologists today do not go much further when they speak of attributing the unknown to the known. In addition, there is a power in similarity in the Latin phrase, *similia similibus curentur* (similar is cured by similar), a phrase that contains the origin of homeopathic medicine (as opposed to the other, *contrariis curentur* [cured by the contrary], which is the principle of the allopathic school).

Even if an important stage of establishing similarity is the beginning of confusion and grappling with the indistinct, it still remains a positive fact that similarities, when they appear, compensate for differences (Aron 1987).

If difference means separation, similarity takes us back to the opposite phenomenon, that is, reunification: *the body is assimilated to the machine, objects become technological, technologies become "intelligent."* The tendencies to mechanize human beings and anthropomorphize objects intermingle with one another. It was the coming of serial production of goods that pushed similarity to the extreme, to identicalness, because every piece had to respond to precise standards. And it was this event that attenuated the uniqueness of human beings and their behavior, setting into motion powerful processes of uniformity, standardization, and homogeneity of the labor force both at a domestic and social level. Now, post-industrialism, through the development of technology, takes similarities between objects to their furthest stage. This does not mean the disappearance *tout court* of differences, but that the basis of sharing common conditions of human beings widens. On this basis, slighter and slighter differences establish themselves, which take place on a higher level and which are produced in a less hierarchical and more diversified way than before. Production of the similar, furthermore, is reinforced almost automatically socially in that it sets into motion at the same time psychosocial processes of simulation of the similar. That is, there is a tendency established to dissimulate differences between objects, and subjects, which makes possible and necessary, cooperation on the part of the public, consumers, and people.

In what way is this cooperation managed? In the way that the forces that create similarity or identicalness at a social level are aided and supported by the unwitting willingness of users. These users, in fact, cooperate with these forces, accepting to live out this fiction as if it were not one. This cooperation can be given also because human beings as spectators, consumers, or the like, tend to convince themselves that what appears similar is actually the same as the object or subject that it claims to be, or the object/subject purports to be similar to the claimed object/subject. This is in virtue of the psychological tendency innate in human beings to stress similarities between objects that belong to the same category (Tajel 1981). This tendency of the development of similarity, and therefore, of reunification, just because it has "worked" both for objects and human beings, has gone and modified the ontology of post-modern human beings, the very structures and fundamental modalities for their being in the world. Therefore, the path of the becoming of the body supports the potent forces at work not only of separation, but also of integration and union. Separations are weakening also under the blows of biotechnologies such as genetic engineering. A new order is being born, a new system, where the hybrid is the key figure that passes from the imaginary to the statute of the real.

### Technologies Inside the Body: Humanization of Objects

Another reason ICTs have been enabled to conjoin with the body is due to our attitude and relationship with objects in general. The means of production, distribution, and consumption, and the significance and that we attribute to objects, has greatly changed. We mean objects in general, because technologies not only form part of the family of objects, but also can in a certain sense be considered their more "noble" part. In fact they are able, as opposed to objects that are immobile, to produce movement. In virtue of this precious capacity of theirs, technologies border more closely than objects on the human and animal. Even so, our attitude toward technology is still influenced by our general attitude towards objects, which, in turn, shapes the former.

Ever since matter and energy have been intensely linked with information as an element capable of determining evolution, the characteristics that attract us most in contemporary objects have changed. We analyze only one of these, an object's humanization, because it is a good example to delineate our relation with technologies as forming part of the great family of objects.

Humanization of machines and technologies signals the acquisition of capacities and competence that so far have only belonged to humans. Let's start from technologies: the family of objects is the most similar to human beings because they can produce movement, and thus, the illusion of life. So, technologies becoming "intelligent" could be interpreted as a strengthening of the virtue of movement that machines had stolen from the human. And, as movement is life, producing movement means producing in a certain sense a central modality among those pertinent to human beings. But an object becoming "intelligent" today is a leap in quality, in the sense that all objects are becoming humanized through the development of information and the capacity to disseminate it. While the mechanization of humans is developing rapidly in a direction that has been tried out for centuries, the new event is the exportation of intelligence into things, bestowing objects with a "mind," of a new quality that is, above all, pertinent to the human kingdom. Making and constructing "intelligent" objects like technological textures, means that we are domesticating these objects, as we have done with animals. We make them similar to us, attenuating the differences between them and us, while specializing their properties and capacities in a complementary mode to ours; in other words, we make "intelligent" objects do what we are unable to do. Indeed, we have to resort to an "inferior" role to accomplish things that exceed our abilities.

But what is artificial intelligence? It is not an extension of human intelligence— in some ways it is a more powerful form, and in others, artificial intelligence is more limited and distorted than ours since it only manages to activate a small part of human intelligence: the part relative to formal logic without regard to common sense, emotive intelligence, or linguistic competence. Clearly the entire conceit is a playing out of a social process (Collins 1990). If we look at the everyday, artificial intelligence is not successful in interacting with its complexity. In fact, it only resolves a few marginal problems. "Intelligent" objects are indeed often a parody, a simulacrum of human intelligence. But notice that once they have been incorporated into everyday, they have the power to shape reality inside a new social order in which their basic distortion becomes a new normality, the new tight boundaries inside which normality is forced to pass. For instance, the "smart house," which may offer a lot of things, will not in itself likely be able to offer basic social needs. That is an important limitation, and one that suggests life will continue on them physically mobile dimensions with which we are presently familiar (Katz 1999).

This discussion so far helps us to understand the current developed characteristics of ICTs that approach the body in order to penetrate it. This aspect develops the incorporeity of the technological object and consequently allows technologies to get inside the body, to escape the forces of surveillance and therefore make individuals aware of their technological penetration.

## Problems Unresolved

The technology that penetrates our bodies often saves our lives, returns us to health, broadens our means of communication, or gives us control—but technology always, paradoxically, results in our devaluation. Technology modifies us radically in ways that inevitably cause some type of suffering or limitation. Technology, while mitigating insufficiencies that have been produced in the body, also reveals the marvels of the human body and how little we still know about it. We must in fact remember that "the West, lord of machines," as Lévi-Strauss writes (1952, It. tr. 1967, p.121), "has very elementary knowledge of the use and resources of that supreme machine that is the human body."

In conclusion, the following list shall identify today's questions and structural problems that remain unresolved in the process of hybridization of the body with the machine. The list is in no way exhaustive, since these problems and questions are complex and still evolving. This list is composed of both the questions and problems with which the epistemological debate has dealt with thus far, and those issues that have not yet been resolved. This attempt to list unresolved problems and questions is important, because we must at least make a start in empirical research around these themes, if only to try and assemble a dual list of the problems that machines help us to resolve, and those that they create afresh.

1.    There are various modes of use and of permanence of machines inside our body. For instance, there are machines that stay inside the body permanently (e.g., valves), machines that go in and out (probes, drills), machines to which we connect regularly (dialysis), and machines that we need occasionally (intensive care unit, operating theater). Does our attitude toward machines change according to their mode of use and the duration of our relationship with them?

2.    What does the machine inside the body mean in respect to the mind-body unit? We know that there is an interrelation between the mind and the body. A machine can substitute or restart one or more functions of an organ, for example. But how can it interact in a complex way with the mind? Up to what point is it an impairment of the body?

3.    What does intimacy mean with a machine at the affective and emotional level, when it enters into our most intimate sphere, that is, inside our body? Very probably our first reaction is a not very intimate one. But, with time, does this probable initial extraneousness remain, or does it become progressively assimilated into the complexity of our bodily image? That is, does the "coenaesthesis," which is the internal perception of our body, change (Starobinski 1981)?

4.    The general and unresolved problem of the responsibility of machines becomes more serious. In fact, when the machine is inside us, up to what point does the way it performs fall under our individual responsibility (Longo 2000)? If the machine makes a mistake, who is responsible for the damage?

5.    One of the relevant general problems that must be faced is delegating many duties to machines (computing, archiving). Inevitably, human beings risk losing the competence that the execution of these responsibilities entails, thereby placing themselves in a situation of dependence on machines. When machines, especially machines of communication, are inside us, the problem of delegation and therefore of our dependence on them will be even more relevant (Longo 2000).

6.    Like everything, machines wear out or become obsolete. What is the implication of knowing that the machine will need to be changed or replaced? We count on our organs to work efficiently until the onset of illness, when we try to heal the organ with an effective therapy. But the entire body takes part in the healing process —will our body manage to heal a machine inside us without having to replace it? Many problems of restructuring the body/machine present themselves at the moment in which the equilibrium is destroyed.

7.    For what kind of problem do we accept machines? For health (diagnosis, therapy), for cosmetic reasons, for communication, as a status symbol, or just because it is fashionable? That is, in what cases are we justified in seeking the aid of a machine?

8.    Body and machine can have a different average life span. When the body dies, what does the machine that is inside the body do? Does it die with the body or can it survive? Can it be reused? That is, do the boundaries of the dead body, the soma, include machines also?

9.    The machines that derive from Turing's famous black box are ingenuous technology because they are evident and direct and respond to other invisible technologies—but they are much more pernicious and perhaps more dangerous as well. Today's com-

puters also have become smaller, tending to disappear inside objects, fabrics, walls, and so on. What does miniaturization of machines, this tendency to become "invisible," signify in terms of self-perception and control? Today they make computers as small as a pinhead for microsurgery. What effects will the invisibility of computers, in addition to other technologies, have on our capacity to control the everyday, and us alongside it?

10.  The idea is becoming more and more common of the machine as a spare part for the body (Katz 1999). That is, machines potentially becoming capable of granting "immortality," or at least capable of extending the average span of life. What does this mean? And, in addition, up to what point can a person become a machine, or vice versa, at what point does a machine become human?

11.  Are there too few or too many machines? Humankind has always negotiated a measure, at a social level, of metabolizing technology with the producers of machines. Are we still able to carry on a negotiation that defends our interests, or is the speed of change in technology and production such that we have difficulty even at a cognitive level to understand what is happening?

12.  There is a problem that is becoming more and more urgent: the aesthetics of machines. In order to approach the body or to penetrate it, does the machine have to be beautiful?

13.  Should machines embrace a gender? Although we do not wish to go as far as to cogitate on the provocative thesis of Samuel Butler, according to whom the human being might be nothing else but a means for the reproduction of machines, we need to ask ourselves the following question: will machines acquire determination of gender? Will there be female and male machines, or machines, for instance, capable of producing and reproducing other machines? The twentieth century produced bachelor machines with their incapability to procreate (not eroticism) and their paradoxical, improbable nature (*Le macchine celibi* [trans. *Bachelor machines*] 1975). The twentieth century also produced the possibility of building a machine that is a universal builder, capable of building other machines (Odifreddi 2000, pp. 209–211). However, machines, writes Baudrillard (1999, p. 110) "do not experience the inebriation of functioning, living, pleasure...they cannot be metaphorical, imaginative, excessive. They do not have that ironic extra of functioning, that suffering, they do not succumb to narcissistic temptations and are not even seduced by their own knowledge. All this explains their profound melancholy, the sadness of the computer. All machines are bachelors"(p. 111).

14.  The usability of machines is not always optimal, which creates further problems of loss of time, economic investment, interruption of work, the need to find solutions. In drawing up balances of the pros and cons, we must always include the second-degree labor and machine downtime (learning, updating, simple maintenance, and repair). To be realistic, we must draw up a balance sheet to see what machines have to offer in terms of performance, costs, and rewards, both at a personal and social level, and also in view of a sustainable development (Poggio 2000).

15.  The secret of machines. According to Marx's nineteenth-century view of the world, the incipient communist society would be able to set up a process of liberation from work by means of the machine and the development of technology. In this century too, the liberating myth and the magic of the object machine has been very powerful;

that is, of the object that manages to produce movement (and hence, energy and then information). In the twentieth century, however, machines began to reveal their secret: they did not free society from work *tout court*, but only from some forms of work. In the meantime, work has turned out to be more complex than expected: even if machines eliminate one part of it, it reappears elsewhere in another form. In addition, machines require continuous maintenance and surveillance.

When the import of these theoretical perspectives, or perhaps more accurately, theoretical snapshots are considered, we see that there are some intriguing questions that remain about the process in which machines increasingly enter us. At the same time, though, they highlight the fact that as machines indeed become us, it remains a socially predicated and inflected process. As machines become us, they also become more social in context and performance.

## References

Aron, J. P. 1987. La tragédie de l'apparence à l'époque contemporaine. In "Parure, pruderie, étiquette," *Communications* 46: 305–314.

Baudrillard J. 1995. *Le crime parfait.* Paris: Editions Galilée (It. trans. Il delitto perfetto. Milano: Cortina, 1996).

Baudrillard J. 1987. Silenzio delle masse, silenzio del deserto (Silence of Masses, Silence of the Desert). In *Media & Messaggi* 4: 38–45.

Baudrillard J. 1999. L'Echange impossible. *Editions Galilée.* Paris (It. trans. Lo scambio impossibile, Asterios, Trieste, 2000).

Collins, H. M. 1990. *Artifical Experts: Social Knowledge and Intelligent Machines.* Cambridge, MA: MIT Press.

Colombo, F. 1999. Segnali di oggetti (Signals of Objects). In *Techne,* no. 2: 52–57.

Durand, G. 1963. *Les structures anthropologiques de l'Imaginaire.* Paris, France: P.U.F.

Fortunati, L. 1995. *The Arcane of Reproduction.* New York: Autonomedia (It. trans. L'arcano della riproduzione. Venezia: Marsilio, 1981).

Fortunati, L. 1998. "Introduzione." (Introduction) In *Telecomunicando in Europa (Telecommunicating in Europe),* ed. L. Fortunati. Milano: Angeli.

Fortunati, L. Real People, Artificial Bodies (forthcoming).

Gras, A. 1993. *Grandeur et dépendance.* Paris: P.U.F.

Hardt M. and N. Negri. 1994. "Labor of Dionysus." *A Critique of the State-Form.* Minneapolis and London: University of Minnesota Press.

Hegel, G. W. F. Phänomenologie des Geistes. 1807. (Republished tr. It. Fenomenologia dello Spirito, La Nuova Italia, Firenze, 1960).

Katz, James E. 1999. Communication in the year 2075. *Science and the Future. Year 2000.* Annual Supplement of the *Encyclopedia Britannica.* Chicago and London: Encyclopedia Britannica, pp. 176-200.

Katz, J. and M. Aakhus, eds. 2002. *Perpetual Contact: Mobile Communication, Private Talk, Public Performance.* Cambridge and New York: Cambridge University Press.

Latour, B. 1998. Fatti, artefatti, fatticci (Facts, Artefacts, Factish). In *Oggetti d'uso quotidiano,* ed. M. Nacci. Venezia: Marsilio, pp.17–36.

Le macchine celibi (Bachelor Machines). 1975. *Catalogo della mostra.* Venezia: Alfieri.

Léroi-Gourhan, A. 1943 and 1945. Evolution et Technique; I: L'Homme et la Matière; II: Milieu et Technique. Paris: Michel.

Lévi-Strauss, C. 1952. *Race et Histoire.* Paris: Unesco. (Republished It. trans. Razza e Storia e altri studi di Antropologia. Torino: Einaudi, 1967).

*L'universo del corpo (Universe of the Human Body).* 1999. vols. I and II. Roma: Instituto della Enciclopedia Italiana.

Longo, G. O. 2000. *Homo Technologicus.*

Longo, G. O. 1999–2000. Mente e tecnologia (Mind and Technology). In *Pluriverso* 4 and 1.

Maldonado, T. 1992. *Reale e virtuale (Real and Virtual).* Milano: Feltrinelli.

Maldonado, T. 1997. *Critica della ragione informatica* (Critics of the Information Reason). Milano: Feltrinelli.

Maldonado, T. 1998. Ancora la tecnica. Un "tour d'horizon." In *Oggetti d'uso quotidiano.* (Again the technique. A "tour d'horizon." In *Objects of Everyday Use*), ed. M. Nacci, Venezia: Marsilio, pp. 197–227.

Marx, K. 1957. *Das Kapital,* vols. I–III. Berlin: Dietz. (Republished It. tr. Il capitale, 3 vols. Roma: Editori Riuniti, vol. I, 1964; vols. II and III, 1965).

Marx, K. 1953. *Grundrisse der Kritik der politischen Oekonomie* (Rohentwurf). Berlin: Dietz Verlag.

Meyrowitz, J. 1985. No Sense of Place. In *The Impact of Electronic Media on Social Behavior.* New York: Oxford University Press.

Negri, A. 2000. Kairòs. In *Alma Venus, Multitudo.* Roma: manifestolibri.

Odifreddi, P. 2000. *Il computer di Dio.* (The computer of God) Milano: Cortina.

Polhemus, T. 1999. The Postmodern Body. In *Body in Transition,* ed. D. Bartlett, Zagreb: Tiskara Puljko, pp.181–184.

Poggio, P. P. 2000. Postfordismo e sviluppo sostenibile (Post-Fordism and Sustainable Development). In *Altronovecento* 2 (http://www.altronovecento.quipo.it).

Starobinski, J. 1981. Breve storia della coscienza del corpo (Short Story of the Body Conscience). In *Intersezioni* 1, pp. 27–42.

Tajel, H. 1981. *Human Groups and Social Categories.* Cambridge: Cambridge University Press (Republished It. trans. Gruppi umani e categorie sociali. Bologna: Il Mulino, 1985).

Virilio, P. 1993. *L'art du moteur.* Ed. Galilée, Paris (Republished It. trans. *Lo schermo e l'oblio.* Anabasi, Milano, 1994).

Volli, U. Body Fetish. 1999. In *Body in Transition,* ed. D. Bartlett, Zagreb: Tiskara Puljko, pp. 131–134.

# Part 2

# National and Cross-Cultural Studies

# 7

# Digital Divides of the Internet and Mobile Phone: Structural Determinants of the Social Context of Communication Technologies

*Ronald E. Rice and James E. Katz*

Overcoming the digital divide—the gap between those who have and do not have information and communication technologies (ICTs)—is a fundamental component of most industrialized countries' telecommunications policy; certainly equity and universal service has been a hallmark historically of U.S. telecommunication policy (Hadden and Rhodes, 1995). This axiomatic commitment may be seen in the U.S.'s universal service tradition (Katz, 1988). Moreover, there appear to be noticeable economic and social benefits to having access to information and communication technologies (ICTs) (Katz and Rice, 2002). But research on the digital divide is almost entirely devoted to the Internet. Clearly this is an important topic, but this emphasis needs to be complemented by consideration of other ICTs such as the mobile phone. This is because the social and economic importance of the mobile phone is quite substantial, even as worldwide ownership rates are rivaling that of TV set ownership (Katz and Aakhus, 2002).

### Evidence about an Internet Digital Divide

Cultural, rather than strict economic, education, and racial differences are receiving increased attention from both government and commercial studies as the source of differential access and usage patterns (Katz and Rice 2002; Cultural Access Group 2001). Haddon (2001) argues that "social exclusion" is context-dependent (neither necessarily economically based nor equivalent across all domains of a person's life), involves not only political and civic involvement but also people's ability to occupy social roles, and may also involve rejection of or lack of interest in, new technologies and pressing issues such as day care. (See also his chapter, this volume.)

There are other aspects of access than just equal distribution across demographic and national boundaries. People who have hearing, sight, movement, and other disabilities may also be disadvantaged by limitations on their ability to access information, contacts, and opportunities for expression on the Internet. The disabled have half the access rate of those who are not disabled (McConnaughey 2001). And even those who do overcome all these obstacles do not necessarily benefit in ways proposed by those concerned with the digital divide. For example, low-skill information- or knowledge-worker jobs are rising as fast as higher-skill jobs, information-based jobs are frequently rationalized and fragmented, and initiatives to help overcome employment opportunity divides often end up simply subsidizing training for organizations with low-paying computer-based jobs (Tufekcioglu 2001).

Recent studies (Jupiter Communications 2000; Katz, Rice, and Aspden 2001), have been finding that at least racial and gender differences in Internet use disappear after other variables are taken into account statistically. A Pew Internet and American Life study (Yahoo!News 2001) found that by the end of 2000, 58 percent of men and 54 percent of women were Internet users; figures for Hispanics were 47 percent and for blacks 43 percent. According to the AOL survey (2000), more women (53 percent) starting Internet use in 2000 than did men; overall, 49 percent of Internet users were women. By June of 2001, a Nielsen/NetRatings study (Net users..., 2001) reported that Internet users mirror the national distribution of women and men, with 53.33 million women using the Internet and 49.83 million men. Men do use the Internet a bit more, about 10.5 hours per week compared to nine hours per week, and view about 31 percent more pages than do women (Net users 2001). Looking at the gender divide from an historical viewpoint, the longer a user cohort had been online, the higher was its proportion of men (AOL, 2000); Katz et al. (2001) found similar trends.

A representative postal mail survey of 80,000 U.S. households conducted by Forrester research in January 2000 (Walsh, Gazala, and Ham, 2001) found that Asian Americans have the highest Internet penetration rate, and Hispanic Americans have a higher adoption rate than Caucasians. Connection to the Internet grew for all ethnic groups who bought personal computers. There are still differences in Internet access, based primarily on income, but also age, education, and technology optimism; but once these are statistically controlled, there are no remaining differences on the basis of race. Indeed, the survey showed that consumers of all ethnicities use the Internet for the same general reasons: communicating with others, accessing information, having fun, and shopping.

## Social Structural Issues for Access to ICTs

Although there are points of disagreement concerning research on the digital divide, the bulk of evidence indicates that the digital divide is decreasing or even disappearing with respect to gender and race. Differences in income and education are still great, and in some studies, increasing. The general lag in access and use may inflict enduring social damage that lingers or appears even after later adopters achieve full access. There are many obstacles to more equitable access, some of which may be deeply embedded in cultural contexts. Of particular interest to the present study is that there may be multiple kinds of communication technology digital divide, and we do not yet know much about any mobile phone digital divide, or about how Internet and mobile phone use are related. The present study, then, focuses on:

1. What other usage differences exist beyond the traditional divide of users and nonusers?

2. To what extent are Internet usage and mobile phone usage similar or different?

3. What are some national policy implications of the various potential digital divides?

## The Syntopia Project and the Social Context of Personal Communication Technology

This study is part of a larger project, which we now call the Syntopia Project. Our joint aim has been to create through a series of national random telephone surveys, as well as case studies, in-depth observations, focus groups, and website analysis, a multi-year program charting social aspects of Americans' mediated communication behavior.

We chose the name "Syntopia" for five reasons given. First, an important aspect of the Syntopia concept is that the Internet is part of a much larger synthesis of communication and social interaction. People's physical and social situation and history influence their actions online, and what they learn and do online spills over to their real world experiences. The term Syntopia underscores this synergy across media and between mediated and unmediated activities. Second, the term Syntopia draws together the words "syn" and "utopia." Derived from ancient Greek, the word means literally "together place," which is how we see the Internet and associated mobile communication and its interaction with unmediated interpersonal and community relations. Third, the term Syntopia invokes both utopian and dystopian visions of what new media such as the Internet and mobile telephony does and could mean. At the same time, the term also alludes to the dark side of new media in the homophone "sin." Fourth, while mediated communication may be critiqued as "impersonal" or "synthetic," we would argue that the research to date shows that mediated communication can provide wider, more diverse, and possibly more real—even hyperpersonal—communication than traditional face-to-face communication. Fifth, "synthesis" also implies being able to put things together in a new way. People of every ethnic group, gender, political and sexual orientation, and economic resource level have shown incredible creativity cobbling together various ICTs at hand to perpetuate and expand their communication networks (Katz 1999; Katz and Rice 2002).

In this application of Syntopia, we seek to understand the digital divide by contrasting two communication media, and contrasting users and non-users in terms of their social drivers. As to the first, the Internet, it has been deeply studied since at least 1995 (Katz and Aspden 1997), except for the dropout phenomena discovered in 1995 (Katz and Aspden 1998) and which has only recently captured attention (Mante and Thomas 2002). As to the second, the mobile phone, its potential digital divide has is only been infrequently analyzed (e.g., Katz 1999).

### Data for a Perspective on Digital Divides

Our analysis is based upon a national probability telephone survey conducted in March 2000, designed by us but administered by a commercial survey firm. The survey data collection procedure followed rigorous sampling protocols, and used random-digit dialing, to produce a statistically representative sample of the adult U.S. population.

We measured usage for the Internet and mobile phone by whether the respondent was a current user, a former user, or never a user (for mobile phone, also whether one's spouse/best friend was a current, former, or never user); the year each medium was first adopted (dichotomized at the median of 1997, creating "veteran" and "recent" users. Reasons for stopping using the Internet or mobile phone included cost, complexity, usefulness, interesting, and access. (Details of the study are presented in Rice and Katz, 2002.)

**Table 7.1**
**Summary details on overall sample sizes, and numbers of Internet and Mobile phone nonusers, users, and former users.**

| User Category | Internet | Mobile Phone |
|---|---|---|
| Current users | 59.7% | 54.4% |
| Former users | | |
| • percent of respondents | 10.5% | 14.9% |
| • percent of current and former users | 9.0% | 14.2% |
| Never used | 29.7% | 36.5% |
| N | 1305 | 1329 |
| Adopted before or during 1997 | 53.8% | 53.8% |
| Adopted after 1997 | 46.2% | 46.2% |
| N | 1000 | 725 |

Demographic variables include gender, age (dichotomized at forty years), income (at $35,000), education (at college degree), race (due to sample sizes, only African-American and white non-Hispanic), marital status (other, or married), children (at none, or any), work (at full time, or other).

Media use measures include number of letters sent weekly (dichotomized at none, or any), phone calls made weekly (up to nine, ten, or more), and email messages sent weekly (at none, or any). General social involvement was measured by number of religious organizations, leisure organizations, and community organizations (each dichotomized at none, or any).

## Apparent Similarity of Internet and Mobile Phone Usage

We asked users the year they started using the Internet (referred to in the surveys as "the Internet, also known as the Information or Electronic Superhighway") or owning mobile phones. Respondents were grouped into those starting in 1997 or before ("veteran users"), and those starting in 1998 or after ("recent users") (based on a median split). We also grouped respondents in two ways according to their usage: whether they were a current or former user, and whether they were a current user or not (including never and former user). Of the over 1,300 respondents, 59.7 percent were current Internet and 54.4 percent current mobile phone users; 10.5 percent had stopped using the Internet, and 9.0 percent had stopped using mobile phones (relative to the total current and former users, the percentages were 14.9 percent and 14.2 percent); 29.7 percent had never used the Internet, and 36.5 percent had never had a mobile phone. For both media, 53.8 percent of those who indicated the year they first adopted the medium did so before or during 1997, and 46.2 percent from 1998 on. On the surface, these aggregate statistics indicate that adoption, former, and nonuse of these two media were about the same in 2000. This might imply that Internet and mobile phone usage is indicative of similar demographic, personal and media use characteristics; that is, that their users are quite similar, and that the two media are quite similar in general communication function. It also implies that the only basic difference for both media is between adopters and non-adopters, the traditional criterion for identifying the "digital divide."

*Different Usage Categories and Their Relation to Demographic Differences*

As table 7.2 portrays, relationships among categories of Internet and Mobile phone users, while significantly positively associated, are not exact. Considering all three categories of current, former, and never, 17 percent of respondents do not occupy similar categories across the two media. Grouping former users with never users, the divergence rises to 38.3 percent. Time of adoption (grouped as through 1997 or after 1997) shows a similar divergence: of the 616 who reported their year of first adoption, 42.5 percent adopted each medium in different time periods. So while these two media appear quite similar in terms of

Table 7.2
Relationship of Internet and Mobile Phone Usage Categories

| Internet Use | Mobile Phone Use | | |
|---|---|---|---|
| | Never | Former | Current |
| Never | 146 / 60.6% | 27 / 11.2% | 68 /28.2% |
| Former | 41 / 27.3% | 22 / 14.7% | 87 / 58.0% |
| Current | 259 / 30.5% | 62 / 7.3% | 529 / 62.2% |
| Chi-square = 100.0 *** | | | |

| Internet Use | Mobile Phone Use | |
|---|---|---|
| | Non (Never & Former) | Current |
| Non (Never & Former) | 236 / 60.4% | 155 / 39.6% |
| Current | 321 / 37.8% | 529 / 62.2% |
| Chi-square = 55.3 *** | | |

| When Started Using Internet | Mobile Phone Use | |
|---|---|---|
| | Veteran: 1997 or Before | Recent: 1998 or After |
| Veteran: 1997 or Before | 211 / 62.6% | 126 / 37.4% |
| Recent: 1998 or After | 136 / 48.7% | 143 / 51.3% |
| Chi-square = 11.9 *** | | |

*** p<.001

aggregate usage and adoption, there are still substantial percentages of respondents who represent different categories of users or adopters for the two media.

The following three sections attempt to identify whether there are noticeable differences in respondents' demographic and media characteristics across these usage categories. We seek to succinctly describe some rather detailed statistical analysis.

*Internet Non-Users Compared to Users.* Non-users were more likely to be female, older, have less income, have less education, be slightly disproportionately African-American, have no children, not work full time, be more satisfied, (obviously) send no emails, and belong to fewer community organizations.

*Internet Veteran Users Compared to Recent Users.* Compared to veteran users, recent users are more likely to be female, have lower income, have less education, have more children, make fewer phone calls, and send fewer e-mails.

*Internet Dropouts Compared to Current Users.* Internet dropouts, compared to current users, were more likely to be younger, have lower income, have less education, have never been married or have a partner, have more general satisfaction with life and communication, feel less overloaded/rushed, (obviously) send fewer emails, and belong to fewer community organizations.

The surveys offered responding dropouts several reasons for their decision. Considering respondents choosing a reason as "extremely important" or "important," too hard/complex was the most frequently named reason (65.4 percent), followed by cost (54.5 percent), lost access (48.2 percent) and not interesting (46.4 percent). A recent U.S. Department of Commerce report (2000), surveying some 48,000 households, also reported on those who discontinued Internet usage. Extrapolating to the entire nation, it estimated there were about 4 million drop-outs in both 1998 and 2000. The three primary reasons given in 2000 for discontinuing where "no longer owns a computer" (17 percent), "can use it elsewhere" (13 percent), and "cost, too expensive" (12 percent). Other reasons were "don't want it" (10.3 percent), "not enough time" (10 percent), "computer requires repair" (9.7 percent), "moved" (6.1 percent), "not useful" (4.2 percent), "problems with ISP" (2.9 percent), "concern with children" (2.3 percent), "not user friendly" (1.5 percent) and "computer capacity issues" (1.2 percent). For those with incomes less than $25,000, cost was the first or second most important reason for non-access at home. For those with higher incomes, "no longer owns computers" or "can use elsewhere" were the most important reasons. The report notes that these reasons differ from the primary reason given by non-users for never connecting at all with the Internet, which is "don't want it."

*Mobile Phone Non-Users Compared to Current Users.* Compared to current mobile phone users, non-users had lower income, less education, were more likely to be never married or not have a partner, not have children, not work full time, feel more overloaded/rushed, and belong to fewer community organizations. Reasons for stopping owning a mobile phone that were rated as "important" or "extremely important," in decreasing order, were "too complicated" (78.4 percent), "lost access" (74.7 percent), "too distracting" (58.3 percent), "not useful" (52.7 percent) and "too expensive" (44.0 percent).

*Veteran Mobile Phone Users Compared to Recent Users.* Compared to veteran mobile phone users, recent users are more likely to be younger, have lower income, have less education, be African-American, not be married/have a partner, not work full time, not belong to religious organizations, and not belong to community organizations.

*Mobile Phone Dropouts Compared to Current Users.* Mobile phone dropouts, compared to current users, were more likely to have lower income, make fewer phone calls, and send fewer emails.

*Multivariate Influences on Internet and Mobile Phone Usage Categories.* Because the various demographic and other variables tend to be intercorrelated, it is useful to combine all those variables that were statistically significant across dropouts and users, into a logistic regression equation, which then controls for shared variance across the predictors. A final logistic equation was run with only significant predictors retained.

Table 7.3 provides the results for Internet usage. Internet users, compared to non-users (never and former), were older and had greater income (explaining 15 percent of the variance). Recent, compared to veteran, users, older, had less

**Table 7.3**
**Logistic Regressions Predicting Internet User Categories**

| NonUsers (0) / Users (1) | | | Veteran (0) / Recent (1) | | | Dropouts (0) / Users (1) | | |
|---|---|---|---|---|---|---|---|---|
| **Predictor** | **B** | **Exp (B)** | **Predictor** | **B** | **Exp (B)** | **Predictor** | **B** | **Exp (B)** |
| Age | -.66 *** | .52 | Age | .35 * | 1.4 | Education | 1.2 *** | 3.4 |
| Income | 1.4 *** | 4.1 | Education | -.68 *** | .7 | | | |
| | | | Income | -.36 * | .7 | | | |
| | | | Gender | .34 * | 1.4 | | | |
| | | | Children | .37 ** | 1.4 | | | |
| | | | Phone | -.33 * | .7 | | | |
| | | | Religious organizations | .26 + | 1.3 | | | |
| Chi-square | 124.5 *** | | | 53.3 *** | | | 37.1 *** | |
| Nagelkerke R-Sq | .15 | | | .08 | | | .06 | |
| Correctly predicted | 71.4% | | | 60.9% | | | 85.0% | |
| N | 1061 | | | 828 | | | 1000 | |

$+ p<.1;$ * $p<.05;$ ** $p<.01;$ *** $p<.001$

education, lower income, were more likely to be female, more children, used the phone less, and had a slight, nonsignificant tendency to belong to more religious organizations (8 percent of the variance). This means that early Internet adopters (before 1998) were younger, had higher education and income, were more likely male with fewer children, and used the phone more and belonged to fewer religious organizations. Finally, users, compared to dropouts, were more likely to have more education (6 percent of the variance). Note that more factors distinguished earlier from recent users than distinguished users from non-users, though age and income explained nearly twice as much variance in the distinction between current users and others. Also, dropouts are distinguished from users by different factors than are nonusers (dropouts as well as those who have never used).

Table 7.4 provides the same analyses for mobile phone data. Mobile phone users, compared to non-users, were more likely to have full-time jobs, have higher income, and be currently married (explaining 12 percent of the variance). Recent, compared to veteran mobile phone users, are more likely to not work full time, be younger, not be married or have a partner, and have a slight

Table 7.4

Logistic Regressions Predicting Mobile Phone User Categories

| NonUsers (0) / Users (1) | | | Veteran (0) / Recent (1) | | | Dropouts (0) / Users (1) | | |
|---|---|---|---|---|---|---|---|---|
| Predictor | B | Exp (B) | Predictor | B | Exp (B) | Predictor | B | Exp (B) |
| Work | -.58 *** | .56 | Work | .73 *** | | Income | .99 *** | 2.7 |
| Income | .99 *** | 2.7 | Age | -.64 *** | | Weekly phone calls | .47 + | 1.6 |
| Marital | .27 * | 1.3 | Marital | -.69 *** | | | | |
| | | | Religious organizations | -.3 + | | | | |
| Chi-square | 102.1 | | | 71.8 *** | | | 16.2 *** | |
| Nagelkerke R-Sq | .12 | | | .13 | | | .05 | |
| Correctly predicted | 64.3% | | | 64.4% | | | 87.5% | |
| N | 1100 | | | 710 | | | 590 | |

+ $p<.1$; * $p<.05$; ** $p<.01$; *** $p<.001$

tendency to belong to fewer religious organizations (13 percent of the variance). Users, compared to mobile phone dropouts, were more likely to have higher income and make more weekly phone calls on a regular phone (5 percent of the variance). Again, different factors distinguish among these three usage measures. Current usage is influenced by characteristics of work, income, and marital status. Later adoption is influenced by work, age, and marital status. Mobile phone dropouts are characterized by income and regular phone usage.

The recent/veteran divide is characterized by the most influences (six for Internet and three for mobile phone), the familiar user/nonuser divide involves two influences for the Internet and three for mobile phone, and the user/dropout divide is characterized by only one significant (though different) influence for each medium. Thus, there is moderate diversity in the factors that influence each of the three kinds of Internet and mobile phone divides. On these grounds, we can conclude that Internet and mobile phone users (and thus nonusers, and therefore digital divides) are not completely the same.

## Contrasting Groups of Internet and Mobile Phone Users

The above analyses showed a variety of influences within each of the three kinds of divides, and across the two media. But those analyses did not assess the extent to which usage categories across the two media overlap, a more stringent test of the basic question as to whether Internet and mobile phone users are essentially the same, or, alternatively, whether the Internet and mobile phones are fulfilling substantially the same needs for the same kinds of users. Here, we consider current Internet and mobile phone users versus Internet and mobile phone non-users, resulting in four categories: current use neither, use Internet only, use mobile phone only, and currently use both Internet and mobile phone. The user/nonuser distinction is the most familiar of the digital divides, and here also takes into account the most respondents.

The first approach is to conduct simple one-way analyses of variance, across the four user/nonuser categories as the factor, and the demographic variables that were significant influences across the media categories in tables 7.3 and 7.4: that is, work, age, education, income, gender, weekly phone calls, and marital status. Table 7.5 shows that all of these varied significantly across the four interdependent categories of Internet and mobile phone users. Income showed the greatest difference, with users of both media having the highest

**Table 7.5**
**Demographic Differences of Internet/Mobile Phone Usage Categories**

| Variable | No Use | Internet Use | Mobile phone Use | Both Use | F-ratio |
|---|---|---|---|---|---|
| Work 0 full time 1 other | .58 236 | .45 a 321 | .39 ab 155 | .33 b 529 | 15.7 *** |
| Age 0 <40 1 >40 | .64 226 | .41 a 309 | .48 a 153 | .47 a 518 | 9.9 *** |
| Education 0 < college 1 >= college | .17 a 236 | .41 b 321 | .21 a 155 | .46 b 529 | 27.2 *** |
| Income 0 < $35K 1 >=$35K | .40 188 | .65 a 263 | .59 a 131 | .84 446 | 48.2 *** |
| Gender 0 male 1 female | .61 b 236 | .49 a 321 | .58 ab 155 | .51 a 529 | 3.5 ** |
| Phone Calls 0 < 10 1 >=10 | .49 a 63 | .59 a 321 | .72 b 87 | .61 ab 529 | 3.0 * |
| Marital 0 other 1 married | .45 ab 236 | .37 a 321 | .47 b 155 | .56 529 | 9.5 *** |

* p<.05; ** p<.01; *** p<.001
Values in cells are mean percent of cases with the "1" value of each demographic variables, and the cell sample size. Letters indicate which means are not significantly different across the user categories, by Duncan's pairwise comparisons.

income, Internet only users and mobile phone users constituting a homogenous group but still in the high-income category, and users of neither media in the low-income category. Education was the next most significant influence, with non-users and mobile phone users constituting one group (more education), and Internet users and users of both media constituting another group (less education). Work status followed in significance, with nonusers least likely to be working full time, Internet only users and mobile phone users constituting one group more likely to be working full time, and mobile phone users and users of both media as a homogenous group with the greatest likelihood of working full time. Non-users were likely to be over forty, while all the other three kinds of users were equally likely to be under forty. Concerning marital status, nonusers and Internet users were similarly most likely to not be married, nonusers and mobile phone users to be less likely to be not married, and users of both media most likely to be married. Nonusers and mobile phone users were likely to be female, while Internet users, mobile phone users and users of both media were similarly about equally distributed between males and females. Making more phone calls characterized mobile phone users and users of both media, while nonusers, Internet users and users of both media were not distinguishable with respect to a lower level of phone usage.

Those who currently do not use either the Internet or mobile phones were significantly distinct for three of the demographic variables, while those who used both media were distinct for two of the demographic variables. So nonusers seem the most "different" or "unique" of the four usage groups.

There may indeed be some grouping within the four categories, and it most likely distinguishes non-users from other kinds of users, but it is not likely to be highly distinguishable on the basis of these demographic influences.

### Digital Divides Come in Two Flavors

*Distinguishing Among Types of Media Digital Divides*

*Veteran versus Recent Users.* Clearly, another terminology for these two categories of uses is "early adopters" and "later adopters." These data show quite a distinction between these two categories of adopters, as diffusion theory would expect. For both media, age is a significant multivariate predictor, but in opposite ways: veteran Internet users were younger, but veteran mobile phone users were older. Amazingly, there is no other common influence. Early adopters of the Internet fit the traditional digital divide model (younger, more education, higher education, male) as well as having some other characteristics (more children, more regular phone use). But early adopters of the mobile phone were more likely to work full time, and be married.

*Dropouts.* The divide between users and former users, or dropouts, for the Internet is primarily associated with being less educated, but for the mobile phone it is lower income and less frequent telephone calling. The two primary reasons for Internet dropout are complexity and cost (with access the third), while for mobile phone dropout they are complexity and access, with cost the least important reason. Note, then, that the first and common reason for dropping out of Internet or mobile phone adoption is complexity. Thus understanding and being able to use the technical features is the single most important named reason for dropping out (though only as rated by around 100 respondents in the survey).

Dropping out of, or disadopting, a new medium, unlike decisions to adopt it in the first place, have hardly been studied. The topic would seem to be of considerable relevance to both the policy community and service providers, including educators. At the same time, the issue of dropouts may be only transient; that is, nearly all dropouts may once again become—and remain—users. While the ultimate future of the Internet and mobile phone communication cannot be known, there seems at present to be millions of former users of both media. Given the substantial economic and social equity stakes, the causes and consequences of this phenomenon require further investigation.

*Distinguishing Among Combinations of Internet and Mobile Phone Users and Non-Users*

While the distinction among the categories of Internet and mobile phone users and nonusers is not completely explicit or predictable, we do have evidence that there is a difference between Internet users and mobile phone users. The distinction comes primarily between those who use only the Internet and those who use only mobile phones. People who use both are somewhat more like those who use only mobile phones, and people who use neither are somewhat more like those who use only the Internet. The primary influence on this distinction is income, followed by education. Intriguingly, this particular digital divide occurs in opposite directions: higher income and lower education are associated with the mobile phone distinction, while lower income and higher education are associated with the Internet distinction. In this sense, there are two opposing digital divides involving the Internet and the mobile phone. Those who use both tend to those with the highest income and somewhat higher education.

## Conclusion

While summaries of national survey data from 2000 suggest that Internet and mobile phone adoption patterns were quite similar, in fact there is considerable divergence in usage patterns and demographic and media influences on those usage patterns. Significantly from a policy and conceptual viewpoint, rather than there being "just" an Internet digital divide, there is also a mobile phone digital divide. Moreover, instead of the Internet or mobile phone digital divides being limited to the first and most common distinction (that is between users and nonusers) there also seems to be a noticeable digital divide between ongoing users and dropouts, and possibly more distinctively between earlier and later adopters.

Further, Internet and mobile phone users (or non-users) are not necessarily the same set of people (or, conversely, the two media do not fulfill similar needs or utilities for the same demographic groups). The simplest distinction seems to be between a group of people who are not currently using either medium or are currently using only the Internet, and a group of people who are using only the mobile phone or are currently using both media. These two groups are distinguished primarily on the basis of income, and secondarily by education, and in opposite directions.

As research and the federal studies of Internet use have argued, people on the short end of the various digital divides (non-users, dropouts, and in some sense the most recent adopters) could benefit from the social, economic and personal resources that new communication technologies can provide. This is clearly recognized in the case of the Internet. Indeed, up until mid-February of 2002, the U.S. government had been pumping billions of dollars annually into social programs to subsidize the Internet's deployment and support social programs to advance training and access to the technology, especially at schools and hospitals. The administration of President George W. Bush has signaled that it is turning away from such programs, arguing that there is no longer a consequential Internet digital divide, at least not one worth spending federal resources on. By contrast, the mobile phone appears to be the stepchild of social programs, and no "universal service," "lifeline," or training and subsidy programs exist. (All of which makes the success of the mobile phone among so many income and education sectors of United States society all the more significant.) It is difficult to explain this disproportionate attention to the two technologies on the part of social policy advocates. Even more mysterious to us is why the federal government seems to be ignoring so much socially beneficial potential of mobile phones. Clearly, the "voice" side, namely mobile phone technology, has not received the attention it deserves, neither in absolute terms nor in terms relative to the "graphical" side, namely the Internet. (It would seem SMS text messaging would be of enormous consequence both in the U.S. and elsewhere. Yet even in Europe, where so much text messaging takes place, the governments there have shown practically no interest in harnessing the power of SMS for social service.)

Our analysis, then, seeks to increase highlight the structural determinants of communication technology adoption and use, especially the relationship between mobile phone and Internet technology. By being more aware of the variety of usage digital divides within and across the Internet and mobile phones, policymakers and researchers might have improved justifications, choices and strategies available for narrowing the several digital divides. Moreover, in line with our interest in Syntopia, it allows a more complete understanding of human communication behavior than would be the case were we to focus exclusively on a prominent technology (e.g., the Internet) ignoring other new communication technology (e.g., the mobile phone) whose user base may soon surpass it.

## References

An earlier version of this paper appeared in B. Wellman and C. Haythornthwaite (eds.) 2002. The Internet in Everyday Life. London: Blackwells.

AOL 2000. *American Online/Roper Starch Cyberstudy 2000*. Roper #CNT375.
Cultural Access Group 2001. *Ethnicity in the Electronic Age: Looking at the Internet through Multicultural Lens*. Los Angeles: Access Worldwide Communications, Inc.
Hadden, S. and Lodis Rhodes (eds.). 1995, November. Evolution of Universal Service Policy. Lyndon B. Johnson School of Public Affairs, University of Texas, Austin.
Hadden, L. 2001. Social Exclusion and Information and Communication Technologies. *New Media & Society*, 2(4), 387-406.
Jupiter Communications. 2000. Assessing the Digital Divide. New York: Jupiter Communications press release, June 15. http://www.jup.com/company/pressrelease.jsp?doc=pr000615.
Katz, J. E., Rice, Ronald E. and Aspden, Philip. 2001. The Internet, 1995-2000: Access, Civic Involvement, and Social Interaction. *American Behavioral Scientist*, 45(3), 404-419.
Katz, James E. and Philip Aspden. 1998. Internet Dropouts: The Invisible Group. *Telecommunications Policy*, 22, (4/5, June), 327-339.
Katz, James E. 1988. Telecommunications Privacy Policy in the U.S.A.: Socio-Political Responses to Technological Advances." *Telecommunications Policy*, 12 (4): 353-68.
Mante, Enid and Frank Thomas. 2002 Internet Have and Have Nots in Europe. Unpublished paper. EURESCOM/COST.
McConnaughey, J. 2001. Taking the Measure of the Digital Divide: Net Effects of Research and Policy (summarizing results of the U.S. Department of Commerce, 2000). Presented to Web Workshop at University of Maryland Dept. of Sociology, June.
Media Metrix. 1997. *Online press release*. http://www.mediametric.com/pcmpr33.htm
Net Users Mirror Nation's Gender Breakdown. 2001. USA Today, June 15. http://www.usatoday.com/life/cyber/nb/nb5.htm
Rice, Ronald E., McCreadie, M. and Chang, S-J. 2001. *Accessing and Browsing Information and Communication: A Multidisciplinary Approach*. Cambridge, MA: The MIT Press.
Rice, Ronald E. and Katz, James E. 2002. Comparing Internet and Mobile Phone Usage. Unpublished report from the Syntopia project, Department of Communication, Rutgers University (mimeo). Available from the authors.
Tufekcioglu, Zeynep. 2001. Rethinking the Theory Behind the Digital Divide Initiatives: It's Not All Good All the Time in the Age of Deskilled, Low-Paying "Hi-Tech" Jobs. Austin: University of Texas Department of Communication. Paper presented to the International Communication Association Conference, Washington, DC, May.
U. S. Department of Commerce. 2000. *Falling through the Net: Toward Digital Inclusion*. Washington, DC: Government Printing Office.
Walsh, E., Gazala, M. and Ham, C. 2001. The Truth about the Digital Divide. In B. Compaine (ed.), *The Digital Divide: Facing a Crisis or Creating a Myth?* (pp. 279-284.) Cambridge, MA: The MIT Press.
Yahoo!News. February 19, 2001. Hispanics, Blacks and Women Surfing the Internet in Greater Numbers. http://dailynews.hayoo.com/h/ll/20010219/co/hispanics_blacks_and_women_surfing_the_internet_ingreater_numbers.

# 8

# Social Capital and the New Communication Technologies

*Axel Franzen*

## Introduction

The rise of the Internet has led to acrimonious though unclear debate and speculation about its influence on society. These discussions could benefit from being organized by distinctions originally suggested by James S. Coleman (1988, 1990). According to Coleman, human beings have three fundamental resources at their disposal: financial capital, human capital, and social capital. Each can be related to new technologies in general and the Internet in particular.

The term *financial capital* refers to the material resources individuals have at their disposal. For most individuals, the prime source of financial capital is the income he or she receives through participation in the labor market. However, financial capital also includes inherited wealth and all types of monetary transfers, even among household members. New technology influences individuals' financial capital when it affects the working market by creating new professions (e.g., computer programmers) or by making certain types of work places more productive. Thus, economists debate how the introduction of PCs influenced productivity and consequently earnings (see for instance Krueger 1993, DiNardo and Pischke 1997, Entorf et al. 1999, Haisken-DeNew and Schmidt 1999, Franzen 2001a). This discussion also applies to the diffusion of Internet access at the work place. The initial assumption with respect to the Internet could be that it facilitates certain types of market activity (e.g., information search) and thus enhances work productivity. Further, the Internet could increase the global exchange of products and services and thereby global competition. In such a case, standard economic reasoning would conclude that the Internet should increase the wealth of all exchange partners. Whether these arguments are empirically valid, though, is still not known. Most of the studies cited were unable to detect a wage bonus for on-the-job PC use and empirical studies that have looked at the wealth effect of the diffusion of the Internet have not yielded definitive results (see Katz and Rice 2002).

The term *human capital* is commonly attributed to Becker (1975) and Mincer (1974). It refers to all skills and abilities individuals acquire through education or on-the-job training that can be used in the work market. Human capital is highly consequential for the creation of financial capital. In market economies, at least, occupational positions are usually filled according to qualification and, thus, it is human capital that is the most important determinant of an individual's earnings. The Internet is a useful tool for spreading information and knowledge and has consequently diffused through educational institutions in industrialized societies. Thus, it has the potential to increase the human capital of those who have access to the Internet and know how to use it properly. As with financial capital, there has so far been very little research that deals with the Internet's effects on human capital.

*Social capital* refers to the amount and quality of an individual's social relations. Within sociology, the term was popularized by Bourdieu (1986) and Coleman (1988, 1990), and has since become a popular term in sociological research. (Yet, according to Palloni et al. [2001], the concept of social capital was first introduced by the economist Glenn Loury [1977]. For recent discussions of this debate, see Portes [1998], Paxton [1999], or Parcel and Dufur [2001].) In particular, there is abundant literature pointing out how important social relations are with respect to issues such as children's success in school (e.g., Parcel and Dufur 2001), individuals' psychological well-being (e.g., Kadushin 1982; Umberson et al. 1996), individuals' ability to find jobs (e.g., Granovetter 1973; 1974), and an individual's ability to build a career (Burt 1999). Thus, the evidence of these studies suggests that social capital is a significant factor in an individual's human and financial capital.

The "decline of social capital" has long been a topic of discussion, although it has also been discussed under other terms, such as "community spirit," "participation," and "neighborliness." Recently, though, the intensity of the discussion has increased; leading social scientists have been concerned that social capital is declining. Putnam (1995), for instance, believes that social capital declined in the U.S. because of an increase in TV consumption. Others have suggested that social capital declined due to increased wealth (Lindenberg 1986). The association stems from the fact that wealth creates privatization in consumption—as individuals become more affluent, they can afford to buy goods for private consumption that formerly had to be shared with others. As a result, affluent individuals do not need to spend time with others because they are not obligated to share houses, apartments, or cars. However, this type of privatization of consumption deprives individuals of face-to-face communication and social approval that accompanies the use of shared goods. But just as the reason for the U.S.'s decline in social capital is debated, so to is the decline's reality. Paxton (1999) actually suggests that the overall social capital did not decline in the U.S. Still Putnam (2000) has assembled an impressive array of evidence and other studies (e.g., Robinson 1990, Franzen 2001b) that find an inverse relationship between TV consumption and social involvement. (See also Katz and Rice 2002.)

The diffusion of the Internet (the "net") has revived the concern that social capital may be declining (cf. Katz and Aspden, 1998). This concern is based on two reasons: first, using the Internet is predominantly an individual activity, as is watching TV (or, for that mater, reading newspapers and books). Internet users have to take time out of other activities to surf the net. Obviously, if Internet users take the time for surfing the net away from other individual activity then no negative consequences with respect to social involvement are to be expected. However, if Internet users cut down on time they would communicate with others, then it would deprive them of social communication. Thus, if the Internet increases the individualization of leisure time it could lead to a decrease in social interaction and eventually to a decrease in individuals' networks or social capital.

Second, the Internet makes it increasingly unnecessary to leave home for personal tasks, such as shopping or banking. As a result, many daily transactions can be done without face-to-face communication, which could eventually reduce social contacts.

There are also reasons why the Internet could increase social involvement. First, the Internet is a fast and cost efficient communication tool. In particular, electronic mail (e-mail) offers the opportunity to maintain geographically diverse networks. Further, the Internet allows for some professions (e.g., journalists, computer programmers) to work from a home-based office. This could increase time flexibility and allow more social contact within families.

To summarize, there are different theoretical expectations of how the diffusion of the Internet affects peoples' lives. The general notion is that the Internet can be very helpful to increase human and financial capital. However, some social scientists are concerned that it is also a technology that increases the privatization of leisure time in a similar way to TV and thus reduces social contact. The real effect of the Internet is an empirical question that may also depend on how it is used. So far, there has been little research with respect to the issue of how human or financial capital are affected—most research deals with the question of how it influences social capital. In the second section of this chapter, evidence on social capital will be presented based on studies conducted in the U.S. In the third section, the results of a longitudinal study recently conducted in Switzerland will be presented.

### Empirical Evidence of the Internet's Effects on Social Involvement

The first national random study of the social effects of the Internet (which, significantly, includes both Internet users and non-users) appears to be Katz and Aspden's 1995 survey (Katz and Aspden 1997). Public concern that Internet use reduces social contacts was heightened by the widespread press coverage devoted to a study conducted which found increased loneliness among heavy Internet users, conducted by Kraut et al. (1998). The Kraut study, which found negative effects of Internet use, based its premise on an attack on the earlier Katz and Aspden research that had found Internet use had no deleterious effect on social capital (Katz and Aspden 1997). For their part, Kraut and colleagues used a non-random opportunity sample to recruit 169 non-users in 73 non-using households for their study. They provided them with free Internet access and observed their usage patterns over a period of two years. Participants received a pre-test questionnaire before they started to use the Internet and a follow-up questionnaire after 12 to 24 months of Internet use. The study found that a small number of individuals who used the Internet more intensely communicated less with family members, had less social contact with their friends, and showed more symptoms of loneliness and depression. (The team's subsequent analysis of additional data showed no such effects.) Although the design of Kraut's et al. study has been broadly criticized elsewhere (e.g., Franzen 2000), its findings were puzzling and inspired further investigations. Kraut's et al. findings received additional support via a large-scale empirical investigation conducted by Nie and Erbring (2000) from the Stanford Institute for the Quantitative Study of Society. This study did use a random sample that included more than 4,000 Americans. The authors found that "up to a quarter of the respondents who use the Internet regularly (more than five hours a week, 36 percent of the whole sample) feel that it has reduced their time with friends and family members or attending events outside the home" (Nie and Erbring 2000). Noteworthy is also the result that 25 percent of regular users reported that they spent less time shopping in stores. Thus, Nie and Erbring provide empirical evidence for both the individualization of leisure time and the privatization of transactions.

But despite the publicity these studies received, they have been among the few that found negative results of Internet use. Katz, Rice, and Aspden (2001, see also Katz and Aspden 1997) recently presented the results of four random national surveys that were conducted in 1995, 1996, 1997, and 2000. The authors compared users and non-users with respect to their involvement in leisure organizations as well as in political activity. They found no evidence that users show less political activity or belonged to fewer leisure time organizations. Quite the contrary: results from the 1995 survey with 2,500 respondents, as well as from the 2000 survey with 1,300 respondents, even suggest that users are more active in both types of activities. Furthermore, Katz, Rice, and Aspden (2001) compared the number of friends respondents met prior to the week of the interviews; the results suggest that long-term Internet users met more friends than non-users.

These contradictory findings are puzzling and raise the question of how the opposing results can be reconciled. One possible answer could be that the reviewed studies differ in design and method. First of all, the study by Katz, Rice, and Aspden (2001) differs from the work of Nie and Erbring (2000) in terms of the measurement of social involvement they applied. Katz, Rice, and Aspden (2001) ask respondents for facts such as the number of memberships or the number of friends they met during a specific period. Nie and Erbring (2000), on the other hand, rely on respondents' subjective interpretations such as whether respondents "feel" that they spent less time with friends and family members. Asking respondents about opinions, feelings, and interpretations and asking them about factual behavior are two different methods—the latter is generally a far more reliable measurement.

A second possible reason for the discrepancies between the studies may be the use of cross-sectional data—both studies by Katz, Rice, and Aspden (2001), Katz and Aspden (1997) and that of Nie and Erbring (2000) use cross-sectional data. Results that are based on the analysis of cross-sectional data are generally sensitive to model specification. Thus, one might find bivariate associations between two variables, such as Internet use and measures of social involvement—but those associations may be due to other variables that correlate with both Internet use and social activities. It could be the case that Internet adopters belong to a generally active group of people that also participate more often in social and political activities. One can try to control for such intervening variables by using multivariate statistical models such as ordinary least-squares regression. However, controlling by corroborating other variables may be incomplete due to difficulty in measuring latent concepts such as "the general activity level." Thus, different control variables between models or studies might explain different results.

Stronger conclusions can generally be drawn on the basis of longitudinal data such as the study by Kraut et al. (1998). A longitudinal design observes the same group of individuals over a certain period of time. Thus, a change in one variable (e.g., Internet use) can be related to a change in another variable (e.g., social involvement). However, the study by Kraut et al. (1998) involved only a small group that was unusual in its composition. Given the other evidence, it seems reasonable to conduct further investigations on the Internet's effects on peoples' social lives, particularly by using longitudinal designs. The results of such a study will be described in the following section.

## A Longitudinal Study on the Social Consequences of Internet Use in Switzerland

The study described below was conducted at the University of Bern in Switzerland under the supervision of the author.[1] In the spring of 1998, a written survey was conducted among a random sample of the Swiss population living in the German-speaking part of the country. Switzerland is trilingual. About 5 percent of the population lives in the Italian-speaking part and about 20 percent in the French-speaking part of the country. We restricted the survey to the

German-speaking part to save translation costs. Also, the German-speaking part is culturally and economically rather similar to Germany.

Of the 2,500 households addressed, 1,196 valid questionnaires were received (a response rate of 50 percent). Of the selected addresses, 138 were invalid due to address changes and were thus excluded from the original sample. Random selection within the household was accomplished by asking that person for participation with the most recent birthday. A 50 percent response rate constitutes a decent response rate for written surveys conducted in Switzerland. Even telephone surveys that usually reach higher participation rates than written surveys exceed rarely participation rates of 60 percent in Switzerland or Germany.

Simultaneously, we conducted an Internet-based survey of the customers of Switzerland's largest Internet service provider (ISP). At that time, the provider had 76,806 customers in the German-speaking part of the country. All customers received an e-mail that introduced the survey and asked for participation. The e-mail contained a link leading to the questionnaire. We received 15,852 valid responses from the Internet survey (a response rate of 20 percent). Both the questionnaire and e-mail respondents were recontacted in the spring of 2001 by again mailing a written questionnaire and e-mailing the Internet link to the on-line questionnaire. The written survey of the random sample was answered by 843 participants (a response rate of 80 percent for the second wave). We were able to recontact 12,000 participants of the Internet survey in 1998 of whom 5,766 individuals responded (a response rate of 47 percent for the second Internet sample).

Both questionnaires (the written questionnaire, addressed to the random sample, and the online questionnaire, addressed to the Internet sample) contained about seventy questions on social involvement, Internet use, socio-demographics and leisure time activities. (Detailed statistical analysis of the responses may be found in Franzen (2000 and 2001[b].)

All four surveys contain two measurements of social involvement. Respondents were asked how many people outside of their household they count as close friends and how much time they spent with these friends during the week prior to answering the questionnaire. The key assumption is that the first question is an indicator of the individuals' network size and the second question is an indicator of the intensity of these relationships. Of course, both measurements are simply indicators that are assumed to correlate with the concept of social capital. Thus, the more friends a person reports and the more time he or she spent with them, the more social capital this person should have. Both indicators are used in studies on social involvement (e.g., Fisher 1982) and the first indicator is similar to the one used by Kraut et al. (1998). The second wave of the surveys in 2001 also asks how many friends the respondent met during the previous four weeks, and also contains a short version of the UCLA Loneliness Scale that measures individuals subjective feelings of loneliness.

The average number of close friends reported in the random sample in 1998 is 10.8 and in 2001 it is 11. Thus, the average network size did not change significantly, as seen also by the amount of time respondents spent with friends— 3.6 hours per week in 1998 and 3.3 hours per week in 2001. The numbers remained stable despite the fact that Internet use increased greatly during the same time. In 1998 only 12 percent of the random sample reported using the Internet regularly and 15 percent said that they were occasional users; in 2001 the percentage of regular users increased to 33 percent and that of occasional users to 28 percent.

Figures 8.1 and 8.2 show the mean number of friends reported by regular Internet users and non-users, as well as the amount of hours users and non-users spent with their friends. Users reported having more friends and spending more

**Figure 8.1**
**Average Number of Friends: Internet Users (Upper Line)**
**and Non-Users (Lower Line)**

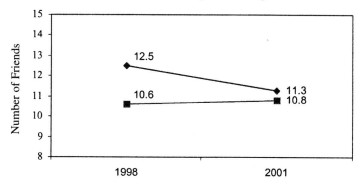

**Figure 8.2**
**Average Time Spent with Friends per Week:**
**Internet Users (Upper Line) and Non-Users (Lower Line)**

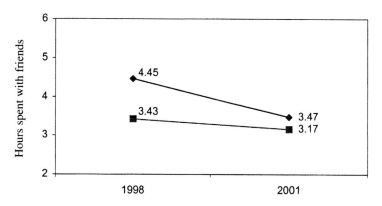

hours with them than non-users in 1998. However, the gap of social involvement dissolved in 2001.

Change in network size and the time spent with the network was correlated with the change in Internet use, controlling for respondents' change, change in socio-economic variables (e.g., income, employment status, marriage status) and other changes in leisure time activity (e.g., watching TV, reading books, playing sports). The results suggest that Internet users' decrease in network size and the time spent with the network are not related to Internet use. The observed decrease in users' social involvement is simply due to the fact that Internet usage has diffused through the sample and that the group of users became more similar to non-users with respect to social involvement.

The measurement of Internet use is rather crude in the random sample since respondents were simply asked whether they use the Internet regularly, occasionally, or not at all. However, finer measurement was applied in the online survey. In particular, respondents were asked for the year they started to use the Internet and how many hours a week they use it. Both measurements of Internet use were then related to the reported number of friends and the time spent with friends. The results (not shown here) indicate that neither the duration nor the intensity of Internet use are related to either the number of friends or the time respondents spent socializing with their friends.

The third indicator of social involvement was the respondents' subjective feelings of loneliness. The survey in 2001 contained the UCLA Loneliness Scale (Russell et al. 1980, Russell 1996). The scale was modified by adopting five items of the original twenty-item German version of the UCLA Loneliness Scale suggested by Lamm and Stephan (1986). The included items are

1.    I am too often alone;

2.    I feel isolated from others;

3.    No one really knows me well;

4.    People around me have different interests and ideas;

5.    I often feel left out.

Respondents were able to note their degree of agreement in five categories. All five items are highly correlated and summed up in an index that ranges from 5 (individuals that do not feel lonely) to 25 (individuals that feel very lonely). Tests show that this abbreviated loneliness scale reliably measures feelings of loneliness. (Cronbach's alpha equals 0.74). The results of a comparison of the loneliness scale between regular Internet users, occasional users, and non-users is shown in figure 8.3. As can be seen, regular users express the lowest feelings of loneliness as measured by the scale. However, the differences are very small and not significant statistically.

**Figure 8.3**
**Modified UCLA Loneliness Scale and Internet Use**

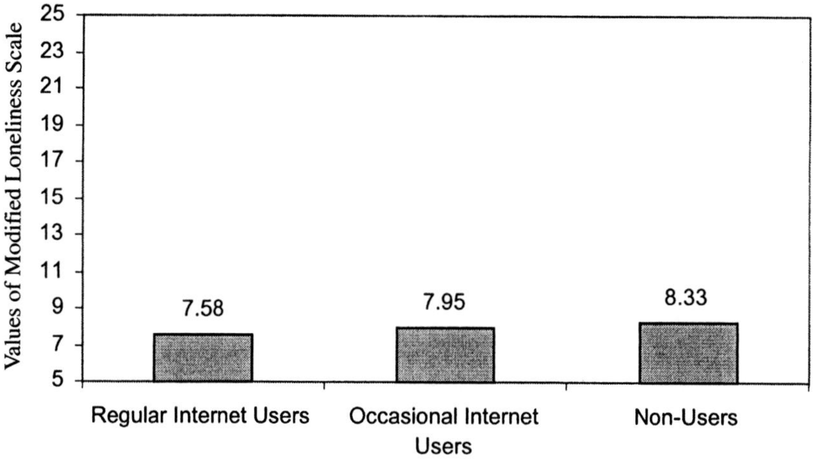

## Conclusions

Whenever a new technology emerges in society, questions naturally arise about its consequences, making the Internet a prime focus for these kinds of questions. Many discussions focus on the assumed positive consequences such as the increased exchange of products, services, and knowledge—in other words, the increase in financial and human capital. However, some social scientists are concerned that it might also reduce individuals' social involvement. This concern is based on two considerations. First, surfing the Internet is predominantly an individual activity. Thus, the Internet could lead to a further increase in the individualization of leisure time and thereby reduce users' face-to-face communication and interaction. Secondly, the Internet allows people to conduct many transactions without leaving home. Thus, it could contribute to a privatization of transaction, which could also reduce social involvement.

These concerns have inspired some empirical investigations on the social consequences of the spread of Internet use. Studies conducted mainly within the U.S. result in contradictory conclusions. In this article, the results of a longitudinal study conducted in Switzerland on the Internet's social effects are reported. The study consists of a random sample among the German-speaking population and a large sample of the customers of Switzerland's largest Internet provider. Both samples were questioned in 1998 and again in 2001. The study contains three measures of social involvement: respondents' number of close friends, their time spent with those friends the week before the (written) interview, and information on individuals' socio-demographic features (e.g., education, income, household composition) and leisure time (e.g., time spent watching TV, playing sports, reading books).

The results, summarized here (details in Franzen 2000, 2001b), indicate that Internet use does not reduce social involvement. In 1998, Internet users even reported a larger number of friends and also spent more time with their social network. However, as the group of Internet users increase, the difference between users and non-users diminishes. Multivariate analysis that relates the change in social involvement to the change in Internet use, together with other changes in the socio-demographic composition, indicate that the decrease of social involvement is not related to Internet use. Further, the measure of individuals' subjective feelings of loneliness (only included in the 2001 follow-up survey) did not indicate that Internet users feel lonelier than non-users.

One might question the relevance of this study to a larger population since this study was conducted in only a portion of one country. It is true that the samples are based only on the German-speaking population living in Switzerland, limiting its general applicability. However, Switzerland is economically and culturally quite similar to Germany and Austria. Therefore, it seems reasonable to expect that the results hold true at least for the German-speaking part of the European population. There is no obvious argument that would suggest that Internet use would have different effects in Germany or even in the U.S. Thus, the study presented confirms those studies in the U.S. that were unable to find any decrease in social relations that could be attributed to the use of the Internet.

This study focuses only on the question of whether Internet use affects social involvement—it did not differentiate between types of Internet use, which may yield more valuable information. This study also did not address how the Internet affects people's human capital, and given the fact that the Internet is widely used in educational institutions, addressing this issue could be another fruitful route for future research.

## Note

1.    I would like to thank my students who were enrolled in the applied social research classes in 1998/99 and 2000/01 for their valuable help with the project.

## References

Becker, Gary S. 1975. *Human Capital*. Chicago: University of Chicago Press.
Bourdieu, Pierre. 1986. The Forms of Capital. Pp. 241–58 in *Handbook of Theory and Research for the Sociology of Education*, ed. John G. Richardson. New York: Greenwood Press.
Burt, Ronald. S. 1999. The Social Capital of Opinion Leaders. *The Annals* 566: 37–54.
Campbell, Karen E. and Barrett A. Lee. 1991. Name Generators in Surveys of Personal Networks. *Social Networks* 13: 203-221.

Coleman, James S. 1988. Social Capital in the Creation of Human Capital. *American Journal of Sociology* 94: S95–S120.

Coleman, James S. 1990. *Foundations of Social Theory.* Cambridge, MA: The Belknap Press of Harvard University Press.

DiNardo, John E. and Jörn Steffen Pischke. 1997. The Returns to Computer Use Revisited: Have Pencils Changed the Wage Structure Too? *Quarterly Journal of Economics,* pp. 291–303.

Entorf, Horst, Michel Gollac, and Francis Kramarz. 1999. New Technologies, Wages, and Worker Selection. *Journal of Labor Economics* 17: 464–491.

Fischer, Claude S. 1982. *To Dwell Among Friends.* Chicago: University of Chicago Press.

Franzen, Axel. 2000. Does the Internet Make Us Lonely? *European Sociological Review* 16: 427-438.

Franzen, Axel. 2001(a). Wages and the Use of New Technologies: An Empirical Analysis of the Swiss Labor Market. *Swiss Journal of Economics and Statistics.* 137: 505–523.

Franzen, Axel. 2001(b). Social Capital and the Internet: A Longitudinal Study on the Consequences of Internet Use. Forthcoming.

Granovetter, Mark. 1973. The Strengths of Weak Ties. *American Journal of Sociology* 73: 1361-1380.

Granovetter, Mark. 1974. *Getting a Job: A Study of Contacts and Careers.* Cambridge, MA: Harvard University Press.

Haisken-DeNew, John P. and Christoph M. Schmidt. 1999. Money for Nothing and Your Chips for Free? The Anatomy of the PC Wage Differential. German Institute for Economic Research, Berlin: Mimeo.

Kadushin, Charles. 1982. Social Density and Metal Health. Pp. 147–58 in *Social Structure and Network Analysis,* eds. Peter V. Marsden and N. Lin. Beverly Kills, CA: Sage.

Katz, James E. and Philip Aspden. 1997. A Nation of Strangers? *Communications of the ACM* 40: 81–86.

Katz, James E. and Philip Aspden. June 1998, Internet Dropouts: The Invisible Group. *Telecommunications Policy* 22, no. 4/5: 327–339.

Katz, James E. and Ronald E. Rice. 2002. Social Consequences of the Internet Use: Access, Involvement and Expression. Cambridge, MA: MIT Press.

Katz, James E., Ronald E. Rice, and Philip Aspden. 2001. The Internet, 1995–2000: Access, Civic involvement, and Social Interaction. *American Behavioral Scientist* (in print).

Kraut, Robert, Vicki Lundmark, Michael Patterson, Sara Kiesler, Tridas Mukopadhyay, and William Scherlis. 1998. Internet Paradox: A Social Technology that Reduces Social Involvement and Psychological Well-Being? *American Psychologist* 53: 1017–1031.

Krueger, Alan B. 1993. Have Computers Changed the Wage Structure: Evidence from Microdata, 1984–1989. *Quarterly Journal of Economics* 108: 33-60.

Lamm, Helmut and Ekkehard Stephan. 1986. Zur Messung von Einsamkeit: Entwicklung einer deutschen Fassung des Fragebogens von Russell and Peplau. *Psychologie und Praxis* 30: 132–134.

Lindenberg, Siegwart. 1986. The Paradox of Privatization in Consumption. Pp. 297-310 in Paradoxical Effects of Social Behavior, edited by Andreas Diekmann and Peter Mitter. Heidelberg: Physica Verlag.

Loury, Glenn C. 1977. A Dynamic Theory of Racial Income Differences. Pp. 153-86 in *Women, Minorities, and Employment Discrimination,* eds. Phyllis A. Wallace and Anette M. LaMond. Lexington, MA: D.C. Heath and Company.

Mincer, Jacob. 1974. *Schooling, Experience, and Earnings.* New York: National Bureau of Economic Research.

Nie, Norman H. and Lutz Erbring. 2000. Internet and Society. A Preliminary Report. Stanford Institute for the Quantitative Study of Society.

Palloni, Alberto, Douglas S. Massey, Miguel Ceballos, Kristin Espinosa, and Michael Spittel. 2001. Social Capital and International Migration: A Test Using Information on Family Networks. *American Journal of Sociology* 106: 1262–1298.

Parcel, Toby L. and Mikaela J. Dufur. 2001. Capital at Home and at School: Effects on Student Achievement. *Social Forces 79: 881-912.*

Paxton, Pamela. 1999. Is Social Capital Declining in the United States? *American Journal of Sociology* 105: 88-127.

Portes, Alejandro. 1998. Social Capital: Its Origin and Application in Modern Sociology. *Annual Review of Sociology* 24: 1-24.

Putnam, Robert D. 1995. Bowling Alone: America's Declining Social Capital. *Journal of Democracy* 6: 65–78.

———. 2000. Bowling Alone. *The Collapse and Revival of American Community*. New York: Simon and Schuster.

Robinson, John P. 1990. Television's Effects on Families' Use of Time. Pp. 195–209 in *Television and the American Family*, edited by J. Bryant. Hillsdale, NJ, Lawrence Erlbaum.

Russell, Daniel W. 1996. The UCLA Loneliness Scale (Version 3): Reliability, Validity, and Factor Structure. *Journal of Personality Assessment* 66: 20–40.

Russell, Daniel W., Letitia A. Peplau, and Carolyn E. Cutrona C. E. 1980. The Revised UCLA Loneliness Scale. Concurrent and Discriminant Validity Evidence. *Journal of Personality and Social Psychology* 39: 472-480.

Umberson, Debra, Meichu D. Chen, James S. House, Kristine Hopkins, and Ellen Slaten. 1996. The Effect of Social Relationships on Psychological Well-Being: Are Men and Women Really so Different? *American Sociological Review* 61: 837–856.

Wellman, Barry. 1999. *Networks in the Global Village*. Boulder, CO: Westview Press.

# 9

# Information and Communication Technology in Russian Families: Results of Sociological Research

*Olga Vershinskaya*

## Objective

For many years, the idea that Russia was perpetually lagging in the sphere of information technology prevailed among Russian and Western academics. The objective of this chapter is to demonstrate the changes that have occurred in this area, especially since the mid-1990s, and to illustrate the evolution of the information and communication technology (ICT) usage by Russian families based on four sociologically oriented surveys which I conducted.

Although Russia may have been lagging behind the West in terms of ICTs, Russia has certainly been a leader in the statistical sciences, which in turn have helped make its survey research methods more efficient. So despite the fact that there have been some surveys on ICTs in the West, the Russian intelligentsia has encouraged the continuous and detailed exploration of the situation in what was the Soviet Union. And even in this regard, the West must be further subdivided between Western Europe, where the leadership and exploration of issues has been intense and insightful, and the United States and Japan. In the case of the latter, it seems that Russia despite its reputation for lagging behind the West, was perhaps even ahead of the United States in some spheres. Hence, with a few outstanding exceptions (e.g., the formidable work of James Katz and colleagues, viz. Katz and Aspden 1997; 1998; Katz and Rice 2002), one might even say that the United States lagged the former Communist bloc in terms of understanding the social role of ICTs in the national social structure.

Thus to place my work in the context of the worldwide pursuit of social scientific understanding of the Internet revolution, the work from Russia can now be seen as joining the vital intellectual records that have been established for Europe (Fortunati 1998; Haddon and Silverstone 1995) and the United States (Katz and Rice 2002; Wellman and Haythornthwaite 2002).

Russia's experiences with ICTs can be divided, albeit coarsely, into three periods. These are:

1.  The USSR period (1960s–1980s). During this time quite a lot of attention was devoted to computers. There were achievements in library and management informatics, mostly in the theoretical spheres. Much of the state's attention was given to the development and implementation of management information systems. However, most initiatives yielded few positive results.

2.  Glasnost policy and perestroika policy. Mikhail Gorbachev initiated the policies and processes of *perestroika* (restructuring), *demokratizatsiya* (democratization) and *glasnost* (openness) in the period of 1985–1991/1992. Through these initiatives came the development of the state program of information technology dissemination that focused mainly on infrastructure development. Socio–economic issues were also present: a countrywide program to computerize education was launched, and the study of knowledge economy was planned. This last initiative died together with Gosplan, the USSR planning committee, when the transition to the market started.

3.  Transition to market reforms started with the liberalization of the telecommunication market in 1992. In 1993 and 1994 the Russian ICT revolution began; PC market growth in 1996, according to the data of European IT Observatory, was up 25 percent a year while the world as a whole saw growth of only 16 percent a year. A commercial information sector of the economy was formed in the early 1990s. Since then, production of informational goods and services has been growing: the production of Russian-built PCs has grown by 40 percent a year; consultancy firms have seen their number of clients increase by ten times between 1998–1999. Between 1999 and 2000, production of communication services has grown by 139 percent. The year 1998 saw the beginning of the Internet revolution in Russia. Although the current Russian Internet audience does not exceed 6 percent (with 3 percent being active users), usage has increased 2.5 times between 1999-2000; another 24 percent of the population are willing to begin using the Internet. The quickest growth of usage has taken place in Moscow and St. Petersburg, with 8 percent of Moscow residents and 6.6 percent St. Petersburg residents using the Internet. A group of researchers from the Institute for Socio-Economic Studies of Population (ISESP) has studied families and ICTs from 1987–1988.

## Surveys

Four surveys were conducted. These are described below.

The *first survey* (1989), called "Culture and Information" was a part of big quantitative survey of the big provincial city of Taganrog (1,000 households sampled). From a statistical point of view, this city represents the urban population of Russia.

During 1988–1989, great changes were taking place in Russia. Computers and videos began coming into the country, and, at the same time, the social value of information was low—an attitude demonstrated by the slogan "every cook can manage a state."

The study's hypothesis was that the population was "informationally passive"—not interested in information when making decisions, and not informed about or interested in information technology.

Studying the presence of information technology in families found that 26.2 percent of families had telephones, 98.1 percent had TVs, 74.4 percent had radio receivers and transistors, 3 percent had video recorders, 0.5 percent of families had PCs. TVs and radios were the main source of information at the end of 1980s. There was no market of foreign information technology, and Russian technology was of bad quality and in poor supply.

A study of the population's everyday informational needs found that people did not use technology as a resource. During this time of shortages, most people (58 percent) walked from one shop or a drug store to another in search of the necessary item; most of the population visited the railway station (55.5 percent) to find out the schedule instead of taking advantage of the telephone. For other information, such as cultural events, people relied on posters in the street. to find out answers to their questions even though such services were available.

More than a half (62 percent) of respondents claimed that they did not need any consultation services and 22 percent did not know that there were no such services in the city. Only 2.6 percent used consultancy firms' services.

The survey proved that the study's hypothesis: people demonstrated "informational passivity" by their lack of interest in information services, and seemed to be unaware that life can be more comfortable with the help of information.

The *second survey,* called "Family and Information and Telecommunication Technology," was conducted from 1991–1992 in Moscow. This was a qualitative study of the first users of PCs and home video recorders.

This period can be called the Russian technological "awakening." It was the prime time of perestroika when continuing shortages (including ICTs) coexisted with a feeling of freedom and openness— videos became an object of dreams and envy and the first users of home PCs appeared. Our research was carried out in a quickly changing socio-economic situation, which greatly influenced respondents' behavior. Deep social transformations and the economic crisis challenged self-identity and confidence in Russians' everyday life.

This qualitative survey was conducted with the help of colleagues from Berlin Technical University and Essex University. The biographic interview method, developed by Dr. Sibylle Mayer and Dr. Eva Schulze (Berlin Technical University) was used in the study.

Nuclear families, which possessed three out of four items of ICTs: phone, TV, video, and computer were studied.

The study found two main channels of ICT supply to Russian families in the beginning of the 1990s that allowed them to overcome constraints of market shortages: trips abroad and the special system of goods distribution through barter trade in the enterprises. The first adopters were people who had access to these channels. Barter trade led to the emergence of a specific form of consumption behavior driven not by rational needs and demands but by casual opportunities.

Motivations for buying new information technology were quite common: entertainment, prestige, children, and investment. Unlike in the West, buying technology in Moscow was an investment, since prices had remained high for several years (one could buy a cottage for the price of a VCR in 1991).

The study revealed changes in family entertainment and communication modes. For the older generation, "entertainment" meant mostly "having guests"; for the study's respondents entertainment meant "home viewing." Though all generations communicated often, the older generation usually had face-to-face contact while the younger generation used a telephone.

The study found that people enjoyed the expanding set of cultural channels because they created the possibility of consuming information of their own choice. The study found that this led to the increasing role of information in Russian society.

In 1997, the *third survey*, "Russian Families and ICT" had been conducted in Taganrog, a follow-up to the 1989 survey. It was a quantitative-qualitative survey with 1,000 households sampled. The objective was to define ownership of ICTs, awareness of new possibilities, access to new technology, and interest in its usage.

*Ownership*

The statistical survey showed that only 2.5 percent families had PCs at home and only 0.6 percent had a connection to the Internet. The study argues that under the conditions of an unstable and constantly changing society the number of computers is not an accurate indicator of society's informational development. Empirical data have proven that computers penetrate into everyday life much faster than their number grows. Only 2.5 percent of families had PCs (five times more than in 1989) and 9 percent of respondents said that they have access to home computers (if not in their own apartment then at their friends' or colleagues').

*Awareness*

The statistical survey showed large differences in awareness: 47 percent said they are well informed about PCs and 20 percent claimed they know nothing about them.

*Access*

In 1997, while 90 percent of respondents had no access to the Internet, the 10 percent of those who did have access comprised a strong social group.

The survey revealed low demand for communication services (2.3 percent used e-mail, 0.6 percent had access to the Internet).

*Interest*

The survey showed that 40 percent among those who did not use PCs at the time were interested in their usage while 50 percent were not interested at all.

People's attitudes and behavior changed dramatically. The qualitative survey of 1997 yielded striking results: changes were observed not only in possibilities but also in priorities and values. This period was designated as the "PCs versus bicycles," stage since PCs became the first priority in families with children.

Observed changes:

1.    ICTs became widely accessible; anyone could buy ICTs if they had the money.

      Software, games, and VCRs were also widely available; any item was available for purchase or order.

2.    The level of awareness about the PC's possibilities greatly increased and the social value of technology was acknowledged.

3.    The upgrading of home computers was occurring; Pentiums were in demand.

4.    PC and video usage changed: they were now used not only for entertainment but also for working purposes.

5.    New modes of behavior appeared:

      •    New forms of entertainment for adults, such as using the computer to play cards or various other electronic games.

      •    Children began playing computer games and watching videos instead of strolling down the streets and playing outside, a traditionally important Russian pastime.

      •    Gifts of technology became popular. Expensive gifts would be a PC, while much more modest might be a videotape.

6.    Big changes in the educational field were observed. During the five years that passed since the previous survey, the very concept of education had changed. In 1997, children entering the better schools were asked whether they had access to a computer. It became "bad form" to submit papers that were not PC-printed; there were no traces of such a situation in the 1992 Moscow survey. One of the respondents was even participating in distance learning at Edinburgh University.

7.    Communication had not changed much—no cases of Internet or e-mail usage among the respondents of the qualitative study were registered. Mobile telephones were very expensive and only present in wealthy families.

**Table 9.1**
**ICT Usage in Russian Families**

| ICT at home | 1988 | 1991–1992 | 1997 | 1999–2000 |
|---|---|---|---|---|
| VCR | – | + | ++ | ++ |
| PC: | – | + | ++ | ++ |
| –entertainment | – | – | + | + |
| –telecommuting | – | – | + | ++ |
| –e-mail | – | – | + | ++ |
| Internet | – | – | + | ++ |
| Mobile phone | – | – | + | ++ |
| Pager | – | – | + | ++ |

Note: ( – ) absent; ( + ) rare; ( ++ ) common.

The *fourth survey,* "Advanced Users of Internet" was a qualitative survey conducted in Moscow 1999–2000.

The focus of the research was the Internet as a social phenomenon, not as means of technical communication. The survey attempted to explore how the Internet influenced respondents' way of life to illustrate qualitative changes in everyday life and work.

The three groups of the most advanced users (according to the data of the commercial information agencies) of the Internet were interviewed: business-men, researchers, and students. The study showed that there are differences in the current Internet use by groups of users.

### Businesspeople

Status was stressed as the main reason for having an Internet address—"No electronic address, no firm" was the attitude of many respondents. Business-men who are active users of the Internet are active users of e-mail and mobile phones also. They are always connected; one respondent explained, "When I switch off my mobile phone, the e-mail brings me messages," which changes life profoundly: "I have forgotten what free time means; all time is working time; no more weekends and Sundays."

None of the respondents defined their business as "electronic" since "gen-eral business procedure changes very slowly in the country." Electronic data interchange (EDI) is very poorly developed, as one respondent expressed, you cannot have it alone, it has to be all." The Internet is used mostly for communi-cation and information retrieval purposes. There are restrictions on Internet access, even in the big firms, since it is expensive; only those who constantly need current information are given access.

## Researchers

Researchers usually use the Internet in the office since they have free access. They use it for three main purposes: information retrieval, self-advertising, and e-mail. Most of researchers' Internet time is spent on information retrieval. Level of sophistication in retrieval strategies is a new characteristic of the consumers of modern ICTs.

For researchers, publishing papers on the Internet is considered a way of self-advertising and of connecting to colleagues. Like everywhere in the world, Russian researchers use the Internet as a way to enhance professional communication. They look for relevant conferences and exchange letters with colleagues all over the world.

## Students

Students were one of the first groups to start using Internet. PCs and the Internet are a necessity for this group; as one respondent noted, "You cannot live without a PC now. My parents cannot buy it for me so I worked everywhere I could to get the money." The study showed that students use all possible applications, but their main interest is in communication.

In studying students' behavior, an interesting observation was made: it is considered bad form to pay for Internet services. The answer to the question of how they manage is: "If you do not have a free access at your job or your parents' job, you find a friend who has." Students believe that "experienced" users and ICT professionals do not pay for Internet services.

Students look for all kinds of information on the Internet: prices for snowboards, information for diplomas, entertainment, information, and so on. For communication, students who work use e-mail instead of faxes, noting that "it is much quicker and easier." The study showed that students' communication preference is not e-mail but live chat technology. Even more, students tend to prefer virtual over personal communication: "To chat on the Internet is much more interesting than to speak over the phone or to walk in the streets." Using the Internet as a tool for marriage is considered normal among the students.

The study showed that, in general, advanced Internet users are socially active and adapt easily to innovation and change. For Russian businessmen, the Internet is mostly a symbol of prestige and means of communication; for researchers, it is basically another means of information retrieval—for students, the Internet is a way of life.

## Conclusion

We can summarize the main results of the survey thusly:

1.  All respondents demonstrated high interest in the Internet and e-mail usage and rated the value of communication services highly.

2.    Two groups of advanced users of the Internet in Russia, researchers and students, are well integrated into the global information space.

3.    Using the Internet to make decisions both at work and in everyday life is a big change from pre-perestroika times.

4.    Usage of the Internet resources depends on the individual user: the ability to select relevant information, establish communication networks, and their enthusiasm and effort.

5.    Acceleration of information retrieval and the speed of information exchange do not increase free time. The division between "free time" and "working time" becomes vague for all three groups of users.

6.    A digital divide exists even within a group of advanced users. Those working in the new economy differ from others in many ways: they spend many more hours in the electronic world, they use more applications, they speak a different language using English "webbish" in their Russian speech, and they feel superior to other groups.

Under the conditions of the socio–economic crisis, a positive process of information society development is taking place in Russia. The information revolution coincided with basic socio–economic transformations, which demonstrates that social adaptation and inclusion into digital world are closely interconnected.

It is worthwhile to note that there are similar patterns of integration of Internet technology in people's lives in Russia as well as in the United States and Western Europe. This would suggest some parallels about the interaction of a technology and cultural patterns and strains. Among the potential explanations for this are that (1) the cultures are fundamentally similar; (2) people themselves tend to be similar and so react in similar ways when they have an opportunity to use a technology for communication; (3) that there are inherent characteristics of the Internet that require or induce its users or usages to evolve in a certain way. None of this should discount the reality that indeed there is cultural variation in technology usage patterns. Yet it would also suggest that each technology has inherent characteristics that lead users to strain their usages in certain directions. It will be interesting to see how the structural of the Internet lead to specific characteristics in the way people live their lives, both in Russia and beyond.

## References

Fortunati, Leopoldina, ed. 1998. *Telecomunicando in Europa*. Milano: Franco Angeli.
Haddon, L. and R. Silverstone. 1993. Teleworking in the 1990s: A View from the Home. SPRU/CICT Report Series 10, University of Sussex, Falmer.
Katz, James E. and Philip Aspden. June 1998, Internet Dropouts: The Invisible Group. *Telecommunications Policy* 22, no. 4/5: 327–339.
Katz, James E. and Ronald E. Rice. 2002. *Social Consequences of Internet Use: Access, Involvement and Expression*. Cambridge, MA: MIT Press.

Katz, James E. and Philip Aspden. 1997. Barriers to and Motivations for Using the Internet: Results of a National Opinion Survey. *Internet Research Journal: Technology, Policy & Applications,* volume 7 (3), Fall, 1997: 170-188.

Wellman, Barry and Caroline Haythornthwaite. 2002. *The Internet in Everyday Life*. London: Blackwell's.

# 10

# Face and Place: The Mobile Phone and Internet in the Netherlands

*Enid Mante and Jeroen Heres*

## Introduction

The concept "Machines that become us" incorporates technology in our daily lives, especially relative to our bodies and self-identity. With society becoming ever more complex and infused with technology, an important question is whether, ultimately, we ourselves will become unwitting instruments of technology.

To answer this question, we focus on the social integration of technology: how it becomes part of our daily lives and how we react to both its positive and negative characteristics. Clearly, too, attitudes toward technology change during its introductory period—sometimes at an extremely rapid pace, as was the case of the telephone's introduction at the beginning of the twentieth century (Katz 1999). What factors may lead one to maintain a critical stance towards technology? (as has been the case with interactive voice response systems or IVRs). What factors will lead one to perceive technology as a "natural" way of life—seamless and unquestioned?

## Three Aspects of Technology Integration

To determine the aforementioned factors, we will consider the following three aspects of social and physical integration of technology, or, if you will, of machines, by looking at the adoption process of the mobile phone and Internet. We look at these technologies from the vantage point of a modern Western society at the beginning of the twenty-first century.

The first aspect is the adoption of technology by the individual, and the diffusion of the innovation in society as a whole. The second is the personal integration of technology in one's daily life, by making it part of everything one does. The third aspect is the positioning among the other technologies used daily.

*Adoption and Diffusion*

In 1962 Rogers devised a simple model on the adoption of innovations; at that time his model of the process ended with the actual purchase of the innovation. In later editions (e.g., 1983, Rogers 1983) he extended his model to the phases after the primary adoption. Herein, the person, by using it, obtains knowledge and develops an attitude toward the innovation, decides to adopt or reject it, puts the innovation to use, and finally confirms the innovation by making the decision to either continue or stop the use.

The individual adoption is part of a collective adoption process in which some people adopt innovations early, while others do this at a far later moment. This diffusion of technology is a standard process—from innovation until late adoption, to eventual out-phasing of technology by replacement by newer, more adequate solutions. This standard process follows an S curve, starting with innovators, followed by early adopters, and taken over by early majority, late majority, and laggards. Until the phase of the early majority taking over the innovation, the S curve becomes steeper, and at the end of the adoption stage, it flattens.

Early innovators are different from later adopters. Innovators are interested in novelty as such and like to try out all possibilities. Later diffusion groups start using a technology when it fulfills a certain need for which they do not have a solution or for which it could be a better solution than the one currently used. Need as such, and the circumstances that bring forth need, are not subjects of Rogers' study.

*Integration*

Silverstone and Haddon provide a model that also depicts adoption of new technology, but goes deeper into the process of adoption in everyday life itself, putting the emphasis on *consumption* of the innovation instead of the *use* as such (Silverstone 1992; 1994) (Silverstone and Haddon 1996). It is the domestication, or the taming of the innovation by the individual, that integrates it in everyday life, that proves the real adoption. It is a process during which the innovation becomes an integral part of oneself and one's daily behavior. This taming process has four stages: from contemplation, acquisition, domestication, to articulation. During this process, the meaning of the innovation changes from something strange and maybe even questionable, to a trusted commodity that we stop thinking about. In the domestication process also the attitude of the user changes from a more distant to a positive feeling. If we talk about machines that become us, it is this aspect of the domestication in which we are most interested.

*Positioning*

Integration is also a question of positioning the technology in our daily lives. What are the dimensions in which people place their technology? Is the technology something that is functional for the special needs one wants to fulfill, or is it something that is subsidiary under certain circumstances? This difference in positioning could be the cause of adoption and domestication developing more quickly, at a slower pace, or even being terminated by rejection. What are the key factors for people to decide on purchases, and choose among competing purchases? What are the perceptual differences among (potential) users of the device that is offered on the market (Katz and Batt 1999)? Is the position fixed, or is it dynamic, making lateral migration possible from one position to another position within one dimension, or making migration possible from one dimension to another?

Katz and Batt (Katz, 1999; Batt and Katz, 1998; Batt and Katz, 1999) have studied the positioning of household technologies in the space of everyday life values, especially on the dimensions of:

- necessity – luxury,
- entertainment – non-entertainment,
- time saving – time consuming,
- enhancing privacy – endangering privacy.

These perceptual dimensions could be expressed on attitude scales, ranging from 1 to 10. When Katz and Batt replicated in 1999 their study from the early 90s, they were able to show that household technologies generated more positive assessments along each of these dimensions. They concluded that this increasingly positive evaluation occurred as people became more accustomed to the technologies and services. But at precisely which point in the adoption process this change of attitude happens is not clear.

## Gender

Katz's research and that of others have shown that attitudes to and positioning of technology is driven by social location, that is, particular socio-economics and demographics of individuals and families. In Katz and Batt (1999) and Katz (1999), the researchers show that there were distinctive differences between males and females, age groups, ethnicity, occupation, and education. In this chapter we examine only the variable of gender since it appears to be highly linked to use (and non-use) of ICTs. (Wyatt 2000) among others claims that gender differences gradually disappear when the technology becomes common practice. Also Katz et al. (2001) remark that new users of the Internet in recent years are more likely to be female.

## Framing Questions

This chapter inquires further into the positioning of the mobile phone and Internet at a time when there already has been substantial diffusion of the device. It also endeavors to look into changes in attitude, during the process of integration. Our main question is: What is the positioning of the mobile phone and Internet in the Netherlands, considering this question is posed less than two years after the Katz-Batt research in 1999?

Sub-questions are:

1.    Is there a shift in attitudes in time that could point to a shift in positioning?

2.    Does this shift in positioning take place on the same dimension or across dimensions?

3.    At which point during the domestication process this shift in attitudes occur: already in the phase of contemplation or after acquisition?

4.    Do we observe the same phenomenon for women as for men?

## Whence Comes Our Evidence?

Data come from the following sources:

- A qualitative comparative study Katz, Batt, Mante and van 't Land, conducted in the first half of 1999 both in the U.S. and in the Netherlands, on the positioning of fixed telephone, mobile phone, and Internet in daily life.

- A quantitative study by Katz and Batt on the positioning of household technology in the U.S. on the dimensions of: necessity – luxury, entertainment – non-entertainment, time saving – time consuming, and enhancing privacy – endangering privacy

- Some primary survey material of a study by EURESCOM on cross-cultural attitudes to ICTs in everyday life in nine European countries. The material is focused on the Netherlands as being a country with a rather high diffusion rate, both on mobile telephone and Internet, and the country that was used for comparison in the qualitative study that preceded the Katz and Batt quantitative study.

To be able to decide on changing attitudes during domestication, strictly speaking it is necessary to follow the same group of users in time. The EURESCOM data do not offer this longitudinal possibility, as it is a one-shot survey study. We are however able to relate changing attitudes more indirectly to the adoption process, by combining them with the number of years people use the application. In the attitude change, the domestication process of each diffusion group will be mirrored. The domestication process of course, is affected by happenings and experiences in the period the process is measured. When we follow a group over time, it is possible to include these factors in the interpretation. Diffusion groups, during the adoption process, also have these experiences. However, as we only ask them at a certain moment in time, we do not know which influences have colored the attitudes during the domestication process. Hence the diffusion groups are not completely comparable, as they are different cohorts in time and different influences have played a role for each cohort. Nevertheless it is plausible to assume that we may draw reasonable valid conclusions on changes in attitude being related to the duration of use.

To be able to look into the effects of use over time, we divided the respondents into six diffusion groups: non-users, and five user groups according to the moment of adoption consisting of early adopters (group 1), early to late majority (groups 2 to 5). To be able to obtain the most valid estimation, we controlled the groups for *real private use*, that is, only the respondents that had personal access to a mobile phone or Internet, *and* had used the device during the last month for at least one hour of private use, were included. This of course means that the number of non-users is larger than we find in the total database. Hence, some differences in percentages between the total database and the tables we present here will be observed.

## What We Found

*Mobile Phone*

*Positioning.* The Katz-Batt research in the U.S. positions the mobile phone on the perceptual dimensions of non-entertaining luxuries. In 1999, at the time of the published work, mobile phone use was moderate in the U.S., but the available technology was well known. This means that people had a distinct idea about it, had used it themselves, or had seen others using it in their surroundings. Katz and Batt also show that, compared with research on the same topic in the early 1990s, the mobile phone had moved in 1999 in the direction of (secondary) necessity.

Simultaneously, the Dutch focus group research (Katz et al. 1999) took place. It showed that the mobile phone was already adopted by the early adopters, but was still rather uncommon. At that moment, the Dutch had some experiences abroad and in their own country with mobile phone use and had very clear opinions on the device. With some hindsight, we could say that the focus group interviews were held at the moment the user interest in mobile phone communications was "taking off." It was remarkable that between the time of invitation to participate in the Dutch focus groups and the moment the focus groups were held, some of the participants of the non-mobile groups in the meantime, had acquired a mobile phone. Nevertheless, it still was far more difficult to find owners of mobile phones than non-owners.

At the moment of the focus groups, the mobile phone was undoubtedly still considered as a luxury, both by owners and non-owners. The Dutch focus group-owner participants qualified it at that moment as a "nice luxury."

Since the focus group research in 1999, the adoption of the mobile telephone in the Netherlands has risen with an enormous pace, up to 80 percent access for the Dutch population from the age of fifteen and up at the end of

2000. This shows that it has become a common device, only slightly less common than telephone, radio, and TV. Hence, it has moved from the realm of luxury to the realm of common devices.

It is to be expected that this change should reflect the attitudes toward the device in the data of the EURESCOM survey.

The EURESCOM research asked participants for attitudes toward the mobile phone in a battery of seventeen items, mostly expressed during focus groups in the qualitative phase of the project. These opinions cover a wide range of uses in the realm of social contact, functional use and leisure, also including social norms about behavior with the mobile phone. These items form three scales, respectively:

- Integration in everyday life, consisting of three sub-scales respectively: coordination (alpha .71), close contact with loved ones (alpha .73), and communication anywhere and anyplace (alpha .67). Two items close to the concept of entertainment, "the mobile phone helps you to enjoy more of your leisure time" and "the mobile phone is fun" also cluster on this integration scale. As an item that drew moderate scores (around 2.5 on the five-point scale) in combination with the other items it seems to not indicate entertainment, but rather pleasure in being in contact with people one likes.

- Mobile phone to notify others in cases of need: emergency, notify others when running late, when it is not too difficult to get access to.

- Negative feelings: fear for health, disturbing for others, dangerous while driving, costly.

Looking at the three subscales of integration in everyday life, non-users score significantly lower on the scales "coordination" and "communication anywhere" than the user groups. As could be seen in table 10.1, the mean for the non-users is respectively 2.28, and 1.97, while the means for the users are 2.98 and 2.99. Thus, attitudes show that mobile phone users rate functionality relatively high. A mobile phone is something useful for coordination and being reachable when outside the home.

Also on the second subscale, "close contact with loved ones," non-users and users differ consistently and significantly (means 2.79 and 3.55).

In 1999, quite a few users and all non-users depicted the mobile phone as something useful in cases of need, but also as very disturbing to others and dangerous while driving. These attitudes come back in the fourth and fifth scale. Score differences between non-users and user groups on the fourth scale are, although statistically significant, not large; users and non-users are both convinced that the mobile is a good means for emergencies. Looking at the "disturbance" scale, we see that non-users are only slightly more convinced of this disturbing nature of the mobile phone, than the last user group.

The scores on the scales illustrate that the mobile phone since 1999 has migrated from something of dubious luxury to something close to a necessity.

**Table 10.1**
**Differences in Attitudes between Users and Non-Users of Mobile Telephone**

| Subscales | Mean score for people with (former or current) access to a mobile telephone (N=798) | Mean score for people with no (current or former) access to a mobile telephone (N=201) | Significance level |
|---|---|---|---|
| Mobile phone to coordinate everyday life | 2.98 | 2.28 | p < .001 |
| Mobile phone to have close contacts with your dear ones | 3.55 | 2.79 | p < .001 |
| Mobile telephone to communicate every time and everywhere | 2.99 | 1.97 | p < .001 |
| Mobile phone to notify others | 4.81 | 4.61 | p < .001 |
| Mobile phone has negative effect on ones surroundings | 3.91 | 4.25 | p < .001 |

**Attitude Over Time**

One of the expectations we had when we were analyzing the attitude scales was that the more years a technical device is used, the more the likelihood it would have become domesticated. By domestication, we mean that the longer the use, the more people would think positively about the device they are using, as it becomes a necessary part of their daily lives. Seen in that light, we hypothesized that there would be significant differences in attitude among non-users and the different diffusion groups, ranging from late adopters to early adopters. When we looked into the mean scores for non-users and five groups of users, within the dimension of period of use, we found the differences we expected for "integration in everyday life" and on the three sub-scales: "coordination," "communication from any place," and "social contact."

Non-users scored significantly lower on the scales, while the scores went up consistently beginning from the latest user group to the earlier user groups.

However, the score differences between the non-users and the latest user group were far more pronounced than those among the diffusion groups. So it seems that the attitude "flattens out" after the first year of use.

For the scales, "close contact" and "communication from any place," we see that the earliest adopters show a small dip compared to the group that came directly behind. This cannot be explained with the material we have, but might be due to specific characteristics of the group innovators and early adopters who look less to utility and gravitate more to novelty. See figures 10.1, 10.2, and 10.3.

The fourth scale, "notifying others," did not show a clear change in attitude. The difference between non-users and latest adopters were very small and the differences between the next adoption groups were almost non-existent. This scale reflects the most elementary use of mobile phone, such as the case of emergencies. It seems that this is something everybody can agree upon even when one does not use a mobile phone. It might show the domestication of the device in the general culture of the country.

| **Legend** | | | | | |
|---|---|---|---|---|---|
| **Diffusion group** | | | | | |
| 1 | = | first users | 4 | = | later users |
| 2 | = | early users | 5 | = | last users |
| 3 | = | mid-range users | 9 | = | non-users |

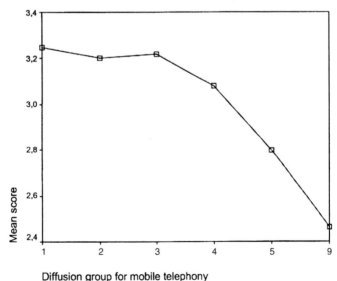

**Figure 10.1**
**Mobile Phone to Coordinate Everyday Life**

Diffusion group for mobile telephony

**Figure 10.2**
**Mobile Telephone to Have Close Contacts with your Dear Ones**

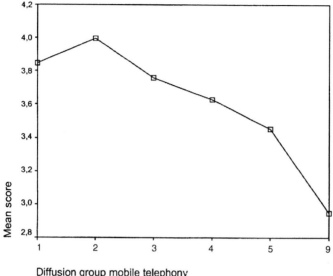

**Figure 10.3**
**Mobile Telephone to Communicate Everytime and Everywhere**

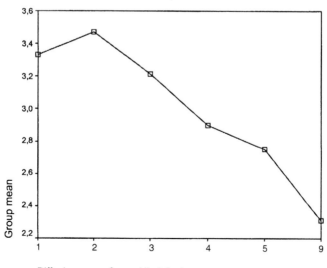

The fifth scale, "negative feelings," also does not follow the general pattern of domestication. Again, there is not much difference of opinion between non-users and the latest adoption group, both highly agreed on the disturbing aspects of the mobile phone. Between the latest adoption group and the before last, we see however a rather steep decline in the scores. After that the scores stay at about the same level, going slightly down again for the early adopters. Apparently, when one uses the mobile, one initially has some misgivings, emphasizing the dangers and the nuisance with the device. With longer use, one sees the mobile in a different, less threatening light. Nevertheless, even the early adopters score way above the mean on this scale. This means that, although users get a more balanced picture, they still recognize the negative side of the device. See figures 10.4 and 10.5.

*Internet*

*Positioning.* The Katz-Batt survey positioned the Internet as a slightly entertaining luxury. It shared its place with the PC and candy (one of the non-technocial consumption items in the scale), closer to the non-entertaining part of the dimension than for example, games, music, video-on-demand, and so on. The non-users of the Internet among the Dutch focus groups perceived the Internet as something beneficial for children's education, a resource for information, and something to have warm feelings about, but indicated that it was

**Figure 10.4**
**Mobile Phone to Notify Others**

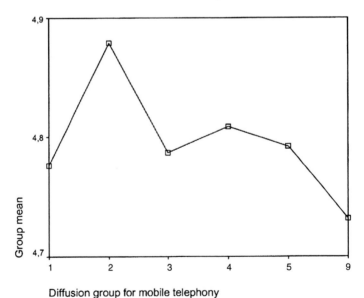

Diffusion group for mobile telephony

**Figure 10.5**
**Mobile Telephone has a Negative Effect on One's Direct Surroundings**

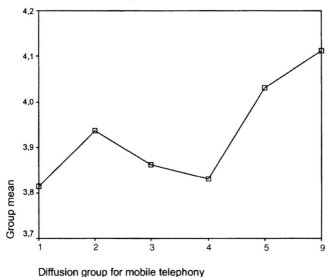

Diffusion group for mobile telephony

"not for me," noting that it was too time consuming. It was apparent from the non-user focus groups that they did not have a clear picture in their minds of what the Internet really was. Since they lacked information on the Internet, unlike the mobile phone, it did not fuel negative attitudes, except for the point that use for children should be controlled because it keeps children from playing outside and it could be enslaving.

In the first half of 1999, the Internet in the Netherlands was not yet fully utilized. Access was under 30 percent, as actual use was low. Also other research by KPN Research during that period showed that people quite often did not know what the Internet was and had never heard about it. That quickly changed in the course of 1999 and later, among other reasons, because of consistent campaigns by the Dutch government and the media, focusing attention to the WWW (World Wide Web). Through all types of media, either in papers, radio, or on TV, a particular service or corporation consistently advertised to the public the corresponding Internet address. Also, both the ICT industry and the Dutch government constantly advertised the benefits of "becoming wired" or connected to the Internet. During the second half of 1999, a lot of free or very cheap web-servers, such as "Het Net" of KPN Telecom, became available to the public. This has contributed to an enormous rise of Internet access, resulting in an access of over 50 percent of the Dutch population by the end of 2000.

In the EURESCOM research, seventeen statements, mostly obtained from the focus groups of 1999, measured attitudes toward the Internet. These statements formed four scales:

- Positive vs. indifferent attitude toward Internet, containing items like "not familiar, not useful."
- Internet as tool to make friends (social function), containing items like: "enables people to make new friends, get in contact with people with the same interests."
- Internet is time consuming (saves time – costs time dimension of Katz-Batt).
- Trust in internet: "friendships are superficial, one cannot trust using a credit card, too much pornography."

The dimension necessity—luxury, as per Katz-Batt, is similar to the EURESCOM study in statement items like: "easier ways, useful, gather information, all being part of the first scale." Again, as with the mobile phone in Katz-Batt, the item "using the Internet is fun," is a comparable factor, but is not included in the scale. The earliest adopters have a higher opinion on the fun item than the later adopters (means ranging from 3.8 for the latest diffusion group to close to 4.5 for the early adopters). However, looking at the uses of the Internet makes clear, that, even in a rather Internet-wise population as that of the Netherlands, the Internet is not directly associated with entertainment—its function is mainly functional. The top five Internet services used in the Netherlands are e-mail, search engines, and accessing information on travel, directories, and traffic. The first (and only) entertainment item in the top ten is "downloading music," which is positioned in sixth place, used by 38 percent of Internet users. Games, horoscopes, adult entertainment, and radio come far lower in the list of uses. Hence, there is no indication that the Internet moves to the entertainment side of the Katz-Batt dimension. Fun, again, should be interpreted as the pleasure of doing things on Internet.

### Attitude Over Time

Looking at the differences over time, we see the same phenomenon occurring for mobile phone use in the Netherlands—the largest difference in attitude is between the non-user and the user. This holds for all Internet scales. The items with the largest differences between users and non-users are the items: "not familiar, not useful, and using the Internet is fun."

When we compare the four adopter groups, the differences are small between groups on the scale "indifference toward Internet" and "the Internet is time consuming." However, the attitude is most positive for the first group of early adopters and a little less positive for each later adopter group. Taking the difference between the last adopters and the non-users as a starting point, it seems that after one year of initial use, the attitude changes in the expected direction, but only in a very moderate way. See figures 10.6, 10.7, 10.8, and 10.9.

The difference of opinion between users and non-users on the social function of the Internet is lowest of all. Scores are however relatively high (means around 3.8). Here we see that the attitude of the second adoption group is lower than of the others. The difference is small, and could be due to specific characteristics of this group.

**Figure 10.6**
**Indifference Toward the Internet**

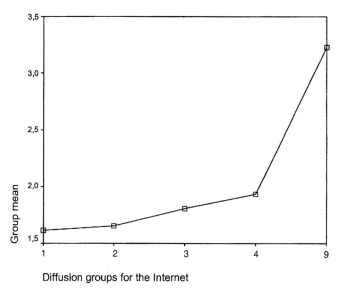

Diffusion groups for the Internet

**Figure 10.7**
**Internet as a Tool to Make New Friends**

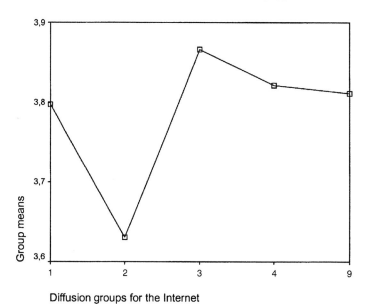

Diffusion groups for the Internet

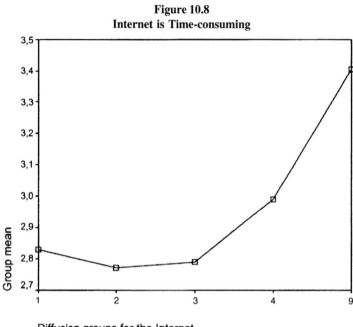

**Figure 10.8**
**Internet is Time-consuming**

Diffusion groups for the Internet

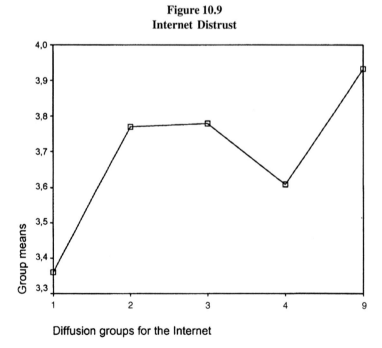

**Figure 10.9**
**Internet Distrust**

Diffusion groups for the Internet

The largest differences between the adoption groups occur on the scale "distrust in the Internet." Here we see that non-users score very high on negative ideas about Internet. The latest adoption group has a clearly more positive opinion than the non-users.

It is interesting that the next two diffusion groups show slightly more negative attitudes than the latest group. Early adopters show by far the lowest distrust. When we look at the items that form the scale, we consistently see the same pattern. It is plausible that experiences in time are the cause of this fluctuation in opinion. The very positive attitude of the first adopter group could be explained either by a different use of the Internet over time, or the fact that they, as early adopters, have different attitudes towards technology.

## Males and Females

Technology is often associated with male behavior. This is especially the case in the innovation and early adoption stage of technology. In the beginning, when the Internet had just become adopted in a country, women were far outnumbered by men when it came to Internet access. Due to the introduction of the Internet in schools and at work, and the predominance of female labor within office functions, the gender gap has strongly diminished in countries with a strong female office workforce and a high Internet penetration or has even turned the other way around (Nurmela et al. 2000). A Eurobarometer survey held in 2000 shows that females are catching up in the high penetration countries, remaining only a few percentages behind the males. In countries with less penetration, the differences are far higher (Thomas and Mante 2001).

Nevertheless, it could be expected that patterns of adoption would differ along gender lines (Wyatt 2000). So it could very well be hypothesized that women's attitudes would be more positive about the social functions both of the mobile phone and the Internet, while men's attitudes would lean more toward the functionalities.

To see what gender differences in attitude look like, we looked at the mean differences on the mobile phone scales and the Internet scales for males and females.

### Mobile Phone

*Gender Division.* The percentage of males is nearly twice that of females among the two earliest adoption groups. As the deployment time available for adoption unfolds later adoption groups have much higher rates of uptake among women, even to the point of surpassing males in the last-to-adopt groups. This confirms the general trend that the innovators are male, but shows also that women catch up (and may surpass) men over time. This finding offers further confirmation for gender change over time in the U.S. context (Katz 1999).

*Attitudes*. Looking at the mean scores for women and men on the mobile phone scales, we see on the integration scale and the underlying sub-scales, that females show a somewhat lower score than males. Although the differences are not always significant, the tendency is very consistent. This pattern is reflected in the scores for the non-users and in all diffusion groups, with one exception: women in the fourth diffusion group show consistently higher scores than men. This diffusion group is the first group in which the women form the majority of the new adopters. It looks as if here we see an effect of the transition between early adopters and early majority, where other reasons to adopt play a role. It is plausible that at that point in diffusion, women discovered the mobile phone as handy for the coordination of their personal lives. Why, however, do we not see the same for the last adoption group that also has a majority of women? It could be that the first adopters and the late adopters have in common that the main motive they are adopting a new technology is that they are curious: the first adopters because they are innovative, the late adopters because they have seen and heard so much about it and are heeding the message not to fall behind in technology usage. The adoption is then less consciously motivated. In that case, the "natural differences" between male and female attitudes become again stronger.

## Internet

### Gender Division

The gender division on the use of the Internet shows the same characteristics of mobile phone use. Males are almost twice as likely to be early adopters. But then over time, females catch up and then become in the majority among the waves of new users. Then, again, the percentage of women surpasses that of males in the last-to-adopt groups. This again mirrors the situation in the United States (Katz, Rice, and Aspden, 2001).

### Attitudes

Again, we see differences in the mean scores on the Internet scales by men and women. On the whole, the women score a little less positively than the men do, especially on the indifference scale and on "tool to make friends." Apparently their outlook on the Internet is a little more reserved. The picture is somewhat mixed concerning items depicting the hazards and toil of the Internet: "time consuming" and "distrust in the Internet." Here the males in the early adopter group are the most positive. Especially on "distrust toward the Internet," the differences between men and women are large (mean scores respectively 3.1 and 3.7), while in the other diffusion groups, men and women only differ slightly both on their opinion on distrust as on their opinion on the time consuming nature of the Internet.

## Conclusion

In seeking an answer to the question, "Do machines become us?" we translated it into the realm of adoption and domestication. What happens in the domestication process and do we find evidence that something like that takes place in the adoption of mobile phone and Internet usage?

Four aspects we thought important are the following:

1.  The positioning of new technology in daily life on the dimensions of luxury and necessity;

2.  The likelihood that a shift will take place from non-entertainment functionality to the realm of entertainment;

3.  The shift in attitude when users move from the realm of non-user to long-time user;

4.  The role of gender in these shifts.

In the following, we attempt to provide answers on all four points.

### Positioning

Compared to the Katz-Batt positioning in 1999, the data of the EURESCOM survey show that both the mobile phone and the Internet are clearly located close to the non-entertainment side of the dimension, entertainment—non-entertainment. Scores on the functional use of the mobile phone are always above the mean of the scale; the usefulness for emergencies being highly recognized even by the non-users. Although using the mobile phone is associated with fun, the fun element forms a part of the sub-scale on social use, being associated with talking to loved ones and not related to entertainment as such.

When we look at the services the Internet is used for, it is clear that it is on the non-entertainment side of the dimension and is mainly associated with functional use. Among the first five services used, there is no entertainment attribute. Among the top ten, only downloading of music may be associated with entertainment.

### Shift in Positioning

The fact that even non-users recognize the functionality of the mobile phone for emergencies gives an indication that for the Dutch, the mobile phone has become to most people something of necessity. Unlike the mobile phone, however, the Internet is not yet commonly associated with something necessary for everyone. There is still a large difference of opinion between users and non-users on the scale "indifference toward Internet," and on the idea that "the Internet is a waste of time."

Hence, if there is a shifting along dimensions, it is more a shifting along the dimension—from luxury to necessity. At the moment, there is no sign that a shift takes place from functionality to entertainment.

*Change in Attitudes*

Do we find proof of a change in attitudes in a more favorable direction when Internet and mobile phone are used over time?

When we compare the diffusion groups for both devices, most of the findings do corroborate the hypothesis that over time, attitudes switch to more favorable. This effect, however, is often not as large as we had expected. How can it be explained?

1.    The items we used were not the correct items, discriminating insufficiently. However, these items came out of the focus group discussions as typical expressions from either users or non-users. Also in most cases, there is a rather large gap between non-users and newest/latest users and often too, albeit a smaller one, between new users and the older adoption groups.

2.    Domestication means that people treat the technology more and more as a commodity. After some time, people use the item in the ways that best fits within their daily lives. The technology provides a natural function in their lives evidenced in that the technology doesn't need to be discussed anymore. Apparently this process takes place soon after adoption.

3.    Domestication is, apart from an individual phenomenon, also a collective phenomenon. The perception of each cohort of users changes along with the changes in society. Perception differs, not only because people use the device differently in their personal life, but also because the context, norms, and values in society shift. Since the data we used are not longitudinal data, but data from a one-shot survey, it might very well be that the fact that the longest user group also belongs to the early adopters, confounds the effects of use over time.

The general tendency of more favorable attitudes was not found for the mobile phone scale of "notifying others." The last showed only very small variances, staying very positive for all diffusion groups. It almost seemed an "open door" statement, showing the general acceptance in the society of the mobile phone.

*Gender*

When we look at the gender gap as one of the most recognized obstructions to adopting and domesticating new technology, we see that women are catching up. Although when the technology took off, women had less access to the technology, both for mobile phone and for Internet use, the latest diffusion groups consist of more women than men. This phenomenon we observed in all countries that were part of the EURESCOM survey, for mobile phone and in all countries where the Internet was well established, for the Internet.

We also see that the attitudes of the sexes follow the same pattern—attitudes of women and men becoming more favorable along the diffusion groups. These differences between men and women are mostly not large. However, on all scales and all diffusion groups, with one clear exception, female scores are a little less favorable than the male scores. This is consistent with the results of earlier research on gender differences that show women a bit more critical than men on technology. The exception is for the fourth diffusion group on the mobile phone.

The scores for males and females on mobile telephony along the diffusion groups seem to show a kind of innovator effect for women: women entering the market in the fourth adoption group belong to the early majority of women coming into the market. It is noted that the motivation for technological innovation is different for the early adopters than for the later adopters, being more functional for the last group. As most of the mobile phone attitude scales are tapping the functional and social use of the mobile phone, it is plausible that in the fourth diffusion group, women entered because they had discovered the mobile as handy for the coordination of their daily lives. Why the last diffusion group does not show the same pattern, of course, is unclear, unless we can describe them as followers, who, like innovators are more motivated by curiosity than personal need. No such innovator effects were discovered for the Internet. This might be due to the fact that the Internet has only recently been discovered by the mass of people, the new users being still closer to the early adopters than to the late majority.

Our data show that the technologies of the mobile phone and Internet are moving into the realm of daily life necessities. Compared to the mobile phone, though, the Internet is slower moving, as during domestication the technologies are becoming increasingly seen as mere commodities. For non-users in these regards, the mobile phone and the Internet are becoming simply acceptable "facts of life." This is true even if the non-user has no immediate plans to use these technologies. This metamorphosis has occurred in a highly compressed time span. Machines and new devices can clearly become accepted into our everyday lives.

Does this mean that gradually machines will become unchallenged facts of life that will govern our lives without fear or acrimony? The scores on the negative side both for the mobile phone, and especially for the Internet, make clear that this is unlikely. Based on our data, people clearly maintain a wary stance toward the possible dangers of the new machines.

## References

Batt, Carl E. and James E. Katz. 1998. Consumer Spending Behavior and Telecommunication Services: A Multi-Method Inquiry. *Telecommunications Policy* 22 (3): 23–46.

Haddon, L. 1992. Explaining ICT Consumption: The Case of the Home Computer. In *Consuming Technologies: Media and Information in Domestic Spaces* (pp. 82-97), eds. R. Silverstone and E. Hirsch ,London: Routledge.

Katz, James E. 1999. *Connections: Social and Cultural Studies of the Telephone in American Life.* New Brunswick, NJ: Transaction Publishers.

Katz, James E., Ronald E. Rice, and P. Aspden. 2001. The Internet 1995–2000: Access, Civic Involvement and Social Interaction. *American Behavioral Scientist,* 45 (3), pp. 404–419.

Katz, James E. and Carl Batt. 1999. *Telecommunication Services in Context,* Morristown, NJ: Center for Research on the Information Society.

Katz, James E., Carl Batt, Enid Mante, and H. Van't Land. 1998. Focus Groups: Telecommunication Services in Context (USA and the Netherlands), Mimeo report KPN, Leidschendam, NL.

Ling, Richard, Frank Thomas, Pedro Concejero, Zbigniew Smoreda, Jeroen Heres, Iris Vrieling, and Enid Mante. 2001. Cross-Cultural Attitudes to ICTs in Everyday Life. Report of EURESCOM P-903, Heidelberg, Germany.

Nurmela J. and M. Vihera. 2000. *The Mobile Phone and the Computer in the Everyday Life of The Finnish, 2000/2 Statistics Finland & Sonera, Helsinki,* pp. 14–15.

Rogers, E. M. 1962. *Diffusion of Innovations,* New York: The Free Press.

Thomas, Frank and Enid Mante. 2001. Internet Have Nots in Europe—A Structural or a Passing Phenomenon. Paper for the International Conference on Uses and Services in Telecommunication (ICUST), France Telecom, Paris, France, June.

Wyatt, Sally. Non-Users also Matter: The Construction of Users and Non-Users of the Internet. 2000. Forthcoming publication in *How Users Matter: The Co-Construction of Users and Technology,* eds. Nelly Oudshoorn and Trevor Pinch.

# 11

# Computer Anxiety Among "Smart" Dutch Computer Users

*J.J. Beckers, E. Mante, and H.G. Schmidt*

### Smart People and Smart Technology

"Do smart homes require smart people?" This question was posed at the April 2001 Rutgers conference, "Machines That Become Us." The terms *smart homes* and *smart people* require further definition, but one aspect of "smartness" suggests that a "smart" person would have no difficulties using technology.

This chapter will first address whether Dutch people experience anxiety when using new technology. This is especially pertinent since there has been significant infiltration of computers, the Internet, and mobile phones into the daily life of those in the Netherlands. Second, this article will address the causes of computer anxiety as it occurs in Dutch society.

To study these questions, KPN Research's Technology Panel was used. KPN Research is part of KPN Telecom, the leading Dutch telecommunication operator, originally state owned and now privatized. The Technology Panel was established in the early 1990s to represent the people of the Netherlands. Panel members might be asked to try or judge technological innovations or to participate in group discussions and be interviewed on ICT (information and communication technology) issues. Participants were drawn from households in the vicinity of The Hague and consisted of diverse socio-economic, educational, and age groups. Panel members often happened to have an affinity for new technology, which made them appropriate targets for questions about computer anxiety.

This chapter uses the term *smart people* to refer to people that (1) have an affinity for computer-related technology; (2) are frequent users of computer-related technology; (3) are skilled in using this technology; and (4) have used this technology in the past without anxiety.

A vast amount of literature addresses the issue of how people relate to new technology. Levine and Donitsa-Schmidt (1998) explored how attitudes towards computers relate to a person's belief about their own computer ability, knowledge, and experience. They found that computer use has a positive effect on perceived computer self-confidence and on computer-related attitudes. Some researchers have focused on possible negative aspects of using new technology, such as anxiety. Computer anxiety refers to having a fear of computers or the tendency to be uneasy, apprehensive, and phobic towards current or future use of computers (Loyd and Loyd 1985; Chua et al. 1999). Computer-anxious people resist talking or thinking about computers and may harbor worries that they will be embarrassed, appear inadequate, or damage the equipment (Nelson et al. 1991). Computer anxiety has often been studied in relation to computer experience, gender, and age. Most studies find that computer experience and anxiety are negatively related, although negative initial experiences may further contribute to anxiety (Maurer, 1994; Weil et al. 1990). In recent years, some have argued that it is worthwhile for people to strive for computer literacy, which is defined as "the collection of skills, knowledge, understanding, values, and relationships that allow a person to function comfortably as a productive citizen in a computer-oriented society" (Watt 1980, p. 3). In terms of being "technologically smart," some authors point out that a positive, anxiety-free attitude toward computers is a prerequisite to, and a component of, computer literacy (Simonson et al. 1987). Consequently, the definition of "technologically smart" requires that the user be anxiety free.

Evidence is mounting that the average Dutch citizen fits the definition of "technologically smart"; by the 1980s, nearly every Dutch household owned a fixed telephone. By 2001, most households owned a PC (76 percent), over half the Dutch population had Internet access, and currently mobile phones are reaching a saturation point (80 percent) (EURESCOM 2000).

However, Beckers and Schmidt (2001) conclude that the introduction of ICTs into everyday life has had negative effects, and other studies in The Netherlands also support this conclusion. A major 1997 study on digital skills and attitudes towards computers found that there was a digital divide between those over the age of fifty and those under fifty, with the older population being less well-equipped to handle technology. Seniors also held less positive attitudes towards the digitization of society (Doets and Huisman 1997), and people with a low level of education or who were unemployed were also more negative in their attitudes. Although there is much evidence that Dutch society is rapidly transforming into an "e-society."

Therefore, the question remains of how "smart" the Dutch are in terms of their comfort and mastery of digital technology—the study in this article provides possible new answers. The entire panel (N = 750) was sent a questionnaire about their

- Socio-economic and educational background;

- Telecommunication and computer devices in their homes;

- Experiences with computers and the Internet; and

- A composite scale measuring computer anxiety.

### Study Participants and Responses

The participants in this study consisted of 565 members of the KPN Research Technology Panel (out of 750 people, or 75 percent participation rate). Not all respondents were computer users, so a subset was formed consisting of those who indicated occasional computer use. This group (n=495) was the particular focus of our study of computer anxiety.

In March 2001, a written questionnaire was sent to the panel members. Questions included

1. Socio-demographic variables such as age, sex, level of education, income, main daily activity, type of job, and vocation.

2. Telecommunication and computer appliances present in the household, such as a fixed phone, a wireless phone, a mobile phone, a computer, a laptop, or a personal digital assistant (PDA).

3. Ownership of a PC and accessibility to the Internet at work, in the home, or in school.

4. Type of applications used, such as word processing, programming, spreadsheets, e-mail, surfing, and downloading.

5. The level of necessity of using a computer for work, for school, and as a hobby.

6. Self-perceived skills with respect to the use of these applications.

7. Average number of hours spent using various computer and Internet applications.

8. Location of computers usage at work, at home, and in school.

Furthermore, to test the participants' level of computer anxiety, a composite anxiety scale was used based on the six-factor model of computer anxiety proposed by Beckers and Schmidt (2001). The six factors measured are

1. Computer literacy (in terms of acquired computer skills),

2. Self-efficacy (confidence in learning to use computers)

3. Physical symptoms in the presence of computers (such as sweaty palms, shortness of breath),

4. Feelings towards computers (like and dislike),

5. Positive beliefs about the benefits for society of using computers, and

6. Negative beliefs about the dehumanizing impact of computers.

For each of the seventy-seven items in the inventory, a five-point scale was used ranging from 1 (entirely disagree) to 5 (entirely agree). The composite anxiety score was a weighted sum of the 6 sub-scale averages, with a value ranging between 0 (low anxiety) and 18 (high anxiety).

A second questionnaire was used to measure how persons recall their first computer experiences in terms of control (e.g., "When you were using the computer did you usually feel pretty much/more or less/seldom in control") and comfort level ("Was your early computer experience generally very/fairly relaxed/fairly tense/very tense"). In addition, the quality of the help available at the first experience (e.g., "friendly and supportive" or "bossy and made you feel stupid") was measured. Finally, respondents were asked about how eager they were to work with computers today (e.g., "Given a choice of procedures for carrying out a task, would you be keen to use/indifferent towards using to-wards/actively avoid using a computer"). The latter questionnaire, consisting of eleven items, was developed by Todman and Donahue (1994).

Through stepwise multiple regression, several variables were explored for people's relative contribution to statistically explaining computer anxiety: Age, sex, highest level of education received, primary daily activity, net income, Internet connection at work, Internet connection at home, e-mail address at work, e-mail address at home, PC owner, total number of PC appliances, total number of telecommunication appliances, total number of hours on the PC, total number of hours on the Internet, frequency of computer use, self-perceived PC skills, self-perceived Internet skills, amount of control felt at first experience, preference for using a computer, necessity for using a computer, comfort level during first experience, and available support at first experience.

## Composition of KPN Research Technology Panel

The KPN Research Technology Panel was designed to be a representative sample of the Dutch population. To test this assumption, a number of socio-demographic variables were compared with available population statistics from the Dutch Central Bureau of Statistics (CBS). These variables were sex, age, and education. The distribution of these variables is given in table 11.1. The data refer to the total group of respondents, a subset of computer users, and the general Dutch population.

As shown in the table, males are somewhat overrepresented in the technology panel and among the computer users. Those in the age category 40–65 were also overrepresented, while those in the age category 0–19 were underrepresented. The technology panel members and the computer users are more educated than the general population. Those with vocational education were also overrepresented, especially in the senior category. The demographics of computer users are consistent with the fact that the technology panel mem-

**Table 11.1**
**Composition of Technology Panel, Subset Users, and Dutch Population**
**with Regard to Sex, Age, and Education (Percentage)**

| Socio-demographic variables | Technology Panel | Subset of Users | Dutch Population |
|---|---|---|---|
| **Sex** | | | |
| Male | 52.5 | 53.3 | 49.5 |
| Female | 47.5 | 46.7 | 50.5 |
| **Age (in years)** | | | |
| 0–19 | 8.0 | 8.9 | 22.4 |
| 20–39 | 25.5 | 27.4 | 30.0 |
| 40–64 | 49.6 | 52.1 | 32.0 |
| 65–79 | 16.1 | 11.6 | 10.4 |
| 80+ | 0.7 | — | 3.2 |
| **Education** | | | |
| Primary | 1.4 | 0.3 | 8.0 |
| Secondary junior general/vocational | 12.0 | 16.0 | 7.1 |
| Senior general/ pre-university | 10.3 | 26.0 | 13.7 |
| Senior vocational | 18.8 | 18.7 | 5.6 |
| Higher vocational | 36.2 | 39.0 | 37.9 |
| University | 14.5 | 15.3 | 18.4 |

Note—Source for Dutch population statistics is the Dutch Central Bureau of Statistics (CBS), http://www.cbs.nl/nl/statline/index.htm. Statistics on sex and age are derived from the survey of 2000; statistics on education from the survey of 1999.

bers voluntarily participate in panels of this nature. This fact is also an advantage to the study, since it is assumed that an interest in new technology is beneficial to becoming technologically "smart." The EURESCOM P903 study showed that the main reason for non-adoption of mobile phones or the Internet was lack of interest. This is also found in the U.S. studies by Katz (1999); and Katz and Rice (2002).

An examination of their main daily activity reveals that slightly more than half of the technology panel members work in a profession or a company (52 percent), one-fifth (20 percent) are on early retirement, almost one out of ten (11 percent) are students or take daytime courses, one out of eight are homemakers (13 percent), only 5 percent are unemployed or unable to work, 9 percent have their own company or work independently, and 6 percent have an office at home. Respondents work in various vocations and/or branches. The most important are, in descending order: government (13 percent), care and medical sector (12 percent), education (9 percent), services (8 percent), banking and insurance (6 percent). A quarter (26 percent) has managerial jobs. It seems the majority of the technology panel members are white-collar workers.

### Presence of Telecommunication, Computer, and Internet Appliances in the Household

Table 11.2 illustrates the telecommunication, computer, and Internet appliances in technology panel members' household. Clearly, the infiltration of fixed and mobile phones is very high, as is that of the PC.

### Computer Usage and Online Accessibility

The technology panel is highly familiar with computer-related technology. Of the panel members, 89 percent use a computer occasionally, and 82 percent own a computer. Of the remaining 18 percent, nearly all the members have access to a computer. Table 11.3 demonstrates that a sizable part of the technology panel is online, especially from home, and many more members have an e-mail address at home than at work. This may indicate a willingness to participate in modern developments.

Table 11.4 shows the location and amount of time technology panel members spend with a computer. Those respondents that use a computer in the office spend an average of half the week working with a computer. Nearly all of the respondents also use the computer at home, though at a lower rate. This may be due to the fact that home computers are used primarily for e-mail. Another possibility is that the large amount of time spent using the computer at work makes it less appealing for leisure use. (Qualitative interviews among members of the panel, conducted for other research purposes, pointed in this direction.)

**Table 11.2**
**Telecommunication, Computer, and Internet Appliances Present in Households**

| Telecommunication appliances | % | Computer appliances | % |
|---|---|---|---|
| Pushbutton phone | 83.4 | Personal computer | 82.3 |
| Mobile phone | 71.0 | Game computer | 27.1 |
| Wireless phone | 64.8 | Laptop | 22.5 |
| Answering machine | 28.3 | Personal digital assistant (PDA) | 8.1 |
| Fax | 21.9 | ISDN connection | 14.5 |
| Mobile phone with car kit | 12.7 | TV—cable | 95.6 |
| Dial phone | 11.0 | TV—and text | 85.5 |
| Beeper | 6.0 | TV—cable with Internet connection | 21.2 |
| Semaphone | 5.1 | | |
| Message watch | 2.5 | | |
| Charge Counter | 1.2 | | |
| Inbuilt car phone | 0.5 | | |

Note—Total sample size n = 565

**Table 11.3**
**Computer Ownership and Online Characteristics of Panel Members**

| Ownership and online characteristics | % |
|---|---|
| Owner of a PC | 84.0 |
| Internet connection at work | 33.7 |
| Internet connection at home | 61.3 |
| Internet connection mobile | 1.4 |
| E-mail address at work | 34.5 |
| E-mail address at home | 57.9 |

Note—Total sample size n = 565

**Table 11.4**
**Location of and Time Spent Working with Computers by Panel Member**

| Location | Average hours per week | n |
|---|---|---|
| At home | 7.9 | 457 |
| Office/company/shop | 20.4 | 240 |
| At school | 6.4 | 69 |
| Other | 4.6 | 44 |

### The Use of Computer Internet Applications and Self-Perceived Skills

Table 11.5 shows the type of computer and Internet applications the members use and how proficient they judge themselves to be with a particular application. The self-rating is on a 10-point scale, 10 being the highest. As expected, nearly all technology panel members use word processing; this application led the others in the number of users and the average number of hours used. Playing games was a strong second. It was found that the more complex the application became, the lower the members rated their respective skill. With respect to recent Internet applications, unfamiliarity may also be a factor.

To summarize the findings so far, it is clear that the KPN Research Technology Panel represents a group that is "technologically smart." They have an affinity for technology, use it intensely for many purposes, and have homes that are fully equipped with new technology, especially Internet access. But on the qualitative side, many members of this group perceive themselves as having insufficient skills to use more complex computer applications, especially advanced applications such as databases and programming. They also lack skills to use Internet applications for chatting and the newer applications such as telelearning.

**Table 11.5**
**PC and Internet Applications Used and Perceived Skill Level of Panel Member**

| Type of application | n | Mean hours per week | n | Mean perceived skill level |
|---|---|---|---|---|
| PC applications | | | | |
| Word processing | 423 | 6.4 | 404 | 7.1 |
| Games | 279 | 2.4 | 245 | 6.5 |
| Spreadsheets | 204 | 3.5 | 176 | 6.4 |
| Graphics | 138 | 1.9 | 116 | 5.9 |
| D-bases | 137 | 1.4 | 104 | 5.5 |
| Programming | 87 | 1.1 | 57 | 3.4 |
| Internet applications | | | | |
| E-mail | 322 | 3.1 | 296 | 7.4 |
| Surfing | 323 | 3.5 | 296 | 6.8 |
| Chatting | 103 | 1.8 | 75 | 5.3 |
| Downloading | 167 | 2.2 | 144 | 6.5 |
| Telelearning | 41 | 0.3 | 41 | 2.5 |
| Teleworking | 87 | 1.4 | 50 | 4.1 |

The issue that remains is how anxiety free these members are in using this new technology. Subgroup measures of 495 panel members that occasionally (or more frequently) use a computer can help answer this question.

### Anxiety in Using Computer (Related) Technology

To measure whether panel members experience any anxiety when using computer-related technology, the composite computer anxiety scale based on the six-factor model of computer anxiety proposed by Beckers and Schmidt (2001) was used. A low score (close to zero) on this scale indicates that a person experiences little or no anxiety in relation to computers, a high score indicates that the person experiences a considerable amount of anxiety. The maximum score on this scale is 24. As seen in figure 11.1, the scores of the panel members indicate a normal distribution with a mean of 10. On the vertical axis, the number of respondents is reported. The curve drawn in the figure represents a normal distribution.

Finding a "normal" distribution within this sample may be difficult. As the technology panel members supposedly are inclined towards technology, one would expect a skew to the left, indicating that the majority of members would experience little or no anxiety. On the contrary, in spite of the general appearance of being technologically smart, quite a few members of the panel are not anxiety free.

**Figure 11.1**
**Distribution of Computer Anxiety Scores among Panel Members**
**(with Normal Distribution Superimposed)**

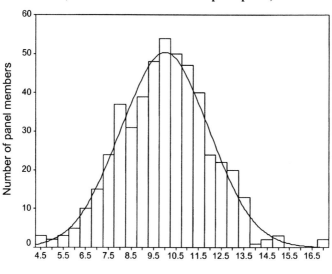

Note—M = 9.99; SD = 1.96; n = 495

Having established that computer anxiety is prevalent among the panel members, the next task is to find which variables explain the variance in the anxiety scores. To this end, two stepwise regression analyses were conducted. The first analysis was done on the basis of socio-demographic variables that were entered stepwise into the analysis: year of birth, sex, highest level of education received, main daily activity, and net income. Table 11.6 presents a summary of the multiple regression analysis with respect to these socio-demographic variables. The dependent variable is computer anxiety.

The variables excluded were main daily activity and net income, which did not significantly contribute to the explanation of computer anxiety. Sex and year of birth contribute in explaining computer anxiety, as females and the elderly experience more computer anxiety. This finding agrees with previous research with respect to these variables, but it is surprising to find that these variables still hold even among the members of a high-tech panel. The regression analysis demonstrates that main daily activity does not relate significantly to computer anxiety—there is no significant relationship between having activities outside the home (e.g., working) and experiencing a lower level of anxiety, or being at home (e.g., housewife, student, unemployed) and experiencing a higher level of anxiety. While one could argue that computers are primarily found in a working environment, this does not currently hold true. Education contributes significantly to the explanation of the variance in computer anxiety; the higher the education, the lower the anxiety. The exact nature of this relationship is still unclear. Do more highly educated people work more with computers, are they more self-reliant, do they like technology more, and are they more skilled in abstract thinking? There is a significant positive relationship between the average number of hours panel members work on a PC and their level of education ($n = 283$, $r = .14$, $p = .01$), but the other questions

**Table 11.6**
**Summary of Multiple Regression Analysis of Socio-Demographic Variables on Computer Anxiety**

| Variable | B | SE B | β | t |
|---|---|---|---|---|
| Year of birth | −.04 | .01 | −.27 | −4.85** |
| Gender | .68 | .23 | .17 | 2.97** |
| Highest level of education received | −.17 | .07 | −.13 | −2.27* |
| Main daily activity | .10 | N.A. | .10 | .95 |
| Net income | −.07 | N.A. | −.07 | .92 |
| Constant | 86.85 | 15.86 | | 5.48** |

Note—df = 299, *p<.05., **p<.01. Model fit: $R^2 = 0.10$. MSE = 1.83. Dependent variable: Composite Computer Anxiety

remain. Net income has no relation to anxiety. Recent research by the Dutch Social Cultural Planning Bureau shows that having a PC in the home is no longer related to income.

As pointed out in the introduction, the literature suggests a negative correlation between computer experience and computer anxiety. The following variables that indicate computer experience were entered into a stepwise regression analysis: total number of hours spent on the PC, total number of hours spent on the Internet, total number of computer appliances at home, total number of telecommunication appliances at home, perceived PC skills, perceived Internet skills, Internet connection at work, Internet connection at home, e-mail address at work, e-mail address at home, computer ownership, frequency of computer use, amount of control felt during first computer experience, feelings about using a computer, necessity of using a computer, comfort level during first computer experience, and available support. The best fitting model is presented in table 11.7.

**Table 11.7**
**Summary of Multiple Regression Analysis of PC and Internet Variables on Computer Anxiety**

| Variable | B | SEB | β | t |
|---|---|---|---|---|
| Self-perceived PC skills | −.04 | .01 | −.24 | −3.67** |
| Self-perceived Internet skills | −.02 | .01 | −.10 | 1.45 |
| Internet connection at work | −.12 | .24 | −.03 | −.51 |
| Internet connection at home | −.29 | .34 | −.06 | -.84 |
| E-mail address at work | −.03 | .26 | .01 | .11 |
| E-mail address at home | .02 | .33 | .00 | .06 |
| PC ownership | .38 | .30 | .06 | 1.26 |
| Total number of PC appliances | .08 | .09 | .05 | .88 |
| Total number of communication appliances | .03 | .06 | .02 | .45 |
| Total number of hours on the PC | −.01 | .01 | −.00 | −.14 |
| Total number of hours on the Internet | .07 | .00 | .05 | .85 |
| Frequency of use | .22 | .25 | .04 | .87 |
| Amount of control felt at first experience | .18 | .06 | .17 | 3.24** |
| Preference for using a computer | .65 | .18 | .18 | 3.56** |
| Necessity for using a PC | .06 | .03 | −.10 | −1.72 |
| Comfort level during first experience | .05 | .02 | .12 | 2.26* |
| Avalable support | .18 | .12 | .08 | 1.57 |
| Constant | 7.43 | .87 | | 8.50** |

Notes—df = 319, *p<.05., **p<.01. Model fit: $R^2$ = 0.35. MSE = 1.52

In the best fitting model, four variables contribute significantly to the explanation of computer anxiety:

1.    Self-perceived computer skills,

2.    Preference for using a computer,

3.    Amount of control felt during first computer experience,

4.    Comfort level during first computer experience.

These four variables can be perceived as part of the general learning process to master a specific skill. Kolb (1984) has developed a theory about experimental learning where he suggests that learning involves a cycle of four discrete steps:

1.    Concrete experience leads to

2.    Reflection and observation on that experience, then

3.    The experience becomes abstracted and generalized on the basis of which

4.    A person actively experiments and gains new experiences.

For example, a learner who begins with a positive early experience will reflect on this experience, find the experience to be enjoyable in terms of control and comfort level, and will develop a preference for repeating the experience—specifically by using computers more frequently and for various purposes, resulting in a high-skills set. The other variables do not significantly contribute to the explanatory power of the equation. Seen from the perspective of a learning process, one could conclude that owning a computer and having access to the Internet and an e-mail address are preconditions for beginning the learning process and in themselves are not related to anxiety. The variable "available support" did not significantly contribute to the explanation of computer anxiety. During their first experiences, most respondents reported their support as high quality, which therefore did not create any difference in the amount of anxiety.

## Conclusion

This study of members of the KPN Research Technology Panel, a fairly representative sample of the Dutch population, had two major findings: respondents have homes well-equipped with telecommunication and computer devices, and that they have high level of access to the Internet both at work and at home. It is noteworthy that nearly twice as many people use a computer at home than in the working environment (n = 457 versus n = 240, respectively). Overall, computer ownership and use is high and multi-faceted. The conclusion can be drawn that these technology panel members live in homes highly equipped with new technology, although most of the products represent what might be called "proven" technology. Moreover, the majority of these "technologically smart" people use computers for work or for school, making it necessary for them to become "technologically smart." With respect to skills level, interestingly many members rate their skills as about average or insufficient (a score of five or less on a ten-point scale), depending on the application used. Computer anxiety was prevalent among the panel members and also showed a normal distribution in those that actually use a computer. In examining the phrase "technologically smart" the conclusion must be drawn that many panel members cannot be defined as "smart" computer users, due to their self-perceived lack of skills and the prevalence of anxiety.

What is the significance of these findings? One may say that the Dutch are progressively becoming "technologically smart" for a variety of reasons. Lower education levels are associated with higher anxiety. As the general level of education in The Netherlands is steadily increasing, and the proliferation of computers in primary schools is also increasing, people will acquire necessary technology skills at a very early age. One is tempted to conclude that computer anxiety will quickly be a thing of the past; while this view seems to be realistic, it is actually optimistic. The fact that a highly computer literate group such as the KPN Research Technology Panel feels insufficiently skilled and anxious indicates that there needs to be improvements made in the interaction between humans and computers. Improvements could include fostering a sense of control, mastery, and comfort level for computer users, especially when novices begin to get acquainted with new computer applications. This would make users more comfortable in using new technology and in embracing the concept that "machines become them," literally and figuratively.

## Acknowledgments

The authors thank KPN Research for permission to use its Technology Panel data. KPN Researchers Roos Bonnier and Hans Kardol were vital to the collection and initial preparation of the data.

## References

Beckers, J. J. and H. G. Schmidt. 2001. The Structure of Computer Anxiety: A Six-Factor Model. *Computers in Human Behavior*, 17: 35–49.

Chu, P. C. and E. E. Spires. 1991. Validating the Computer Anxiety Rating Scale: Effects of Cognitive Style and Computer Courses on Computer Anxiety. *Computers in Human Behavior*, 7(1-2): 7-21.

Chua, S. L., D. T. Chen, and A. F. L. Wong. 1999. Computer Anxiety and its Correlates: A Meta-Analysis. *Computers in Human Behavior*, 15(5): 609–623.

Doets, C. and T. Huisman. 1997. Digital Skills: Contemporary State in the Netherlands. Den Bosch: CINOP.

EURESCOM. 2000. Cross-Cultural Attitudes to ICTs in Everyday Life. Report of EURESCOM P-903, Heidelberg, Germany.

Katz, James E. 1998. *Connections: Social and Cultural Studies of the Telephone in American Life*. New Brunswick, NJ: Transaction Publishers.

Katz, James E. and Ronald E. Rice. 2002. *Social Consequences of Internet Use: Access, Involvement and Interaction*. Cambridge, MA: MIT Press.

Levine, T., and Donitsa S. Schmidt. 1998. Computer Use, Confidence, Attitudes, and Knowledge: A Causal Analysis. *Computers in Human Behavior*, 14(1): 125–146.

Loyd, B. H., and D. E. Loyd. 1985. The Reliability and Validity of an Instrument for the Assessment of Computer Attitudes. *Educational and Psychological Measurement*, 45(4): 903–908.

Maurer, M. M. 1994. Computer Anxiety Correlates and What They Tell Us: A Literature Review. *Computers in Human Behavior*, 10(3): 369–376.

Nelson, L. J., G. M. Wiese, and J. Cooper. 1991. Getting Started with Computers: Experience, Anxiety, and Relational Style. *Computers in Human Behavior*, 7(3): 185–202.

Simonson, M. R., M. Maurer, Torardi, M. Montag. and M. Whitaker. 1987. Development of a Standardized Technology of Computer Literacy and a Computer Anxiety Index. *Journal of Educational Computing Research*, 3(2): 231–247.

Todman, J., and E. Monaghan. 1994. Qualitative Differences in Computer Experience, Computer Anxiety, and Students' Use of Computers: A Path Model. *Computers in Human Behavior* 10(4): 529–539.

Watt. 1980. Computer literacy: What Should Schools be Doing About It? *Classroom Computer News* 1(2): 1–26.

Weil, M. M., L. D. Rosen, and S. E. Wugalter. 1990. The Etiology of Computerphobia. *Computers in Human Behavior* 6: 361-379.

# 12

# The Social Context of the Mobile Phone Use
# of Norwegian Teens

*Truls Erik Johnsen*

## Introduction

During the last few years there has been explosive growth in the number of mobile phones in the Nordic countries, particularly among the youth. Suddenly the mobile phone has turned into a necessity in their daily life, and checking for text-messages has come to be a daily routine (Katz and Aakhus 2002). The mobile phone has, as all new technology, gone through the usual phases from user denial and skepticism to acceptance in most milieus and among most age groups, and we are now able to see some vague contours of the use of future technologies like wireless web-access and so forth.

I will attempt to explain how the mobile phone has come to be a central part of people's lives. This analysis is partly based on my master's thesis in Ethnology from the University of Oslo, which was done on contract from Telenor Research and Development.

I will first present a few examples to try to illustrate the extent of the phenomenon.

During the period from 6 P.M. till 2 A.M. this New Year's Eve, there was sent three million text-messages trough the Telenor Mobile net. The first hour of the New Year the pressure on the system was extremely high, and 150 text-messages passed trough the net every second. During the first hour of year 2000 there was sent a total of 540,000 text messages. This means that every Telenor Mobile GSM-subscriber sent an average of two text messages each. (Telenor Mobil 2000)

These high numbers of text-messages indicate that there is no longer interest in analyzing what the marketing staff at Telenor Mobile has done right; however, it is of interest to evaluate why people have adapted to this communication form to this extent. A sign of what can be the cause is seen in this citation from an article about youth and mobile phones in one of the major newspapers in Norway:

A day without mobile? Then I'd get abstinence. A week without my mobile is unthink-
able, says Eda Syvertsen and shakes her head. (Engh and Vintervoll 2000)

In the following pages I will focus on two different, but very similar perspectives to try to explain citations like this. The following is a short summary of
ethnology and technology, and the definition of "meaningless communication," which is termed thus to explain the explosive growth in mobile phone
use in Norway.

## Ethnological Studies of Technology—A Short Summary

Ethnology—as practiced in Northern Europe—has a long tradition of studying humans and their relations to material objects or artifacts. This has mainly
resulted in studies of "traditional" housing and working techniques, but during
the last years, a number of scientists in the field have shown interest in modern
artifacts and technologies. One of the major contributors to this field is the
Swedish ethnologist Jan Garnert, who with the groundbreaking work, *Anden i
Lampan*, translated as *The Genie of the Lamp* (Garnert 1993), focused on the
social and cultural aspects of technology. This work has also been a major
inspiration in thinking and writing about youth and mobile phones.

Further on there have been done a number of studies related to the understanding of communication and travel, and these studies have also contributed
valuable insight and perspectives. Last, but not least, there are the traditional
studies of how artifacts, tools, and technologies shape the culture they are a part
of, and how the culture shapes them. This is in short the essence of my way of
looking at technology, as shall be seen throughout this chapter.

The perspectives presented here are, as indicated, based on a study of
Norwegian youth and mobile phones done over a period of four months in
the winter of 1999–2000. The main goal has been to uncover the social
processes the mobile phone is a part of, and to understand the said explosive
growth of the phenomenon of sending text messages. During the collection
phase of the study, a number of different approaches were used to procure the
material needed for this study. The main source of information comes from
observing the actions of the group, and studying how, when, and in what
ways they used the mobile phone. This was done in part to be able to understand the use, or to put it another way, understand the use through the informants' eyes. Notes and situational descriptions work through this method in
combination with my own reflections and experiences. To further elaborate
the findings, I have used a combination of formal and informal interviews,
along with the personal impressions of the interviewer (in this study, the
interviewer is the author of this paper), to deepen the understanding of individual social actions.

The four-month duration of interviewing the teenagers provided a solid
base for the final interviews toward the end of the project. It made it possible to

establish a common ground between the teenagers and me, and made it easier to discuss common situations and experiences. Through this it was also possible to allow the teenagers to reflect on their own use of the mobile phone, and describe their own and other experiences of the mobile phone. Phenomenologists usually refer to this social occurrence as *Lebenswelt,* meaning within the informant's own reality. The psychologist Steinar Kvale weighs this as one of the major points in the qualitative research interview, and puts the unique information in this way:

> The qualitative research interview has a unique potential for obtaining access to and describing the lived everyday world. The attempt to obtain unprejudiced descriptions entails a rehabilitation of the *Lebenswelt*—the life world—in relation to the world of science. The life world is the world as it is encountered in everyday life and given direct and immediate experience, independent of and prior to explanations. (Kvale 1996, 54)

The nearness gained through these four months could have been problematic and could also have caused what the ethnologists Ehn and Löfgren have dubbed "being blind to one's own culture" (Ehn and Löfgren 1996). On the contrary, knowledge and understanding gained through this close relation between myself, the researcher, and those studied, have given information of great value. It has enabled what Ehn and Löfgren call a "private cultural-analysis."

## The Mediated Interaction

The mobile phone cannot be understood solely as a part of a technological network but must also be considered as an important part of the social network in which the users are interrelated (Katz 2000). It connects social networks and creates an idea of belonging, and as the ordinary phone does, it strengthens the social ties that already exist in the user's social network (Katz 1999: Wellman and Tindall 1993; Wellman and Hampton 1999).

This means that understanding the communication that takes place over the mobile phone is the key to understanding the aforementioned impact of the mobile phone. We need to establish an understanding of the various functions of the communication to understand how communication technologies act in a society. The Norwegian folklorist Anne Eriksen uses the term "activity-oriented communication" (Eriksen 1989). This gives meaning to the communication whose most important aspect is to sustain and confirm that one belongs to a social network. The communication has, accordingly, a very important function apart from the instrumental exchange of information. It becomes an information-carrier without necessarily having content or function except to sustain the idea of a social fellowship:

> Communication can be understood as a strategy to sustain and activate the fellowship that already exists in the milieu or group. The activity confirms and consolidates the social network that already exists. This form of communization can therefore be called circular... (Eriksen 1989)

The function of the communication is, as we understand in this setting, not necessarily to transfer what one can call information or substance (Album 1994) in an instrumental sense, but to confirm a fellowship. This means that communication also has to exist among people in a close-knit social network. That way the conversation can work in a circular motion, and by only communicating fragments of information confirm membership to the group by referring to common understanding of the information.

In the following we shall focus on two perspectives that might help us to understand the massive impact the mobile phone has had on communication in youth milieus in Norway. These perspectives are based on anthropological works that have analyzed what is commonly known as "gossip" or "chat" (Gluckman 1963, Hannerz 1967, Blehr 1994) and a "gift" perspective on the exchange of text-messages (Mauss 1925, Bourdieu 1996). By using these perspectives I will further elaborate how communication works in a social network, and how the mobile phone acts as a mediator in this process. Through the use of these metaphors it is easier to understand the role of communication and interaction—by "seeing something as something else" we have the opportunity to study the phenomenon closer.

### "Small Talk"—Gossip and Chat

The term *gossip* might be understood as a pejorative concept when one studies the role of the mediated conversation. Therefore, we use the term *chat* as it is used by ethnologist Barbro Blehr in her study of a small community in the northern part of Sweden (Blehr 1994). Chat involves in this matter a number of different aspects and variations, and according to Blehr, it contains both communication that is understood as neutral, but also elements of critique and negative information. The Norwegian sociologist Dag Album has dubbed this form of communication as "Contentless meaningful chat" (1994), which implies the distinction between the substance of the communication and the ceremonial aspect of the "chat." The conversation gets what one can call a high degree of expressive-symbolical content (Album 1994).

Small talk, or chat, is, according to this analysis, an essential part of the studied informants' daily communication. An eighteen-year-old woman exemplifies the role of the mobile phone in the daily contact among her friends this way (author's questions are in italics):

> *Does it happen often? –That people call in the middle of the night?* —Yes, yes, actually it does. —But it's more like... not to chat...except during the weekends. ... But when people call in the night during the week it is usually because they need to talk. —That way I think it is all right to have the mobile phone switched on—so one can be there for them? I couldn't have done that on the ordinary telephone.

The mobile phone gives this young woman the ability to confirm her social status and be a part of the social network. She can "be there for someone" if there's a situation that needs it, or she can supply the "network" with small talk and gossip. As mentioned earlier, it's not the content of the communication that is important, but the mere fact that the communication takes place.

Another aspect of the mobile phone and the way it works in a social network is the way it enables the users to keep up the contact with distant friends and relatives. Due to the relatively limited form of the text message, it is possible to keep up the contact without "investing" too much time and effort. This exchange of information makes it easier to breathe life into a latent social relation, and contributes to the continuity of these (Hannerz 1967). The text message works in this manner as both a way to exchange information and as a way to strengthen the social contacts that exist between the parts in the conversation.

The conversations the users have in situations like this tended to have the characteristics of describing situations or that of storytelling. This implies naturally that it contains elements of gossip, but it's still the fact that the stories are told that is the central element in the communication. By telling each other stories and anecdotes, the participants confirm that they are a part of the same social network. If the conversation and/or story involve a third party, this third party usually is a part of the same network. Through these mechanisms the conversation works more like an expansion and strengthening of the social network rather than a way to filter out certain people in the network. This is exemplified by this extract from an interview with a sixteen-year-old girl in which she talks about how she calls her mother without having anything to say:

*So it happens that you call her without having anything to say?*—Yes, I've done that a few times...it's more like… "Mom call me, I just got to tell you what I've bought"... And other times I just call because I want to talk.

"I want to talk," she says, and confirms by this the main function of the conversation—as a social tie. This exchange of information is extremely important in the adolescence phase, the period that the informants are going through. This is a time in which friends and friendship are very important. This is in contrast to the periods before and after, where parents or parenthood are the most important elements in the daily routine. During adolescence, the social networks are under constant change and keeping contact with friends and peers is considered important. One of the young male informants explains it this way:

*Does it happen that you call without having anything to say?*—Yes…Well, maybe not. Unless the person I'm calling has information that I need. Like when I call people from my old school to know what's happening there.

"What's happening" is, in his words, the main issue in the conversation, and the explanation of the conversation as a way to gain information hinges on the "essence of the chat." The information exchanged during the conversation gives him the opportunity to keep up the contact with his old friends, and gives him the possibility to revitalize these contacts if needed. The information that he gains gives him, in other words, a way to create continuity in the social network.

The function of conversation and communication is seen as something more than the mere exchange of instrumental information. The mobile phone is used on a daily basis as the individuals' contact to their social network. They use it in a number of settings and to cover a number of needs. It becomes an invaluable element in social interaction, and in communication, which is commonly known as meaningless chat, can accordingly not be brushed aside as unnecessary. On the contrary, we need to understand it as one of the most important reasons for the immense growth of mobile phone use. It is this communication that in many ways builds what we like to call the "network society."

## Digital Gift-Giving

The use of the metaphor of the gift in an analysis of the text-message is based on the knowledge of how the gift works toward sustaining social relationships in a society. The short and limited form of the text-message (technical limitations gives only room for 160 characters) gives the user an opportunity to communicate through a mode that is extremely different from speech communication. It is fast, yet asynchronous. It is limited, but still long enough to have room for the most important phrases, like "I love you," or "Hi there!—Where's the party?" Through this different form of communication a whole new pattern of use grows. Communication through text messages often has a different function and is given a different content than the communication that takes place through speech.

I will further elaborate on this communication form that is often used to transfer information with emotional aspects or, expressed through jokes, logos, ring-tones, and so forth. This means that one can understand the communication through the text-message as more expressive than ordinary speech. A parallel to this is seen in the exchange of jokes, chain mail, and animated movies in e-mail where the content is not as important as the fact that it is sent. It is sent to confirm a social tie.

In the essay "The Gift" the anthropologist Marcel Mauss focuses on both the social and the economical implications of gift giving, and a central point in this is what he calls the three aspects of gift giving, namely the duty to give, the duty to receive, and the duty to reciprocate or to give back. These three very basic rules for gift giving have to be fulfilled so that they work in a social system. A similar system is found when teenagers send and receive text-messages. The duty to give, receive, and give back is known to the participants in the communication, and they all know the sanctions that are put upon them if they break this system. This means that even if the content of the text-message seems like nonsense, the mere fact that it takes place is most important. It gives the participants an opportunity to strengthen their social network through giving each other what one could call "digital gifts" even though the messages themselves have little or no economic value.

The importance of this "digital gift-giving" is shown in a number of statements from the informants. And they often favor the positive and nice aspects of sending and receiving text-messages. One boy recalls how he uses text messages to keep in contact with old friends:

> *So has the cell-phone enabled you to keep in contact with old friends?* Yes, probably it has. Yes, at least people from my old school. We tend to drift apart into different milieus.... But we only send each other text-messages…just jokes and stuff (laughs)…
> *So why do you send them then?* Well…I don't know… maybe I thing that some day our roads will meet again…

He uses the phrase "Just jokes and stuff…" but through sending this text message—or gift—he gives strength to the understanding of the expressive side of the communication. What he sends has no value except as "social glue" that keeps the contact between partners in a social network, and as shown here, to keep in contact with old classmates. The text messages are also used to keep in contact with close friends and relatives. One of the girls says it this way:

> *Do you ever get jokes sent to you?* Nooo.... (smiling).... yes, yes, and animations too! ..I've received quite a few really funny ones, but I have saved so many that there isn't room for more in the memory of the phone. I got stuff like this one (shows the message) "Thinking of you," and I got this from my sister "Love you sis." And here's one "You put a smile on my face whenever you send me a message."

Sayings, stories, and jokes that normally are told face-to-face becomes mediated through the text messages of the mobile phone, and give the actors a way to sustain their social network-ties without relation to the spatial distance between the participants in the communication. The communication becomes a part of what James Katz has noted as the capturing of industrial technology for social purposes (Katz 1999). Text messages, and talking on the mobile phone gives the actors—or users—an opportunity to be a part of a social network, which is disembedded from "place" as we know it in a pre-communication technology sense. The communication becomes a part of the daily routine where one gives away a continuous stream of signals to the surroundings. It becomes a part of the social ties that keep the society together.

Attention given to friends and relatives through the text messages becomes the essence of the communication, and as we have seen from the previous statements of the youths, they have a very strong consciousness about this. The text message to the receiver is perceived as an attention-getter, and therefore, demands a reply. A clear parallel to this process is found in the sending and receiving of postcards (Keesing and Keesing 1971). The economical aspect of the gift isn't important, but the fact that it is sent is what counts:

> A gift is a statement about the relationship between giver and receiver. The thing given is a symbol of that relationship, and hence has value and meaning beyond its material worth. Furthermore, the relationship established or continued by the gift implies reciprocity. (Keesing and Keesing 1971)

Reciprocity is, in other words, the central element in the process, and it is one of the key elements that make the "digital gift-giving" possible. But as has been shown, this is not unique to the exchange of messages, as it is the norm in all exchange of gifts in nearly all known culture.

The reciprocity and the time between giving and giving back are crucial elements in gift-giving, and knowledge of these elements is required to establish a common understanding of the exchange. The Norwegian anthropologist Thomas Hylland Eriksen has phrased it like this: "Exchange of gifts creates this way social obligation and establishes permanents ties between the parties of the communication. There's nothing like a free gift" (Eriksen 1995). One of the girls explains how she looks at how time interacts with the duty to reciprocate:

> If you send a message to a friend...how fast do you need to be answered? On the minute maybe? —Actually I demand an instant answer. Most people in my age group actually do, because we have the cell-phone nearby all the time. No one leaves it home for a day, and if they do it's just because they've forgotten it. People always carry their mobile phone, and they never turn it off…

There is, in other words, an assumption that the other partner in the communication, or gift giving, replies instantly. If not, the basic rules of gift giving are broken, and the social ties are put under pressure. If the receiver doesn't reply to the message, it is considered a split in the friendship. To break the chain of giving and giving back becomes a way of "waging war" to use a term from Marcel Mauss (1995).

## Summary

The gift and gossip has been seen here in the role of establishing and nurturing social ties and connections, and therefore the mobile phone, all of a sudden, has established a strong position in this process. Through analyzing the role of the mobile phone in an everyday setting, new knowledge, patterns of use, and understanding are established. There is no longer a question about whether the teenagers actually need this form of communication, but the real question lies in what role this mode of communication has in their lives (Wynn and Katz 2000). I have tried to show that voice and text-messaging communication acts more like a part of a social network, than as a "stand-alone" technology outside society or culture. The mobile phone connects people and enables them to communicate in ways we know from face-to-face interaction without the limitations of space. It has become what Anthony Townsend calls the umbilical cord of the network society:

Individuals live in this phonespace—they can never let it go, because it is their primary link to the temporally, spatially fragmented network of friends and colleagues they have constructed for themselves. It has become their new umbilical cord, pulling the Network Society's digital infrastructure into their very bodies. (Townsend 2000)

# References

Album, Dag. 1994. Innholdsløs meningsfull prat. *Sosiologisk Tidsskrift* 2.

Blehr, Barbro. 1994. *Lokala gemenskaper,* Stockholm: Carlssons Bokförlag.

Bordieu, Pierre. 1996. *Symbolsk Makt: Artikler i utvalg*, Oslo, Norway: Pax.

Castells, Manuel. 1996. *The Rise of the Network Society*. Oxford: Blackwell Publishers.

Ehn, Billy and Löfgren, Orvar. 1996a. *Kulturanalys*, Malmö: Gleerups.

Ehn, Billy and Löfgren, Orvar. 1996b. *Vardagslivets Etnologi*, Stockholm: Natur och Kultur.

Engh, Christine and Lene Vintervoll. 2000. Ungdom blir mobiljunkier (Youth Becomes Mobile-junkies). In *Aftenposten,* excerpt translated by T.E. Johnsen, Dec. 29. http://tux1.aftenposten.no/nyheter/iriks/d182549.htm.

Eriksen, Anne. 1989. Massekulturens kommunikasjonsform. In *Budkavlen årg.* 68, excerpt translated by T.E. Johnsen.

Eriksen, Thomas Hylland. 1995. Postscript in Mauss, Marcel. *Gaven* (The Gift). Oslo: Cappelen (originally published 1925).

Garnert. 1993. *Anden i lampan,* Stockholm: Carlssons.

Garnert. 1990. *The Consequences of Modernity.* Cambridge: Polity Press.

Gluckman, Max. 1963. *Gossip and Scandal: Current Anthropology* 4(3).

Hannerz, Ulf. 1967. Gossip, Networks and Culture: *Ethnos* 32.

Hughes, Thomas P. 1987. The Evolution of Large Technological Systems. In *The Social Construction of Technological Systems*, ed. Hughes Bijker and Pinch, Cambridge, MA: MIT Press.

Katz, James E. 1999. *Connections: Social and Cultural Studies of the Telephone in American Life.* New Brunswick, NJ: Transaction Publishers.

Katz, James E. 2001. The Telephone. Entry in the *International Encyclopedia of Social Science* (2nd edition). Amsterdam: Elsevier. 2001. Vol. 23, pages 15558-65.

Katz, James E. and M. Aakhus, eds. 2002. *Perpetual Contact: Mobile Communication, Private Talk, Public Performance.* Cambridge and New York: Cambridge University Press.

Keesing, Roger M. and Felix M. Keesing. 1971. *New Perspectives in Cultural Anthropology.* New York: Holt, Rinehart and Winston, Inc.

Keller, Suzanne, The Telephone in New (and Old) Communities. 1977. In *The Social Impact of the Telephone*, ed. Ithiel de Sola Pool. Cambridege, MA: The MIT Press.

Kvale, Steinar. 1996. *InterViews*, Sage Publications.

Mauss, Marcel. *Gaven* (The Gift). 1995. Oslo: Cappelen (originally published 1925).

Telenor Mobil. 2000. press release (Jan. 1), excerpt translation by T.E. Johnsen. http://presse.telenor.no/PR/200001/798830_1.html

Townsend, Anthony M. 2000. *Life in the Real-Time City: Mobile Telephones and Urban Metabolism* (Aug. 30). http://www.informationcity.org/research/real-time-city/index.htm.

Urry, John. 2000. *Sociology Beyond Societies—Mobilities For The Twenty-First Century*, Routledge: London.

Wellman, Barry and Keith Hampton. 1999. Living Networked in a Wired World. *Contemporary Sociology* 28 (6).

Wellman, Barry and David B. Tindall, 1993. How Telephone Networks Connect Social Networks. *Progress in Communication Sciences, vol. XII.*

Wynn, Eleanor and James E. Katz. 2001. Teens on the Telephone. *Info*, vol. 2 (4): August 2000, 401-419.

# 13

# Two Modes of Maintaining Interpersonal Relations Through Telephone: From the Domestic to the Mobile Phone

*Christian Licoppe*

## Introduction

The social sciences constantly over represent network society, overemphasizing the individual's involvement in relationships. The theory of social networks, for example, is based largely on the idea of connected individuals who calculate their opportunities in a realm of relationships that defines their social capital. (Burt 1992; Lazega 1992; Forsé and Degenne 1994; Katz and Rice 2002). This type of theory is also at the center of discourse on organizations (Veltz 2000), including those of management consultants and theoreticians who, with more operational intents, believe in social flexibility and the network structures thought to maximize it. This thinking has also become a general subject of interest in sociology, forming a process of justification and equivalence between individuals. It also characterizes what Luc Boltanski has suggested calling the *cité connexionniste*: an individual motivated by a desire to be connected, fully equipped with a set of managed relationships that exist among fluctuating objectives and temporary plans. The individual's greatness, then, lies in his capacity to jump from one project to the next and avoid getting stuck in a given position (Boltanski and Chiappello 1999).

As these authors so rightly point out, the individual who operates in the *cité connexionniste* is also heavily equipped in information technologies (Boltanski and Chiappello 1999). James Katz and Ronald Rice see social and political worlds that are increasingly mutually influenced by ever-larger circles of players. Networks become ever denser and richer, and entertainment, personal, and information networks become more intertwined (Katz and Rice 2002). This of course is also related to, and anticipated in, the ideas set forth in James Katz's impressive study of the telephone in American life. Yet beyond the Internet,

171

Katz and Rice are not highly specific as to precisely how these interpersonal networks might change, and while they assert that the Internet is just one of many important technologies of communication, their attention is tightly focused on the Internet, with little attention paid to the mobile telephone.

In this chapter, we aim to demonstrate a new and useful aspect of the sociology of network society, starting with telephone communication (see Katz 2001). Long before the advent of computers and multimedia tools, the telephone was the main medium of interaction between people, either in a vocal mode or in the more recent mode of textual messages sent from telephone terminals (Katz 1999). So my purpose here is to demonstrate how the mobility and particularly the portability recently acquired by telephones, rather than the hypothetical properties of multimedia interaction, constitutes a significant point of entry into a sociological analysis of the network society (Katz and Aakhus 2002).

We can identify two distinct practices in the management of telephone relations between close friends and family. One practice consists of open, often long conversations in which people take their time, at appropriate times of the day; the open dialogue and the "settling down" into phone conversation, is a sign of engagement in the relationship. The other practice consists of short, frequent calls, the content of which is often secondary to the act of calling. The continuous nature of this flow of isolated, short calls maintains an illusion of constant connection, an idea that the link can be activated at any moment; this type of phone relationship is thus reassuring as it relates to the other person's engagement in the relationship.

Through several surveys on the domestic phone, the mobile phone, and SMSs on mobile phones,[1] it is shown how each device, without completely determining its uses, influences patterns of use and contributes to greater clarity in users' representations of such patterns. Noting the time-sequence when these devices are brought to markets introduces a historical dimension; conclusions are drawn on the gradual entrenchment of the "connected" phone practices for the management of relationships and of a social networked representation, regarding the appearance of several mobile devices and services. This serves as an interpretation of the emergence of a network society with regard to practices and representations.

This domestic phone study was carried out in 1997 and 1998, before the sudden upsurge in the use of mobile phones, and is described elsewhere (Smoreda and Licoppe 2001; Licoppe and Smoreda 2001). The results were confirmed by subsequent research carried out in 2000 by Michael Eve, Chantal de Gournay, and Zbigniew Smoreda who provided access to some of their preliminary results for this chapter.

A number of results relating to the mobile phone study have been or are about to be published (Licoppe and Heurtin 2001; Licoppe and Heurtin 2002).

The SMSs on mobile phone section is based on the reinterpretation of a purely qualitative study on uses of the SMS, initiated by Carole-Anne Rivière and Christian Licoppe in 2000, to be published at a later date.

### Maintaining a Distant Link by Taking Time for Telephone Conversations: A Use Repertoire Clearly Observable in the Case of the Domestic Phone

One consistent result of residential fixed-phone usage studies is that a larger geographic distance between callers results in longer conversations and also longer intervals between calls (Claisse and Rowe 1993; Rivière 2000). This effect is even greater when the callers are well acquainted, such as close friends or family. A recent study on the development of telephone behavior before and after people move (Licoppe and Smoreda 2001) produced even more striking results, showing that

- Two people in the same geographical area will have a consistent average duration of time spent on the phone.

- The duration of the call becomes shorter when people move closer together.

- The duration of the call becomes longer when people move further apart.

- As the frequency of calls increases their duration decreases, and vice-versa

The common interpretation of these results is a relation of geographic distance to a decline in face-to-face contact. This interpretation, which is based on the idea that face-to-face is the richest form of contact, equates geographical distance to relational distance. The telephone becomes a resource to maintain the relationship, as the following example of a student indicates: "If I don't call them [her parents] for a week they worry and call me, so I never forget…or hardly ever." Personal expectations crystallize to the point of creating veritable telephone rituals, as in the case of a young woman who calls her father at his home very regularly, and complains of the lack of spontaneity in this type of telephone relationship: "It's difficult, it's not natural for me to phone every Sunday afternoon, for example, like to tell him everything about my week. I prefer it when it's kind of, you know, I think about my father and I call him." In this case, *not* calling can undermine the emotional frame of the relationship.

This type of call tends to be relatively long. People ask about each other, take the time to talk without any clear purpose, as in the case of a young girl who calls her parents "without anything special to say, just to talk," to tell them about "the little incident that happened the day before or something that happened in the street, I don't know, anything. *And important things.*" For both respondents, having an open conversation becomes a sign of a personal bond (Goffman 1971), which is especially important since the relationship has become more vulnerable due to permanent or temporary physical distance. This reflexive interpretation in terms of the maintenance of the relationship is, moreover, fairly explicit, as in the case of the following student whose boyfriend lives far away, and who tells about how she calls him every evening "usually for three-quarters of an hour" to tell him "what we were going to do, when we were going to see each other" but mostly "we told each other about our days…(and then) *we had the impression we weren't so far apart. It brings one closer.*"

Statistical studies on the distribution of these long calls shows that calls made from home are mostly to other domestic phones. Most of the calls are made in the evening after 7 P.M., and tend to last longer the later they are made. This tendency corresponds to the higher probability that the members of the household will be at home and available. The number of calls decreases sharply after 10 P.M., although the average duration of calls increases (Licoppe and Smoreda 2001). This is due to two factors: first, relatively explicit conventions of courtesy make calls after 10 P.M. impolite, except in the case of very close friends and family. Second, after 10 P.M. people are generally expected to be more available since they have finished most constraining routine domestic activities. Because they occur in domestic settings, these long conversations between people who know each other very well are influenced by the rhythms and time frames of each household.

This type of telephone use will be referred to as the "conversational" mode of managing telephone relations between close friends and family, since it consists of open, relatively long conversations in which people ask about each other, at a time often set aside for that purpose. The term "conversational" stresses the open nature of the interaction, which allows time for the conversation to develop rather than following a predetermined dialogue with a sequence of reciprocal turn-taking. In some cases, one of the participants may talk during most or all of the conversation. The aim of this participant is to relate a personal event, no matter how commonplace, and thus to reaffirm the relationship by ratifying a shared memory of events which were not experienced together.

This "conversational" mode is not the only possible type of telephone relationship. Especially among young users, there tend to be occasional, short, targeted calls that take on a distinct relational mode. For example, one of the friends of a young woman leaves multiple messages on her home phone answering machine (a habit in their group): "Sometimes he leaves me five messages in a row: I'm calling you. What're you doing? You're not in, I'm thinking of you." A distinction emerges between several brief calls and calls made in a more "conversational" mode, as in the case of a young girl who makes many practical calls to her boyfriend during the day but calls him every evening in another mode: "On the other hand, in the evening we just tell each other everything that happened in the day." Domestic phone users rarely take part in these multiple, brief call in maintaining relationships between close friends. By contrast, it is frequent among users of the mobile phone.

## Maintaining a Link through a "Continuous" Telephone Presence:
## Use Centred on Connection

Calls made on mobile phones are shorter than those made on fixed phones: calls are, on average, one-and-a-half minutes as opposed to five minutes. In a 1999 study on new mobile phone users whose calls and behaviours were monitored throughout the year, it was observed that calls of less than forty-five seconds accounted for one-half of all mobile phones calls compared to only one-third of calls from domestic phones. This significant statistic of short calls on the mobile phone was even more marked among young users. In all age groups, mobile phone users who participated in the study demonstrated consistent types of phone usage based on short calls with a precise and targeted goal. Users generally gave three reasons for these types of calls:

- Cost.

- Coordination checks—determining arrival times, informing someone of lateness, confirming an appointment, retrieving an access code. Noteworthy uses of the mobile phone almost always include a story of urgent and extraordinary coordination that would not have been possible without the mobile phone.

- Embarrassment—The shortening of calls because of the social situation of the call recipient. Since, in theory, the mobile phone can be used regardless of time or place, it increases the risk of a call being received at an inappropriate time. But often recipients, using voice tone and pace, will make their embarrassment obvious to the caller. This shortens the interaction, and politely allows it to be postponed.

This constant ability to be reached has particularly interesting implications in the case of close relationships between partners or close friends. These relationships in the private sphere are reaffirmed through a series of face-to-face and fixed-phone interactions constituting a "continuous conversation" (Berger and Kellner 1973; Berger and Luckmann 1966). Success of these contacts reaffirms the importance of the relationship and also reaffirms a particular reality constructed in the context of this conversation. These relationships are both structuring and precarious, and their maintenance is important. Consequently, the possibility of being able to reach each other regardless of time or place is both a new resource and a new threat— a resource because the possibilities of making this private continuous conversation even more continuous are enhanced. A threat because, due to this theoretic constant reachability, each failure indicates unavailability, suggesting that one of the relationship participants is too absorbed to maintain contact. In this context, the mobile is used to reassure the other person and to reaffirm the link, by means of very short calls. (This notion of distance is subjective, and is based on the user's perception in terms of reciprocal rights and duties.)

For example, a sailing enthusiast regularly calls his wife "to tell her that I'll be late, to let her know…" In his use of the mobile phone "there is the aspect of security and that of domestic organization." In other words, he distinguishes between one type of call for coordination and the other short call to reassure. The aims of reassurance and of maintaining a close link through small communicative gestures tend to merge, as in the following example of a woman and her husband who is a truck driver:

> With my husband, it is mainly to know where he is. Because he works in Saint Denis, which is quite a way away, and he doesn't have easy hours…so I do like to know where he is.…But on the other hand it's really nice to be able to…because we have access to things we didn't have before. I know when my husband's got a problem with the car, he calls me, or when he's stuck on the road. I tell myself it's one less worry.…Otherwise, I wouldn't even know where he was, and so on. Sometimes he leaves work at five, and when he gets home it's already nine, it's taken him four hours to get home: ring road jammed, Bois de Boulogne jammed.…Well for me who's at home, waiting, for four hours I'm on edge. And for a lot of situations it's like that.

Calling on a mobile becomes an act of domestic devotion in which reassurance is experienced in the mind as well as in the body. Now she can go to sleep.

Two things threaten the success of this mode of maintaining telephone relationships:

- The potential unavailability of the other person, which implies a need for justification that weighs heavily on the participants because they have relied on multiple calls to construct a telephonic presence.

- The threat of calls becomes a method of control or of "policing": "Sometimes when I call my husband and I hear that noise I say 'But where are you, in a bar?' I sense he's uncomfortable and I say 'No, don't feel bad, it's okay.' And the people he's with are going to know who's on the phone. But he knows I'm casual about that. But it's true; he was really embarrassed. But it was two o'clock, and usually he's already at work. And that time he'd left later, he was with his work mates. But so embarrassed!"

Note that unintentional information on context is provided not by what is seen but by what is heard—which places the receiver of the call in the immediate element of their context.

The possibility of being able to call at any time from a mobile phone is in conflict with potential availability of the call's receiver, which means hat the caller has to evaluate when their target will most likely be available. Users' anticipation becomes increasingly complex as they try to imagine other's schedules:

> It depends, I see my husband, depending on the time, well, for example, I know it's a time when I don't really know where he is, if he's on his way home or still at work, so I'll first phone him at work because often he's still at work rather than coming home. But there are times, in the morning for example, it's happened that I've needed to reach him, like when I've got the wrong key or something like that, I get him directly on his mobile, because I know he's still in the car. At lunch I phone on his mobile because I tell myself he's gone to eat, that he's not at work anymore. It depends on the time.

The degree of the person's accessibility—whether calls are taken directly or heard through a message service, which increases chances of successful anticipation of a user's availability—is a decisive factor in the development of mobile traffic (Licoppe and Heurtin 2001).

Availability is not the only element of regulation in mobile phone interaction. The question of cost also plays a part, albeit an ambiguous one. The possibility of phoning free-of-charge stimulates the fantasy of a continuous connection. In the year 2000, operators launched (and immediately withdrew) special offers with free calls in the evenings and on weekends. Several interviewees told of friends who used this to maintain a constant connection, with the mobile phone connected next to their beds so that they could listen to each other sleeping. These "folk stories" of the mobile phone (see Katz and Aakhus 2002) express the desire for constant mobile connection, now exploited in mobile phone ads. But the reality of mobile phone users is prepaid cards and flat rates. Many say they shorten their calls, even if it means giving up interaction that was previously in a "conversational" mode—such as one student's mobile communication with his girlfriend: "Uh, yeah, not for my girlfriend, I prefer the mobile because otherwise it takes hours, just for one call!" In this context, the habit of making multiple short calls makes it possible to maintain a more continuous presence without exceeding the limits of the mobile phone plan.

The result of these factors is a somewhat vague usage in which connections are maintained by an increased "presence" through short and frequent calls from mobile phones, which can make the act of calling more important than what is said. In this sense, the mobile phone becomes an almost indirect way of maintaining a relationship (Jakobson 1973). In the context of a relationship between close friends or family, these calls tend to be more frequent, since an increased presence provides a more reassuring link. This type of relationship tends to detach telephone interaction from place and content; the relationship seems reduced to the series of calls which sustain it. Wherever they go, individuals seem to take along their social network that can ideally be activated at any moment. Making multiple calls, then, is a way of experiencing and reassuring oneself of the connection's permanence.

Sociologist Maurice Hallbwachs (1997) highlights the feelings of permanence created by repeated social interactions in places, giving social groups a collective memory through a sense of place, and, in, turn, the imprint of social groups on place. In this case, a sense of permanence is given by a device that is both technological and social—in this context, the stability of the connection (which is also a "place" in the space of social links) replaces the material place. However, the relationship stability that the mobile phone allows is constantly in flux; contexts are always likely to change the "permanence" of these interactions—for example, the atmospheres created by sound: "No, but sometimes it's maybe just to hear a background noise, something that makes us think of the place where the other person may be. Or silence, as you said when someone calls you at home. You hear the mobile voice, and at the same time no background noise. *It's disturbing!*"

The format of the mobile connection is not directly determined by the nature of the relationship, even if the relationship is more or less adapted to this form of communication. Some relationships are more prone to depend on such practices, especially those involving frequent contact in which alternating telephone calls and face-to-face encounters impact on one another. Age is important because it distinguishes different social stages in life where social networks take on different forms; for example, the younger the users of mobile phones, the larger the proportion of short calls. From one life stage to the next, the question of availability is negotiated differently. The later stages in life which involve later phases of friendship can reduce certain telephone interaction to a "conversational" and quasi-ritual mode, as in the following case of a pensioner and his good friends who live in the country: "our friendship was based on four phone calls a year, except for the times we were able to meet, so these three or four phone calls a year carry on…When I called them I spent a half an hour with them. I found that half hour in the evenings, at 8.30 or 9 P.M." By contrast, with his Parisian friends who are easier to see, occasional phone calls remain a habit: "No, those we see the most are friends or family in Paris, just because it's easier. It's so simple to make a phone call. Can you come round this afternoon?" But the identification of this "connected" management of close relationships as an autonomous practice seems fairly clear in all users of mobile phones; while the intensity of use may vary, its explicit identification largely cuts across differences in age and life-style.

The indirect communication mode and its repertoire of "connected" uses cannot be linked *unequivocally* to a technological device (the domestic phone or the mobile phone), even if the device offers a different type of communication practice. Calls for coordination and reassurance were observed in the case of use of fixed phones (at home, at the office, and elsewhere). Conversely, the mobile phone is not used only for short calls—over 15 percent of the time spent on mobile phones is devoted to conversations of over fifteen minutes, which is enough for a long conversation (taken from a study on the use of mobile phones bought for personal, rather than professional use). Like calls on domestic phones, these long conversations on mobile phones take place after 7 P.M. Even if the constraint of being at home is partly removed by the portability of the mobile terminal, the user's availability is affected. Beyond an apparent demand for decontextualization of mobile phone interaction, conventions of politeness, announcements of calling place location, and domestic time frames remain determining factors for long conversations on mobile phones, due to both parties' need for availability.

Even if technical devices do not entirely determine what social aspects will change, they do add new dimensions to old ways of connecting. The portability of the mobile phone does seem to prompt users to phone more frequently and to create a more defined "connected" mode of telephone interaction that results in meaningful small gestures among close friends and family. Therefore, the introduction of new technology and new devices establishes an historical dimension, both in the variety of uses and in its degree of explanation as a meaningful practice. This idea will now be explored by considering a new possibility for interaction that appeared more recently on mobile phones.

### Development of the SMS, a new Resource for the "Connected" Link Practice

Short message services (SMSs) started to develop significantly in France in 2000. These messages of a maximum of 160 characters in text mode are written and received on mobile phones and billed per unit/message. Because of this structural constraint, the SMS is seen as an additional resource for short, isolated communicative gestures. This section reviews the results of an empirical and qualitative year 2000 study on users of SMSs, from the particular viewpoint of managing personal relations on a mobile terminal.

It is interesting to note that when this survey was conducted, the vast majority of the correspondents of SMS users were very close friends or boy/girlfriends and were often the people they saw most. (These users were mostly in the fifteen-to-thirty-five age group and used mobile phones extensively for vocal communication.) One of the reasons given by users was the limited length of messages. With close friends, the density of the experience shared in an intense and lasting relationship allows the use of codes, allusions, and veiled references—this type of interaction is hardly relevant for an outsider:

> No, but that's really a hard core, it's not the same. I think it's mainly a question of complicity. ...Yes, we allow ourselves more, well yes, that's it, I mean, we're briefer, as I said, we use allusions, things like that. Don't have to make sentences. I can imagine someone we don't know so well, or even that we do know well but who's more of an acquaintance, I can't see myself sending them a message. In this telegraphic style, all that.

This is not their only use; SMSs also serve to sort out problems of coordination, for example.

In the context of interaction between close friends, SMSs contribute significantly to strengthening telephonic presence through frequent small gestures. This mode is clearly distinguished from "conversational" practices: "An SMS is a thought at that moment, and so as not to bother the other person for 5 or 10 minutes, at work. But it's just a little thought, like that. Otherwise, the phone call, rather in the evenings, I'd say, it's short conversations, advice, or anything concerning the couple." Such a description more clearly defines "connected" use as a particular practice. Some SMS users go so far as to oppose the two practices and to reject the "conversational" in favor of the "connected" mode:

Yes, I don't know, for example, *instead of talking for three hours about our lives,* ... for example, our aim would rather be to see each other, to arrange to meet, and directly ask when we can see each other, directly through the message. *Instead of going through: yeah, you okay? and so on, because in a normal call you always go through all that.* But with the SMS you go directly through the message you want to send.

What is striking in these interviews is the extent to which this sense of a "connected" practice comes across clearly, even more so perhaps than in surveys on telephone conversations: "it's not something essential, but it shows when we're far apart like that, that we are thinking of our brother, our sister or sometimes our girlfriend." Sometimes this goes so far as to redefine customary rituals, such as saying goodnight: "It's true that SMSs are great. I've got a friend who sent me one 'Good night sweetie. Have nice dreams about Tom Cruise'— a lot of things like that! It's true that before going to sleep we send short messages to people, to say goodnight. We don't phone them, a message is cooler."

The short message seems to allow users to decontextualize their interactions more than, for example, with a phone conversation. Almost all of them refer to "anywhere, any time," emphasizing the impulsive nature of the message, apparently detached from habits and routines: "It's not related to my daily habits. I mean, I don't get up and say to myself, right, I'm going to send a short message to someone. It's really a question of mood. For the past few weeks I didn't think about it, so I didn't send any." Users also highlight the fact that the message is not assigned to a particular context or place: "Oh no, not at all, no special places, it just depends on where I am, if I absolutely have to send one or if I just feel like it for fun, just a little romantic message or something, it depends. So it can be at work if I've got five minutes, or at home, also because I've got five minutes, it can be in the street, anything. There aren't really special places, no."

The exchange of gestures reaffirming the person's presence and relationship are, in this case, quite typical of social conventions (de Certeau 1990) in which the user takes advantage of inherent situations and opportunities that arise from casual social interaction. This use seems to have become so natural that the materiality of the technologies fades into the background: "As soon as I have five minutes I send one. I never force myself, it's, right, let me tell you, I had five, okay, I sent you a message, there you are. And often, I often think about my kids, my girlfriend, lots of things, and then it's true, I quickly let them know that I haven't forgotten them." This almost systematic discourse of continuous connection becomes a characteristic of the user; the SMS user embraces the value of the "connected" practices that SMSs offer. However, in reality, the actual use of the SMS differs. The same individuals, when questioned further, disclose a more place- and time-dependent representation of their use. The majority say they regularly send mini-messages, especially from home in the evenings, a minority say they send them from work, and most of them describe occasional use in public places or when they are travelling. Even though the "anytime, anywhere" concept does not assert itself in actual SMS usage, the users' ideological belief in this mode of communication demonstrates social acceptance of these "connected" practices.

A second sign of social acceptance of "connected" practices is the fact that the SMS can constitute a strategic resource in managing relationships. In the case of the SMS, the brief nature of interactions, the weaker demand for reciprocity, the written form, or the terminal and its screen tend to act as a barrier between people and thus become a set of mediums for the management of relational difficulties. For example, it can make the expression of aggressiveness in a friendship bearable: "The SMS enables one to stand back. Even when the person calls to send a very aggressive message, *there is always the telephone between you*. It's less violent, I'd say. One flares up less easily, I find, and the memory of vocal aggressiveness doesn't stay in one's mind." The same applies to a loved one. For one interviewee, in love with a dancer with totally different working hours from his own (he has a day-time job, she dances at night), SMSs are part of a strategy to maintain a romantic presence, to be able to say things without seeming to require a potentially awkward reply:

> Yes, I threw in somewhere…like for example…a sentence like 'I'm missing you,' I know that if I say that on the phone there'll be a silence afterwards, not because she doesn't want to reply but because she takes it for herself and she keeps it, in fact, whereas if I put it on the phone, at least, I'm sure there won't be a silence and that I won't have to get the conversation going again afterwards. It's a sentence and then afterwards that's it.

SMSs can therefore be woven into the story of the relationship as an element used to negotiate its evolution or a difficult phase:

> That's exactly what happened with my best friend. We weren't on speaking terms anymore: for two or three months we just sent each other SMSs, but ghastly stuff. I can't even tell you what words we used. He phoned me two weeks ago and said, "listen, in fact, I was half joking in those messages. I loved irritating you and so on 'cause I know you get upset so easily.…" So, for example, if it had been on the phone he wouldn't have been able to backtrack.…You see, it's not the same.…We let it go as if he was just teasing me whereas on the phone he wouldn't have been able to tease me like that.

## Conclusion

By synthesizing several communication studies on the domestic and the mobile phone in the form of conversations or SMSs, two practical patterns of practice were revealed in telephone relationships between close friends and family members. The first consists of conversations that are generally spread out in time, long, and sometimes even ritualized, in which taking one's time to converse is a sign of the strength of each person's commitment to the relationship. The second consists of generally short and frequent communicative gestures: conversations or vocal or textual messages at irregular times. It is the frequency and continuity of this flow, which guarantees the strength of the communicators' mutual engagement in the relationship and not necessarily the content of the communication. In this sense these modalities of interaction, either "conversational" or "connected," constitute variable methods of managing telephone relationships between close friends, with regard to both phone uses and the social implications of these uses. The definitions of the two types of communication are particularly vague due to the wide variety of telephone practices and interactions. This chapter has nevertheless attempted to demonstrate how users distinguish these practices with different levels of clarity and interpretation. This variety of practices demonstrates a wide range in the types of relationships and situations, as well as in the technical devices through which interaction takes place.

It has been seen how the advent of the mobile phone is accompanied by the development of the "connected" mode of telephone interaction and how users now define this mode with greater clarity. This practice is particularly significant in the case of mobile phone use for several reasons:

- It is portable, to the extent of becoming an extension of the user.

- Since there is no mobile directory, users *give* their number to a chosen group (Licoppe and Heurtin 2001). In a "gift and counter-gift" culture, this ritual exchange represents the user's entry into a mode of access in which the frequency and continuity are no longer limited by access to localized communication tools.

- The mobile phone includes an extensively used, portable, and readily consultable address list containing the numbers of those people with whom the user has telephone contact.

Thus equipped, the user feels that it is possible to engage in telephone communication at any time—however, the accessibility and availability of the caller and his or her contact determines communication in a "connected" mode (Rifkin 2000). Mobile phone communication is defined by constraints of availability due to activities, places, and times; availability of the other person is still a question of calculation. Characteristically the discourse of SMS users does not require immediate availability, which most closely follows the ideal of the "anywhere, anytime" communication typical of the connectionist world.

Nevertheless, it would be a mistake to directly relate the development of relationships in a "connected" mode to a particular device. These relationships existed well before mobile phones—for example, frequent and reassuring calls can occur from the closest corded phone: home, work, public booth, place of transit. But even though the technological devices do not determine usage, it does exert an influence—certain aspects of relationships can be more convenient, more visible, more incorporated, and thus more conventional or naturalized by a particular device. Management of relationships in the "connected" mode was already present with the fixed phone, was more firmly entrenched with use of the mobile phone, and solidified with the use of SMSs. This new mobile mode of interaction developed until it constituted a strategic resource in the maintenance of relationships between close friends and family because SMSs are brief, because mediation is more visible and prominent (the screen acts as a barrier between people), and because the demand for reciprocity is considerably reduced. It may seem, then, that the accumulation of communication technology influences history, both in the variety practices and in its potential to become a meaningful practice in itself.

The establishment of a "connected" communication pattern strengthens social structures in which users carry their links around with them, ready to activate them at any moment. The structure of the "connected" link thus seems to be a required condition of the new communication technology described and highlighted in this chapter—connected individuals who must calculate when and where they can connect, which results in a definition of their social connection. What is at issue is not the random emergence of a networked social world and an individual as a bundle of links on her or his own networked ground. Rather, the process of developing these social connections is a gradual anchoring of a structure through multiple modes of communicating that compose this "connected" social arrangement. These communication modes help to define the changing social patterns; not necessarily true but pertaining to the realm of truth, as Michel Foucault would have it.

There is a hypothesis that this "connected" practice of interaction might be given a treatment similar to that of panoptic technologies by Foucault. For him, these was a vast range of diverse but coherent practices scattered throughout a wide variety of contexts, and which subverted the ideal of the Enlightenment. This author would like to propose treatment of the "connected" mode of managing relationships as providing meaning to a vast range of practices in a growing diversity of contexts and communicative technology. These practices would facilitate the use of these technologies and reduce the relevant economic, social, and cognitive costs, and constitute the basis for the representation of a networked social world. It is therefore useful to explore these practices in all of their variations, which transcend the context of the telephone relationship and sociability between close friends and family considered in this chapter.

## Note

1.    This section is based on the reinterpretation of a purely qualitative study on uses of the SMS, initiated by Carole-Anne Rivière and Christian Licoppe in 2000, to be published at a later date. I wish to thank Carole-Anne Rivière for elements relevant to the research developed here.

## References

Berger, Peter and Thomas Luckmann. 1966. *The Social Construction of Reality: A Treatise in the Sociology of Knowledge*. New York: Doubleday.

Berger, Peter and Hansfried Kellner. 1964. Marriage and the Construction of Reality, *Diogenes* 46: 1–24. (Trans. Le mariage et la construction de la réalité, *Dialogue*, 1988(4):6-23).

de Certeau, Michel. 1990. *L'invention du quotidien, tome I. Arts de faire*, Deuxième édition, Paris, Gallimard. (Published originally as *The Practice of Everyday Life*, Berkeley: University of California Press, 1984).

Burt, Ronald. 1992. *Structural Holes: The Social Structure of Competition*. Cambridge, MA: Harvard University Press.

Chabrol, Jean Louis et Périn. 1993. *Les pratiques de communication des Français*. Paris: Télécom/DPS.

Chiappello, Eve and Luc Boltanski. 1999. *Le nouvel esprit du capitalisme*. Paris: Gallimard.

Claisse, Gérard and Frantz Rowe. 1993. Téléphone, communication et sociabilité: des pratiques résidentielles différenciées, *Sociétés contemporaines* 14-15: 163–189, Paris: L'Harmattan.

Degenne, Alain and Michel Forsé. 1994. *Les réseaux sociaux*. Paris: Armand Colin.

Foucault, Michel. *Surveiller et punir. La naissance de la prison*, Paris: Gallimard. (Trans. *Discipline and Punish. Birth of the Prison*, New York: Vintage Books, 1995).

Goffman, Erving. 1971. *Relations in Public*. New York: Basic Books.

de Gournay, Chantal and Smoreda. Technologies de communication et relation de proximité. *Annales de la Recherche Urbaine*, à paraître.

Hallbwachs, Maurice. 1997. *La mémoire collective*. Paris: Albin Michel.

Jakobson, Roman. 1963. *Essai de linguistique générale*. Paris: Les éditions de Minuit.

Katz, James E. 1999. *Connections: Social and Cultural Studies of the Telephone in American Life*. New Brunswick, NJ: Transaction Publishers.

Katz, James E. 2001. "The Telephone." Entry in the *International Encyclopedia of Social Science* (2nd edition). Amsterdam: Elsevier. 2001. Vol. 23, pages 15558-65.

Katz, James E. and M. Aakhus, eds. 2002. *Perpetual Contact: Mobile Communication, Private Talk, Public Performance*. Cambridge and New York: Cambridge University Press.

Katz, James and Ronald E. Rice. 2002. *Social Consequences of Internet Use: Access, Involvement and Expression*. Cambridge, MA: The MIT Press.

Lazega, Emmanuel. 1992. Analyse de réseaux d'une organisation collégiale: les avocats d'affaires, *Revue française de sociologie* XXXIII: 559–589.

Licoppe Christian. 2001. Pratiques et trajectoires de la grande distribution dans le commerce alimentaire sur internet: vers un autre modèle de coordination pour le commerce électronique. *Revue Economique*, Vol. 52, pp. 191-211.

Licoppe Christian and Jean-Philippe Heurtin. 2001. Managing One's Availability to Telephone Communication through Mobile Phones: A French Case Study of the Development Dynamics of the Use of Mobile Phones, *Personal and Ubiquitous Technologies*, 5, 99-108.

Licoppe Christian and Jean-Philippe Heurtin 2002. The Cellular Phone as a Tool for Managing Risk and Trust in Social Bonds: Re-locating Mobile Phone Users and Re-Synchronizing Unexpected Contexts in Cellular Phone Interactions. Pp. 94-109 in *Perpetual Contact: Mobile Communication, Private Talk, Public Performance*, eds. Katz, James and M. Aakhus, Cambridge and New York: Cambridge University Press.

Licoppe Christian and Zbigniew Smoreda. 2000. Liens sociaux et régulations domestiques dans l'usage du téléphone , *Réseaux* 103: 119–141.

Rifkin, Jeremy. 2000. *The Age of Access*. New York: Putnam.

Rivière Carole-Anne. 2000. Les réseaux de sociabilité téléphonique. *Revue Française de Sociologie*, 41–4: 685-717.

Smoreda Zbigniew and Christian Licoppe. 2000. Identités sexuées et statuts interactionnels. De la gestion de la durée des communications téléphoniques. *Réseaux* 103: 255–276.

Veltz, Pierre. 2000. *Le nouveau monde industriel*, Paris: Gallimard.

# 14

# Culture and Design for Mobile Phones for China

*LiAnne Yu and Tai Hou Tng*

## Introduction

China is the world's largest market for mobile phones. Telecommunications technology has played a pivotal role in transforming personal and business relationships in urban China, where lifestyles are becoming increasingly fast-paced, mobile, and commodified (Li and Loconto 1998).

Until the late 1980s, few families in China had private telephone lines. This was due both to cost and the fact that phone installation often required several years' wait. By mid-2001, however, China had 169 million fixed-line users, and another 117 million mobile phone users, allowing contact anytime, anywhere (Lawson 2001). The mobile phone can be purchased instantly, allowing China to "leap-frog" into the age of mobile communication.

Although China's potential market for mobile phones is enormous, little attention has been directed towards designing mobile devices and applications to suit the country's communication culture. Instead, two predominant strategies have been used, the first of which is a universal or global perspective. Within common marketing and design strategies, the vision of a "ubiquitous" communication device is often conflated with the belief that people experience mobile communications in an increasingly homogeneous and globally consistent manner. While there are certain characteristics of communication and wireless device usage that are universally shared, global models have *not* been culturally neutral. Rather, they are based on Western and Japanese models, which have proven successful in their respective spheres.

A second common approach to wireless design employs localization techniques. Already successful devices and applications have been adapted for different market segments. These adaptations involve changes in appearance, language, and references to local customs. For example, localized websites take into account what colors are considered auspicious or attractive, reference appropriate holidays, or utilize colloquialisms. But it can been seen that, by itself, a strategy of adapting already-developed products to suit local "tastes" is insufficient. While localization provides some visible changes, the underlying paradigm upon which products and applications are based remains unchanged.

As this chapter demonstrates, neither universalizing nor localizing approaches (Katz 2001) can fully account for the ways in which wireless technologies acquire culturally specialized meanings that go beyond superficial preferences. Because their usage traverses various locales, wireless technologies have the potential, more than other technologies such as PCs or television, to reflect a unique sense of self as one moves from sites of work, home, leisure, and learning (Katz and Aakhus 2002). And because they are literally worn or carried on the body, mobile phones become associated with one's physical, emotional, and social identities.

By combining ethnography and design, it can be better understood how people envision their world and the rules by which they live. Hence, people's everyday life experiences can be observed regarding communication to generate models of successful interaction. Design considerations allow an understanding of how to visualize and embody these interaction values in actual products and interfaces. The result is a model based on the unmet needs that people articulate through their life stories and everyday interactions.

This chapter illustrates the application of this process in terms of developing unique wireless technologies for China. It reflects collaborative work that has been done between Ericsson Cyberlab in Singapore, and Point Forward, Inc. in Redwood City, California. Ethnographic interviews and participant observation were conducted in China as well as among overseas Chinese communities in the San Francisco Bay area (with a focus on Chinese professionals and university students within the Bay Area community).

### Discovering Chinese Communication and Interaction Models

China is undergoing epochal change. Field studies and the secondary research that was drawn upon revealed two main interaction characteristics that have become particularly salient since the introduction of market reforms in 1978:

- Increased privatization of most realms of everyday life;

- Building social capital, or *guanxi*.

First these themes are explored, and then in the next section, their implications are drawn out for current mobile phone usage and the development of unique wireless devices for the Chinese market.

*Increased Privatization*

Under Mao Zedong, the Chinese Communist state dismantled the private market and instituted a state-run economy. Industrial production was nationalized, agriculture was organized into collective state-run farms, and most commercial activities were banned. From 1949 up until 1990, the majority of urban adults worked in state-owned enterprises and experienced the so-called "iron rice bowl" of lifetime employment, egalitarian wages, and welfare benefits. These socialist "privileges" came at the cost of the private sphere, however. The state mandated that the workplace, or *danwei*, should distribute social welfare benefits, allocate apartments, and provide many consumer items such as a weekly movie, fresh fruit at holidays, plastic sandals for the summer, or a cake to celebrate a baby's birth (Davis 1999). Furthermore, the state sought to control urban growth by instituting the *hukou*, or household registration system. During this forty-year period, Chinese nationals were severely restricted in terms of where they lived, how they lived, and how they earned a living.

Not only was the economy de-privatized and placed under state hegemony, but the Chinese Communist Party also closely monitored and directed personal activity and behavior. What had formerly been personal realms, such as the home, women's reproductive systems, and marriage, became areas that the state could legitimately penetrate and monitor (Fraser 2000). The party sought to transform the private into the public by politicizing the domestic and social spaces through periodic mass campaigns and social movements.

After 1979, the Communist Party initiated a shift towards economic liberalization and a partial retreat from its authoritarian control. In the early 1980s, special economic zones were created in southern China, which have subsequently become booming industrial and commercial cities. By the early 1990s, massive layoffs in the state-owned sector became an additional impetus that drove Chinese nationals into the market economy. Communist Party leadership could no longer control the social consequences of increased commercialization and private entrepreneurship. "Millions of daily commercial exchanges not only calibrated the flow of material goods; they also nurtured individual desires and social networks that challenged official discourse and conventions" (Davis 2000).

The post-Mao decline of the work-unit system and the withdrawal of the state from a dominant role in people's daily lives have created opportunities for social interaction beyond the gaze of the state. While scholars argue about whether the private sphere has reemerged to triumph over the public, what is undeniable is that economic liberalization and the new consumerism of the 1990s have initiated the separation of work and home and expanded the realms of the personal and individual. The creation of new markets and industries, along with the partial withdrawal of the state from domestic and social life, has given rise to increasingly diverse types of personal space. These areas include home ownership, childcare, leisure activities, education, and the rearticulation of gender roles within both work and the domestic sphere.

These macro political economic themes were clearly echoed in the personal experiences of the people that were interviewed. One of the upwardly mobile professionals interviewed, "Grace," was a twenty-six-year-old accountant for a German textile company. She and her husband make an extremely comfortable living working for foreign companies and have just bought their first home in Shanghai. Like an increasing number of young urbanites, their private sector jobs allow them the luxury of living apart from other family members. Grace says living alone gives them a sense of privacy as a young couple that the older generation did not have. The décor of their new condominium declares their liberation from the homogeneity of state-owned property and their full engagement with the culture of consumerism. Every detail, Grace points out, from the Spanish tiling in the kitchen to the flower-motif quilt and pillowcases, was hand picked and personally chosen. Grace was asked to spend some time with the researchers on a typical Saturday afternoon—she went to OBI, a German home furnishing store. Most of the brightly colored pottery, plastic garden furniture, and lace curtains are imported goods. Grace says they are more expensive than locally produced goods, but tend to be more beautiful and unique.

Grace's attitude towards personalizing the domestic sphere is reflected in other arenas formerly controlled by the Communist state. Commercialized leisure spaces, such as multi-level discos, karaoke bars, shopping malls, and bowling alleys, have replaced state-supervised forms of entertainment. In these new spaces of consumption, Chinese nationals are active agents in enacting new identities as cosmopolitan and modern subjects, apart from state surveillance.

What was formerly public and politicized under the Mao regime is now increasingly privatized, both in the sense of becoming commercialized and falling under the realm of personal choice.

### Building Social Capital, or Guanxiwang (Personal Networks)

A second, interrelated phenomenon that was observed is the increased reliance on *guanxiwang*, or personal networks. *Guanxiwang* are based on the cultivation of personal relationships and networks of mutual dependence. They require the manufacturing of obligation and indebtedness through the exchange of gifts, favors, and banquets. Participants in *guanxiwang* are obliged to give, to receive, and to repay (Yang 1994).

During the decades of heavy Communist state penetration into the economy and the private sphere, personal networks helped people secure scarce goods and protection. The transition into a market economy has engendered new venues and modes for socializing with others, expanding and altering social networking. As Davis put it,

Using the language of Pierre Bourdieu, one could say that the expansion and commercialization of leisure enabled people from all strata to accumulate private caches of 'social capital' whose acquisition 'presupposes an unceasing effort of sociability.' Thus to move ahead in the 1990s one did not necessarily need to have privileged access or control over scarce goods; one could also build capital by forging dense and varied social connections. (Davis 2000)

*Guanxiwang* are often based on some commonality in background. Chinese communities within China as well as throughout Southeast Asia and the West frequently organize themselves by means of the *hui*, or same surname associations. In research among overseas Chinese professionals living in the Bay Area, there were hundreds of Chinese associations found based on common surnames, hometowns, dialects, and universities. These clubs provided both formal (banquets with featured speakers, conferences) and informal (potlucks, weekend getaways) venues for both professional and personal networking. Among Overseas Chinese, these associations allow for the experience of community in urban settings. Research revealed that these associations are increasingly being fostered by online communication. While the goal of these groups is to provide face-to-face contact, online discussion groups and e-mail lists provide a means to extend the *guanxiwang*, and thus ability for individuals to build their social capital.

Within China, as well as among Overseas Chinese communities, such horizontal ties are commonly fostered both for their affective and economic dimensions. Gan Wang writes,

Social capital is extremely important for the rising economic elite in Shenzhen because of its potential for conversion into economic capital. Working outside the established state system, private entrepreneurs need networks to get access to scarce economic capital, either internally (often from the state) or externally (e.g., through foreign investment), and because the market is highly unregulated, they seek personal trust in economic transactions to reduce their risks. (Wang 2000)

The research similarly suggested that Chinese who emigrate feel vulnerable in the face of new laws, cultural understandings, economic conditions, and languages. Most believe they are not yet equipped to work "within" the system, and so look to Chinese networks to gain information and job opportunities. They believe that knowledge gained through these networks will be more reliable and appropriate for themselves than something they learn from a non-personalized source, such as a web site or official.

Furthermore, the fieldwork both in China and in the U.S. revealed that individuals with good reputations in various webs of *guanxiwang* acquire social capital that may be leveraged in other interactions. They begin to act as "middlemen," who not only benefit from connections but also actively build them between other parties. By making good introductions between, say, a potential employer and employee, middlemen acquire others' indebtedness to themselves. As Gan Wang writes, "This kind of image becomes symbolic capital that means a person has a reputation for having 'networks that can be used to accomplish a great deal.' As a person becomes someone everybody would like to know, it becomes much easier for him or her to develop networks further" (Wang, 2000).

In the post-Mao era of economic liberalization, personal networks are one of the primary means by which individuals navigate the disjunctures and radical shifts in China's social order. The proliferation of such networks is both an outcome of and a catalyst for increased privatization, of not only the economy but also nearly all realms of life in China.

The next section explores how these two primary characteristics of life in post-Mao urban China have affected mobile phone usage, and how they should continue to be explored in the development of future wireless products for China.

### Developing a Wireless Paradigm for China

In 1990 there were 20,000 mobile phones in China. By 1995 there were 3.4 million. By 2005, China will have the largest number of mobile phone users in the world. The growth in telecommunications over the past decade has dramatically transformed phone calling from an inconvenient and very "public" undertaking to both a symbolic and a real manifestation of China's increasingly privatized and highly mobile urban lifestyle (Erwin 1999, p. 148). In Beijing in 1990, private telephone lines were a rarity. Making a call required one to go to the post office, fill out a form, and wait in line. Receiving a call was even more difficult; an exchange student in a dormitory of 500 students would share one line. The receptionist, upon receiving a call, would ring up to the student's room. If the student happened to be in, the call could be taken in the noisy hallway, usually with the receptionist not even making a pretense of not listening.

With the rapid expansion of mobile phone use, ordinary citizens are now able to make "private" calls at their convenience. Owning a personal phone to carry anywhere, people are no longer forced to make and receive calls in phone centers or with public lines. Phone calling has thus taken on new meanings, as voice-to-voice communication is no longer a rarity that demands only pragmatic and unrevealing conversations.

Ethnographic research has revealed that mobile phones are becoming important tools as well as symbols in China's transition from a state-run to a market-driven society. Specifically, mobile phones are used to express the increase both in the private sphere, and in *guanxiwang* building. These interrelated spheres speak to fundamental shifts in interaction and communication values.

The mobile phone as an artifact of daily living has taken on a set of connotations that are specific to the larger socioeconomic processes occurring in China. Research was conducted not only among mobile phone users but also in places where people buy phones. Mobile phone shoppers were consistently directed towards phones that were either "male" or "female," depending on the gender of the person purchasing the phone. When a female showed interest in a particular Motorola model that was commonly known as a man's phone, she was told that it would make her look too masculine and chubby, and the slimmer women's phones should be considered. Likewise, a Chinese girl said that her peers made so much fun of her father when he purchased the latest and smallest Nokia phone that he decided to give it to her.

The models came from the established names—Ericsson, Nokia, Motorola, and Siemens. These were not styles unique to the China market—the same or similar phones were sold in other places around the world, without such gendered connotations. It can be argued, however, that the shift away from socialist notions of male and female sameness is reflected in people's preoccupation with defining gender differences. The same phenomenon can be observed in fashion, as unisex Mao suits have given way to clothing that celebrates as well as exploits feminine sexuality.

In a larger sense, both men and women view their mobile phones as a kind of jewelry, which is to be worn and shown (Katz and Sugiyama 2002). Interactions with mobile phone users revealed that people commonly took out their phones and placed them on the table in front of them. Men were concerned about how the phone would look on their belts. Women, who usually kept their devices in their purses, expressed concern over whether the phone would look good in their hands or next to their faces, as they were using them.

Such gendered conceptions of mobile phones are unique to China. While a similar preoccupation was found with mobile phones as markers of identity during research in Japan, there are no clear male and female styles. It is not uncommon to see Japanese men using small, pink DoCoMo phones, with Hello Kitty-esque tassels. In the U.S. and Western Europe, mobile phone use is about pragmatism, and the dominant identity they are associated with is the male professional. While there have been attempts to evoke other mobile phone user identities in ad campaigns (e.g., the hip teen user), the default image continues to inform both mobile phone styles and use patterns.

Not only have Chinese users actively manipulated the image of the mobile phone in order to express greater personal choice, but also the subject matter of phone calls has been, to a certain extent, liberated from public surveillance. Kathleen Erwin explores how telephone "hotlines" have reconfigured public and private discourse and practices in the shaping of Chinese modernity. These hotlines included counseling services to help resolve family and sexual problems:

> The emergence and growth of hotlines services stems not only from rapid improvement in the telecommunications infrastructure but also from a shift in both private and official attitudes toward love, marriage, and sexuality. During most of the Maoist decades, and especially during the Cultural Revolution, such personal aspirations were disparaged as bourgeois distractions from revolutionary fervor, and public discussion of them came under close party scrutiny. (Erwin 1999, p. 169)

The growth of these hotlines and the parallel growth in the number of people who own mobile phones have produced a phenomenon in which the public space of the call is becoming privatized—people are discussing issues that are personal and decidedly not state-directed (Katz and Sugiyama 2002). The mobile phone as a symbol of the regeneration and value placed on private matters is vividly illustrated in any public locale, such as buses and restaurants. Urban Chinese—professionals, teens, housewives, and hipsters—loudly and with an almost exaggerated physicality—answer their phones and make no pretense of hiding the fact that they are engaging in private conversations.

Such value placed on publicizing the private differs significantly from mobile phone usage in Japan. Fieldwork in Japan revealed that the mobile phone offered an opportunity to create a private "pocket" in very public contexts. Yet instead of publicizing one's private conversations, Japanese users withdraw from the public gaze by immersing themselves in SMS, a form of text messaging that can be done with the numbered keypad.

The ethnographic research also revealed that mobile phones in China were increasingly seen as tools for augmenting and fostering *guanxiwang,* or personal networks. What was found was that for Chinese users, a contact is not just a name on a phone list, but also a potential ally in multiple situations that require a highly personalized relationship. The immediacy of voice communication offers them the ability to set the groundwork for the giving and accepting of favors, and the creation and fulfillment of indebtedness.

In the networking process, voice calling was not an end in itself, but primarily a means to set up face-to-face contact. Voice calling allowed for gestures of giving when time or space did not permit actual visits. During such calls, typical networkers may give out some special nuggets of knowledge or news, or they may set up appointments to meet for a meal. Like the Japanese SMS users, there is a continual give and take that characterizes mobile phone communication. In the case of Chinese users, however, this give and take must be similar to face-to-face (as in voice-to-voice) communication, even if it can't actually be in person.

Furthermore, these social networks incorporate various spheres of life in China—work, leisure, and family. Unlike findings from the mobile phone research in the U.S., where it was found that users defined fairly strict groups of people (friends vs. colleagues vs. family), research both in China and among Overseas Chinese in the U.S. reveals that a single contact is often thought of in multiple contexts. For example, a superior at work can be someone you do favors for, or who does favors for you in particular situations. A state official can be both someone with whom you interact in a formal matter, as well as someone that you interact with informally over dinner or in your home. The flexibility in these ways of conceiving of contacts allows individuals to maximize their web of relations. Rather than compartmentalizing people, and thus limiting the scope of how they may be of assistance, research indicates a pattern of constantly enlarging each contact's significance.

The fieldwork revealed that people speak loudly on their phones, make appointments, check in with others, and make plans for getting together. Such activities over the phone signify that the person has a strong social network. People often automatically put their mobile phones on the table in front of them, as if to say that they were expecting to be contacted.

While mobile phones allow users to keep in touch and augment their networks, they are also limited by other forms of communication technology in how they facilitate both privatization and Chinese *guanxiwang* building. The latest designs tend to combine phones with PDA features. While such a combination gives the appearance of completeness, the model of the PDA is ultimately inappropriate for Chinese users. PDAs emerged from a Western vision of the world. As a result, PDAs tend to reflect a very compartmentalized way of thinking such as the separation of contacts, schedule, and to-do list. Chinese users, with their interaction models based on flexible social networks and shifting boundaries of public and private, need a more dynamic and integrated model to help them keep in touch.

Moreover, given the success of the i-mode service in Japan, there will be growing emphasis on developing an interactive paradigm for China. This emphasis will include messaging, e-mail and imaging applications for mobile products. Yet, our research on Chinese values and communication styles suggests that these applications will not resonate with potential users precisely because of their interaction models. E-mail, for example, is an appropriate medium for Westerners who are forging business alliances but who have never met. In China, however, it is important that if the first contact cannot be made face-to-face then, at the very least, voice contact is required. The appropriateness of the communication medium for varying contexts thus should guide research and design of mobile applications.

The issue of integrating messaging features into a mobile device furthermore raises the issue of appropriate inputting methods. The development of a new generation of "keyboardless" Asian language solutions such as Apple's Advanced Chinese Input Suite (Sacher 1998) and AsiaWorks' SPK 1.0 for Windows can be seen as a first step in that direction. The focus of these efforts has been to develop an understanding of Chinese interaction and to support such characteristics in the interaction with computer systems. Features that are essential to Chinese are: managing an immense number of ideographs, dealing with ambiguities and dialects of spoken Chinese, handwriting and speaking as complementary channels, maintaining an implicit, perpetual learning process, and enriching expressions with a personal style (e.g., handwriting). Apple's Advanced Chinese Input Suite was the world's first commercial product to permit Chinese-speaking users to enter text into the computer based on language abilities that they attain and apply in daily life (see Sacher 1998).

Although this research was geared towards desktop computing, several issues are equally significant for the development of mobile devices for China. Foremost is the importance of pen use for inputting characters in a form that is natural to Chinese users.  Using the pen, users do not have to translate the characters of their own language into Roman script or other alphabet-based methods (e.g., pinyin, WuBi) that are not part of their native language skills. Pen input does not require users to go through any translation or decoding procedures.

Also of significance to mobile application development is the integration of dictation and handwriting input.  The research conducted on keyboardless Asian language solutions revealed that speaking and writing are closely interrelated activities for native Chinese speakers. It was found that for names and less common words, people simultaneously spoke and wrote (with a finger in the air) these words. The visual augmentation of a "written" character gives the listener more information to understand exactly what words were spoken. Apple's Advanced Chinese Input Suite integrates an application for dictation (speaker-dependent, discrete word), a handwriting input method (user-independent, character-based), and speech synthesis.

In summary, this research points to characteristics of Chinese communication that should be incorporated into a wireless Chinese paradigm since it will better serve the needs and interests of potential users. These characteristics, outlined below, are all aimed at expanding the private sphere and personalizing expression. They include:

1. Gendered preferences

2. The concept of the mobile phone as jewelry

3. The fostering of *guanxiwang*, or personal networks, including:

   a. The non-segmented way of conceptualizing contacts and information
   b. The integration of pen and voice.

While there have been attempts to incorporate some of these characteristics, they have met with relative failure. The Motorola Accompli, for example, is a combination phone and PDA featuring a pen-based interface that allows Chinese users to write Chinese characters "naturally," without resorting to other, non-native techniques to create text.  While this certainly offers Chinese users more appropriate technical solutions, the overall concept did not resonate with the individuals that were interviewed.  They found the appearance of the device difficult to accept—users found its square look and thick frame unattractive, and not a positive reflection of the self they wanted others to see.  Further, they found the notion of a phone combined with a PDA to be incongruent with their communication goals.  The users found the PDA model of information management interesting, but they did not believe that it could facilitate or augment communications with others. In fact, they believed the PDA functionality would "get in the way" of basic voice calling and potentially jeopardize their business or social relations. This mobile phone model thus violated aspects of two interaction characteristics that were identified—the mobile phone as an expression of personal self, and the mobile phone as a tool for augmenting *guanxiwang*.

Since attempts to incorporate certain Chinese-friendly features into mobile communication failed, one could argue for an approach that integrates all of the characteristics listed above. The concluding section discusses the implications of efforts to develop such a device.

## Conclusion: The WuKong Project

Based on Chinese values regarding communication and interaction that have emerged in the post-Mao period, Ericsson Cyberlab in Singapore and members from Point Forward have developed a next-generation mobile communication concept. The objective of this project was to develop a mobile concept that is culturally, emotionally, and technically satisfying for Chinese users. Secondary research on Chinese professional culture, and ethnographic interviews with sixty mobile phone users were conducted. The findings on Chinese communication culture and its impact on mobile phone usage, which have been discussed in this chapter, have been incorporated into an iterative process of research and design. Design concepts that arose out of initial discovery research are taken back out to Chinese respondents, and such designs are then refined or changed according to feedback.

The result is WuKong, a mobile device concept based on the interaction principles that were identified through ethnographic research: the expansion of the privatized, personalized sphere, the fostering of *guanxiwang*, and the integration of pen and voice inputting methods. WuKong is based on a people-centric concept, rather than a Western PDA model of information management. That is, WuKong fosters both voice communication and personal networking through applications that link contacts with knowledge sources. This allows people to engage in *guanxiwang* building. Wukong also features pen input techniques, allowing Chinese speakers to create text in a natural method.

WuKong is only the first manifestation of a mobile concept that integrates the essential characteristics of Chinese communication. The embodiment of these characteristics may and should take many forms within the wireless domain—and that is the challenge this chapter seeks to set forth. From an industry perspective, it is believed that those involved in developing wireless technologies for China cannot remain complacent in the knowledge that the market is so promising. What the research highlights is that young professionals in China are becoming increasingly sensitive to being perceived as modern in their *own right*, rather than being blind followers of anything Western or Japanese. These users are increasingly articulating—in Chinese terms—what that modernity is. Products and services that cater to non-Chinese cultural mind frames will be increasingly perceived as inappropriate as local industries proliferate and Chinese designers take on the challenge of wireless development. Western companies, such as Ericsson, Nokia, and Motorola, should predicate their long-term success in the Chinese market on a profound understanding of their customers. Based on this understanding, they should develop wireless paradigms around the way people envision their world, benefiting both themselves and their customers.

## References

Davis, Deborah (ed.) 1999. *The Consumer Revolution in Urban China*. Berkeley: University of California Press.

Erwin, Kathleen 1999. Heart-to-Heart, Phone-to-Phone: Family Values, Sexuality, and the Politics of Shanghai's Advice Hotlines. Pp. 145-171 in *The Consumer Revolution in Urban China*, edited by Deborah S. Davis. Berkeley: University of California Press.

Katz, James E. 2001. The Telephone. Entry in the *International Encyclopedia of Social Science* (2nd edition). Amsterdam: Elsevier. 2001. Vol. 23, pp. 15558-65.

Katz, James E. and M. Aakhus, eds. 2002. *Perpetual Contact: Mobile Communication, Private Talk, Public Performance*. Cambridge: Cambridge University Press.

Katz, James and S. Sugiyama. 2002. Fashion and Mobile Phones. Paper presented at the International Communication Association Annual Meeting. Seoul, Korea, July 21.

Lawson, Stephen. 2001. China to Add 46M Mobile Users this Year. IDG News Service/ Hong Kong Bureau (10 August). Retrieved on April 27, 2002 from http://www.idg.net/ crdidgsearch666167.html?sc.

Li, Conghua and Pat A. Loconto. 1998. *China: The Consumer Revolution*. New York: John Wiley and Sons.

Sacher, Heiko. 1998. Interactions in Chinese: Designing Interfaces for Asian Languages. *Interactions Magazine* 5 (5), pp. 28–38.

Yang, Mayfair Mei-Hui. 1994. *Gifts, Favors, and Banquets: The Art of Social Relationships in China*. Ithaca, NY: Cornell University Press.

# Part 3

## Subcultures, Technologies, and Fashion

# 15

# Outwardly Mobile: Young People and Mobile Technologies

*Nicola Green*

## Introduction

Considerable empirical and theoretical attention has recently been paid to the relationship between young people and mobile technologies, particularly mobile phones (cell phones) (Green 2001, 2002; Katz 1999; Weilenmann and Larsson 2001; Kasesniemi and Rautiainen 2002; Ling and Yttri 2001). Emerging research is tracing the impact of mobile communication on the lives of young people; indeed, such research also shows how young people themselves have contributed to the distribution and institutionalization of mobile technology (Katz and Aakhus 2002).

In this chapter, we have set two goals. First we aim to contribute to this growing body of empirical data, and detail some of the results of long-term qualitative research among groups of young people in the United Kingdom. Second, we wish to raise wider questions suggested by these empirical findings. We challenge the common assumption about an affinity between young people, technology, and "the future." We also critique the common emphasis on the issue of *difference* between "teenagers" and "others," which by implication, places all teenagers in the same identity and behavioral categories, and implies the formation of youth "subcultures." Rather, our research project suggests multiple and diverse negotiations of identity and social relationships that challenge the notion that researchers can associate "youth" and "technologies" as singular categories, and that all "teenagers" can be understood as forming part of the same generalized group.

## Mobile Teenagers

Over the past two years, a research project entitled "The Socio-technical shaping of Mobile, Multimedia Personal Communications" (STEMPEC) has been carried out at the University of Surrey. The STEMPEC project has been funded for three years by the Economic and Social Research Council and four mobile network operators—Orange, BTCellnet, Vodafone, and One2one—under the Department of Trade and Industry's Foresight Link scheme. One strand of this extensive research has been an investigation of how "teenagers" use and consume mobile technologies.

Our research on young people was conducted in one South Central London High School, and Two "Green Belt" Sixth Form Colleges in the United Kingdom. The high school in South London has around 1,700 students, with an age range from eleven to eighteen. The school serves several London boroughs with a mixed socio-economic and ethnic profile.

According to a deputy-head, the gender ratio is approximately 45 percent girls and 55 percent boys. The ethnic composition of the students is approximately 40 percent Anglo, 30 percent African or Afro-Caribbean, and 30 percent Asian.

The two Sixth Form Colleges in London's "Green Belt" cater to an age range from sixteen to nineteen. Interviews were conducted with three groups of between ten and twenty lower school students, and larger groups of twenty to twenty-five (up to around 150 students) at the Sixth Form Colleges. Both users and non-users were included in the groups of those interviewed in all age brackets. In addition to interviews and observations with young people, members of staff, including teachers and head teachers, were interviewed at all of the schools. Furthermore, around twenty parents of the young people interviewed were contacted by telephone for their views about their teenagers' use of mobiles. In the spirit of an ethnographic approach, observations included not only the use (and non-use) of mobile phones, but also documented the other talk and artifacts associated with the social life of teens in schools, from the magazines shared over the canteen table, to local media reports on school bullying via text messages. These materials served to provide a "rich description" of the social milieu of which the teens are a part.

The level of ownership and uptake of mobile devices steadily increases as young people get older (see also Rautiainen 2002). Among eleven and twelve year olds personal mobile phones are rare, whereas the uptake of personal mobile phones has increased to around half by thirteen and fourteen. Among the sixth form, the uptake has reached around the 70 percent mark, equally divided between males and females.

The focus of the interviews was mobile "phones," as this was the primary definition all the students had of mobile handsets. *Non-users* among teen groups were both *voluntary* and *involuntary* non-users. *Involuntary* non-users were those who said they wanted a phone, but were prevented from getting one because they could not afford the phones or maintenance, and/or their parents refused to buy one for them. There were also *voluntary* non-users among the research groups however, and their number increased with age. Some of these young people said "they preferred to spend their money on something else." Others objected to the devices themselves, particularly their presence in public space, and said things like "I don't want one" or "I don't care about them, I don't have a passion for them," or attributed their non-use to a refusal to "follow fashion." Other young people had once had a mobile, and had either given them away ("I used to have a mobile but I gave it to my mum"), or had stopped using them, on the basis that "they didn't have a need" for them.

### Group Identity and Difference

In our research it quickly became apparent that young people use mobile technologies for "micro-coordination," in much the same ways as adults. This is certainly supported in European research. Ling and Yttri (2001) conducted a study of Norwegian teenagers based on ten group interviews. In particular, they focused on the role of the mobile in managing "nuanced, instrumental co-ordination" and accessibility. Beyond communication for micro-coordination, however, is "hyper-coordination," which involves not only the instrumental aspects of managing accessibility, but also adds an expressive dimension (social and emotional communication), as well as self-presentation within and between groups. Ling and Yttri (2001) argue that hyper-coordination, including these latter elements, is more important for teens than other groups.

Certainly, issues of youth identity and identification, concepts of self and personhood within family and peer groups, are central issues that have been identified beyond Ling and Yttri's study. Nafus and Tracey (2001), for example, argue that the consumption of the mobile phone (among consumption of related devices) is a material and symbolic location for constructing relations of difference and relatedness, and associated concepts of personhood. Similarly, Kasesniemi and Rautiainen (2001) identify a number of salient features of identity for young people, including the decreasing age of young mobile users, issues of gender, and the particular kinds of uses (such as short-text messaging) that are used by peer groups of young people.

As was the case in Ling and Yttri's (2001) research, it was consistently evident in our fieldwork among different groups of young people that the mobile was seen primarily as a communicative device that was often talked about in positive and emotional terms as "connection" with (peer) others. Mobiles also gave young people a greater sense of control over their own affairs (see also Skelton 1989). Phones, both fixed and mobile, "become an extension of peer group relations and close friendships that are other times are conducted away from home. For teenagers, the combination of a private space at home and intimate talk with friends may mean that friends become more influential in their emotional development and well being" (Gillard et al. 1998).

The construction of personal identities among teens via the mediation of mobile devices depends crucially on the social, cultural, and economic *value* those devices represent and enable, as they are situated in complex and shifting relations of solidarity and alliances, and identities and differences in peer group and family identities.

### The Economic Value of Mobile Telephony

Mobile phones have specific economic value in the context of young people's everyday lives. This should not be surprising when we recognize that the term "teenager" itself did not emerge until the 1950s and 1960s, specifically in relation to young people as a new market niche (a social and economic category of consumer) in a time of relative economic affluence. Fowler (1995) makes a convincing argument that social and economic conditions began to change for youth in Britain during the interwar, rather than postwar years, and that it was at this stage that they began to be recognized as an emerging consumer market. It seems that the increasing cross-fertilization between Britain and North America, and the growth of "consumer cultures" in general since the 1950s, have served to create "the teenager" in particular as a consumption category. Since this time, the term "teenager" as a descriptor of physical age, and the term "adolescence" as a descriptor of a period of social transition, has become relatively synonymous. Furthermore, today's "teenagers" are located in a social world increasingly oriented toward consumption in a world marked by increased cross-fertilization of ethnic, class, and national cultures. This has led some contemporary researchers to focus on notions of "global" youth culture, and have drawn attention to the central roles of cultural economies of consumption in the creation of youth subcultural identities.

Shields (1992), for example, identifies a number of changes in urban space, media, and information technologies; and techniques of representation that prompt changes in the ways young people (and others) formulate a sense of self, and identities in relation to others through the activities of consuming goods. Shields argues that "there is a need to treat consumption as an active, committed production of self and of society which, rather than assimilating individuals to styles, appropriates codes and fashions, which are made into one's own." According to de Certeau (1984), we are

> confronted by an entirely different kind of production, called "consumption"... characterized by its ruses, its fragmentation... its poaching, its clandestine nature, its tireless but quiet activity, in short by its quasi-invisibility, since it shows itself not in its own products, but in an art of using those imposed on it.

In effect, cultures of consumption have evolved, which take malls and high streets as their architecture, which generate spectacular representations of commodity and consumption, and become sites of cultural change. Young people's consumption activities in these sites—including social interaction and communication with peers—result in a kind of "tribalism" (Maffesoli 1996). This has become especially the case as (relatively) affluent teenagers of the 1950s and 1960s have become increasingly rare, and living conditions in Europe have changed with increasing recession. According to Langman (1992), the spaces of shopping centers

> allow a degree of contestation, reinterpretation, and often mobilization, if not in fact, in fantasy. For many youth, the school has become the world of submission to boring routine, the mall offers empowerment through hyper-real gratification…. Those groups that are destined to remain peripheral to the spheres of real power and affluence are most likely to embrace the empowerments allocated by popular culture and the commodities of malldom…. Identification with the simulacra of mass media offers "micro-spheres of empowerment" and/or gratification of recognition and dignity that compensate teenagers for exclusion from the ever more distant worlds of bourgeois affluence.

The implication of this for the study of mobile devices is that a commodity is not simply a functional technological object that has an effect on particular social groups (for better or worse), but is rather part of a whole range of commodities, spaces, and relations already bearing meaning (including meanings about identity), in wide range of environments. Each technology may, above and beyond its functional uses, bear meaning that *socially* connects groups of people (in the dynamics of identity and difference), but also socially connects a number of related technologies and objects.

Mobile phones have a very high economic value among young people, particularly because of their simultaneous cultural value. Both economic and cultural value is demonstrated in the extensive discussions the young people had about the "black market" for phones within and among schools. Both money and fashion are factors here, and the economic value of the phones is relative. According to the younger age groups, the objects in the black market included mobile phones, pagers, money, bus passes, walkmans, CDs, handheld game devices, Pokemon cards and items of clothing such as leather jackets or trainers. Mobile phones seemed to be at the top of a hierarchy of value, firstly because they were relatively rare within the school environment (some schools having banned phones); secondly because the older you got, more "serious" things were stolen, and mobiles had high market value as a commodity in general (white) markets.

### The Cultural Value of Mobile Technologies

Key to the commodity value of mobiles for some teenagers was, of course, fashion. Social status within age groups was expressed in terms of "street cred"("credibility") and "flash," (a "look") social distinctions based on cultural values. All the teenagers interviewed displayed extensive knowledge of device styles and designs. Their discussion of styles and features often took place with reference to current advertising, and younger participants would identify the particular make and model of the phone they owned. Mobiles were evaluated on both functional and aesthetic grounds. These teenagers perceived particular devices (branding), particular features (such as the ability to customize and personalize the phone), and rarity as "flash," making the phone more valuable, and raising the status of its owner.

The extent of the influence of fashion and status tended to be more highly emphasized by younger groups. The most enthusiastic of the young people were highly aware of the aesthetic qualities of the device and the way it contributes to their "presentation of self." Among these users, extensive discussion takes place about the look of the device, the use of services such as text messaging, and functions (such as address books or game scores).

> You get into a competition about who's got the best mobile phone.

> It's like with trainers, everyone goes to PE. Everyone looks at your trainers. Or you look at somebody who's got bastard trainers. And it's still the same [with mobiles].

One means to understand the importance of fashion and status among young people is to examine the devices that bear these meanings with reference their place within youth "subcultures." According to the CCCS approach,

> ...culture is a distinctive way of life embodied in beliefs and customs, social relations, institutions and material objects. All these aspects of the subculture were referred to as "maps of meaning," which shape the sub-culture and make it intelligible to its members... Studies of youth subcultural groups examined the way in which these maps of meaning were constituted by focusing on the meanings given to the objects, institutions and practices by the group. (Valentine et al. 1999)

At the same time, however, subcultural approaches have been heavily criticized for making gender and the private sphere invisible in analysis, and ignoring the considerable impact of black and Asian style on European youth cultures. According to analysts such as Hall (1976) and Gilroy (1987), then, any questions addressing youth cultures need to undertake a global analysis that recognizes the links between cross-national expressive cultures. Cultural, ethnic, and national identities are intersected by those identities based on class, age, gender, locality, and peer group. This recognition has led to an emphasis on a "politics of difference," an acknowledgment of diversity among young people, as well as adults.

This diversity was certainly apparent in the meanings young people attributed to mobile technologies, and while some young people emphasized the fashion and "subcultural" possibilities of mobile technologies, others were far more critical. Some users, for example, evaluated the importance of fashion and status in relation to their discretionary spending power (economic value), and made decisions on that basis:

> It's the same cover, always. I'm not going to buy another cover for it. I'm not going to pay fifteen pounds... that's another fifteen pounds on the phone, another two fifteen pounds to buy myself a shirt, some trousers...

Other users, often older, tended more to evaluate a mobile's qualities on the basis of its relevance to their lives, its immediate functional qualities, and only pay some, minimal attention to the make and model of the mobile when it is associated with particular functional shortcomings:

> To me, to some people, as long as their phone works and they can make a call, and they can do whatever they need to do, it's fine.

> As long as it's not a brick. (a "brick" is where the phone is too large to have "cred")

Indeed, some young people are highly critical of the fashion elements of mobile phone use, claim not to participate, and criticize other young people for their preoccupation with it:

> To me, that's what different about fashion. People dressing themselves then dressing their phones. I don't do that...

Still others tended to express negative attitudes toward the advertising and branding of phones and services they see:

> The thing is, it doesn't occur to people until it's there. Like I bet 15 years ago, it wouldn't have occurred to people "yeah, I want to walk around talking, I can't just stay at home"... They say they're supplying a need, but really, they're providing it.

There is considerable diversity then, in the economic and cultural meaning of mobile technology among the teens, which indicates far more critical and negotiated value of mobiles as cultural mediators for teenage identities than has heretofore been extensively recognized. In addition to the expressive cultural values associated with new and mobile technologies, are the social values those devices represent for young people in their everyday lives, that render any analysis even more complex.

*The Social Value of Mobile Technologies*

It became quickly apparent in our fieldwork that teens use mobiles to constitute and accomplish social solidarities and differences, both among themselves, and between themselves and other social groups. Mobile devices are symbols of membership and exclusion, dynamically oriented to the changing forms of the devices, and shifts in the social relationships of teenage social groups. The opportunities for *connection* with their friends that the phones represented, as well as access and availability, were means to *perform* identity and difference both with friends, and to others such as family members, thus creating the social value of the phone beyond its economic or cultural value and meaning. This "performative value" included the presentation of self to both peers and family members. Having the "right" names in the address book to demonstrate one's participation in a peer community, comparing phones on aesthetic and functional grounds, and having friends call during domestic time to demonstrate social networks independent of the family, were all important ways to perform one's identity as a member of teen groups.

Collective differentiation between teenage groups relied not only on the dynamics of everyday *use* for teen activities however. It was also apparent in the ways young people *talked about* their own and others" use of mobile phones. The young people identified several different kinds of users, both to demonstrate themselves as responsible mobile users, considerate of others in public space, and to differentiate themselves from others who were identified as irresponsible and inconsiderate in their use and behavior. "Good users" were those who thought about their use of the mobile in the context they were in, and behaved "appropriately." Young people described these behaviors most often when they were describing their own behaviors:

> I'm one of those people where, if I get on the bus, I'll turn the volume of the phone down, because I know it annoys so many people, and I know it annoys me as well when I hear this really loud ring, so I turn it down. I don't have to shout about my phone.

"Bad users" were those who used their phones "inappropriately" in public space, and were inconsiderate of others there. Most often, the behaviors described were attributed to others, and the young people distanced themselves from them:

> Like if I'm sitting in… like in a café, and someone near me, their phone rings, and it's "HELLO, YES, I'M SITTING ON A TRAIN, I'M SITTING IN A CAFÉ." I don't like them.

> I hate it. I really don't like people talking on the phone in buses. All they have to say is "I'll phone you back."

Young people will also discuss various strategies for responding to what they perceive as "bad users":

> I start listening to what they're saying. And then they'll start talking, and I'll just say exactly the same thing, then they'll realize that I'm paying attention, and they'll turn the phone off.

> Has anyone ever just turned around and said "shut up"?

Sometimes, the teens emphasize age differences to distance themselves from adults who act "badly":

> I heard someone on the bus say, "I'm sorry but you're going to have to turn the phone off now because you're too boring." They were like our age, and he was about 23.

The final category was "incompetent users." These users are most often described as "parents," although when teens talk about their "parents" in this way, they, in fact, talk about their mothers' behavior in particular. Incompetent people can be identified both by their ignorance of the uses and functions of devices, and the provision of services:

> My mum doesn't know how to use it; she doesn't even know how to turn it on. And then she got this rubbish one, and then the service credit runs out, so then the call credit doesn't, so she's got like two hundred pound worth of call credit, but like no service credit, so she can't use it.

> My Aunt's got one, but she's really terrible…like she doesn't know how to use it, and she's scared of it, she doesn't know what to do with it.…So I take it.

## Managing Social Relations and Independence

The young people we spoke to associated particular phone functions with specific sets of social relationships. Family relations tended to be associated with voice, whereas the (by far preferred) text messaging was associated with friends. One parent explains this by saying,

> I suspect what is happening is that kids will sometimes say things in a message that they won't… like the heart sign and things like that. You don't go like "I love you." She had this boyfriend in Liverpool.…I suspect a lot of the messages were more like greeting cards, or soppy…I think if you want to say something like "Pick me up at the station," I'm not sure you would really message that, would you? It is something you need to get an answer to straight away.

Text messaging certainly does rely on a "community of messengers" in the U.K. Young people will not tend to send messages to those that cannot, or do not answer. Sending a text message relies on the possibility or probability of a response, usually in the form of another text message, in a form of ritualized exchange in the "giving of gifts" (Mauss 1973). The "insiders" and "outsiders" thereby created are not so much "excluded" as they are "unconnected" to some of the ongoing conversations among peers (in the form of text messages) that provide resources for building and maintaining peer relationships.

In developmental perspectives, adolescence is seen as the most important site of secondary socialization, where the maturing individual gains social and economic independence from their family of origin, and creates identification with chosen associates (peers) as a replacement for that family. The peer group is a source of social learning in a time of increasing (although sometimes ambivalent) movement toward autonomy. "Developmental tasks" toward a mature personality and adult competence are conceived to be central to the development of a secure self-identity. In the developmental literature, the ability of the adolescent individual to achieve these tasks within the variables of their social context is described as finding a "niche," finding a "pathway," or establishing a "trajectory." How information and communication technologies (ICTs) and mobile technologies provide teens with resources to do this is a question of how such technologies allow them to gain independence from the family.

Beyond this developmental perspective, however, are also the issues of the relative social power of parents and children in defining teen identity and independence, and how this is expressed in the negotiation of behavioral regulation and teen responsibility. More recently, social scientists have shifted their focus to the variables affecting the achievement of growth tasks; from social class, to family, neighborhood, work context, labor markets, and the institutional framework of schools and colleges (Allatt 1997; Chisholm 1997; Coles 1997; Nagel and Wallace 1997).

In this sense, the ways a mobile might be used by teens in domestic space is indicative of its role in mediating growing youth autonomy. For example, whether or not mobile phone use in the home becomes "normal" for teens is a result of three factors: the number of mobile phones within a household and their conventions of use by family members; the network of teenage friends who have mobile phones and call at "domestic" times; and the attitudes of parents to the use of mobile phones and how that is negotiated with their children.

Most of the young people in the middle and older groups will use their mobile phone at home. One of the most important reasons for this is the privacy it affords them. Talking to their friends and conducting their social affairs can all be done in the privacy of their own bedroom, because within the home the landline phone does not always provide for a private conversation. Some parents certainly acknowledged this and also noted that teens can use it to "bypass" them:

> As far as I can see... the two advantages about those messaging things is that 1) I think it is cheaper, and 2) it is if you don't want anyone to hear who has rung you up. That's how [the teenager] uses it anyway.... She gets messages and then rushes upstairs to use the landline. I think she speaks to people I don't approve of! She mentions about when she will ring or something, but it means that I don't ask any questions.... And in a way she didn't like it because the phones are in public places... So she couldn't speak in private so she bought this...

Use of the phones can both maintain and upset domestic order. Some of the older teenagers reported that the noise of the phones continually going off could annoy some members of their families. A number of parents reported that their teens spent considerable time on the house phone, and that it could become a problem with people trying to get through to the parents:

> She bought the mobile herself because she was spending so much time on the landline that first of all people couldn't get through to me, and secondly I couldn't get out... I think this was for a bit of independence too, which in a way I can understand, but I feel, well actually my job is too important... I don't mean it that way, but you know...

Other parents' accounts of phone use among their teens focused less on their need for privacy, and more on their perception of their children's use for "novelty value," or "talking about nothing, really":

...every other street that she is walking down she had to ring someone up to prove that she was on the phone, that she had it out.

Many parents argued that their landlines already provided for the privacy needs of their teenagers, where they could use the house phone either in their rooms, or in common rooms that could be shut off from the rest of the house. One parent outlined calls in the middle of the night as particularly disruptive:

> Friends would call at all times of night, and I don't think that if they were using the house phone they would call up at midnight. But you'd hear the phone go off at midnight.

Parents attempt to lay down various rules when they themselves bore the cost of mobile phones for their teens. For the youngest groups, these rules were laid down beforehand, and were a pre-condition of the phone's purchase and use. At other times, parents did not realize the cost of mobile phones. Particularly in the case of the older groups, the parents assumed (and they sometimes described this assumption as naïve), their children's use of the phone primarily for safety and security, would be similar to their own. One parent commented that she "had no idea about text messaging. I just didn't know."

The parents for whom this was a concern described how they used the situation of high mobile phone bills to discuss levels of use and encourage the teen to accept economic responsibility for their use. Both parents, who bore the cost of the use, and those who didn't, reported that their children were also shocked at the level of the bills. They talked about their children "not realizing" how much the cost of services accumulated:

> My 12 year old son, I'm going to get him one because he has a very long way to go to school, but he's angling for one of those that do things like e-mail, and he doesn't realize that it's all extra, he just doesn't realize.
>     She couldn't speak in private so she bought this and it was one of the pay as you go. Having said that I think she is realizing that it is costing quite a lot of money even though she is trying to cut down.

One mother said,

> We told her that she had to accept responsibility for her use of the phone, so she is now required to bear the cost of the calls she makes, with the exception of calls home and for cabs etc., as well as the cost of long distance calls on the home phone. She seems to be restraining herself more now, and she now understands how much it costs.

In the case of disruption, as well as large mobile phone bills, parents attempt to regulate the use of both mobile and landline phones. Some parents said they tried to encourage their teens to lessen their use of both the house phone and the mobile phone. The dilemma still remained for some parents, however:

> When she rang up such a huge bill on her mobile phone, we tried to get her to use the house phone more instead. But then she rang up huge bills on the home phone calling mobile numbers for someone who lived a mile away, in the local calling area.

Teenagers try to bypass parental rules of mobile use with various "parent management strategies"—getting vouchers from both parents, convincing parents to pay or, when charges for the use of special "contract services" appear on the bill, seeking to explain away these excesses as "accidental calls." Parents are, unsurprisingly, well aware of these strategies, but they feel caught in a dilemma:

> I thought that a pay-as-you-go phone might be better, but what would happen then? I'd give her a £10 voucher so that she can ring home, and have her spend the money on messaging with friends?

Parents also tended to see no solution to this dilemma.

Different groups of students then, find clearly that the phone allowed them a greater sense of independence. The mobile phone overrides the gatekeeper role of parents and teachers and allows them to develop a greater sense of control over their own affairs.

Issues of safety and security of the teen in their growing independence were, however, paramount in the talk of both teens and their parents. Parents and teenagers offer sometimes conflicting accounts of who calls whom when children are out. Some parents acknowledge that they use the teenager's mobile phone number to call them, find out where they are, and to ask if they need a lift home. Other parents, however, maintained that the phone was not so much for them to get in contact with their teenager, but for their teenager to get in contact with them:

> I like to feel, not that I can instantly get hold of her, but that she can get hold of me.

> We don't use it to contact her; we don't use it as a means of checking up on her. There has to be an element of trust there.

Teenagers claimed that parents did use it to check up on them, and outlined their own and parents' strategies to negotiate those contacts, as is evident in the following exchange:

> My mum used to be like that, and hates them, but she always wanted to know where I was, so... that's what I don't like. Everyone knows where you are all the time, that's why I don't like him or her.

> You don't tell them where you are!

> I'll be out, and I'll go to my friend's house... until really late, and mum would get worried, and I won't phone home... and so they're all getting all stressed, and "you're not going anywhere again", and with the phone they can just say "oh, what time are you coming home, are you alright, blah blah"...

> Sometimes they [ask where I am]. If I say, "I'm going there", they'll think I'm still there, and stuff like that... Or I won't say, I'll say, "I'm just out with one of my friends".

You just lie. It's just lying…

Parents are, again, well aware of their children's strategies. Despite some parents' claims that the phone is for the teenager to contact the adult if needed, the same parents will also take special notice when teenagers are employing these strategies:

> Yes, I think sometimes she has said "I'm going round to Vicky's" and then she rings later and you think there is an awful lot of noise in the background for Vicky's house. It sounds a lot like a pub. She will not perhaps directly lie, she will say something like "I'm with Vicky," but you feel a bit…Maybe I'm too naïve at the moment.

### Pragmatic, Enthusiastic, and Critical: Use, Meaning, and Diversity

In our research, the negotiation of the social and cultural value of mobiles in relation to identity, difference, independence, and interdependence, has clearly established patterns of meaning and use, but also has established significant diversity among young people and the contexts of their lives. These uses and meanings are very much contextually based, and depend not only on the age of the young people concerned, but also on the school and household contexts and their relative negotiation of identity, difference, and independence among themselves and with others. Clearly, not all teens consume in the same way. Of most importance perhaps is the growing indication that some teens are restricting or stopping their use of mobiles altogether. Statements such as the following were beginning to emerge:

> I've got a phone, but I prefer to spend my money on something else, so I just receive calls on it now. I never bother texting… I have text and voice mail, but I just receive calls.

This clearly challenges those studies that associate teenagers particularly with "consumption," and that assume teenagers will consume if they are able to do so, in subcultural and "global youth" styles.

We have developed three alternative categories of young users from the research data so far. These categories of user are found among all age groups. They do not describe "sub-groups" or age-based segments. Instead, these categories are more accurately described as "identity categories," based on the words teens use to describe their relationship to mobile devices, their attitudes to the role of mobiles in social life, and the characteristics with which they identify themselves and others as users.

The first category is that of "enthusiastic users." Enthusiastic users were most often found among the youngest groups of teens, although could be distributed throughout all the groups. Enthusiastic users described mobile devices—the services, the features of the phones, how they used them and what they used them for—in great detail, whether in relation to their own mobile, or that of others. They tended to identify strongly with their phones as a part of their presentation of self, and a symbol of their communication with a community of peers. They were generally positive towards (and more heavily used) the current services offered, and positive in their approach to possible future services.

"Pragmatic users" were commonly found across the middle and older age groups. These young users described mobiles as pragmatic and instrumental tools, and part of the "background" of objects that they used to negotiate everyday life. They tended to appreciate the current services offered, but did not necessarily embrace possible future services unless they could see an immediate practical benefit for their lives at present.

"Critical users" were found predominantly among the middle age groups, although they could be found in all age groups. Critical users are so-called because they tended to be negative towards the social effects of mobile phones, particularly their disruption of public space, and were also negative toward the ways mobiles were marketed to them—including the marketing of future services. They would not get a mobile phone, use it only out of necessity, or give it away once they had it (Katz, 2001).

### Conclusion

The boundaries of childhood, adolescence, and adulthood, remain relatively arbitrary. According to Sibley (1995),

> Adolescence is an ambiguous zone within which the child/adult boundary can be variously located according to who is doing the categorizing. Thus, adolescents are denied access to the adult world, but they attempt to distance themselves from the world of the child. At the same time they retain some links with childhood. ...These problems ...demonstrate that the act of drawing the line in the construction of discrete categories interrupts what is naturally continuous.

Often, the boundaries of the teenage years are defined by exclusion—by defining what those of a certain age *cannot* do, or be, or say—as in the case of legislation controlling such diverse activities as paid employment, sexual practice, drinking, voting, or fighting in a war. The social activities and meanings surrounding "teenagers" or "youth," however, neither correspond necessarily to the age of physical bodies, nor do they necessarily imply a decisive difference from the practices of adults (Wynn and Katz 2001).

As has become apparent throughout our research with mobile technologies, teenagers are economically and socially diverse, holding both similarities and differences to other age-based social groups. The categories of childhood and adolescence, youth and adulthood, are socially and situationally specific and negotiated. They can be categories of identity, and the social relationships attached to them. For example, children and adolescents can be considered (and consider themselves) "older" or "younger" when negotiation takes place with their parents about what they are deemed responsible enough to do at any given time. At times, teenagers will seek to identify with adults in order to enjoy some of the privileges of the adult world. At other times, teenagers will seek to distance themselves from the adult world (the identity category of "teenager" comes to mean the opposite of the way adults are defining it— "whatever they say I am, that's what I'm not")(Sacks 1979).

Furthermore, as Sefton-Green (1993) notes,

> ...young people themselves negotiate the social meanings of different age bound-aries.... Digital technologies, or precisely certain uses of them, continue this process of redefinition in seemingly contradictory directions. Thus, on the one hand they seem to offer a kind of "adultification," since young people can act in the digital realm with an equivalence of grown-up power. On the other hand, they seemed to have continued the process of "juvenilization" associated with leisure pastimes, and in particular with notions of playing games.

It is therefore by no means assured that young people will take up new technologies simply because they are young, nor is it assured they will con-tinue to use them in "the future," or use them for the same purposes as they age (Wyatt 1999; Katz and Aspden 1998). These points suggest caution in making any generalizations about "teenage" use of mobile technologies. Our findings suggest that youth "subcultures" and "countercultures" can be extremely con-tradictory. The social worlds of young people are created through the process of both segmentation and legitimation (Strauss 1982, 1984), which are constantly negotiated, and ensure that communities of young people cohere not only around identity, but also difference and diversity.

## References

Abbott, C. 1999. Making Connections: Young People and the Internet. In *Digital Diver-sions: Youth Culture in the Age of Multimedia*, ed., Julian Sefton-Green. London: UCL Press/Taylor and Francis.

Allatt, Pat. 1997. Conceptualising Youth: Transitions, Risk and the Public and The Private. In *Youth, Citizenship and Social Change in a European Context*, eds. John Bynner, Lynne Chisholm, and Andy Furlong. Aldershot, UK: Ashgate.

Bennett, A. 1999. Rappin' on the Tyne: White Hip Hop Culture in Northeast England—an Ethnographic Study. *The Sociological Review* 47( 1): 1–24.

Chisholm, Lynne. 1997. Sensibilities and Occlusions: Vulnerable Youth Between Social Change and Cultural Context. In *Youth, Citizenship and Social Change in a European Context*, eds. John Bynner, Lynne Chisholm, and Andy Furlong. Aldershot, UK: Ashgate.

Coles, Bob. 1997. Vulnerable Youth and Processes of Social Exclusion: A Theoretical Framework, A Review of Recent Research and Suggestions for a Future Research Agenda. In *Youth, Citizenship and Social Change in a European Context*, eds. John Bynner, Lynne Chisholm, and Andy Furlong, Aldershot, UK: Ashgate.

de Certeau, Michel. 1984. *The Practice of Everyday Life*, trans. Steven Rendall. Berkeley: University of California Press.

Evans, Karen and Andy Furlong. 1997. Metaphors of Youth Transitions: Niches, Path-ways, Trajectories or Navigations. In *Youth, Citizenship, and Social Change in a European Context*, eds. John Bynner, Lynne Chisholm, and Andy Furlong. Aldershot, UK: Ashgate.

Fowler, D. 1995. *The First Teenagers: The Lifestyle of Young Wage-Earners in Interwar Britain,* London: Woburn Press.

Gillard, P., K. Wale, and A. Bow. 1998. The Friendly Phone. In *Wired-Up: Young People and the Electronic Media,* ed. Sue Howard. London: UCL/Taylor and Francis.

Gilroy, P. 1987. *There Ain't No Black in the Union Jack: The Cultural Politics of Race and Nation,* London: Hutchinson.

Green, N. 2001. Information Ownership and Control in Mobile Technologies, *Proceedings of E-Usages: Third International Conference on Usage and Services in Telecommunications,* Paris: June.

Green, N. 2002. Who's Watching Whom? Surveillance, Regulation and Accountability in Mobile Relations. In *Wireless World: Social, Cultural and Interactional Issues in Mobile Communications and Computing,* eds. Barry Brown, Nicola Green, and Richard Harper. London: Springer-Verlag.

Hall, S. and T. Jefferson, eds. 1976. *Resistance through Ritual: Youth Subcultures in Postwar Britain.* London: Hutchison.

Howard, S. 1998. Unbalanced Minds? Children Thinking about Television. In *Wired-Up: Young People and the Electronic Media,* ed. Sue Howard, London: UCL/Taylor and Francis.

Kasesniemi, E. and P. Rautiainen. 1999. Mobile Communication of Children and Teenagers: Case Finland 1997–1999. Chapter in James Katz and Mark Aakhus (eds.), *Perpetual Contact.* Cambridge: Cambridge University Press.

Katz, J. 1999. *Connections: Social and Cultural Studies of the Telephone in American Life,* New Brunswick, NJ: Transaction Publishers.

Katz, James E. 2001. The Telephone. *International Encyclopedia of Social Science* (2nd edition). Amsterdam: Elsevier. 2001. Vol. 23, pp. 15558-65.

Katz, James E. and Philip Aspden. 1998. Internet Dropouts in the USA, *Telecommunications Policy* 22 (4/5): 327–39.

Katz, James E. and M. Aakhus, eds. 2002. *Perpetual Contact: Mobile Communication, Private Talk, Public Performance.* Cambridge and New York: Cambridge University Press.

Leblanc, L. 1999. *Pretty in Punk: Girls' Gender-Resistance in a Boys' Subculture,* New Brunswick, NJ: Rutgers University Press.

Ling, R, and B. Yttri. 1999. Nobody Sits at Home and Waits for the Telephone to Ring: Micro and Hyper-Coordination through the Use of the Mobile Telephone. Chapter in James Katz and Mark Aakhus (eds.), *Perpetual Contact.* Cambridge: Cambridge University Press.

Mauss, M. 1973. Techniques of the Body, *Economy and Society* 2 (1): 70–88.

Maffesoli, Michel. 1996. *The Time of the Tribes: The Decline of Individualism in Mass Society,* trans. Don Smith, London: Sage Publications.

Nafus, D., and K. Tracey. 1999. The More Things Change: Mobile Phone Consumption and Concepts of Personhood. Chapter in James Katz and Mark Aakhus (eds.), *Perpetual Contact.* Cambridge: Cambridge University Press.

Nagel, Ulrike, and Claire Wallace. 1997. Participation and Identification in Risk Societies: European Perspectives. In *Youth, Citizenship, and Social Change in a European Context,* eds. John Bynner, Lynne Chisholm, and Andy Furlong. Aldershot, UK: Ashgate.

Rautiainen, P. and Virpi Oksman. 2002. (this volume). Perhaps It Is a Body Part: How the Mobile Phone Became an Organic Part of the Everyday Lives of Finnish Children and Adolescents. In *Machines Become Us,* ed. J. Katz, New Brunswick, NJ: Transaction Publishers.

Sacks, Harvey. 1979. Hotrodder: A Revolutionary Category. In *Everyday Language: Studies in Ethnomethodology,* ed. George Psathas, New York: Irvington Publishers.

Sefton-Green, Julian. 1999. Introduction: Being Young in the Digital Age. In *Digital Diversions: Youth Culture in the Age of Multimedia,* ed. Julian Sefton-Green, London: UCL Press/Taylor and Francis.

Sefton-Green, J., and D. Buckingham. 1999. Digital Visions: Children's Creative Uses of Multimedia Technologies. In *Digital Diversions: Youth Culture in the Age of Multimedia,* ed. Julian Sefton-Green, London: UCL Press/Taylor and Francis.

Sheldon, L. 1998. The Middle Years: Children and Television—Cool or Just Plain Boring? In *Wired-Up: Young People and the Electronic Media,* ed. Sue Howard, London: UCL/Taylor and Francis.

Shields, R., ed. 1992. *Lifestyle Shopping: The Subject of Consumption,* London: Routledge.

Shin, Dong Kim. 1999. The Social and Cultural Conditions for the Diffusion of Mobile Communication Technology in Korea. *Perpetual Contact Workshop,* Rutgers University, December.

Sibley, D. 1995. *Geographies of Exclusion,* London: Routledge.

Skelton, F. 1989. Teenagers and the Telephone. *Australian Journal of Communication* 15: 21–24.

Smith, D. 1988. Femininity as Discourse. In *Becoming Feminine: The Politics of Popular Culture,* eds. L. G. Roman and L. K. Christian-Smith, London: Falmer Press.

Strauss, A. 1982. Social Worlds and Legitimation Processes. In *Studies in Symbolic Interaction,* ed. Norman K. Denzin, JAI Press, Inc., vol. 4, pp. 171–190.

Strauss, A. 1984. Social Worlds and their Segmentation Process. *Studies in Symbolic Interaction,* ed. Norman K. Denzin, JAI Press Inc., vol. 5, pp. 123–139, JAI Press, Inc.

Tobin, J. 1999. An American *otaku* (Or, a Boy's Virtual Life on the Net). In *Digital Diversions: Youth Culture in the Age of Multimedia,* ed. Julian Sefton-Green, London: UCL Press/Taylor and Francis.

Valentine, Gill, Tracey Skelton, and Deborah Chambers. 1999. Cool Places: An Introduction to Youth and Youth Cultures. In *Cool Places: Geographies of Youth Cultures,* eds. Tracey Skelton and Gill Valentine, London: Routledge.

Weilenmann, A. and K. Larsson. 2001. Local Use and Sharing of Mobile Phones. In *Wireless World: Social. Cultural and Interactional Issues in Mobile Technologies,* eds. B. Brown, N. Green, and R. Harper. London: Springer-Verlag.

Willis, P. 1977. *Learning to Labour: How Working Class Kids get Working Class Jobs,* Westmead: Saxon House.

Willis, P. 1978. *Profane Culture,* London: Routledge and Kegan Paul.

Wyatt, S. 1999. They Came, They Surfed, They Went Back to the Beach: Why People Stop Using the Internet. *Society for the Social Studies of Science,* Annual Conference, San Diego, CA, November.

Wynn, Eleanor and James E. Katz. 2001. Teens on the Telephone. *Info,* vol. 2 (4): August 2000, 401-419.

# 16

# Breaking Time and Place: Mobile Technologies and Reconstituted Identities

*Linnda R. Caporael and Bo Xie*

## Introduction

For most of human history, people's relationships have been bound by time and space. Communication and coordination constrained the distances people could be from each other (Katz 2001). Creative inventions have continually extended these distances. As societies changed, new conceptions of time and space emerged as by-products of novel technologies and ways of acting in the world. Information and communication technologies (ICTs) break the bonds of time and space. As in other cultural periods, such a break alters conventional boundaries between conceptions of public and private and self and identity (Katz 1999b). The mobile telephone and the personal digital assistant (PDA), two technologies that are just beginning to merge, are everyday manifestations of deep cultural and global changes. The mobile phone's "anytime/anywhere" characteristic enables the blurring of public and private space/time, and with it, the blurring of identities. The PDA enables people to reconstitute these altered boundaries by listing appointments, tasks, and other information typically associated with highly structured roles (Katz and Aakhus 2002). The mobile phone and the PDA are not just "machines that become us." They are also machines that *we have asked* to become us.

In this chapter, we report a work-in-progress using cross-cultural data from China and the United States. Questionnaires, interviews, and textual sources are used to explore (1) definitions and descriptions of what constitutes private and public time/space; (2) acceptable behavior and conversational topics related to one's location and activity; (3) how people attempt to redesign time and space through the use of personal technology, specifically the mobile phone and the PDA; and (4) how users experience their interpersonal relationships in the context of new time/space structures. At this point in our research, our goal is not to test hypotheses, but to analyze the use of these two devices to suggest

219

directions for future research. We begin in the next section with some general considerations about time/space. Although most social scientists think of time and space as objective and immutable, we suggest that human conceptions of time/space are bound up with technology.

## Time and Space

In human consciousness and history, time and space have always been intertwined (Aveni 1989), and both can be altered by technological innovation. Regularities of biological time, such as the beat of the pulse and the breathing of the lungs, have been modified by artificial time keepers. The most prominent of these has been the mechanical clock. All people have experienced feelings such as, "I'm not feeling tired, but, it is *time* to go to bed," or "I'm not really hungry, but I'll eat because it's *time* to eat." The biological "space" of our bodies has been changed by the artificial time created by the clock. More importantly, these feelings are experienced because the clock has already changed the rhythm of the whole society: most restaurants are open only during "eating time," and it is necessary to go to bed when it is time to sleep because it is necessary to wake up when it is time to work. The clock, one of the earliest products that trained and constrained human behavior, plays such a crucial role in shaping human civilization and society that Mumford was moved to argue that modern industrial society "could do without coal and iron and steam easier than it could do without the clock" (Mumford 1934, 18).

Revolutions in how human possibilities are conceived are also revolutions in how space and time are newly reconceived. Hunters and gatherers and nomadic herders move through space using the natural cues of ecological time. Among many agriculturalists, there are long periods of "in-between times" when fields lay fallow. The religious demands for prayers at intervals during the day led to the mechanical clock, which centuries later harnessed workers of the Industrial Revolution to a scheduled workday and bound railroads to precision timetables. The activity systems of humans are intimately bound to cues in the environment, which can be transformed into temporal cues (e.g., the sun's shadow) or man-made cues such as the clock. In technologically simpler societies of the past, identity was likely to be bounded by ritual times and places. In the technologically complex world of modern society, identity shifts as often as the colors in a kaleidoscope as we respond to emerging technology and move through varied groups organized around different goals.

If the many revolutions in human history have been accompanied by different ways of combining time and space, we would expect that the modern Information Revolution would have its temporal novelties. Calendars are illustrative because they are where power, identity, globalization, and temporal control come together. In the United States and Europe, the Gregorian calendar suffices for almost all purposes. In China, the Gregorian and Chinese calendar are used in business. Most Thais living in urban centers such as Bangkok use three calendars: Gregorian, Chinese, and Thai. Other characteristics of the Information Revolution include "24/7" availability, meaning the nonstop accessibility of services twenty-four hours a day, seven days a week. New information technologies can push practices around time and space. For example, the mobile phone blurs the boundaries between one's personal time and work time, once carefully separated by punch clocks. Space is also altered. A participant in the mobile conversation can be, unbeknownst to his or her partner, speaking from a distant country or from home while still in pajamas. New information technologies enable people to redefine time and space to suit their own purposes. Conceptions of privacy, public behavior and interpersonal relationships accompany new technologies that can be used to alter (or resist alteration) of existing expectations and standards (Katz 1999a).

## Mobile Phones and PDAs

The mobile phone has clearly changed one aspect of an everyday device, the telephone, by eliminating the constraints of a cord. The effects of the PDA are more complicated because they are open-ended. In addition to organizing one's day, the PDA allows one to organize record collections, to play interactive fiction games, to keep track of weight changes, and even to use it as a digital recorder, camera, or a mobile phone.

One approach to understanding the significance of the PDA is through the interrelationship of time and space. Throughout human history, human beings have tended to use space, which is visible, to represent time, which is a more abstract concept, by creating various time-keeping devices such as the mechanical clock, the paper planner, and most recently, the PDA. In its simplest manifestation, the PDA is simply an analogy to the paper planner, with bells. It enables us to coordinate with others using convenient alarms that tell us to make a call or dash off to an appointment, something the voiceless paper planner could not do. Like the mechanical clock or the paper planner, the PDA uses a spatial metaphor for time. Hours are noted on the edge of lines, and these lines can be filled in with tasks and appointments to cue us about the actions to engage next.

The planner, whether paper or electronic, is peculiarly characteristic of knowledge work, activities that require the organization of information, generation of plans of action, and evaluation of outcomes. While past human practices have been cued by physical phenomena, such as the beginning and end of daylight, or the movement of widgets down an assembly line, knowledge work seems to lack similar distinctive cues about what needs to be done next. Substitutes—such as creating stacks of work—feel disappointingly ineffectual. In some ways, the PDA appears to be an attempt to remedy the abstractness of knowledge work by instituting a series of lists and alarms to keep people on track. However, as this article demonstrates, the management of time and space in a world of information becomes increasingly personal and complex.

The lined paper planner with spaces for tasks and appointments appears to have originated in the late 1950s with the invention of a Lawyer's Day calendar by a Pennsylvania attorney. Occupation-specific calendars were later created for other professions and became so popular that a generic form was developed, which became the current DayTimer product line (see *http://www.daytimers.com*). Such planners became not just specific artifacts using space on paper for representing time and organizing activity, but also specific systems for using the artifact. Other popular systems extended the spatial metaphor. For example, Franklin Covey (Allen 2000; Covey, Merrill, and Merrill 1994) uses a quadrant to organize tasks according to importance and urgency. A central goal is to attend to those tasks that are important to one's aspirations, but not urgent, that is, tasks not cued by e-mail, voicemail, or stacks of paper demanding attention—the modern equivalent of mooing cows demanding to be milked. The David Allen Company (Allen 2000) emphasizes list-making according to location, such as "at computer" or "at phone." Unlike mooing cows that "tell" the farmer what to do, phones and computers have such general uses that that they mostly cue only pressing, possibly easy but low-value activities. An "at phone" list tells the user what other, more high-payoff calls can be made when there are a few moments for calls.

Life Balance by Llamagraphics, Inc. (http://www.llamagraphics.com) is a PDA application (originally conceived for Apple's Newton) that, unlike the others, has no paper analog. Life Balance promises to help users not only plan their time, but also to balance the competing demands of career and personal life. Goals are listed in an outline format, with sub-goals and tasks listed under a top-level goal. Tasks can be rated in terms of the effort to do the task and the importance of the task. Algorithms within the program use this and other information to determine when the task appears on the screen. Life Balance also takes the manipulation of time and space to a new level. In addition to listing when to accomplish tasks, Life Balance also enables the user to indicate where to complete the tasks, such as "home," "work," or "store." However, real-life spaces are more complex than a simple bucket such as "store" into which items can be thrown. In real life, the store may be in a mall where errands might be completed at several stores, and sometimes the stores we want to go to may be closed. In a similar way, Life Balance enables the user to create a category such as "mall" and include the names and hours of various stores. This feature, called "Places," reveals the ways in which users attempt to make virtual time and space correspond to real time and space. One user describes the possibilities (direct quotes are given exactly as they appear in the user discussion groups): "Here's how my system works. In addition to my normal 'places' (i.e., home, work, and so forth), I have places for each of the days of the week: Monday, Tuesday, Wednesday, and so forth. Each of the weekday places have certain 'open' times associated with them. Monday is 'open' starting on Mondays, and remains open until Sunday."

The following sections compare the mobile phone and the PDA in a number of dimensions. Ten Americans (four of whom were female) and eleven Chinese (two of whom were female) responded to a questionnaire on their use of mobile phones. Of these participants, four Chinese and four Americans were interviewed by telephone or America Online Instant Messenger (AIM), a free program that enables people to type conversationally in real time (see *http://www.aim.com*). Although our questionnaire included some items on PDAs, our material on personal organizers was drawn primarily from website fora. (We discovered that few Chinese use PDAs because data input involves numerous complex choices and, in China, the devices are prohibitively expensive.) The PDA data consists of 368 threads, which contributed to several Life Balance fora in 2000–2001. At the time, there were about 360 active members of the fora. As in many such discussion groups, there are a few people who have posted a large number of contributions and many who have posted one or two. Most of the contributions sampled for this paper come from about a dozen people who made numerous contributions and are most familiar with the application.

## Private and Public Time/Space

Judging from the popular media, a company takes considerable pride in having continuous ("24/7") availability, and the Internet has provided a convenient way of meeting this goal. However, with individuals, continuous availability seems to dissolve familiar distinctions between the public time and space of work and the private time and space of non-work hours. In the exploratory study of the mobile phone, we asked about the acceptability of employers calling employees outside of usual business hours. Among Chinese participants, work calls during non-work hours were acceptable to all the participants. Six of the eleven Chinese participants thought such calls were acceptable because of the importance of work, and four people said the business calls were usually an emergency. This pattern of responses contrasted with the American group, which found calls during non-work hours to be largely unacceptable. Unlike the Chinese, the Americans tended to use screening devices (caller ID, voice mail, pagers, etc.) to control their interactions. Much of the screening was to detect "emergencies," which were considered to be acceptable reasons to have a business-related conversation during non-work hours.

In addition to the screening practiced by the Americans, another way to separate public time from private time is to turn the mobile phone off. Although the Chinese participants did not use screening devices, they typically indicated (8/11) that they turned off their phones to avoid being disturbed during sleep. In contrast, Americans had several reasons for turning off their phones, including that they turned off their phones when not calling out or while re-charging batteries.

Where privacy with mobile phones appears to refer to screening off or com-partmentalizing parts of one's life, "private" and "public" initially seem to have different meanings for PDA users. *Private* refers to hiding information so that other people can't see it. Credit card information, pin numbers, and dan-gerous liaisons might be marked "private" and require a secret password to view them. However, other uses of PDAs do approximate the screening of mobile phone usage. For example, in some companies, PDAs are synchronized with group calendars; everything that is not marked *private* by the PDA user is public by default. The PDA default categories enable marking some items as *business* and others as *personal*. The user can then choose which category to view thus screening off the other. Life Balance extends this capability. Where the PDA default categories require the user to flip back and forth between business and personal, Life Balance can automatically screen categories so that only categories relevant to a specific time and/or place will appear on the PDA screen.

## Norms and Expectations

Mobile phones can be turned off to protect personal privacy, and they can also be turned off to protect the collective good. Both Chinese and Americans participants turn their phones off or switch them to silent mode in theatres, concert halls, churches, and some meetings. What is interesting about occa-sions for turning off the phone is what is *not* mentioned—turning off the phone on social occasions with friends and family. While several participants voiced concerns about "disturbing others" during public events, the same concerns were not raised for more personal relationships.

We asked mobile phone users about the acceptability of specific topics of conversation in public places. Chinese and Americans agreed that sex and money were improper topics for discussion in a crowd. Common reasons had to do with privacy around strangers. In some ways, this is a curious response—if one does not know or anticipate knowing strangers in a crowd, why would discussions of sex and money be any more personal than making appoint-ments, a topic all agreed was acceptable for public discussions? One possibil-ity is that sex and money are intrinsically interesting and draws the attention of strangers. You might not know or ever know the stranger enjoying your sexy conversation, yet somehow another's interest in your conversation makes her less a stranger and her gaze more personal. Alternatively, being an object of attention may be seen as "disturbing others" in the way that leaving the phone on in a concert is disturbing—or perhaps we have misread the concert situation in the first place and the reason to turn off the phone is to avoid having people stare.

Norms and expectations *for* PDA use were not studied, and the Life Balance fora did not mention this topic frequently (except concerning the relief of boring meetings by appearing to take notes while actually playing games). However, many PDA users use their devices to help them meet the norms and expectations of everyday life. On the Life Balance online fora, much of the advice exchanged involves setting up recurring tasks in order to remember birthdays, anniversaries, and other social events. While it is fairly simple to set a PDA to remember fixed rituals of social expectations, Life Balance users are able to use the program to help them perform "roles," a discourse drawn from the Franklin Covey (FC) time management system (Covey et al., 1994). A key objective in the FC system is to help the user achieve both inner peace and increased productivity by balancing responsibilities, obligations, and ambitions. This is done by identifying one's roles, the goals for each role, then assigning tasks ("Big Rocks") that have the highest payoff for achieving the role. Common examples of roles are "parent," "community leader," and "sales manager."

A typical FC strategy involves listing roles as the top-level items on Life Balance's outline and listing various goals beneath the role as a way of organizing categories of activity. As a user explains,

> All of your life's roles plus a category for "Sharpening the Saw" [e.g., exercise, friendships] can be put at the top level of the Life Balance outline. (Or alternately, the top level can be dedicated to the fundamental development areas: Physical, Mental, Spiritual and Social.) Below, individual goals can be listed for each role or development area. Relative priorities are assigned to each goal; these priorities can be easily revised as your thinking evolves. Once you set up your goals, you refer to the Life Balance to-do list to see what needs attention. Important goals start at the top of the list. Slightly less important goals are further down but if you ignore them for a long time, they move up in priority. This usually has the effect of making you act on them or prompts you to reassess the priorities.

A new user writes to the other members of a Life Balance forum, "I'm reevaluating the organization of my outline. I'd like to have a list of TLIs [Top Level Items of the to-do outline] that are fundamental to human life in general, then work to specifics from those. What's your idea of the most fundamental categories?" A quick reply goes,

Interesting. My TLI's are my roles, but my categories under my role as an individual are eerily close to your fundamentals.

I have / You have:

Goals / Planning

Physical / Health

Mental / Knowledge

Financial / Means

Social / Relationships

Spiritual / Reason

Creative / Pleasure

As this particular thread unwinds, other users join in and compare their roles and categories. The developer of Life Balance, Catherine White, cuts through this discussion. She objects to subdividing her life into roles partly because they have no clear meaning. Does the "good mother" role mean being like June Cleaver (of the popular 1950s TV program, *Leave it to Beaver*), she asks. Catherine continues, writing that, "Life Balance is the product of my struggle for a way to just be one authentic person, all the time, rather than to adopt twenty different roles like so many suit jackets. One Life, One list. (One little ME!)" Another user, expanding on Catherine's discussion, notes that the issue is to discover who you are deep down, thinking about whom you want to be, and addressing the schism between them. This discussion, however, instigates a return to an application focus by another user.

Obviously, there is no way of knowing how many users resolve the challenges of using Life Balance to employ its features. Most Life Balance owners do not participate in the fora, which we would expect to be heavily weighted toward those needing help and others wanting to give help. A few participants, however, appear to be highly skilled at having the right role appear at the right time. One user, correcting an earlier error reveals, "...was typing to fast...this promotion is going to kill me, how am I going to play on the web when I'm so busy. Last night my wife asked me who I was when I got home at 6 pm."

### Interpersonal Relationships

Most Chinese participants also reported that the mobile phone had not changed their interpersonal relationships. Among the Americans, those who reported the most interaction with family, friends, or co-workers also reported the least change, but these were infrequent users who paid their own phone bills. In both groups, the most frequent callers were those who had their phone costs covered by employers—and these users were young and male. One young man reported having had a mobile phone "the whole time" (meaning since reaching adult status) and explained that he did not report any change in relationships because he was very busy and did not talk to his friends and family much. The data suggest that more research is needed to investigate the interactions among gender, the source of payment for the phone, and changes in interpersonal relationships. People whose phone costs are paid by the employer tended to use the phone more frequently. However, more use could be associated with less interaction with family and friends unless these interpersonal relationships were specifically targeted for phone use.

We were disappointed to find few reports of changes in interpersonal relationships in the mobile phone pilot study.   Although there are many possible explanations, a significant possibility is that questionnaires are not the best way to detect changes in interpersonal relationships, partly because people do not accurately notice or report such changes. If this were the case, it would be necessary to turn to more informative (and expensive) research methods that enable studying phone use in the original environment. Other studies have been more successful. For example, a telephone interview study conducted with nineteen middle-class women in the Chicago area in July 1991, Rakow and Navarro (1993) found that women creatively used the mobile phone to manage their responsibilities for home and children. While the authors of this study argue that the use of mobile phones reproduced familiar gender inequalities, their descriptions of "remote mothering" suggest that there are changes yet to be understood. Anecdotal evidence suggests that mobile phones can smooth interpersonal relationships simply by making it easier to coordinate meeting times.

Relationships are important to some Life Balance users and are related for many to their concepts of roles, both of which often blend in discussions. By combining the different features of Life Balance, users are able to have tasks appropriate to a particular role appear on the screen or even have an alarm go off to remind them that a particular role-relevant task should be done.   For example, one Life Balance forum member described how the category Leisure came up reminding her that no activity had been planned, so she immediately called a friend to arrange dinner.

As relationships among family and friends become more complicated, many forum participants (especially women) struggle to create order and demonstrate their strategies so that they might help others. One woman writes,

> Maybe my approach to keeping up with family and friends can be of use to you. One of my top-level categories is "Connection." Under that I have "Charles" (my spouse), "Family" (each of our grown children and their spouses), "My extended family" (includes elderly aunts who need regular contact, cousins, etc.), "Charles' extended family" (ditto on the aunts), and "Friends." Under each grandchild level of the outline I've entered the names of the people I want to stay in touch with: "Call Chris" or "write Laura and Holland" or "visit Toni and Bill," and the time detail for each of those is whatever frequency I've found to be realistic for my schedule and theirs. I want to call Chris once a week, but we only visit Toni and Bill twice a year (it's a long trip). But this way LB helps me not let our connections slip.

In a similar vein, a man explains in an asterisked footnote to his category scheme why he has Romantic Relationships as a top level item: "*Yeah, right. Romantic relationships. As if I can remember what they're like. And I know it seems strange and a bit impersonal to have something like that in a ToDo system, but I need this because I have a bad memory and I do not want important things to slip."

In addition to the handy built-in alarm feature, Life Balance has another action motivator, a system for giving credit for completed tasks. One of the available screens features two pie charts representing the "Desired" and "Actual" balance in one's life. The sections of the pie chart represent the top-level items of the outline (which in turn may represent goals, roles, projects, etc.) A user can manipulate the size of the sections in the "Desired" pie chart, and then the trick is to complete and check off to-do items so that the "Actual" pie chart matches the "Desired." A large gap between the two charts represents a "life out of balance" (or a user who has yet to master the feature). Simply completing a task, however, does not determine the credit received. When a user taps out a task on the PDA, various algorithms that use the "Effort" and "Importance" ratings of the task determine the size of the pie chart. This method can present a problem; while the pie chart is meant to represent effort or achievement of goals, many users find it difficult to not to think in terms of time spent. One user, Rev. Brown, frets that, "If i have a task of 'spend TEN hours at the beach with family,' LB credits that as ONE task. whereas, if i spend ONE hour answering TEN phone calls at the office, LB credits that as completing TEN tasks. according to LB i have spent TEN times the 'effort' (to use the llama lingo) at work as i have with family. however that would be wrong."

While others sympathize, another forum participant explains that there is a difference between "chronos," time measured by the clock, and "kairos," time "measured by 'rightness' or 'quality' instead of quantity. The day at the beach has to be seen as "a synergy of different roles you may have in life," that could be measured in relationship goals such as "time spent with my wife," or "talking to my daughter about school difficulties." This explanation completely satisfies the reverend who replies, "you've come up with what seems to be an excellent solution…this would satisfy my need. again, llamas be praise[d]."

There are at least three interesting effects of the PDA on interpersonal relationships. One is the reflection on role, relationship, and identity as users try to construct, fit into, or otherwise amend one or another "system" for representing and acting on their interpersonal relationships. The Franklin Covey approach is an example of such a system. A second effect includes the changes that might actually occur (e.g., calling someone for dinner, taking painting lessons) prompted by interaction with the PDA. The third is the indirect effect of the PDA as a social object, one around which people create virtual relationships in the various fora.

### Breaking Time and Space

Like its land-based predecessor, the mobile phone breaks the proximal bonds of space by enabling a conversation to occur without requiring proximity. For these technologies, time *is* space. It's a different time, even a different day, when a call from China is received in New York. But that time is abridged by the immediacy of the conversation, the ability to talk without the speakers having to travel. The advantage of the mobile phone is that it eliminates the constraints of a telephone cord. In doing so, it requires people to actively substitute with behavior the constraints that would typically be imposed by place. The substitution can be seen in the way that privacy, and especially "private" conversations, such as those involving sex or money, are handled (or fail to be handled. In public spaces, the privacy of walls is substituted by hands over the phone, quick glances around the space, and a hurried request to talk another time. (The same behavior also occurs in the home when that private space has been "invaded" by undesired listeners.) A more interesting substitution may occur when one party to the conversation believes that the person to whom they're speaking is in one place, such as an office, and is really in another, such as an amusement park or at a funeral. Because the communication codes of one place are not the same as the other, the mobile phone user may have to undertake the more or less difficult performance of being "in two different places" (that of her physical location and that of the other speaker's location) at the same time.

The conflation of time and space is particularly interesting in the case of the PDA. Life Balance has a feature that enables its users to identify "Places," that can be nested within each other (e.g., the place Main Street may include another place such as Drugstore). In addition, Places can be set to be open for particular hours. So in addition to being assigned "Effort" and "Importance," a task tapped into the PDA could also be assigned to a Place. When the Place is open and the priority is high enough, the task will appear in the task list on the screen. Most participants in the Life Balance forums (including one of the developers), use Places for "real" places (bank, office, home, etc.). As they go from one place to another, they pick their Place at the top of the to-do list and tasks for that place appear. More knowledgeable users combine Place and time, as in "Home Morning," "Home Evening," "Home–Telephone," and "Home–Computer." Properly set up, Places open and close during the day and the user does not even have to select the Place; Places previously set to open and close on specific days at specific times will automatically appear. Other users, especially as they become more experienced, develop creative ways of combining time and place, sometimes utilizing dozens of line entries.

## Machines That Become Us

The first question, of course, is what constitutes "us"? Identity is a matter of where and when as much as inclusion and exclusion. The anytime/anyplace character of the mobile phone can deceive the caller. At the same time, it can demand that the receiver adopt an identity unrelated or even amusingly contradictory to the current time and place. Interpersonally, the mobile phone's side effects can be revelations about identity, as when a hip teenager out with his friends flips out his Nokia and says with disappointment, "Oh. . . hi, Ma," or the lover receives a call from his ex-girlfriend while dining with his new flame. The mobile phone can also be an extension of us (Latour 1995), embarrassing us at concerts or theatres with its rude noises. Unlike the corded phone, the mobile phone demands a nimbleness of us even as it pretends to mere convenience.

The PDA with a program like Life Balance is an ideal candidate for a machine that we can ask to become us. The rare user reports a return to lost goals and ambitions. After organizing his roles and goals, one user reported his daily study of Taoism, finishing a lingering short story, and signing up for Taijiquan lessons. More frequently, users struggle to make the machine become them. They post settings on the fora comparing Top Level Items, the organization of time in terms of Places, setting alarms, and waiting for Life Balance to "tell" them it's is time to move on to a new task or role. One user, for example, writes, "To do's that are overdue or must be done on a given day show up RED/YELLOW/GREEN. That is almost a must for me and it allows LB show me what I should be doing, and what I have to do, just by scrolling up and down real quickly." After he finishes a lengthy description of his system for organizing his life, he concludes, " …it's taken me forever to come up with this combination, but I'm finally content that I have enough FC princ[i]ples, palm portability, and drudgery automation in a solution that let me focus more on doing tasks and less on managing the programs."

Arguably, Life Balance, if not a *necessary* tool, is certainly a useful one for the mobile worker in the information age. Lacking stable cues from veridical place and time—a home where tasks and relationships in the home cue behavior or a workplace where the next stack of widgets and an assembly line drive activity—Life Balance and similar PDA to-do and date book programs help to create an activity system where things can get done (Gollwitzer 1999; Hutchins 1996). These PDA applications not only distribute cognition between user and artifact; they also reveal the dependence of human cognition and activity on a material world too often ignored in our theories of psychology (Lave 1988).

The constant activity of the 24/7 mobile phone and the PDA we hope will balance our lives points to the profound irony of modern technology. The mid-twentieth-century fantasy was that technology would increase leisure time for activities such as gardening, music, and baseball games. The fantasy was that robots and machines would do the work. Instead, we have become the cyborgs (Haraway, 1991) as the world of work enlarged, and we now need devices to contain our lives that formerly existed solely within our bodies.

### Acknowledgements

We are deeply indebted to the participants in our study, especially the mobile phone users and Catherine E. White, president and founder of Llamagraphics, Inc., (*http://www.llamagraphics.com/*) for permission to use fora material for this project. Support for this research was provided by the National Science Foundation Grant 98-1898207. We also thank Judith Gregory for her comments on early versions of this paper

## References

Allen, D. 2000. *Getting Things Fone.* New York: Viking Press.

Covey, S. R., Merrill, A. R., and Merrill, R. R. 1994. *First Things First.* New York: Simon and Schuster.

Gollwitzer, P. M. 1999. Implementation Intentions: Strong Effects of Simple Plans. *American Psychologist* 54: 493–503.

Haraway, D. J. 1991. *Simians, Cyborgs, and Women: The Reinvention of Nature.* New York: Routledge, Chapman and Hall.

Hutchins, E. 1996. *Cognition in the Wild.* Cambridge, MA: The MIT Press.

Katz, James E. 2001. The Telephone. Entry in the *International Encyclopedia of Social Science* (2nd edition). Amsterdam: Elsevier. 2001. Vol. 23, pp. 15558-65.

Katz, James E. 1999a. *Connections: Social and Cultural Studies of the Telephone in American Life.* New Brunswick, NJ: Transaction Publishers.

Katz, James E. 1999b. Communication in the Year 2075. *Science and the Future. Year 2000.* Annual Supplement of the *Encyclopedia Britannica.* Chicago and London: Encyclopedia Britannica, pp. 176-200.

Katz, James E. and M. Aakhus, eds. 2002. *Perpetual Contact: Mobile Communication, Private Talk, Public Performance.* Cambridge: Cambridge University Press.

Latour, B. 1995. Mixing Humans And Nonhumans Together: The Sociology of a Doorcloser. In *Ecologies of Knowledge: Work and Politics in Science and Technology,* ed. S. L. Star, 257–277, State University of New York Press.

Lave, J. 1988. *Cognition in practice.* New York: Cambridge University Press.

Mumford, L. 1934. *Technics and Civilization.* San Diego, New York, and London: Harcourt Brace & Company.

Rakow, L. F. and V. Navarro. 1993. Remote Mothering and the Parallel Shift: Women Meet the Cellular Phone. *Critical Studies in Mass Communication* 10: 144–157.

# 17

# Crossbreeding Wearable and Ubiquitous Computing: A Design Experience

*Jennica Falk and Staffan Björk*

**Crossbreeding Wearable and Ubiquitous Computing:
A Design Experience**

Many technological approaches have been proposed during recent years to transform the personal computer (PC) and make it usable in new places and situations. As computer use spreads to novel situations and locations, as well as begins to support activities currently not supported by conventional computers, they will have an even greater impact on everyday life. Continuous access to devices that provide enhanced communication and information processing functionality will change the environment in which we live as the devices influence the way we communicate and interact socially. While the approaches to transform PCs differ from each other, not only in their view of how computers should be designed, but also in how they imply different use and relationship to computers, they, in one sense, promise the same thing: to free the user from the boundaries of the desktop and the limitations of the desktop computer interfaces.

In ubiquitous computing (Weiser 1991), computers are envisioned as invisible and omnipresent, having moved away from the desktop to become seamlessly integrated with the physical environments in which we work and live. In this approach, the PC moves away from the user into the environment to become, in one sense, less personal. In wearable computing (Mann 1998), the personal computer is turned into a device that is worn like clothing with the goal of becoming seamlessly integrated with the wearer. Aspiring to create the "truly personal computer," the wearable computer approach moves the PC away from the desktop closer to the user, and thus becomes more personal (Katz 1999). Given the goals of the approaches, ubiquitous computing and wearable computers can be placed on opposite ends of a scale describing how "close" we should be to computer technology. Put in other words, they articulate the question: should computers be "close" to their users, as wearable computing proposes, or should they be "distanced" from their users, as proposed by ubiquitous computing?

Our hypothesis is that, despite this polarity, crossbreeding between these two "extremes" is both productive and feasible as it challenges conventional conceptions and categorizations, reaffirming or redefining approach attributes (Katz 2001). By designing such prototype devices, we believe that one can learn more about how they affect how we present ourselves, how we communicate person-to-person, and ultimately, how social boundaries in society are changed by the introduction of such technology.

To test this hypothesis, we designed a prototype device, the *BubbleBadge*, which highlights some of the possibilities and challenges of communicating and presenting ourselves in an environment saturated with information technology. In this chapter, we wish to bring forth and discuss the questions raised by the BubbleBadge design as well as to share the lessons we have learned. The following section serves two purposes: to provide a general design framework for both ubiquitous computing and wearable computers, and to draw some conclusions about what design implications these approaches suggest. We thereafter point to related works and finally articulate and discuss questions raised by the BubbleBadge and its related examples.

## Background

The answer to the question, *"Where is the computer?"* can be seen as a main design decision that separates the process of designing wearable computers from that of designing ubiquitous computing environments. This answer not only has implications for how to physically design computers but also how users should relate to them. As we describe the general design frameworks of these approaches, we will do so with the above question in mind. The investigation arrives at a number of common-sense connotations that serve as a starting point for the design of the BubbleBadge by requiring their transgression.

## Ubiquitous Computing

Ubiquitous computing envisions a seamless interaction with manifold and omnipresent computational resources in the physical environment, strongly emphasizing that the computer should disappear into the background of attention. Rather than equipping users with personal desktop computers or even laptop computers, the physical environment should contain numerous computers that can be used by anyone as needed. The power of ubiquitous computing according to Weiser, "comes not from any one of these devices; it emerges from the interaction of all of them. The hundreds of processors and displays are not a 'user interface' like a mouse and windows, just a pleasant and effective 'place' to get things done" (Weiser 1991).

The idea of ubiquitous computing originally emerged from the observation that office workers are not always stationed at their desktops, that is, not all work is, nor should be, carried out on a desktop computer. Although ubiquitous computing has since evolved to encompass environments beyond the workplace, its essence remains—the user should not have to bring the task to the computer or the computer to the task. Instead, computational facilities that match their intended use should be as readily available and as easy to use as pen and paper. If each and every one of these devices were to demand the same amount of attention from the user, as the PC tends to do, the environment as a whole would become overwhelming and unmanageable. Therefore, challenges for ubiquitous computing are to make large parts of the interaction disappear to avoid making the presence of many potentially attention-demanding tasks too stressful (so-called Calm Technology), and to reduce the complexity of using many different devices. In conclusion, ubiquitous computing offers several non-personal computers that effectively should be "invisible" to their users.

Some of the first ubiquitous computing systems, perhaps most noticeably the ParcTabs in the ParcTab system (Want et al. 1995), are specifically designed to be personal. However, the now common devices that are most similar to this primordial device, Personal Digital Assistants (PDA) and mobile phones, are not typically regarded as being examples of ubiquitous computing. This is probably at least partly due to the fact that although these popular devices are ubiquitous in the sense that one can find people carrying them everywhere, they are not accessible for use to everyone present in a physical environment. In order to avoid confusion in how we categorize devices in this paper, we refer to ubiquitous computing environments as environments that contain computational devices and resources that are available to all people in an environment.

*Communal Devices, Public Information*

Because of their placement in public spaces, items such as cafeteria message boards, street signs, and information displays are well suited to convey information to several people. Speaking generally, such objects are shared resources, or communal, and the information they convey is public. Even if the information is intended for a specific person, for example, a broadcast personal message or a personal note posted on a message board, the nature of the medium used to convey it will cause the information to be publicly available.

Similarly, if we embed computational power into walls and objects that are easily noticed, effectively turning them into information resources, they are well suited to provide people with information. In ubiquitous computing environments, such information resources are regarded as communal since nobody can claim ownership to them. However, the fact that computation and information is contained in the environment causes privacy concerns. It therefore makes sense that ubiquitous computing environments should distribute public information or information that is non-sensitive. Many successful ubiquitous computing environments can be found in "smart room" applications that support collaboration between co-located people (Streitz 1999; Abowd 1996), where the system has been designed to be communal. This suggests the connotation that computer systems based on communal devices are particularly suitable for public information or services.

*Wearable Computers*

The idea of wearable computers, as the name implies, is the idea of body-worn computing systems. They are described as highly personal devices, always powered on and always accessible, serving their users throughout all aspects of daily life. Wearable computers support accessing personal information at all times while securing control of that information by minimizing the need for external infrastructure. The systems are intended to be constant companions, literally encapsulating their wearers with computational functionality to allow a close and personal association with the user, and are envisioned as evolving over time to suit every need or preference of its wearer. Put in other words, the core of wearable computing is according to Mann (1998), "personal empowerment, through its ability to equip the individual with a personalized, customizable, information space owned, operated, and controlled by the wearer."

One of the design challenges of wearable computing is to create computer systems that function well without limiting users in their everyday activities. One of the proposed defined attributes (Mann 1998) of these computers is that they should be prosthetic devices that are so closely integrated with their wearers that they become one with the people wearing them. An important corollary of the goal that wearable computers should not restrict everyday activities is that they should not be perceived as socially inhibiting or alienating by others, as this would disturb normal social interaction.

Similar to the case of ubiquitous computing, many increasingly common devices such as PDAs, mobile phones, and computational watches, are carried (or worn) by people and are constantly available for use. Since these devices are not explicitly regarded as wearable computers in the research community, we will be more generous in our definition of a wearable computer. For example, we include devices that are picked up from a table, or worn in pocket or on a belt clip.

*Personal Devices, Private Information*

Diaries, wallets, and safe-deposit boxes are examples of objects owned by or associated with specific people, that is, they are personal, and content is maintained and controlled by specific people. By being physically in control of how the objects are accessed, one is also in control of the content.

In terms of computing, the PC is one such container, and even more so, if it can be worn. Because of how wearable computers are designed, it is difficult, if not impossible, for outsiders to access the information unless the user explicitly makes it available. Therefore, it makes sense to use such computers for private information. Many wearable computing applications (Rhodes 1997) are designed as such, for example, e-mail or personal notes, suggesting the connotation that highly personal computing devices are suitable for handling private information.

### The BubbleBadge

We designed the BubbleBadge with the goal of creating a device that was both communal and personal, and that handled both public and private information—but we were interested in how challenging was the proposed connotations that personal devices should handle private information and communal devices should handle public information. We wanted to turn the wearable computer inside out to face the public and let the ubiquitous computing environment be worn bodily.

After evaluating several design concepts, we decided to construct a wearable device that borrowed characteristics from jewelry. The advantages of basing a design on jewelry was easy to motivate: they are conventional "wearables," highly personal, and in continuous contact with the wearer, but at the same time also public, as they are viewed primarily by other people. We soon concluded that a brooch design would be especially suitable because they afford viewing by other people than the wearer, a property that we capitalized on in our design. The final BubbleBadge design became that of a computer display residing in a brooch-like frame that is pinned to a wearer's clothing, making it a *public wearable display*.

Its design suggested that the BubbleBadge could function well in face-to-face conversations. Not only is it placed near the face, but also a quick glance on the display does not necessarily interrupt a conversation and the BubbleBadge can thus be an unobtrusive part of the interaction between people. Figure 17.1 depicts the first generation of the BubbleBadge hardware.

**Figure 17.1**
**First Prototype of the BubbleBadge**

**Figure 17.2**
**Second Prototype of the BubbleBadge**

The first generation of the BubbleBadge was based on the Nintendo™ GameBoy, an off-the-shelf handheld video game, from which we detached the display. The display was then encased in the brooch frame and reconnected to the video game by a long cable, allowing the game computer to be worn separate from the display, for example, on a belt. The second generation, as depicted in figure 17.2, was designed with the Color GameBoy. For a brief technical description of this work, see Ljungstrand et al. 1999.

Interacting with the BubbleBadge. By designing the BubbleBadge as a brooch it is naturally directed away from the wearer and towards the people with whom the wearer interacts. This is in contrast to a typical wearable computing system that provides information solely for the wearer. Interestingly, this makes the viewer of the BubbleBadge the actual user rather than the wearer. This has the implication that the information displayed should be of relevance to the viewer, either because the information is addressing that person or because the information is of contextual relevance to that person.

As the BubbleBadge is attached to a person who is not its actual user we deliberately omitted input mechanisms such as buttons, making physical interaction with the device unnecessary. Lacking input from the viewer, the BubbleBadge requests and retrieves information from other sources. In the current design, local servers and other BubbleBadges (e.g., the *viewer's* own device) provide this information. Below is a sample use scenario that highlights how the BubbleBadges may function in face-to-face conversations:

> Liza and John meet in the corridor and stop for a chat. Their BubbleBadges identify each other via infrared communication so that Liza's BubbleBadge is set to present information related to John, and vice versa. Liza's BubbleBadge runs an e-mail notification program that queries a local server for new e-mail, and when she has new e-mail, it requests that the message "Liza, You have new e-mail!" is shown on John's display. As John has allowed trusted sources to use his BubbleBadge to display such messages, Liza is notified about her new e-mail while she is talking to John without explicitly having to pick up any device or otherwise interrupt the conversation. A few minutes later both BubbleBadges pick up a message, this time broadcast from a local server,

reminding everyone about the weekly lunch meeting. John and Liza have both autho-
rized this type of message, and this time, their BubbleBadges show the message on its
own display, instead of forwarding it to the other device.

As with wearable computers, BubbleBadges are personal devices because
individual people wear them. However, BubbleBadges do not provide wearers
with information that are private to them. Because the display is directed away
from the wearers, such information would make little sense to display. Hence,
BubbleBadges lack one of the main properties of wearable computers—the
ability to display private information to the wearer.

When public announcements are broadcast, such as in the case of the lunch
meeting announcement, the BubbleBadges are used to display public information. This illustrates how the devices challenge the connotation between private information and personal devices by showing public information on personal devices. In addition, BubbleBadges may function, to viewers, as display
devices of private information. In the scenario, Liza reads a private message
(i.e., that she has new e-mail) on John's personal display. Thus, BubbleBadges
contradict the connotation of using communal devices as a source for public
information in two ways: by using a personal device as a communal resource
for information and by using that resource to show private information. Although one may claim that private information presented in a public medium
makes the information public, in the context of the BubbleBadge it is still
regarded as private (or perhaps personal) as it is addressed to one particular
person.

### Related Work

Work conducted by Horovitz (1999) to combine agents and direct manipulation, or the works of Want et al. (1999), and Ishii and Ullmer (1997) to couple
digital information with physical objects, suggest that it is possible to combine
paradigms and arrive at interesting and novel conclusions. One explicit example of interest to the BubbleBadge is the work of Rhodes et al. (1999), where
a system combining wearable computers and ubiquitous computing is described.
However, the system uses ubiquitous computational devices to support and
enable functionality for wearable computers rather than explore the possibilities of merging the concepts. Below, we discuss in greater detail two devices
that are of specific relevance to the BubbleBadge as they have several characteristics in common.

The *Meme Tag* (Borovoy et al. 1998) is a display device worn around the
neck. It hosts text messages, or *memes*, that can propagate via infrared communication over a "network" of devices. It is based on the idea of computer enhancing nametags used at social events such as conferences. Similar to the
BubbleBadge, the Meme Tags have displays that are directed toward viewers
rather than their wearers. The Meme Tag can be viewed as a device that chal-

lenges our proposed connotations for similar reasons as the BubbleBadge. The devices are worn and perform their own computation, but the information displayed is not intended for the wearers of the devices, but rather for the viewers. The main difference from the BubbleBadge is that the information displayed depends on information locally stored on the individual Meme Tags, which differs from user to user. In essence, it matters whom you talk to.

The Active Badge (Want et al. 1992) is related to our discussion because it is a personal device used in a ubiquitous computing environment where information about the wearer is made public. Active Badges communicate their presence to infrared beacons mounted throughout a physical space in order to infer location information about people. This location information was made available on ordinary computer displays where the name and location of the Active Badge wearers were presented.

## Discussion

The BubbleBadge is interesting because its design raises interesting questions rather than offering novel technology or functionality. How should we relate to a public wearable display? Is this wearable or ubiquitous computing? How should we understand such a device? It is not important that the BubbleBadge is a brooch since a baseball cap with an electronic display or a T-shirt using the whole backside as a display area would bring forth the same type of questions. Although its physical appearance, that is, a display that you wear like a brooch is very simple, the answers to questions regarding how we should relate to such a display seem to be unexplored and potentially rewarding to how we view computers and their role in society.

The initial reaction from people about the BubbleBadge design primarily concerned the question of how public wearable displays could benefit them. Not surprisingly, the answer depended to a large extent on whether the people questioned saw themselves as viewers or wearers of such a display. Nearly everyone expressed that it is more interesting to be the viewer of the BubbleBadge than the wearer. This was expected, and while people could relatively easily find scenarios where BubbleBadges offer useful functionality to them as viewers, it seemed more difficult for them to find reasons for wearing one. We believe that this partly is due to the pervasive preconceptions about computers as tools in service to the user most obviously associated with them, and partly due to the fact that people did not have the opportunity to get familiar with wearing BubbleBadges over an extended amount of time. Claiming that the BubbleBadge is not interesting in terms of functionality does however not mean we dismiss the importance of providing it with meaningful applications. We believe that finding even only one good reason to wear it might suffice to increase our understanding of these types of devices. We therefore identified a number of possible uses of a computational device that is worn but presents output to other people.

If we make the parallel between the BubbleBadge and some of the artifacts we use to make statements ourselves, e.g. jewelry, clothes, hairdos, all of which we make very conscious choices about and often have very strong feelings about we might find one kind of answer. Another answer is to view the BubbleBadge as the wearer's puppet or the messenger that expresses or presents personal information or information that the wearer would like to express. Both these ideas are concerned with making the wearer feel a stronger personal attachment to the BubbleBadge. An alternative approach could be to do the opposite and make the wearer feel disassociated with it. The idea is to create a use for the BubbleBadge where it is easily accepted as not a part of the wearer's usual image. One example of such an application area is within constructed events, such as role-playing or game-playing situations where the BubbleBadge can be seen as a theatrical prop that has some importance, either in the narrative play or to the character. The final area of use we proposed for the BubbleBadge is as an icebreaker in arranged social situations, for example, conference receptions, much like the proposed use of the Meme Tag. We believe that a prime requirement to the answer of why a person would want to wear a BubbleBadge lies in making the experience of wearing it a comfortable one, which will differ from person to person and from situation to situation.

Naturally, whether a person would want to wear a BubbleBadge largely depends on the information it presents. The most salient objection to wearing one was the uncertainty about the nature of the presented information simply because the wearers could not see the display themselves. Because the display was attached to them, the wearers felt tempted to look down and see what the viewer saw. Nevertheless, they suggested situations where it would be beneficial to present information about the wearer. One suggestion, besides variations of the ones described above, was to let hospital patients wear BubbleBadges that displayed physiological information, for example, heart rate or blood pressure. Another proposition was to let conference participants wear the Bubble-Badges and present context-aware and tailored information when people meet.

In the case of the BubbleBadge, four sources of information can be categorized: *the wearer, the viewer, information relating to both,* and *information relating to the location.* The wearer has, as we have seen, been an obvious choice and easy for people to relate to. A more radical idea is to let the viewer be the source of information, as illustrated in the e-mail notification example in the scenario. In addition, it is interesting to let the information be a result of the specific people that interact (Meme Tag are examples of devices that displays such information). The information displayed could for example, relate to the persons previous encounters, or their mutual interests (Borovoy et al. 1996). Finally, the information could be provided by the location, also illustrated in the scenario above where a message was broadcast from a server.

In order to infer more general conclusions about public wearable displays, it is necessary to test the BubbleBadge in various situations as well as to explore what reasons compel people to be the wearers of public wearable displays. Further, additional types of public wearable displays and devices that are hybrids between the two approaches need to be constructed to gain a richer understanding of this design space.

## Conclusion

In this chapter we have described the BubbleBadge, which is a public wearable display that provides information to viewers of the device. Further, we have given examples of use situations along with a discussion on how the interaction with a BubbleBadge differs from other personal computing devices.

During the process of designing the BubbleBadge we identified two connotations regarding ubiquitous computing and wearable computers: *communal-public* and *personal-private*. Although the BubbleBadge can be at least partially described in terms of both wearable and ubiquitous computing, it does not completely fit into either category. It questions the connotations by being a device that is both communal-private (in the case where it showed e-mail) and personal-public (in the case where it showed public announcements). This disparity has let us articulate and explore questions concerning crossbreeding wearable computers and ubiquitous computing. By doing so, we can not only identify new areas of information technology use, but also open up a route to gain a richer understanding of wearable computers and ubiquitous computing in general, and of hybrids between them in particular.

## References

Abowd, G.D., C.G. Atkeson, and A. Feinstein, et al. 1996. Teaching and Learning as Multimedia Authoring: The Classroom 2000 Project. *Proceedings of MM '96*, ACM Press, pp. 187–198.

Borovoy, R., F. Martin, S. Vemuri, et al. 1998. Meme Tags and Community Mirrors: Moving from Conferences to Collaboration. *Proceedings of CSCW'98*, ACM Press, pp. 159–168.

Borovoy, R., M. McDonald, F. Martin, and M. Resnick. 1996. Things that Blink: Computationally Augmented Name Tags. *IBM Systems Journal* 35 (3-4): 488–495.

Horovitz, E. 1999. Principles of Mixed-Initiative User Interfaces. *Proceedings of CHI'99*, ACM Press, pp. 159–166.

Ishii, H., and B. Ullmer, Tangible Bits: Towards Seamless Interfaces Between People, Bits and Atoms. *Proceedings of CHI'97*, ACM Press: 1997, pp. 234–241.

Katz, James E. 2001. The Telephone. Entry in the *International Encyclopedia of Social Science* (2nd edition). Amsterdam: Elsevier. 2001. Vol. 23, pp. 15558-65.

Katz, James E. 1999. Communication in the year 2075. *Science and the Future. Year 2000.* Annual Supplement of the *Encyclopedia Britannica*. Chicago and London: Encyclopedia Britannica, pp. 176-200.

Ljungstrand, P., S. Björk, and J. Falk. 1999. The WearBoy: A Platform for Low-Cost Public Wearable Devices. *Proceedings of ISWC'99*, IEEE Computer Society, pp. 195–196.

Mann, S. 1998. Wearable Computing as Means for Personal Empowerment. Retrieved September 10, 2001 from http://wearcam.org/icwckeynote.html

Rhodes, B. 1997. The Wearable Remembrance Agent: A System for Augmented Memory. *Proceedings of ISWC'97*. IEEE Computer Society: Rhodes, B., N. Minar, and J. Weaver, Wearable Computing Meets Ubiquitous Computing: Reaping the Best of Both Worlds. *Proceedings of ISWC'99*: 141-149. IEEE Computer Society, 1999.

Streitz, N., J. Geißler, T. Holmer, et al. 1999. i-LAND: An Interactive Landscape for Creativity and Innovation, *Proceedings of CHI'99*, ACM Press, pp. 120–127.

Want, R., K. P. Fishkin, A. Gujar, and B. L. Harrison. 1999. Bridging Physical and Virtual Worlds with Electronic Tags. *Proceedings of CHI'99*, ACM Press, pp. 370–377.

Want, R., A. Hopper, V. Falcão, and J. Gibbons. 1992. The Active Badge Location System, *Transactions on Information Systems* 10 (1), ACM Press, pp. 91–102.

Want, R., B. N. Schilit, N. I. Adams, et al. 1995. The Parctab Ubiquitous Computing Experiment. Technical Report, CSL-95-1, Xerox Palo Alto Research Center.

Weiser, M. 1991. The Computer for the 21st Century, *Scientific American* 265 (3): 94–104.

# 18

# Mobile Telephony, Mobility, and the Coordination of Everyday Life

*Rich Ling and Leslie Haddon*

### Introduction

Against the backdrop of extensive urban expansion and suburbanization (Chen 2000; Crawford 1994; Haddon 2001; Hall 1989; Thorns 1972) telephony is seen as a way to coordinate interaction (Katz 1999). However, there are also a number of claims about the potential effects that telecommunications can have on mobility (Katz 2001). For example, there is the suggestion that telephony and transportation stimulate each other (Falk and Abler 1980). Others argue that telephony modifies travel rather than reducing demand (Salomon 1985), and still others note the contrary idea that telephony replaces transportation (Claisse and Rowe 1993; 1988).

Invariably, these discussions concern fixed telephony, and in an historical context. Yet there has been recently a growing range of studies about mobile telephones (Katz and Aakhus 2002) and though many of these are qualitative studies of the mobile phone, they often suggest a variety of implications for physical mobility. The first step in this chapter is to assemble and review this material in relation to certain key issues. These include:

- The role of the mobile phone in the micro-coordination of activities and modification of travel;

- Gender differences in relation to mobility, coordination, and mobile telephone use;

- The question as to whether mobile telephony promotes or reduces travel;

- The location of mobile phone use.

Next, we report on the findings of a Norwegian quantitative study of the relationship between mobility and the mobile phone.

Reflecting on this study, the final part of the chapter considers how this whole line of investigation might be further developed.

*Mobile Phone's Role in Changing the Coordination of Mobility*

Looking broadly at the way in which mobility has been coordinated, one can see three general phases. The first phase comprises the period before telegraphy, where communications regarding mobility could only be delivered by being mobile. That is, the speed of the message was the speed of physical transport. With the development of the second phase, telegraphy, the speed of the messages that could potentially cause or save travel was able to move at many times the speed of physical travel. Thus, one could send a message to a remote person asking them to come or not come without the need for a messenger to actually make the physical trip to the "interlocutor." The limitation on this system is that, in order for the message to come through, the person sending a messaged needs access to a sending device, at a fixed location, and also needs to know the physical location of the person who is receiving the message, as encoded, for example, in a telephone number. The third phase, which we are now experiencing, removes the condition on fixed locations for the sending and receiving equipment. A person interested in sending a message is, within some very broad boundaries, free to choose where they will initiate the communication. In addition, there is no need to know the location of the person to whom they wish to speak. The development of mobile telephony thus "softens time" in that one does not necessarily need to agree upon an absolute point in time but rather can, to some degree negotiate, or micro-coordinate, over where and when to meet. Given these technical considerations, the nuances with which mobility can be synchronized, and the social norms of giving and receiving messages in places where this was previously not possible, are both changing.

In this chapter, we further examine the role of the mobile telephone in the coordination of everyday life. This issue has arisen in qualitative analyses (Ling 2000a; Ling and Yttri 2002). Material from both individual and group interviews over the last three to five years indicates that, broadly speaking, there are several motives associated with the adoption of the mobile telephone. Depending on the group interviewed, these motives include accessibility, display, coordination, and safety or security. This material also indicates there are generational effects at work here. Specifically, the accessibility and display issues are particularly pronounced among teens and young adults. The use of the mobile telephone for micro-coordination is most noticeable among families with children. Finally, issues associated with safety and security is common among older users. The placement of these age groups within the confines of the various orientations is not, however, absolute. For example, teens (in conjunction with their parents) employ the mobile telephone as a type of security system in certain situations. Teens coordinate activities with friends and family via the device, and so on.

In the material from group interviews one often comes across parents describing the use of the mobile telephone to coordinate or perhaps micro-coordinate, their activities (Ling and Yttri 2002). The informants described the arrangement and reorganization of various logistical details on a real-time basis. These comments included such things as driving children to music lessons, purchasing things at the store, or relaying messages. There is, however the coda that "It is something that we need." This is key here. The informant is describing the exchange of information regarding the ongoing routine maintenance everyday life. This type of call is not intended as social interaction. Rather the call is concrete and focused. Thus, the qualitative material points to the sense that the mobile telephone is a device that allows for the redirection of already established trips. There is the suggestion here that the more functional purpose of the mobile phone results in a more efficient use of the transportation system. Rather than having to move from fixed telephone to fixed telephone in order to give and receive messages, one can do this, to use Townsend's phrase, on a "real-time" basis (2000). The mobile telephone allows for the nuanced coordination of transportation such that meetings can be arranged, errands can be carried out, and people can be reached.

There are different types of micro-coordination that affect transport and travel. In earlier work, it was found that the mobile telephone is used in the coordination of various types of work. For, example, in the case of construction work, the mobile phone is used to coordinate the delivery of various types of equipment and also to check plans with central decision-makers. The variations used in the family do not necessarily have the same economic motivation, but previous work has shown that the device is used in the same way.

*Gender, Mobility, and the Mobile Phone*

The fourth area of interest concerns gender. Both mobility and telecommunications have been considered specifically in relation to women's role in the maintenance of the home and domestic life. Analysis has shown, for example, that women often have more complex, and thus more limited transportation alternatives, precisely because of that domestic commitment (Hayden 1984). Hjorthol (2000) has demonstrated that women work closer to home, and because of this they have fewer choices concerning the geographical labor market. Women's mobility is contingent upon domestic responsibility, and thus, their trips are more often the combination of several tasks. This is particularly true in families with pre-school or primary school children. Put into the Falk and Abler's context (1980), women have greater "effort distances" than men.

Looking into the telecommunications portion of this equation, there is the sense in which the telephone allows for a type of multi-tasking, enabling women to be both away from the home but also in contact with it, and so able to carry out those responsibilities. Rakow and Navarro, as well as Vestby, speak of "remote mothering," that is, using the telephone to communicate with children who have come home from school and need to check in with their parents. (Rakow and Navarro 1993; Vestby 1996; Moyal 1989; Rakow 1988; 1992).

The mobile telephone has also been considered in this light—parenting by proxy. Indeed, Rakow and Navarro considered this technology specifically for this purpose. More generally, this has to be placed within the argument that because of the mobile, one is not chained to a specific location (Lange 1993). In the context considered here, we have empirical examples of how the mobile allows one, for example, to attend to domestic errands while also being available for job related interaction (Klamer et al. 2000). This is done against the backdrop of the increasingly private use of public space (Keane 2000; Ling 1997).

*Mobile Telephony and the Promotion or Reduction of Mobility*

Apart from the role of mobile telephony in changing journeys already in progress via the process of micro-coordination, there is the question of whether this technology generates or reduces mobility overall, that is, whether it leads to extra or lesser traveling. As a first step to understanding the significance of this issue, we need to reflect upon more general discussions of mobility in society.

Taken in a wider perspective, the degree to which we are mobile on the whole is an important issue for a number of reasons. Certainly, mobility is a concern for transportation planners. Moreover, one key issue from an environmental perspective concerns sustainable travel—especially in relation to the pollution from cars—given the green critique pointing to the unsustainability of current levels of mobility, or what has been termed "hypermobility" (Adams 2000). Questions have also been raised concerning the limits to mobility because of the amount of time that people are ultimately willing to spend on traveling (Vilhelmson 1999). Meanwhile, other authors have drawn attention to work processes affecting the "nomadization" of our lives (de Gournay 1996); to how we are locked into certain levels of mobility by spatial locations of work, shops, leisure facilities, etc., which have created a need for certain types of travel (Sørensen 1999); and to the subjective imperative to travel in which the very experience of being modern is linked to our mobility (Sørensen 1999).

Against this background of interest in mobility, we have the question of how much information and communication technologies (ICTs) may reduce or indeed create more journeys. For example, we have one strand of writings about telework, (and by implication the ICTs involved in that work), which deal with the possible effects of this work practice on travel. This was captured in the original term "telecommuting" explicitly suggesting that transport would be replaced by telecommunications (Nilles 1991) and more recent appraisals by those such as Gillespie et. al., (1995). That optimism has been replaced by a generally more sober estimation of its potential (Haddon 1999).

Moreover, we question the potential effects on mobility of communications and transactions in the form of activities such as home shopping, home banking, distance learning. (The COST269 Mobility Workgroup 2001). To date, though, far more emphasis has been placed on ICTs such as the Internet rather than the relation of the mobile phone to mobility.

What evidence, then, do we have that specifically relates to the mobile phone? There are some, albeit contradictory, clues about the mobile phone's influence on mobility from the following recent European study. The EUROSCOM-P903 project contained a qualitative using six focus groups among six countries: the Czech Republic, Denmark, France, Italy, The Netherlands, and Spain.

- There were instances of people who were out of the home using the mobile phone to ask another to join them, leading to journeys that otherwise might not have taken place (Klamer et al. 2000). Certainly some participants thought that in general the mobile phone had led to an increase in their own mobility.

- In that same study, some participants claimed they actually made fewer journeys for socializing because of the mobile phone. However, others argued that it was, in reality, other factors, such as time pressures, which really made such journeys problematic. It was only when people could not travel for these reasons that the mobile phone was used and was useful for making contact. Hence, the mobile phone did not itself necessarily directly cause a reduction in mobility, but rather compensated for it.

- Some participants doubted whether the mobile phone had much effect overall compared to other more important factors influencing the total degree to which people traveled.

There is one further question not addressed in this study and that is whether the option provided by mobile telephony enables us, indeed tempts us, to pack in more activities into the day. In one sense, this relates to the wider issue of time use, the timing of activities and the "busyness" of life, but this all has implications for mobility.

*Location and Mobile Phone Calls*

A third question, somewhat distinct from the various changes in mobility discussed above, relates to the issue of where we use mobile phones. One distinction within the study of mobility in everyday life can be made between the use of ICTs generally when traveling, that is, when underway, as opposed to their use in sites away from the home (and perhaps away from work) (Haddon 2000). However, to date, we do not actually know how much the mobile phone is used en route as opposed to in these other sites and hence, this will be addressed in the findings reported below.

To clarify the distinction a little further, we have a set of questions and research that focus on the relation between ICTs and travel behavior—and this would include micro-coordination en route, the utilization of travel time to make mobile phone calls, calling from the mobile to say when you will arrive, be late, etc. (The COST 269 Mobility Workgroup 2001). The picture is made slightly more complicated by the organization of mobility by ICTs prior to travel; thus, calls may relate to or even initiate mobility but they do not take place actually en route.

On the other hand, we have studies of particular sites and events, that is, particular space-times such as the restaurant meal (Ling 1997) or the holiday in the Norwegian *hytte* (Ling et al. 1997) that have their own specific social dynamics, expectations, rules etc. These space and time factors in turn have a bearing on the experience of using ICTs such as the mobile phone.

Turning to existing studies, there seems to be little research on where phones are used, but there is at least some on where mobiles are switched on. A European five-country quantitative study examined how often mobile phones were switched on in one's own home, restaurants and bars, shops, shows or plays, buses or trains, cars or other people's homes (Haddon 1998). The study, which covered France, Germany, Italy, Spain, and the U.K., was conducted for Telecom Italia in 1996. In all of those countries, the location where mobile phone users were least likely to have their phones switched on was when attending some event like a play or show, adhering to the rules of those particular settings. In contrast, the car, as a relatively private space, was where people from all the countries said they were most likely to have the mobile on—with the likelihood that they had them on while underway.

However, this study also highlighted another factor about location. Most of the discussion about the mobile phone and representations of its use refer to spaces outside of the home. Yet between about a fifth (18 percent in the UK, 22 percent in Germany) and about a third (32 percent in France, 31 percent in Spain, and 29 percent in Italy) of interviewees always had their phones switched on when they were at home. This, then, might count as a first sign that at least some are adopting the mobile phone as their personal terminal through which they can be contacted at all times—as opposed to just using it when they are out of the home and reverting to the domestic line when at home.

Accordingly, the survey reported in this paper asked not only about the use of mobile phones at other sites and about use when traveling but also about mobile calls made and received at home as well as at work, a site that seems to have received very little attention in discussions of mobile phone use so far.

## Collecting Evidence

The material described below was gathered in a "diary" survey involving ninety-three persons living in Bærum, a suburb immediately west of Oslo, Norway. The area is generally upper middle-class with a high percentage of single-family homes. Since the sample was somewhat small and since we were interested in focusing on the ways in which the mobile telephone is used in the coordination of mobility, respondents were selected according to criteria intended to expose these characteristics. Thus, it is neither possible to claim that these statistics can be generalized, nor that confidence intervals are particularly small. Of course, if we considered other groups on a national basis, it is possible that the findings here would be contradicted. This stated, the results nonetheless point toward the fact that mobile telephony has an impact on transport for the families included in the sample.

The instrument used to collect the data was a diary wherein the respondents were asked to describe each private telephone call made or received (from both fixed and mobile terminals) as well as mobile-based text messages during a twenty-four-hour period. E-mail messages were not considered in this analysis. In addition, respondents were asked to describe each trip taken during the same twenty-four-hour period. Trips included those taken on foot, bicycle, automobile, public transport, or a combination of these types. In addition, the respondents were asked to record and describe each trip made during the course of the day, regardless of which type of transport was used.

In order to be included in the sample, a person had to be a parent in an intact "dual-income" family wherein there were children under the age of twelve. In addition, the family needed to have a car and at least one mobile telephone. These dimensions describe a relatively small group of persons when considering the total population. The justification for the requirements was to try to find those persons who were the most likely to have a need for routine coordination. We know from earlier work, that the demands on this group are particularly stringent (Hjorthol 2000). The everyday demands for delivering children to various daycares, schools, and extracurricular activities, particularly in a suburban setting, means that the parents need to pay special attention to the coordination of the various activities. From a methods perspective, it is not quite legitimate to prefigure the analysis in this way. However, given the limited budget for the analysis, the desire to take the first steps at quantifying the results of qualitative analysis and also the quasi-exploratory nature of the work this must be allowed as an acceptable strategy. Obviously there is the open research question associated with describing other age, gender, life cycle, and income groups.

Looking quickly at the respondents, there were 93 persons who filled out the diary. Of these, there were 52 (approx. 56 percent) men and 40 (44 percent) women. The ages of the informants ranged from 24 to 61 with the mean age being 39. With the exception of one missing answer, all the informants had a driver's license, and all but 4 percent of the spouses had a driver's license. Interestingly this 4 percent of spouses without a license were all women. The material shows that 41 percent of the respondents had only one automobile in their households while 59 percent had two or more. This is a high rate of car ownership for Norway but it reflects the affluence of the suburb in which the trial took place. When looking at their working lives, with only one exception the men were employed in full-time jobs. By contrast, 56 percent of the women were in full-time jobs.

When looking at the location of one's work, 67 percent of the men worked in Oslo, that is, the local metropolitan center, where half of the women said the same. By contrast, 47 percent of the women worked locally in Bærum while only 24 percent of the men said the same. The remaining respondents worked in other locations. Thus, the men were significantly more likely to work in the city while women worked locally (Pearson chi$^2$ = 4.523 [1], sig. = 0.03).

Finally, the respondents indicated that in 81 percent of the cases, their spouses had a mobile telephone (this in addition to the respondent's mobile). Looking at this by gender, however, 96 percent of the women said that their husband had a mobile telephone while only 71 percent of the men said that their wives had a one. Again, this is a statistically significant difference (Pearson chi$^2$ = 6.843 [1], sig. = 0.03).

The picture that emerges here is that the respondents are well off when compared to the general population of Norway. However, there are gender differences in the commuting (women are more local) and also in the access to mobile telephony (women have less access). These two latter trends are characteristic for women in Norway (Hjorthol 2000; Ling 2000b).

The travel diary showed that there were 361 trips reported by the respondents. The median length of the trips reported was 7 km and the time was fifteen minutes. A trip was travel from one point to a second point. Thus, a trip could include several legs, each of which was reported separately. The statistics here are for the "legs" of a trip. When looking at the daily pattern of both the calls and trips there are two obvious peaks for both travel and calling. The first occurs from 7:00 to 9:00 and the second from about 16:00 to 18:00. The valley between peaks is deeper for calling than for travel. The other interesting point is that the morning call peak comes slightly calling than for travel peak. The other interesting point is that the morning call peak comes slightly before that travel peak. We will come back to this in the discussion below.

### What We Found Out About Mobile Telephones

*Use of the Mobile Telephone*

Taking the use of the mobile telephone first, 43 percent of the personal calls reported were either made or received via a mobile terminal. As with possession on mobile phones, there is a statistically significant gender difference that follows from men's greater access to the mobile telephone via their job (Ling 2000b). This will be examined in more detail below.

When looking at the private calls reported in the diary, the respondents reported a total of 394 calls. Of these calls, 77 were related to the arrangement of travel. The data shows that 48 of these travel-related calls were made via the fixed-line telephone, and the remaining 29 were made via the mobile telephone.

*The Effect of the Telephone on Travel*

Turning now to our first two areas of interest, the 77 travel-related calls, one question asked whether the telephone call had any effect on respondent's use of the car, offering the options of (a) the call resulted in a trip, (b) the call changed a trip already underway, and (c) the call saved a trip. Table 18.1 shows that mobile use is roughly evenly balanced between causing, changing, and saving trips, with slightly more calls causing additional car journeys. There are, however, more substantial differences when looking at travel arranged through the fixed-line telephone. More than half of the travel-related calls made via the fixed-line telephone caused travel. This is almost 20 percent more than with the mobile telephone. In addition, when considering changing travel, this was twice as common with less than half of the calls. This, of course points to the advantage of the mobile telephone in that it allows for this type of real-time coordination.

*Gender and the Use of the Mobile Telephony in Mobility and Coordination*

As the reader will recall, one of the informant selection criteria was that the household should have a mobile telephone that is in active use. The data show the men dominated in this use of the device. The men reported receiving or making 53 percent of their private calls via the mobile telephone while only 32 percent of the women said the same (Pearson chi$^2$ = 16.957[1], sig. < 0.001 [n = 389]). This finding is also supported by earlier analysis of gender-based use of the mobile telephone (Ling and Vaage 2000).

When considering only the 77 travel-related calls, that is, calls that either generated, saved, or changed travel, there were several gender-based differ-

**Table 18.1**
**Effect of Calls on Travel Behavior (in Percent) by Terminal Type**

Effect on travel

| Terminal type | Caused | Changed | Saved |
|---------------|--------|---------|-------|
| Mobile | 37.93 | 31.03 | 31.03 |
| Fixed | 56.25 | 14.58 | 29.17 |

n=77

**Table 18.2**
**Calls made to various persons by terminal type (in Percent)**

| Relation | Mobile | Fixed |
|---|---|---|
| Partner* | 31 | 22 |
| Kids | 9 | 10 |
| Kin* | 8 | 16 |
| Friends** | 7 | 18 |
| Acquaintances | 4 | 5 |
| Other** | 41 | 29 |

n = 169 mobile and 223 fixed
* = < 0.05, ** = 0.05 to 0.001.

ences. First, women made or received more of these types of calls. Where men made about 41 percent of the travel-related calls, women made 58 percent of these. These findings are in concert with the general way in which women are often more deeply involved in the everyday coordination of the household (Ling 1998). When considering the type of terminal used, men were evenly split between making travel-related calls on the mobile telephone (52 percent) and the fixed-line telephone (48 percent). With the women, about 69 percent of their travel calls were via the fixed-line telephone. The remaining 31 percent were made on the mobile telephone.

*Who was Called*

Of the 392 calls recorded in the diaries, about 25 percent were to the respondent's partner, 10 percent were to children living at home, and 12 percent were to other kin. The material shows that about 13 percent of the calls were to friends and 5 percent to acquaintances. The remaining 35 percent were to other unspecified persons. In 1988, Claisse and Rowe (1988) reported that 40 percent of household traffic is with members of the family, 36 percent with friends and acquaintances. While not being exactly the same distribution, the material here is not too different from this earlier analysis.

Comparing the use of mobile to fixed telephony in table 18.2 one can see that there are different emphases in their use. The major differences are first that the mobile is used more than one would expect to call one's partner and perhaps more surprisingly, for calls to the "other" category. This latter group can include instrumental communications such as control and follow-up of various types of repair personnel and services having to do with the management of the home. It is interesting to note, however that mobile calls to this group have become so commonplace.

The groups that were underrepresented vis-à-vis, the mobile telephone are kin and friends. Previous research and also the material in this analysis show that calls to friends and kin are typically the domain of women in their role as the maintainers of the social network (Ling 1998). As we will see below, their more limited access to the mobile telephone is a likely explanation for this difference.

*Peak Time Calls*

As noted above, there were peak times for both calling and traveling. When looking at the calling data, the peaks came early in the morning and also late in the afternoon. Interestingly, however, the data shows that men are generally responsible for the morning peak of mobile telephone calls (Person chi$^2$ = 6.112 [1], sig. < 0.013 [n = 107]) while women contributed more to the afternoon peak. Indeed, the material shows that almost 27 percent of all men's calls were between 8:00 and 10:00. For women, the peak is somewhat more distributed but between 14:00 and 18:00, they reported more than 43 percent of their calls.

Looking specifically at these peak calls provides some insight into where the men and women are and the types of things they are doing during these periods. The material shows that men who called during their early morning peak period were far more likely to be either at work or en route, whereas women who called in their afternoon peak were likely to be at home. The difference in location is also seen in the fact that in the morning peak men used a mobile telephone while women used a traditional fixed device. One can see indications that women were more likely to place calls to children living at home during the morning peak time.

Looking at the men, the morning peak time calls seem to be a type of time displacement, that is, use of the mobile phone to coordinate extra-domestic private life while driving to the job. The findings underscore that the mobile telephone is used disproportionately to make calls related to functionality in terms of men vs. women users. If we consider specifically at private mobile-based calls made during the morning peak to non-family/friends, men dominated almost completely (Pearson chi$^2$ = 12.813 [1], sig. < 0.001. [n = 51]). Women were more likely to call friends during the afternoon peak when considering both mobile and fixed telephony (Pearson chi$^2$ = 11.297 [1], sig. < 0.001 [n = 119]). The data show that the women were more likely to call in order to make an agreement with their interlocutor, whereas men noted that they either gave or received a message in these peak-time calls.

*Location and the Use of the Mobile Telephone*

When looking at all private calls, the respondents indicated that more than 77 percent of these were made or received either from their homes or from work.

**Table 18.3**
**Distribution of Call Location by Mobile and Fixed Telephone Use (in Percent)**

|  | Mobile | Fixed |
|---|---|---|
| Home | 8 | 49 |
| Job | 43 | 49 |
| Other location | 16 | 2 |
| En route | 34 | 0 |

n mobile = 169, n fixed = 223

When considering only those calls made from the mobile telephone, the picture is quite different as can be seen in table 18.3. As one would suspect and in the light of the research cited earlier, some, but only a few, calls are made from the home (7.7 percent). This is because one has access to a cheap and accessible alternative, that is, the fixed telephone. Looking at the calls made or received at work, the respondents reported about the same proportion of calls for both the mobile and the fixed systems, that is, 43 percent of all mobile calls and 49 percent of all fixed-line calls. The large proportion of mobile calls is likely a reflection of the fact that the mobile telephones for this group of respondents were paid for by employers and they felt free to use the telephones in this context for personal calls. One third of the calls from mobile telephones were made while the respondents were en route, and the remaining 16 percent were made at other locations away from the home. The picture for the fixed-line telephone is quite different. As noted, about 50 percent of the calls were made at work and the other 50 percent were made at home. Only about 2 percent were made from other locations. Thus, for this group, the mobile telephone has almost completely replaced the use of telephone booths or the borrowing of a telephone in locations along the way.

*Speculation about Travel Generated and Saved*

Beyond these rather broad analyses, we also have more targeted data. In a small questionnaire carried out in 2000, we have tried to determine the degree to which mobile and fixed telephony generate or save automobile traffic.

The method for calculating this analysis was that calls that stimulated traffic were multiplied by the median trip length reported in the questionnaire. The same was done for the calls that replaced trips. The calls that changed travel en route were treated as being about 40 percent of a median trip since the trip was already begun and since the rerouting might not have been carried out if the respondent did not have a mobile telephone.

Table 18.4
Kilometers Generated And Saved Via the Use of Fixed and Mobile Telephones,
Bærum Norway, 2000

|  | Generated travel | Saved travel |
|---|---|---|
| Mobile | 77 km (48 miles) | 88 km (48 miles) |
| Fixed | 189 km (118 miles) | 118 km (74 miles) |

From the small analysis we did in Bærum, it appears that mobile telephony actually saves more automobile traffic than it generates. The material in Table 18.4 shows that for the day covered by respondents' diaries, the mobile telephone generated about a total of 77 km (48 miles) in travel while it save almost 90 (56 miles). The situation with the fixed telephone is somewhat different. According to the data, the fixed-line telephone generated about 190 km (119 miles) while it saved just under 120 km (75 miles).

## Meaning and Interpretation

Now we turn to a discussion of the material presented above. In this portion of the paper we will look into some of the gender aspects of mobility and mobile telephony, potential cohort effects, and finally some speculations as to future work.

### Gender and the Need for Micro-Coordination

The question arises as to why women should use the mobile less for micro-coordination. This is counter-intuitive: in terms of the social expectations of their role one would anticipate that they should be more active users of the device. There is more use of the fixed telephone for the coordination of everyday life and there are also more geographically remote tasks to be carried out by women. One would expect that the more logistics to be managed, the more naturally the device would fit into their lives.

The material here as well as that reported in other literature shows that women generally have less access to the mobile telephone. A partial clarification is that they also have less access to mobile telephones as a perquisite of their jobs (Claisse and Rowe 1988; Moyal 1989; Ling 1998; Rakow 1988). Women's telephone use comes out of the private economy, while that of men comes out of their employers'. Thus, one sees a curious type of cross subsidizing, that is, the job telephone for men subsidizes their coordination of private life while the woman's privately held mobile telephone subsidizes her ability to juggle work and home.

One sees another dimension of this when looking into the question of who women call during the morning peak. For those few calls that they made during this period, women were more active calling to children living at home during the morning peak time. However, for men living in homes where there were small children (0–3 years of age) or where there were pre-adolescents (9–12 years of age), they were generally more active in their use of the telephone, that is, they used their telephones during this period *but not to call home*. As suggested above, their calling may have been focused on instrumental mainte-nance coordination. The data seems to show, however, that it was the women who were calling home to awaken their pre-teen children and make sure that they were on their way to school, a type of remote mothering (Katz 1999, Rakow and Navarro 1993).

*Cohort Effects*

The material here shows that mature women are not the biggest users of mobile telephony in spite of their apparent need. However, other analysis has shown that teenaged girls are heavy mobile telephone users. Indeed, in some situations they use them more intensely than same aged boys (Ling and Vaage 2000). The similarity holds for those younger than their mid-twenties. Among older age groups, men dominate both the ownership and use of the mobile telephone as we have seen in the material here. The general question is the degree to which this is a characteristic of a life phase or of a cohort. That is, to what degree will today's teen girls carry the habit of mobile telephone use with them as they mature? If, indeed the life phase effect were static, then one would expect that teen girls would reduce their use of the device as they moved into young adulthood. On the other hand, it is perhaps more likely that as they mature, they will carry their use with them as they move into other phases of life (Wynn and Katz 2000).

Thus, one might anticipate that the expectations associated with mobile telephony will become a part of their adult perspective. This would mean that the differences seen in the material here might well be minimized with time. However, there is still the question of payment. While there have been adjust-ments in the income levels of men and women in order to narrow a gap, there are still disparities. In addition, there are disparities in access to jobs where perqui-sites such as mobile telephone access are available. Thus, one might expect that some of the differences in mobile telephone use will be reduced in the near future as the current generation of teens establishes themselves in the job mar-ket; it is more difficult to fathom that it will be eliminated.

*Mobile Phones and the Generation of Reduction of Mobility*

When we look at the figures concerning where calls affected travel we have to ask how are the respondents interpreting this and what is the causality implied. The interest in the initial discussion is if more or less travel takes place overall because of the existence of the technology per se. So, for example, one might imagine the following line of thought: "I had planned to see someone, but when I phoned her, we discussed what we needed to, and as a result, there was no need for that trip." Or, alternatively "I am in the vicinity of someone, and because I have a mobile phone, I phone suggesting they come and join me or I join them," whereas "without the mobile I would never have thought of this."

But one can also imagine another scenario where "I had already talked about meeting someone when we last met, and I use the mobile to finalize the details. If I had not had a mobile phone, I might have used a fixed-line telephone, or we might have agreed all the journey details at the last meeting." But the point is that the travel behavior would have occurred anyway and using a phone of some sort to make contact was only the last action—a trip resulted out of the call but the phone itself or the call did not provide the motivation for the trip.

We are inclined to interpret the figures in the former sense where the mobile replaced travel, because certainly in the case of the qualitative research on the mobile phone cited earlier, participants spontaneously generated examples of this sort when asked to think about what difference a mobile made to mobility. We also find examples of this sort in other qualitative research.

In either case, a few observations can be made. First, we seem to see here one more way in which mobile phones and fixed-line telephones are perceived to be different from each other, here in terms of outcomes—fixed lines seem to generate more trips. Although the paper did not specifically seek to address observations about the fixed-line telephone, it is interesting given the claims that effects of traditional telephony have replaced transportation. While there were some percentage differences, the most striking thing about the mobile calls is that the various examples seen in the qualitative research, some of leading to new travel, some to less, seem to roughly balance out. Indeed, if the other data on car use were to be generalized, then some travel might be reduced. So from this initial data, those concerned with the sustainability of the transportation industry need not be too anxious about this mobile phone technology.

*Location*

It is perhaps a little surprising that so many of the mobile phone calls in this study took place at the workplace of the respondents. This may be accounted for using different explanations. More and more, the mobile telephone is seen as a type of perquisite associated with one's job. Thus, its use for private calls is simply a type of "bad" habit that one picks up. From the perspective of the employer, it may well be that by tolerating the private use of the mobile telephone at work, they, in turn can extend their, and their customer's ability to reach the individual in the more traditionally private spheres of life. Thus, there is a type of overall efficiency argument that is in the background here. Further, one can only speculate that some of these employees move around at work but need to be reachable immediately. There is some research on the private use of the fixed-line phone at work (deGournay 1997) but more on private use of the whole range of telecommunications options (mobile, e-mail) in this context deserves more attention, particularly when different workplaces have different rules about private use of such communication media.

The limited use of the mobile in the home is in line with previous research and has already been interpreted from two perspectives: usage is low because of the cheaper fixed-line phone alternative, and it exists because some people use the mobile as their main personal phone.

In the Norwegian context (and considering this particular sample), we would speculate that use en route would often mean use when in a car. (More than 76 percent of the trips reported in the travel section of the diary were made by car; another 10 percent were made using public transportation.) Therefore, before generalizing too much from these results, one would want to consider how the patterns might differ for those sections of the population using public transportation, and in countries where there is relatively more use of public transportation. However, the fact that use en route is substantive in this study, accounting for a third of all mobile calls, means we can ask about the extent to which the mobile has changed the experience of traveling, and in particular, how it has changed the way we can utilize travel time. It might also be interesting to explore how much of that use underway is actually for the micro-coordination discussed previously, in which case the logistics of everyday life might increasingly be organized "just-in-time."

*Developing Further Research*

The general points about the small and unrepresentative sample have already been made in the discussion of methods. Nevertheless, the research reflects the first steps toward investigating the relationships between mobility and mobile phones, indicating, for example, how the mobile telephony has some impacts on travel behavior. Obviously, the areas of study indicated in this paper could be explored with different samples, but in this last section, we would like to explore other ways in which such research could be developed. One first observation is that this study has only considered cases when it is claimed that the mobile phone or fixed-line phone is leading directly to (or changing or reducing) travel. Yet, we can already point to qualitative research on mobile phones, which note the "gifting" or "social grooming" calls where it is the symbolic act of calling that matters as much as the content or what is achieved (Nafus and Tracey 2002; Ling and Yttri 2002). The point is that such social calls may help to create generally closer relationships and enhance sociability that, in turn may indirectly influence the desire to make personal contact. Clearly, this process of calls indirectly influencing travel patterns is not measured in the structure of the present survey. Although this issue is worthwhile to flag, it is perhaps less obvious how one would incorporate this finding into future research.

However, there are some facets where it is clearer to see how one might incorporate them into future studies. For example, behind any hard statistical data there are always the cognitive and social processes by which responses are constructed. In relation to this particular field of mobility it would be interesting to know how the participants of this (or any future) study made the judgments they did when they reached an evaluation that certain telephone calls generated, changed, or saved the need for trips. For instance, were some journeys, or types of journeys, more prominent, or prominent in their memory, than others? In future quantitative research we would certainly procure a more detailed picture, and hence perhaps more understanding of which journeys people are considering if we offered more categories in order to explore what types of travel were involved. For instance, a qualitative component of future research could entail interviews to explore the criteria in classifying a call as either generating or reducing travel, which might also provide more insight into exactly how and why calls had an influence on mobility. The upshot is that there are both quantitative and qualitative steps one could take to enhance future studies.

Although we stated our initial interest was in mobile phones, we have already in this analysis started to make comparisons between the mobile phone and the fixed-line phone. A further step would be to locate the use of mobile telephony within people's entire (electronic) communications behavior. For example, even if the primary interest is in mobile phones we could also consider media such as e-mail or indeed, the mobile could be relegated to being just one medium among others, shifting the focus to telecommunications and mobility.

But this immediately introduces questions of how these different media interrelate and how we shift between them over time. For example, if someone makes a mobile phone call that changes travel behavior, in the past an equivalent call may have been made using the fixed line. In which case, there might not be any overall change in someone's mobility compared to the past. On the other hand, there might be occasions where mobile calls do not substitute for fixed-line ones but complement them, constituting additional communications, which in turn might lead to "real" increases, changes, or reductions in people's travel behavior. Other research suggests that the picture is indeed complex with both processes of substitution and balancing of old and new media of communications (Haddon 2000). This is certainly a dimension that could generate a more complex analysis of the "impact" of the mobile phone. Haddon's study drew upon quantitative and qualitative research conducted by British Telecom, which include direct questions on the degree to which mobile telephony and e-mail displaced fixed telephony.

The introduction to this chapter focused on how much difference mobile phone made to mobility—at least in terms of the frequency of traveling. But this preliminary analysis reported here from the survey has clearly counted trips as if they are all the same. The next step to a more detailed analysis would be to take into account the fact that this is clearly not the case, certainly in terms of the distances covered and the time taken. A trip to the local shops is not the same as a journey to visit relatives in another part of the country or a holiday abroad. Once again, we have the potential for more complex analyses. The minor study that was also reported in this chapter has started on the first steps to considering distances.

Our original question was posed about mobility in general, but clearly this was asked in terms of practicality in certain questions with respect to car travel. Now the very important, and in certain senses, culturally specific role of the car, both practically and symbolically, in Norwegian society has been documented elsewhere (Sørensen 1990). But if we want to consider more general travel behavior we would want to broaden also the scope to cover other modes of traveling.

Finally, there are also some considerations that depart from the original reasons given for having an interest in mobility in society: there is the question of what different types of mobility mean to people. For example, in the recent qualitative multicultural study (Klamer et al. 2000), certain types of travel had for many people become relatively taken-for-granted, rather than problematic experiences, including, perhaps surprisingly, commuting. In contrast, leisure travel was seen positively and where it increased in people's lives over a long period, it was regarded as a welcome development. If communication, in this case via the mobile phone, does have (potential) outcomes for travel behavior, we might also address the issue of how this is subjectively perceived (Katz, 2001).

## Conclusion

In this chapter we have delineated some areas of study concerning the relationship between mobile telephony and mobility. While there has been some speculation and argument about fixed telephony, mobility, and coordination in the literature, there has been little quantitative research on this aspect of mobile telephony. Our first contribution was to determine the questions to be addressed and to assemble relevant material from both qualitative studies of the mobile as well as other pertinent studies.

Our findings underscore the fact that fixed-line telephone calls in general, and mobile phone calls specifically, can be used for many purposes such as increasing security, maintaining a social network, and personal status enhancement via display of a terminal. This study shows that only a minority of calls specifically has a bearing upon coordination and travel. However, that minority still accounts for roughly one fifth of calls made and received in this study overall. While a majority of the travel-related calls were from a fixed-line phone, over a third were from a mobile.

In terms of gender, women make and receive more travel-related calls than men. This was expected, given their role in the coordination of domestic life. However, it is the fixed line that, for a variety of reasons discussed in this chapter, still predominates over the mobile telephone.

If we consider the effect of private mobile calls on travel, as anticipated, the mobile was more important for modifying travel, reflecting the discussion of micro-coordination. Again, one third of travel-related calls had this outcome and the data on who was called would lead us to speculate that this dynamic is often, as expected, taking place between partners—at least in this type of "busy" household.

When looking only at the generation or avoidance of travel, the mobile phone seems to be neutral in that calls generating travel are balanced by calls reducing it. In contrast, it is the fixed line that is far more likely to generate travel. When the modification of travel is added to the equation, coordination via the mobile telephone appears to save more travel than it generates. The contrast is starker if one considers the distances traveled by car, as shown in the secondary study. In this context, the mobile phone saves some time on travel while the fixed line still generates it overall.

In relation to the question of where private calls are made and received, it turned out that the locale of work dominated, even though the use of the mobile in this setting has been so little discussed. Fitting previous research, the mobile was used at home, but admittedly in a minority of cases. When we turn to that distinction between calling en route and calling from sites outside of the home and work, the former calls were reported to be twice as common.

## Acknowledgement

The authors want to acknowledge Randi Hjorthol of the Transport Økonomisk Institutt for her work in the development of the questionnaire.

## References

Adams, J. 2000. Hypermobility. *Prospect* (March). (http://www.prospect-magazine.co.uk/highlights/hypermobility/index.htlm)

Chen, D. 2000. The Science of Smart Growth. *Scientific American.* (Dec.): 60–67.

Claisse, G and Rowe, F. 1988. The Telephone in Question: Questions on Communication. *Computer Networks and ISDN Systems* 14: 207–219.

Claisse, G and Rowe, F. 1993. Domestic Telephone Habits and Daily Mobility. *Trans Res* 27 (4): 277–290.

COST269 Mobility Workgroup. 2001. From Mobile to Mobility: The Consumption of ICTs and Mobility in Everyday Life. Report for COST269.

Crawford, M. 1994. The World in a Shopping Mall. In *Variations on a Theme Park: The New American City and the End of Public Space,* pp. 3-30, ed. Sorkin, M., New York: Hill and Wang.

de Gournay, C. 1996. Waiting for the Nomads: Mobile Telephony and Social Change. *Reseaux: The French Journal of Communication* 4 (2).

de Gournay, C. 1997. C'est personnel...La Communication Priveé hors de ses Murs. *Reseaux* 82/83 (Mar.–June).

Falk, T. and R. Abler. 1980. Intercommunications, Distance and Geographical Theory. *Geografiska annaler* 62 (2): 59–67.

Frolich, D. M., K. Chilton, and P. Drew. 1997. Remote and Homeplace Communication: What Is It Like and How Might We Support It? *Proceedings of the HCI '97*.

Gillespie, A., R. Richardson, and J. Cornford. 1995. Review of Telework in Britain: Implications for Public Policy. A report for the Parliamentary Office of Science and Technology, Sheffield, Employment Department, February.

Haddon, L. 1998. Il controllo della comunicazione. Imposizione di limiti all'uso del telefono. In *Telecomunicando in Europa,* ed. L. Fortunati. Milano: Franco Angeli.

Haddon, L. 1999. Approaches to Understanding Teleworking. *Telektronikk* 4, Oslo, Norway: Telenor.

Haddon, L. 2000a. An agenda for "Mobility in Everyday Life" for ICT researchers. Paper prepared for the COST269 Mobility Workgroup.

Haddon, L. 2000b. Old and New Forms of Communication: E-mail and Mobile Telephony. A report for British Telecom, November.

Hall, P. 1989. *Cities of Tomorrow.* Oxford: Blackwell.

Hayden, D. 1984. *Redesigning the American Dream: The Future of Housing, Work and Family Life.* New York: W.W. Norton.

Hjorthol, R.J. 2000. Same City—Different Options: An Analysis of the Work Trips of Married Couples In The Metropolitan Area of Oslo. *Journal of Transportation Geography* 8: 213– 220.

Katz, James E. 1999. *Connections: Social and Cultural Studies of the Telephone in American Life.* New Burnswick, NJ: Transaction Publishers.

Katz, James E. 2001. The Telephone. Entry in the *International Encyclopedia of Social Science* (2nd edition). Amsterdam: Elsevier. 2001. Vol. 23, pp. 15558-65.

Keane, J. 1995. Structural Transformations of the Public Sphere. *The Communication Review,* 1 (1): 1–22.

Klamer, L., L. Haddon, R. Ling. 2000. The Qualitative Analysis of ICTs and Mobility, Time, Stress, and Social Networking. Report of EURESCOM P-903.

Lange, K. 1993. Some Concerns About the Future of Mobile Communications in Residential Markets. In *Telecommunication: Limits to Deregulation?* eds. M. Christoffersen and A. Henten, pp. 197-210. Amsterdam: IOS Press.

Laurier, E. 2000. Why People Say Where They are During Mobile Phone Calls. *Environmental and Planning D: Society and Space.* (http//jimmy.qmced.ac.uk/usr/cilaur/dynamic/S&Swhere2-Title.html.18.08.02).

Ling, R. 1997. One Can Talk about Common Manners! Use of Mobile Telephones in Inappropriate Situations. In *Communications on The Move: Experience of Mobile Telephony in the 1990s,* ed. L. Haddon, COST 268 Report, Telia, Farsta,

Ling, R. 1998. She Calls, [but] It's for Both of Us You Know: The Use of Traditional Fixed and Mobile Telephony for Social Networking among Norwegian Parents. R&D Report 33/98, Telenor, Kjeller, Norway.

Ling, R. 2000a. We Will be Reached: The Use of Mobile Telephony among Norwegian Youth. *Information Technology and People* 13 (2): 102–120.

Ling, R. 2000b. The Ownership and Use of Mobile Telephones by Norwegians in 1999. R&D Notat 62 Telenor FoU, Kjeller.

Ling, R. and O. Vaage. 2000. Internett og mobiltelefon—ikke lenger bare for de få. *Samfunnsspeilet* 6.

Ling, R. and B. Yttri. 2002. Nobody Sits at Home and Waits for the Telephone to Ring: Micro and Hyper-coordination Through the Use of the Mobile Telephone. In *Perpetual*

*Contact: Mobile Communication, Private Talk, And Public Performance*, eds. J. Katz and M. Aakhus, Cambridge and New York: Cambridge University Press.

Ling, R., T. Julsrud, and E. Krogh. 1997. The Goretex Principle: The Hytte and Mobile Telephones in Norway. In *Communications on the Move: The Experience of Mobile Telephony in the 1990s*, ed. Haddon, L., COST248 Report.

Moyal, A. 1989. The Feminine Culture of the Telephone: People Patterns and Policy. *Promethius* 7(1): 5–31.

Nafus, D. and K. Tracey. 2002. The More Things Change: Mobile Phone Consumption and Concepts of Personhood. In *Perpetual Contact*, eds. J. Katz and M. Aakhus, Cambridge and New York: Cambridge University Press.

Nilles, J. M. 199. Telecommuting and Urban Sprawl: Mitigator or Inciter. *Transportation* 18: 411–432.

Rakow, L. F. 1988. Women and the Telephone: The Gendering of a Communications Technology. *Technology and Women's Voices: Keeping in Touch*, ed. C. Kramarae.

Rakow, L. F. 1992. *Gender on the Line*. Urbana: University of Illinois Press.

Rakow, L. F. and V. Navarro. 1993. Remote Mothering and the Parallel Shift: Women Meet the Cellular Telephone. *Critical Studies in Mass Communication* 10: 144–157.

Salomon, I. 1985. Telecommunication and Travel: Substitution or Modified Mobility? *Journal of Transport Economics and Policy* (Sept. 19): 219–235.

Sørensen, K. 1990. The Norwegian Car. The Cultural Adaption and Integration of an Imported Artifact. In *Technology and Everyday Life: Trajectories and Transformations*, eds. Sørensen, K. and A. Berg, Trondheim: University of Trondheim.

Sørensen, K. 1999. Rush-Hour: Blues of the Whistle of Freedom? Understanding Modern Mobility. STS-Working Paper. Center for teknologi og samfunn (March), Trondheim.

Thorns, D.C. 1972. *Suburbia*. London: MacGibbin and Kee.

Townsend, A. M. 2000. Life in the Real-Time City: Mobile Telephones and Urban Metabolism. *Journal of Urban Technology* 7 (2): 85–104.

Vestby, G. M. 1996. Technologies of Autonomy?: Parenthood In Contemporary Modern Times. In *Making Technologies Our Own: Domesticating Technology Into Everyday Life*, eds. M. Lie and K. E. Sørensen, 65–90. Oslo: Scandinavian University Press.

Vilhelmson, B. 1999. Daily Travel: Trends, Limits and Susceptibility to Influence. In *Changing Environmental Behaviour*, ed. L. Ludgren. Swedish Council for Building Research, Stockholm.

Wellman, B. 1999. *Networks in the Global Village: Life in Contemporary Communities*. Oxford: Westview.

Wynn, Eleanor and James E. Katz. 2001. Teens on the Telephone. *Info*, vol. 2 (4): August 2000, 401-419.

# 19

# Soft Machine

*Elda Danese*

"The soft machine is the human body under constant siege from a vast hungry host of parasites with many names," wrote Burroughs (1961) about the meaning of the title of his fourth book. *"The Soft Machine"* represented, in a frame without hope, his obsession of control that post-technological society wields on humans and the social body.

According to David Porush (1985), the writing of Burroughs represents a form of techno-paranoia, an answer to a cybernetic threat. In his critical essay, which adapts the title of "soft machines" from Burroughs' book, Porush considers both the scientific and literary sources of cybernetics, inquiring the way in which this technology has penetrated and inspired literature.

From Porush's point of view, cybernetics is the more recent mechanical model that, like the earlier Copernican, Darwinian, and Freudian ones, is also a model for a cultural revolution. In this cultural form, human nature and society are conceptualized as machines. The ultimate machine model is the achievement of a techno-myth: the "mechanical" idea of the human body began with the earliest physiological investigations and anatomical dissections and flourished in the seventeenth-century world of science, with the speculations of Descartes and Harvey. In the eighteenth century, after a long line of automaton-builders and inventors dating back to ancient times, Jacques de Vaucanson's machines, termed *automates,* received the applause of the Paris public (Beaune 1989; Ugo 2000).

But the tendency to simulate vital human functions with mechanical systems shifts to the superposition of these two realities: the attribution of softness to the machine indicates the identification of the automaton with the human body (Katz 1999b). The propensity to create an enhanced man-machine hybrid brought several scholars to investigate the implications of such a phenomenon on our life and culture. For instance, the exhibition "Soft Machine—Design in the Cyborg Age," (O'Mahony 1999) held from November 1998 to January 1999 at the Stedelijk Museum, examined cyborgs from the point of view of designers, showing jewelry, clothing, video, sculptures, and product design.

But if the word *soft* signifies an attribute of matter, in our time its meaning is broadened to include the concept of immateriality. *Soft,* as opposed to *hard,* is the term adopted to designate the immaterial product, the "intelligence" of computer equipment.

In this chapter, the term *softness* is analyzed from a different perspective apart from the past genre of machine technology: it is not considered metaphorically, but defines the present technological tendency towards the use of flexible, light, and elastic media, first of all textile materials. Since the term *soft,* moreover, has a series of different meanings (smooth, flexible, malleable, round, squashy), it aptly represents the idea of a more extended transformation, a new appearance of machines and technology.

The materials which, according to a consolidated image, characterize machines are metals and, in general, solid, heavy, and rigid substances. For this reason, even if plastics have already gained an important role among the elements constituting not only the casing but also the internal components of machines, the images signifying technology are connected to the brilliance, the solidity, and the rigidity of metal. According to Ezio Manzini, "the clash between the world of metals and the world of plastics can be seen as a contrast between a technical culture of solid and a technical culture of solid-fluid" (1989). The fact that they can be shaped, which is the main characteristic of plastics and an important reason for their success, has been underlined in the rounded forms and the rounded corners of many objects. The growing number of new materials and composites and their ability to take on different appearances and to offer different performances, however, hinders their identification with a specific and definite aspect: the reality of materials has acquired a kaleidoscopic complexity (Manzini 1989). Such ambiguity clashes with the general human need to recognize and identify things and functions. Images and symbols that endure the passing of time are in contrast with the rapid environmental and technological changes (Fortunati, Katz, and Riccini 2002). Softness, though, does not apply to technological determinism, which is rejected here, both hard and soft (Katz 1999a; Maldonado 1999); culture and human will rule outcomes within technologically defined constraints (Katz and Aakhus 2002).

One of the functions of a designer is the creation of a dialectic relation between these contrasting aspects. On some occasions, the gap between culture and technique becomes wider: this is what happens, for instance, when the image of heaviness and solidity of a building is obtained through the use of light materials (Manzini 1989). In this example, heaviness is more a cultural and symbolic expression than a technical requirement: thickness and heaviness communicate the idea of stability and stasis.

According to recent theories, static expression in architecture does not result from a dynamic equilibrium of forces, but is derived from the Descartes model of gravity, in which time and force are excluded from the system (Lynn 1999). For these reasons it is argued that architectural theory and representation up to now have not shared the complexity of contemporary scientific thought. The redefinition of architectural space, according to Lynn (1999), is bound to find a theoretical model in the concept of gravity proposed by Leibniz: "In such an abstract active space, the statics of fixed points in neutral space is replaced by the stability of vectors that balance one another in a phase space" (Lynn 1999). The articulated topological surfaces of buildings created by these architects are the expression of the virtual change that results, with the passing of time, from the action of forces that are internal and external to the form.

The need to explore movement, that is mutability in all its forms, has determined the orientation of our scientific thought (Giedion 1980 [1948]). This aspect of modernity implies an oscillation between the need to define and identify, which is necessary to human comprehension, and the variety and multiplicity inherent in the change. Besides, the use of computer animation as a visualizing tool for the architects implies the shift from volume defined by Cartesian coordinates to topological surfaces (Lynn 1999; Perbellini and Pongratz 2000).

This change in the system of graphic representation, by allowing the visualization of deformations and transformations of a surface, influenced the forms of these new architectures and also of other products designed with digital tools. The stereographic representation of a surface, whose deformations result from the action of forces, which can be expressed using mathematical calculus, is one of the important possibilities offered by digital systems of graphic description to designers and manufacturers.

With these tools, some researchers in the field of industrial engineering succeeded in simulating the behavior of surfaces like textiles: their visualization is achieved by taking into consideration the physical and mechanical properties of different types of materials and textures, and the effect of external forces, like gravity and wind, or collisions with obstacles, etc. (Cugini et al. 2000).

Through this change in the representation system it is possible nowadays to describe what was previously not defined by Euclidean geometry. The mutability of textiles, of adaptable and flexible surfaces, can be described by topological geometry. This characteristic allows them to be used mostly as a coating for solid forms, but this is one of the reasons why the interest of designers and researchers is focused on them: textiles follow the movement and the variation of other forms.

The clearest example of such a tendency is the concept of "wearable computers." By this term we refer to accessories and clothes that incorporate electronic devices that can have different functions: communicating, entertaining, monitoring, and so on. The identity of "wearable computers," however, is still uncertain: in various conferences dedicated to this subject, in fact, we have seen many attempts at defining them through the determination of a series of parameters, like "portable while operational and always on," "context and environment sensing," "equipped with a hand free or nearly hands free user interface," "able to augment the users perception of the reality," and so on (Billinghorst 1999).

Even if many enterprises and universities are involved in these research efforts, and despite all progress, wearable computing today is described as "a very exciting field very much in its infancy" (Billinghorst 1999). Of fundamental importance in such developments is the advent of widespread wireless communication and the downsizing of electronic devices, factors that already allow us to carry many of them with us in our pockets or bags.

The downsizing of electronic parts caused them to disappear from our sight, a phenomenon that contributed to promoting the idea of a tendency towards their "dematerialization." What we can now verify is that the possibility of producing ever-smaller devices, which are therefore not perceivable, generates the illusion of an absence of matter. In this case, as in others, the relationship between perception and comprehension of phenomena requires frequent and rapid updating. Moreover, both the discovery and the production of new materials tend to transform the appearance and the consistency of things. Some Japanese researchers, for instance, created a polymer gel with a sponge-like structure that can absorb large quantities of an organic liquid called THF. A piece of THF swollen-gel placed on water will dart: this is a rough description of a "gel motor," which has been named, to keep to the subject of this paper, "Soft machine." (Mitsumata et al. 2000) Or, in another example, Aerogel is a silicon-based solid with a porous, sponge-like structure in which 99 percent of the volume is empty space. Technological research tends to create and produce materials that possess greatly enhanced properties in comparison to existing substances. As clearly shown by our second example, the increase in lightness is an important aim of many research projects, and it is also a crucial aspect of the design of wearable computers, because it allows us to carry a great number of devices capable of multiple functions. In this way our clothes become machines, soft machines.

In many wearable computers, moreover, as in other technological tools, the fabric is not just a covering bearing the various components: on the contrary, it is one of the components, with the function of carrying information and connecting various functions within an integrated system of products.

The soft phone and the fabric keyboard are examples of personal technologies integrating fabric with conductive fibers. In these products, an electric textile structure offers the capability of reading the location of a point of pressure. This function is applicable also in an elastic sheet structure, allowing the fabric to conform to a three-dimensional shape, including compound curves, while still measuring the x-y coordinates to identify the position of points of pressure (Antonelli 2001).

According to Stefano Manzano, director of Philips Design, "the 'connector' of the new function systems will become the fabric. This fabric...will simultaneously handle the functional and aesthetic performance" (Gambara 2000).

The co-existence of these two aspects in the design and realization of wearable computers involves two industries that for a long time seemed to belong to distant and antithetical worlds: fashion and electronics. The design of these new clothes revolves around the definition of their potential users: the categories of consumers identified are "the business professional," "kids and youth street wear," and "performance sports" (Philips research). The high technological content and the targeted market segments determine the choice of a design oriented toward forms derived from workgear and sportswear. While it is true that the twentieth century witnessed an increased influence of sports clothing on the renovation of dressing forms, the tendency to identify sportswear as models for more informal and practical clothes had already emerged in the second half of the eighteenth century (Coppola 1991).

Yet, the specific characteristics of wearable computers have induced their designers to abandon the historical and cultural references to fashion, on account of the belief that "the moment has arrived to study new kinds of clothing for the functions that they express. Until recently the functions performed by technology were synthesized and expressed in a product, in an item, in varying levels of complexity but still perceivable as a single product. Today we are faced with functions which have lost their outer clothing. Often the performance remains but the envelope which expressed it is gone. From this comes the need to provide a new vehicle to these functions" (Gambara 2000).

Clothes are thus conceived with the aim of performing and representing technological functions and not with the intention emphasizing the gender, the culture, or the personality of the person wearing them. But if it is true that "one cannot escape fashion" (Baudrillard 1979), then technology probably is also one of the terms of this symbolic language. The technical aspect of materials and finishing, the simple forms, the Velcro fastening seem to answer the question posed by Rudofsky who, after having counted in a man's suit up to seventy buttons (most of which are of no use) and more or less twenty pockets, asked himself whether these clothes were really modern (Rudofsky 1947).

In the above quoted interview, however, Stefano Manzano states the necessity of signifying the new technological functions by redefining the aspect of machines, not just clothes.

In the imagery of the twentieth century, technology had been represented through big metal monsters—heavy, powerful, and dark; nowadays, all devices become smaller and smaller, so that we tend to forget their existence and even confuse the human with the technological. The propensity to create myths around technology is not a new phenomenon: Futurism, like other artistic currents of the twentieth century, elevated machines, glorifying them as a new symbol of might and modernity.

The fancy of animating objects is a recurrent theme in literature, art, and other expressive forms of human imagery. Through the automata and the other anthropomorphic objects that can be found in fairy tales, movies, and fiction, human thought fluctuates between the desire to control reality and the world of things and the fear of a rebellion of things, capable of turning upside down the domination typical of the relationship between mankind and objects (Fortunati 1995).

The complexity of new electronic devices and equipment, together with the rapid development of new interfaces capable of reacting to sound, temperature, light etc., favors such an illusion (Fortunati 2001). On the contemporary scene, moreover, we can detect other changes that distinguish new machines from their ancestors: their colors, their materials, color schemes, size, decorations, sound, and, of course, performance. Such changes are particularly evident in all equipment of personal use (like the mobile phone, the computer, and even the automobile): their friendly appearance encourages a greater familiarity with technology. Moreover, due to their prolonged closeness to the body, they can be compared to accessories, to the corollary of objects that connote the identity of their users.

On the other hand, while personal technologies enter the fashion system and machines become clothes, in some recent proposals of fashion designers, we can find clothes that become portable furniture. According to Ezio Manzini, "the new availability of prosthesis with a high performance density, coupled with a similarly great variety of means of transport, generates the very important result of a high-tech nomadism" (Manzini 1989).

In such a scenario, it looks as if not only the communication sphere, but also the habitat sphere becomes a bodily prosthesis, in tension between movement and stasis.

Fashion is raiding the furnishing design sector. A Japanese fashion designer has integrated into clothing some elements of "furniture": in a recent collection, soft body-shaped poufs were wrapped around the body or used as seats or rugs. The same willingness to create clothes with multiple functions emerges from the proposals of other fashion designers: nylon cloaks that can be transformed into hammocks or camping tents, padded overcoats that become sleeping bags, and skirts that become small tables. The interest in the integration of fashion with furnishings comes primarily from the peculiarity of the solutions adopted and their transformability, even if some of these proposals, rather than reactions to social changes, seem to be stylistic exercises practiced in a new territory. They express, basically, a "functionalist" tendency with a low decorative content and a high degree of technological representation, coexisting with the ornamental flourishing which is present in most textiles and clothes proposed nowadays by fashion designers.

On the other hand, in the design of furniture and other objects of personal use, we can find a plurality of languages, which goes alongside the many languages of fashion. Recently we have witnessed the creation of "a feedback loop between fashion and furnishings: clothing becomes decor and living spaces, like bodies, dressed up to transform. Fabric becomes the go-between in a more engaging relationship between people and objects, offering added functions

for furnishing and new, colorful, variegated skins for everyday useful objects."
(Morozzi 2000) This relation between fashion and furnishing is a recent phenomenon, which becomes visible through an ever-greater involvement of fashion designers in the creation of furniture and home accessories, and also in the
birth of specialized magazines dealing with both subjects. Interior design has
been traditionally conceived as something to be left to architectural authority,
but now we have prêt-à-porter for furniture.

During the 1970s magazines of design and architecture began to cover also
the fields of apparel and fashion. The presence of the feminist movement, with
its reference to body and reproduction, has certainly been an important factor
in stimulating this widening interest. Other reasons, like the desire to redefine
the forms of self-expression, motivated the shift toward such uniquely feminine
issues. In some cases, choosing to deal with "surfaces" meant the coincidence
of project with life, therefore its dissolution. "A process generated and lived by
thinking of something else, corresponding more to life than to design" (Mendini
1982) is opposed to projects that assert ideal rules and functions. Designer
Alessandro Mendini's (1982) dissent from the principles governing the rigor of
planning methods induced him to prefer a soft and sensual dimension because
"a world all in fabric won't be cruel. Architecture is made of nude and cold
parts, which fabric covers and warms. Fabric alleviates the hardness of life, it
quietens [sic] the inside of the house and leads back into the material womb."
This is another instance in which material acquires a symbolic role, corresponding more to an archetypical, interior, and protective image than to the
reality of women's domestic life.

If, on the one hand, this relation interior/exterior has deep, archetypal roots,
then on the other hand, the idea of interior as the place of intimacy and comfort,
as opposed to the concept of exterior as a hard and public territory, has historical and cultural origins linked with the emergence of the bourgeois class
(Maldonado 1987).

A clear distinction between a private/interior sphere and a social/external
one has been correlated for a long time to a strict definition of sexual roles. In
this separation, women's main role is to take care of home interiors and, at the
same time, provide comfort to the lives of others: an essential activity in the
productive process, ignored from the economic point of view, and scarcely
valued at the social level. In recent times the division between interior and
exterior is becoming less rigid: "in the post-modern society, the social system
of differences developed in the modern age is being completely restructured.
Many differences, even between men and women, between the world of production and reproduction, have disappeared or are at least less clear-cut"
(Fortunati 2001).

These changing relationships do not appear in our everyday material life: in
home interiors, for instance, furniture and objects still express, among other
aspirations, a desire for intimacy and protection (Bocchi and Scarzella 2000).

Very often we expect from objects to recreate our reality, to answer our unknown or unanswered need. But the concept of comfort, besides gaining importance in many dressing styles, is also spreading into workplaces. The confines between home and workplace are vanishing as, at the same time, the separation between time of leisure and time of work is fading.

For this reason in the preface of the catalog of the exhibition *Workspheres,* "soft" and "fuzzy" are attributes used to define the new image of work. If they "sound more like a blanket than a place, it isn't such a bad metaphor" because: "being 'wrapped up with your work' is a phrase that has an all new meaning in *Workspheres"* (Antonelli 2001).

The designer Hella Jongerius gives form to this idea by designing a series of domestic objects that incorporate technology into their very fabric, like a bed with a computer screen at the foot. The keyboard and the mouse of the computer are embedded in "smart pillows" that utilize touch-sensor technology. By changing the rigid quality of technological objects and letting them embrace and caress us, designers give us the illusion that the machine, or "daughter born without mother"—described by the artist Francis Picabia—have finally found a mother.

In the same exhibition designers Naziha Mestaoui, Yacine Ait Kaci, and Christophe Beaujays, presented the "Communicating Scarf" that, like a wearable computer includes a telephone, a screen, a keyboard, and a camera. More so than other wearable PCs, the scarf allows the wearer, being wrapped around the neck, to be physically and acoustically isolated from the outside world (Antonelli 2001).

These examples are representative of a significant, if not widespread, tendency: the penetration of machines in our personal sphere is driving producers and designers to give higher consideration to the emotional and "sensorial" aspects of our relation with them. From this point of view, textiles, besides giving computers "wearability," offer the machines a caressing quality, a more private character. Moreover, they encourage the diffusion of technology at an everyday level. In this way, like we suggested before, the idea of comfort joins the idea of work. This concept is clearly expressed in the words of the designer of *Soft bed*: "The use of color and textile helps to discard the negative associations one may have of bringing work into the home."

## References

Antonelli, P., ed. 2001. *Workspheres. Design and Contemporary Work Styles,* (catalog of exhibition). New York: Museum of Modern Art.

Baudrillard, J. 1979. *Lo scambio simbolico e la morte.* Milan: Feltrinelli.

Beaune, J. C. 1989. The Classical Age of Automata: An Impressionistic Survey from the Sixteenth to the Nineteenth Century. Trans. Ian Patterson. In *Fragments for a History of the Human Body*, eds. M. Feher, R. Naddaff, and N. Tazi, vol. 3, Part 1 (431-480), New York: Zone Books.

Billinghorst, M. 1999. Wearable Computers: Beyond Handheld Computing. Tutorial given at first International Symposium on Handheld and Ubiquitous Computing (HUC'99), Karlsruhe. In *The vision and reality of wearable computing*. (http:/ www.weareble.ethz.ch/vision.htm).

Bocchi, L. and P. Scarzella. 2000. *Dentro le case italiane nel*. Milan: I Saloni spa and assArredo/Federlegno–Arredo.

Burroughs, W. 1961. *The Soft Machine*. London: Paladin.

Coppola, E. 1991. Effetto maschio: moda modi miti dal cortigiano al borghese. In *L'uniforme borghese*, eds. G. Butazzi and A. Mottola Molfino. Novara: Istituto Geografico De Agostini.

Cugini, U., A. Galimberti, and C. Rizzi. 2000. Industrial Research in Woman Clothing Industry: Project and Results. Paper presented at the conference *Virtualità e modellistica* organized by Venice University Institute of Architecture and Province of Treviso Industrialists' Association. Treviso: Chamber of Commerce.

Fortunati, L. 1995. *I mostri nell'immaginario*. Milan: Franco Angeli.

Fortunati, L.2001. Italy: Stereotypes, True and False. In *Perpetual Contact: Mobile Communication, Private Talk, Public Performance*, eds. J. Katz and M. Aakhus. Cambridge and New York: Cambridge University Press.

Fortunati, L. 2001. The Human Body: Natural and Artificial Technology. Paper presented at *Machines That Become Us* conference (published in this volume). New Brunswick, NJ: Rutgers University.

Fortunati, L., J. E. Katz, and R. Riccini, eds. 2002. *Corpo futuro: Il corpo umano tra tecnologie, communicazione e moda*. Milan, Italy: Franco Angeli.

Gambara, M. 2000. A New Kind of Clothing for Technology. Trans. Spazio Lingue and Patrizia Quattrocchi, *Active design management* 23 (8): 90–92.

Giedion, S. 1980. *La mécanisation au pouvoir*, Paris, France: Centre George Pompidou/ CCI (French transl. of: *Mechanization Takes Command: A Contribution To Anonymous History*). New York: Oxford University Press Inc., 1948.

Katz, James E. 1999a. *Connections: Social and Cultural Studies of the Telephone in American Life*. New Brunswick, NJ: Transaction Publishers.

Katz, James E. 1999b. Communication in the year 2075. *Science and the Future. Year 2000*. Annual Supplement of the *Encyclopedia Britannica*. Chicago and London: Encyclopedia Britannica, pp. 176-200.

Katz, James E. and M. Aakhus, eds. 2002. *Perpetual Contact: Mobile Communication, Private Talk, Public Performance*. Cambridge and New York: Cambridge University Press.

Lynn, G. 1999. *Animate Form*. New York: Princeton Architectural Press.

Maldonado, T. 1999. Possiamo vivere in un sogno, ma alla fine dobbiamo svegliarci. *Telèma* 16 (5): 8–12.

Maldonado, T. 1987. *Il futuro della modernità*. Milan: Feltrinelli.

Manzini, E. 1989. *La materia dell'invenzione*. Milan: Arcadia Edizioni.

Mendini A. 1982. In Praise of Fabric. *Domus* 626: 1.

Mitsumata, T., K. Ikeda, J. P. Gong, and Y. Osada. 2000. Controlled Motion of Solvent-Driven Gel Motor and Its Application as a Generator. *Langmuir* 16: 307.

Morozzi, C. 2000. From Dress to the House. *Interni* 507: 140–143.

O'Mahony, M., ed. 1999. *The Soft Machine: Design in the Cyborg Age* (Catalog of exhibition, 18 November 1998–10 January 1999), Amsterdam: Stedelijk Museum of Modern Art.

Perbellini, R. and Pongratz, C. 2000. *Nati con il computer. Giovani architetti americani*. Turin: Testo & Immagine.

*Philips Research Into Marriage Of Electronics And Clothing,* http://www.research.
 philips.com/pressmedia/releases/990802.html.
Porush, D. 1985. *Soft Machine: Cybernetic Fiction.* London: Methuen.
Rudofsky, B. 1947. *Are Clothes Modern?* Chicago: Paul Theobald.
Ugo, V. 2000. Il corpo costruito. *Modo* 202: 41–44.

# 20

# Aesthetics in Microgravity

*Annalisa Dominoni*

**For the Second Skin, the New Frontier**

Exploring behavioral dynamics in relation to aesthetics in an extreme environment is a rare opportunity. The situation of astronauts in microgravity, or more informally, outer space, enables us to focus on special human problems. Moreover, it allows us to examine the psychological and social implications that are derived from these dynamics. The conditions of constant emergency for crewmembers on board the International Space Station (ISS), the confined environment, and the microgravity effects cause heavy stresses that make astronauts more sensitive and vulnerable. Interpersonal relationships are altered and the harmony of social interaction may be seriously compromised. The culturally unique aspects of various crew members may also be important. For a perceptive examination of psychological and social effects of isolation during space missions, see Bluth (1985); and, more generally, Katz (1985).

In this context, behaviors may be magnified and actions or gestures may be interpreted with severe meanings that on Earth would be of only secondary importance. The aesthetics in microgravity must also be included this principle. The extreme conditions in which astronauts live require particular attention to aesthetic values in order to encourage a high level of personal satisfaction and, therefore, a calm acceptance of one's self.

On board the ISS, equipment performance must be extreme, the clothing inclusive; therefore, it is necessary to study the high technological level of materials and production processes utilized for space compared to products used on Earth. This means that the clothing worn by astronauts should be great improvements over the aesthetics and comfort of ordinary life.

These issues are being studied in the research project, VEST. The Italian Space Agency (ASI) has given SpaceLab a task to develop the project VEST in order to provide astronauts with suitable clothing systems for microgravity

277

environment. The feasibility stage was finished in June 2001, and the first experiment in orbit on the International Space Station was Roberto Vittori's April 2002 mission.

The VEST research project team is composed of Milan Polytechnic's SpaceLab, responsible for scientific coordination, with the Benetton Group, responsible for technical and industrial aspects, and with Altec, responsible for the system spatialization.

This effort entails the development of an integrated clothing support system of Intra Vehicular Activities (IVA) for the International Space Station, which could provide an effective dual spin-off in terms of both aesthetics and technology. It should be noted that the study of life in space is still in its early stages and that space itself, is after all, a relatively new environment for human beings. Its effects have been recorded by collating the experiences of a few people, most of whom have spent but a few days in space, while only a few have spent several months there.

At present, astronauts wear the same kind of clothes they wear on Earth, which are obviously unsuited to the peculiar environmental conditions to be found on board. Current space clothing is not suitable to the negative effects of microgravity, confinement, and radiation sustained by humans inside the ISS. It is easy to observe, for example, broadcasted media images and photos of astronauts wearing polo shirts whose collars curl toward the neck, or astronauts wearing T-shirts that are cut low in the back because the clothing wearability doesn't consider the neutral posture of the body in microgravity environs and the physiological alterations caused by microgravity (Antonutto and di Prampero 1992). The end result is that the crew experiences disorder and discomfort.

This project recognizes that clothing wearability requirements for the space environmental should be built on the neutral posture that crew members adopt in conditions of microgravity similar to that of the posture adopted by the body under water. This posture seems to result, above all, from a newly found balance between the muscles and the tension of fabrics acting on the different joints (Wichman et al. 1996). From the research project, we have discovered that the neutral posture is very similar to the posture adopted by snowboarders—limbs bent, knees and elbows upward, and head bent forward. Some functional devices for better wearability of snowboard clothing have even been directly applied to space clothing.

Limited attention has been given to the aesthetics of space clothing. Much of the focus on clothing for microgravity environments has been centered on the issue of technological research.

Technological research on clothing has been concentrated on fibers and materials in order to offer a high level of hygiene for astronauts, thanks to a special small silver-particle finish that fights bacterial proliferation and body odor, and the use of thermoregulating fibers and fabrics, which absorb excess heat and release it when the body's temperature falls, while it also curbs the noxious effects of perspiration by transferring excess sweat to the outside.

If, in common earthly conditions, to have a positive perception of one's self means feeling at ease with one's body and one's clothing or one's "second skin"—which leads to an overall improvement in social relations and, therefore, increased efficiency in terms of both operativity and performance—in outer space, the aesthetic values are essential for the well being of each individual and considered fundamental for the mission's success.

### Rigorous Problems Require Innovative Approaches

During the feasibility stages of research project VEST, we have pinpointed a series of new parameters to meet the needs of living in space. These parameters are essentially founded on two objectives: counter-measures and style. The following questions and reflections have emerged during the research project while working in close contact with the astronauts, who actively participated in all the design phases of the project.

How important are style and image to the astronauts? And if they are important, where should the inspirations for designs come from? Could there be an exclusive style and design for astronauts that might evolve independently from the styles for society on Earth? Do the astronauts prefer a futuristic and ultramodern style? Or do they want clothing that is traditional, casual, or just comfortable? Do the requirements imposed by their environment and NASA have an impact on this project and, as a result, affect aesthetics overall? Are uniforms still important? Are astronauts content to wear uniforms or would they prefer an individualistic and more personal style?

Many of these questions have more than one answer, and often, these answers contradict one another. Other answers reflect, and are a direct consequence of, design choices—but these are simpler and easier to manage in formulating an explanation. The objective of this paper is to encourage reflection on these issues by providing an interpretative key that extracts the experience and culture of industrial design.

The project objectives adopted to counter the adverse effects of the space environment and to improve living conditions within confined spaces are to increase the degree of well being and efficiency of the astronauts; to ensure garment wearability, bodily thermal stability, hygiene, and the monitoring of biologic and physiologic functions. Such project requirements fully respect NASA indications as to fabric composition, weight, volume, and storage and, therefore, greatly influence overall aesthetics.

From which sources do designers draw inspiration when creating styles for space clothing? They are a far cry from the kind of clothing described in books and viewed in science fiction films. What does the industrial designer deem to be of paramount importance when setting out to create a new and aesthetically pleasing integrated clothing system?

The solution consists in striking a balance between functional needs (comfort and the counter-measures called for by the microgravity environment) and subjective needs (personal taste and individual satisfaction). The whole clothing system VEST is based on the concept of flexibility so as to answer the project requirements and objectives identified, notably those of comfort or operative efficiency, and wearability.

The inclination of the "human factors specialist" and the industrial designer is to converge on a new form—halfway between design and human sciences—exemplifying growing attention toward users' needs and the emotional value of the products on the one hand, and major involvement in the processes of technical and scientific innovation on the other (Dominoni 2001).

In project development, the industrial designer must therefore take into account the needs of the astronauts, but at the same time, meet the requirements imposed by space agencies, notably NASA and ESA, and find counter-measures for the adverse effects suffered by the crew on-board, owing to microgravity and confinement.

In the aerospace sector, the role of mediation played by industrial design is made all the easier by the participation of the astronauts themselves in recording project briefs and in following checks and experiments. Moreover, the instrumental nature of space products, along with user feedback on design considerations, help determine parameters for the design itself.

To make up for the scant knowledge of the space environment, given the small number of missions carried out thus far and the limited number of recorded experiences, industrial designers must rely on ever more sophisticated electronic and digital systems. These systems make it possible to which makes it possible to anticipate possible results. It is therefore advisable for both the designer and the user to have recourse to well-consolidated schemes, where the designer can operate in a manageable known field regulated by pre-defined conventions, and where the user can feel more self-assured when performing familiar tasks and gestures. To gain credibility with aerospace industries and agencies, the industrial designer must be prepared to submit specific proposals for equipment, specifically in this instance, items of clothing, which should be considered state-of-the-art solutions that have been well tested and proven to be safe. (Here nothing suffices as well as items demonstrated in orbit to be useful and safe.)

If we then wish to analyze the issues of style and aesthetics, astronauts, like most users, are rarely a source of clear ideas. It is indeed the task of industrial designers to create a number of aesthetic solutions with just as many variables, by giving shape to the needs expressed by the users in addition to embodying potential ones in real and usable products.

### Steps Forward

When addressing the issues of style and aesthetics in relation to astronauts' clothing, it is necessary to distinguish between the astronauts' activities carried out on Earth and those carried out in orbit and, in both instances, specify whether they need a variety of clothing both to reflect official situations, for example PR events or communications with Earth, as well as informal situations, for example, routine life and work on-board.

To ask "Do uniforms still have any value?" without specifying whether they are to be used for public or private occasions would lead to but a partial reply, and therefore, useless information in terms of the clothing project.

As far as astronauts are concerned, uniforms may serve three main purposes: they can create team spirit, identify their wearers as belonging to the astronauts' corps, and describe, through badges and pins, both the missions carried out and the qualifications obtained. One should, however, note that uniforms clearly reminiscent of the military tend to be disliked.

Apart from official occasions, when working and living on board, astronauts prefer to wear garments that are not standardized uniforms, so as to avoid the stress of feeling as if they were always on a mission. Privately everybody wants to feel free to affirm his or her identity and dress according to personal tastes. It is also important to point out that the ISS crew consists not only of astronauts, who in some cases have received military training, but also of scientists, researchers, and tourists, who are even less inclined to wear uniforms in their daily on-board activities. It is, however, always necessary for all astronauts to have in their wardrobe an official uniform, along with all the other necessary items of clothing.

Astronauts highlight the importance of style, which should be modern, in the contemporary sense of the word, and futuristic so as to stimulate people's imagination at large; but above all, style should never be pretentious if this means sacrificing functionality. The term "functionality" refers to the parameters of comfort, making for increased operative efficiency, and wearability, but above all, the term refers to those characteristics that, thanks to the innovative features of fibers, fabrics, and finish, ensure thermal stability, immediate antiperspiration relief, and increased overall hygiene.

The study of fabrics, shapes, styles, accessories, and colors aimed at diversifying garments and at providing astronauts wider choices, is essential in improving the level of well being, the quality of life, and on-board social relations. Just as important is the pleasure derived from wearing clothes that do not necessarily smack of military uniforms, but enhance instead the personality and identity of the astronauts. This parameter becomes very important if we consider the confined environment in which the mixed-sex multi-ethnic crews have to live.

The integrated clothing system for space, VEST, must therefore coordinate clothing to the various specific roles of astronauts, while at the same time accounting for new parameters of wearability closely associated with microgravity environments.

Moreover, the need to create items of clothing for specific purposes with the specifications to be universal in style emerged in the course of meetings with the astronauts. These parameters have led to the development of three kinds of clothing utilizing specific garments based on the activities of work, rest, and physical exercise.

Differently colored bands characterize the three kinds of clothing, corresponding to the three above-listed activities. In the first feasibility stage of the integrated clothing project, the colors were chosen at random. However, during the implementation stage, the study will explore in depth the perception and use of color in microgravity environments.

The integrated clothing system VEST will thus highlight the differences in roles among the astronauts while taking into account the new parameters of wearability. Contrary to expectations regarding the formal and aesthetic choices of the integrated clothing system, astronauts feel the need when in orbit to wear clothes not all that dissimilar from those used during training on Earth, so as to facilitate the adjustment of the crew to life on board. We have concluded that recreating a domestic and family environment is the best approach and the one that best meets the user requirements of the ISS clothing system.

The integrated clothing system VEST may therefore consider designing garments both for ground and in-orbit activities tailored to the differences in wearability with respect to environments, without renouncing comfort and aesthetics. The integrated clothing system would additionally keep the current typologies, shades of color, and accessories, and have recourse to the current thermoregulating, anti-perspiration, anti-bacterial, anti-odor, and anti-static treatment for fabrics.

VEST also will consider the role of functionality and its impact on the designing of clothing for astronauts, that is, ascertaining the extent of the impact of the requirements imposed by environmental peculiarities and by NASA itself on the integrated clothing system and, therefore, on its overall aesthetics.

The task of industrial design is, therefore, to translate project requirements into opportunities that can be expressed through aesthetic values. Given this premise, there is value in providing modular flexibility in answer design solution. The whole clothing system of VEST is based on the concept of flexibility so as to respond to project requirements as they are identified. In this context, it is notable that the two that the largest influences have been the design and style of clothing. This can be translated into comfort (operative efficiency) and wearability. For example, the integrated clothing system VEST foresees devices and solutions ensuring that, once the garments have been put on, the adherence and elasticity of sleeves, trouser legs, and around the waist may be adjusted thanks to strings threaded through the single items of clothing, which may be widened or tightened up and secured with Velcro.

This makes it possible to adapt single garments to the changes the body undergoes in conditions of microgravity, be they physiological (fluids tend to shift to the upper part of the body, causing it to swell), morphological (atrophy of the lower limbs and lengthening of the spine), or postural (when in orbit one assumes a neutral semi-curled position). Moreover, the possibility to modify adherence and elasticity in relation to the microgravity environment enables the astronauts to wear the same kind of clothing also on Earth, during training and the preparatory stages of space missions.

## Conclusions

Far from being final, the findings of this study have opened up new vistas and provided questions in need of exploration. Yet we may synthesize our various findings in the following.

Astronauts' dislike for uniforms used on board for non-official occasions is evident in their desire to affirm their identity through clothing. As much as possible, the cultural and ethnic peculiarities of the different crew members should be respected and mirrored in the clothing they wear as well. Obviously, in the European astronauts' corps, differences are not so marked as to call for different garments. The clothing of ESA staff might however be different from that of American, Russian, Japanese, or Canadian personnel (something like the uniforms worn by national teams on the occasion of the Olympic games). But it is more likely that for reasons of image and popular recognition, during public and institutional occasions, it might be decided to create a collection of garments common to all world astronauts as this would in all likelihood lead to the creation of group identity.

It certainly seems that people like a feeling of belonging that clothing can give them, that is belonging to a culture, reference group or "tribe." At the same time, they also like items that reinforce a degree of uniqueness, personal identity and self-worth (Fortunati, Katz, and Riccini 2002).

Issues of self-perception and the perception of others are also considered important in space. What concerns seem to prevail relative to space clothing are not only solutions ensuring functionality and comfort, but also stylistic considerations. The term "functionality" covers parameters of comfort, making for increased operative efficiency and wearability, but above all those characteristics, are the concerns of thermal stability, immediate anti-perspiration relief, and guarantee increased overall hygiene. So-called "intelligent" fabrics are meeting the latter expectations.

Contrary to expectations, in regard to the formal and aesthetic choices of the integrated clothing system, astronauts feel the need when in orbit to wear clothes not all that dissimilar from those used during training on Earth, so as to facilitate their adjustment to life on board.

The study concludes that recreating a domestic and family environment is the best approach and the one best answering the requirements of the users who will make use of the ISS clothing system.

The role of industrial design, in this case, consists in mediating the needs of the user/astronaut with the peculiarities of the space environment, and consequently, considers designing garments both for ground and in-orbit activities, by differentiating wearability relative to the different environments, without renouncing comfort, aesthetics, favorite typologies, shades of color and accessories, while utilizing the current technology of thermoregulating, anti-perspiration, antibacterial, antiodor and antistatic treatment for fabrics.

Finally, by considering the impact of functionality on global aesthetics, one can identify those project requirements that have been adopted owing to the peculiarities of the environment.

The need to improve the crew's comfort and efficiency, to foresee new parameters of wearability, to guarantee thermal stability and personal hygiene, and to ensure the monitoring of the astronauts' vital, biological, and physiological functions are the project requirements adopted to counter the adverse effects of the space environment and to improve living conditions in confined cramped environments under constant physical and mental stress (Connors et al. 1999). As previously mentioned, the task of industrial design is to transform project requirements into opportunities that can be expressed through aesthetic values.

## References

Antonutto, G. and P.E. di Prampero. 1992. *Human Physiology in Microgravity: An Overview.*

Bluth, B. J. 1985. The Social Psychology of Space Travel. *People In Space,* ed. J. E. Katz. New Brunswick, NJ: Transaction Publishers.

Connors, M., A. Harrison, and F. Akins. 1999. *Living Aloft: Human Requirements for Extended Spaceflight,* NASA Ames Research Center, Washington, DC (April 22).

Dominoni, A. 2001. Space Design. *Techne World Wide Magazine* 6, ed. Milan: Medianet.

Fortunati, L., J. E. Katz, and R. Riccini, eds. 2002. *Corpo futuro: Il corpo umano tra tecnologie, communicazione e moda.* Milan: Franco Angeli.

Katz, J. E. 1985. *People in Space.* New Brunswick, NJ: Transaction Publishers.

Wichman, H., Harvey, and S. Donaldson. 1996. Remote Ergonomic Research in Space: SpaceLab Findings and a Proposal. *Aviation, Space, and Environmental Medicine* 67 (2), Alexandria, VA.

# 21

# Piercing, Tattoos, and Branding: Latent and Profound Reasons for Body Manipulations

*Anna Maria Grossi*

This chapter explores the underlying meanings of body manipulation such as tattoos, piercing, and branding. My aim is to explore what I see as the latent significance for youngsters regarding their attraction to the placement and viewing of marks on the skin. This placement, it must be noted in a way that is essential to my argument, can in general only be achieved through the voluntary submission to a painful procedure.

The general theme of this book is "machines that become us." My essay, though, is less directly involved with the mechanical than it is with the process of "becoming" and the quality of "us." Yet, although not central to the more technologically oriented theme of the book, my chapter nonetheless can be related to the theme of machines and the social context of technology in the following way: my exploration deals with the process of people changing their physical appearance, and thus their public persona, in such a way that they signal to themselves and to their friends (as well as to those who are strictly defined to be outside their group of respected and desirable persons, that is, their anti-reference groups). One of the three meanings that the editor has for the phrase "machines that become us" alludes to way in which people use machines and communication devices to portray, alter, and confirm their identity. In this sense, machines are a way of defining ourselves. So too are tattooing and other skin decorations. I would suggest that skin decorations are both throw-backs and throw-forwards. They not only relate and derive from our atavistic past, but allow us to anticipate what the future might hold.

In essence, then, my essay is, in the phrase of Professor Ronald Day, an examination of the use of tattoos as "a mode of technological inscription upon the body" (Day 2002). My supporting framework is based on formulations drawn from the literature in psychoanalysis, philosophy, and from cultural theory.

Ultimately, though, my argument relies largely on an appeal to observing common practice among adolescents in modern Western cultures. Having taught many such youth, I have a degree of familiarity with them. Others may agree or disagree based on their own observations and readings.

I describe this practice using the argumentative poles of proximity and distance, arguing that tattoos represent a unique practice of writing the body into social being via technology applied to the body itself. Through tattoos, the body and technology combine to express a combined public and private meaning. This mode of social appearance of the body has the paradoxical characteristic of expressing the "I" (or ego) in an internal sense and yet despite this private connotation, is also done in a mode of public representation. It also combines both private choices among symbols (though of course heavily guided by reference group ideals) and by using conventionally recognized symbols. As such, it not only calls attention to ways that people may technologically inscribe public space into their bodies (e.g., though inscribed language upon the body), but also in ways that the body may wish to inscribe itself into the public. Hence, I see the public and private connections that people use on their bodies can be extrapolated to a yet-to-be-determined degree to the way that people use machines. Both can be, and increasingly are, used as a method to inscribe bodies. The moreover, the notion of tattooing can be associated with a prediction of how the futuristic devices with fashion and function components may be integrated onto and into our flesh (Day 2002).

Ultimately, then, these inscriptions are generators of meaning and significance, created and propagated by individuals. In a sense, they give the body the appearance of speaking. Although the term "voice" is doubtless over-used, it is germane here. For certainly these decorative and interpretive elements tend to lend a voice to the body's original and archetypal representation. In prehistoric times, it would seem clear that such body decorations were important, and certainly they continue to be so in premodern (and contemporary) societies.

We can refer to the I-skin, or the ego-skin, first defined by Didier Anzieu. This reference is to an attempt at defining one's own identity as personalized and distinguished; an attempt by the body to free itself from those techno structures of which language and fashion are two prime examples (Anzieu 1985).

However tattooing, piercing, or other inscriptions executed, for instance, on the scalp, still reflect the fashion system whose strength can drive people to extremes of sacrifice, on the physical and fiscal levels, and even to the extent of sacrificing one's life. Yet, short of these extremes, other forms predominate of what could better be termed investments in oneself and ones' niche. (It is perhaps worth pointing out that "investments" is also a play on words in the Romance language-derived terms vestments, vests, and the like).

Nothing is less permanent than what is commonly considered fashionable, yet for many, the preoccupation with fashion and being fashionable is a permanent condition (Katz and Sugiyama 2002). "Fashion does not push anything away, it offers itself to both those who escape obsessive repetition, and those who are looking for it because they are following a dream of identity" (Galimberti 1983; translation by chapter author). Certain also is the fact that this fashion plays with the hottest and most serious theme in human existence, the theme of identity, of "who am I?" (Skog 2002). Fashion is a game and representation of what one dare not be, is not capable of being, or will dramatically become. According to this view, piercing and tattooing would also offer a defense against the anguish of separation and of being different, typical of adolescence and of a possible failure in one's own social birth. The recourse to ferocious and indelible manipulations would be able, according to G. P. Charmet (2000), to placate the anguish that originates from the perception of one's own social invisibility in a society no longer able to organize reactions of jubilation for "new births." "The manipulations indicate a rise in the level of defences compared to the past decades during which manipulating clothes and hair seemed to kids enough to be noted and to try to tell a social tale about themselves" (Charmet 2000).

Body inscription retrieves in adolescents its original meaning, namely a sacred test that snatches bodies and individuals away from their deep relationship with nature; we could talk about permanent and temporary manipulations of the body as "marks of civilization" through which the individual separates himself and his own body from that undetermined origin that is nature, securing on the body the signs of a symbolic order out of which nature transcends, and begins to communicate through, to become an active part of the social body. It is a sort of primordial initiation ritual that presumes the end of an old existence and the beginning of a new; a symbolic death and resurrection that only the pain of flesh can seal.

In a society where the indications of belonging to a role and to a social identity is usually established by clothes and accessories, and which tends to homogenize individuality to the populace (Kaiser 2002), it seems necessary to have an even more distinguished indelible mark. All this would explain the unrelated diffusion of Body Art, which perhaps serves also to demystify the art, thought to be taboo by modern society. The body art ritual in tribal societies has the aim of releasing the latent tension of a threatening desire lived by the entire community; this is however circumscribed to the short-lived circumstances of breaking a taboo, and therefore body art shows its necessarily fleeting and transient character.

A different thing is the disturbing and terse description of body art given by Don De Lillo in his most recent work, *The Body Artist*. The process of the body art itself becomes slow, lean, and painful. The protagonist body artist, Hartke, undergoes a shocking transformation, and even after the few repeats of her performance have ended, she continues to be devastated. Hartke is a body artist who tries to free herself from the body—her own body. "Hartke acts, and during the performance she constantly transforms herself into other male and female characters, she explores deep identities." (De Lillo 2001) Once again, a mark on a body, even though it represents a fleeting moment, takes us back to problems regarding the process of individuation.

Going back to the theme of fear of social invisibility and the awe of "not being," of "not hearing," one resorts to the pain induced by these practices that we remember as ferocious and imposing. A pain with significance; The "I feel, therefore I exist" pronouncement hides the anxiety of not being able to feel the heartbeat of one's own true self, the traces of which one fears having lost. We find analogies of other violent body manipulations during adolescence. The skeleton images of anorexic young girls remind us that there is no difference between the body and itself; in both instances we are confronted by the modifications, which alter the natural state of the body, introducing cultural and symbolic elements.

If we take into consideration Anzieu's thoughts on the concept-theory of I-skin, we can see how he highlights both the internal differentiation of the body surface toward the center (mind-thought, which originates from the body) and the principle of containment, foreseen by Freud in 1895. If we take into consideration the psychophysiology of the skin, it gives us indications of its paradoxical function, where what is paradoxical to the psyche finds part of its support on the skin. The semi-verbal messages of our persona that the skin reveals are then intentionally manipulated in a more or less reversible way. It can become the preferred place to vent aggressiveness and unsolved conflicts, while the signs of the symptoms become apparent. Therefore, mutilations of the skin would then be dramatic attempts to preserve the limits of the body and of the self, to re-establish the feeling of being intact and whole. Many artists expressed their art through their body, thus catching and representing the specific bond between perverse masochism and the skin, even before writers and scholars of the psyche did so.

According to Joni Lomatz, body piercing "allows people to be individuals, and to use their freedom. I also believe it to be a positive form of expression given its non-violent nature and because it transcends all barriers, these being race, religion, age, or profession" (Lomatz 1996; translation by chapter author). Another person with passion for piercing declares that in the short instant when the needle pierces your flesh, you could reach enlightenment about your being.

These manipulations, despite such claims, are of course also signds of subcultural conformity and affiliation. Yet they also serve individual memory: indelible trace dug into the flesh of an existence threatened by confusion with others. So a tattoo becomes both a symbolic barrier that puts limits to the progress of the undetermined, and represents a very personal sentimental journey, which aspires to the uniqueness of one's own consciousness.

According to the investigations of Charmet, it seems that the dilemma to the prescribing and ratifying aspect of this fashion of body art is solved through being able to follow it without becoming part of a crowd of people who appear identical. It would seem that the experience of an adolescent is that of making an alternative and courageous gesture, at once both solitary and against the tide. Here lies the deception of fashion, and its power—the power of recruitment, and the ability to let adolescents use it under the illusion that they have invented it themselves. The same research shows how the grouping function of friends doesn't necessarily determine choices. Manipulating one's own body can be a personal decision, a journey within, in search of the true self. One can trace the effects of an initiation ritual in that the experience might be shared by one's companion with whom one can celebrate it, as well as being the one who guarantees that it happens.

Beyond the choice of the adolescent to get a piercing or a tattoo, no strong motivations or intentions seem to arise; they are not directly at the receiving end of such a message, as in the circumstance of anorexia. Family disapproval and sorrow toward the enduringly marked body persists in the family as parents tend to defend the values of naturalization and, even more so, of family resemblance. Evident are the worries related to hygiene and to possible infections that such acts might involve. It is important to emphasize how in Italy, even now, there is a lack of adequate sanitary control and regulations for operator establishments of body manipulations. It is also possible that in the older generations (at least in Italy) prevail principles of Catholic imprint, according to which incisions and stigmata would disfigure the image of God reflected in the human figure.

Moreover, there would come into play a transformation of the classical principles operated by the monumental Neo-Platonic mediation, which establishes moral superiority of the psyche over the body. As Michel Foucault puts it, "we are inclined to think of the practice of taking care of ourselves as something immoral. . . successors, as we are, to the Christian tradition where self-renunciation is the condition for salvation" (Foucault 1913; translation by chapter author).

It seems undeniable to me that tattooing is an essentially sexual practice and evokes sexual symbols: long, sharp needles, under-skin penetration and the release of a liquid, and the strange union of pleasure and pain. This form of eroticism unravels yearnings of total ecstatic and fetishist possession of the body. The majority of terms in the glossary of piercing presents application to the most intimate points, and piercing of female genitalia is ever more diffused. Other piercings are often in places such as lips, tongue, breasts, and parts of the body clearly related to sexuality.

The adolescents of today spend most of their day in tightly bound to a variety of new communication technologies. These electronic devices affect their eyes, ears, postures, and hands. But most importantly, they affect their minds.

In contrast to agricultural or industrial era, children of the information era spend much of their time in a virtual world, losing their human and physical contacts and context. This is most especially telling in their social life, where people meet and get to know one another, and even revise their identities via mediated technology (Wynn and Katz 2000; takes place in the virtual world of the Internet, which inevitably deprives a relationship of its tactile, bodily, sensory aspects. In this regard, it would seem difficult to imagine anything more distant from the cold, hard dry technological reality than the soft, warm wet processes body manipulation.

We are now witnessing an explosion of interest and utilization of both "polarities," especially in the age group commonly thought of as young—virtual and erasable information on one side, physical and indelible information on the other. It is as if society was developing two parallel but antithetical forms of communication, that see the man and woman of today hovering between the explosion of scientific knowledge, which elude the body, and an atavistic need of the body to reaffirm its existence, its reason, and its truth. Friedrich Nietzsche reflects this sentiment in *Thus Spake Zarathustra*, where he writes, "There is more reason in your body than in your best wisdom" (Nietzsche 1954, 146.) With the power of the machine looming ever larger, and the dessication of physical connection due to virtual dominance ever more commong, I expect the body will also in ever-more pronounced ways to seek its own Nietzschean reason. The body will be increasingly celebrated, modified and, yes, let us say the word, worshipped. What the body can be in terms of decoration and symbolic communication will continue to be explored and exhibilited. The cross-pressures of revolt against the machine and desire to incorporate it will continue. Tattooing and related practices will cointinue to be partial reflections of these mixed messages and feelings. The social sphere will continue its celebration of the body's strong voice (via tattooing and related practices) and its special and intriguing interaction with the graphic and mechanical. The polar worlds of the interior—psychological and physiological, atavistic and adumbratory, spirit and mechanical—will cotinue to be explored and reflected by the themes that appear on the body's surface. machines may disappear inside us, or ride on us in various niches. but for those who know where to look and how to read, the stories will continue to be told on our outsides.

## Acknowledgements

I thank Ron Day for his incisive, instructive comments.

## References

Anzieu, Didier. 1985. *Le Moi-peau*. Paris: Bordas.
Charmet, Pietropolli Gustavo. 2000. *Piercing e Tatuaggio*. Milan: Franco Angeli.
Day, Ronald. 2002. Personal communication, March 26.
De Lillo, Don. 2001. *The Body Artist*. Turin: Einaudi.
Foucault, Michel.1969.*Opere*. Turin: Einaudi.
Galimberti, Umberto.1983. *Il Corpo*. Milan: Feltrinelli.

Kaiser, Susan. 2002. Chapter 18 in Fortunati, L., James E. Katz, and R. Riccini, eds. , *Corpo futuro: Il corpo umano tra tecnologie, communicazione e moda*. Milan: Franco Angeli.

Katz, James and Sugiyama, 2002. Fashion Attentiveness and Fashion Interest: An Empirical Test of a New Scale. Paper presented at the International Communication Assocation annual meeting, July. Seoul, Korea.

Lomatz, Joni. 1996. Piercing e Tattoo. Milan: Tea.

Nietzsche, Friederich. 1954. *Thus Spake Zarathustra: A Book for All and None* (Walter Kaufmann, translator). New York: Modern Library.

Skog, Berit. 2002. Identity. Pages 255-73 in Katz, James E. and M. Aakhus, eds., *Perpetual Contact: Mobile Communication, Private Talk, Public Performance*. Cambridge: Cambridge University Press.

Wynn, Eleanor and James E. Katz. 2001. Teens on the Telephone. *Info*, vol. 2 (4): August 2000, 401-419.

# 22

# "Perhaps It is a Body Part": How the Mobile Phone Became an Organic Part of the Everyday Lives of Finnish Children and Teenagers

*Virpi Oksman and Pirjo Rautiainen*

## Introduction

This chapter investigates young people's relationship to mobile telephony within a cultural and social perspective. Unlike quantitative examinations of telephone behavior (Katz 1999), our emphasis is on ethnographic approaches. We look at the meanings children and their families attribute to the mobile telephone (and other new technologies) and the emotions directed towards them. This line of inquiry complements the social-structural and organizational understandings of the telephone (Katz 2001). The spread of mobile phone use to ever-younger age groups continues in Finland, despite the absence of related marketing targeted at children and their parents. Finland has one of the highest penetration rates of mobile phones in the world (Katz and Aakhus 2002). Currently, 85 percent of Finnish households have at least one operational mobile phone (Nurmela et al. 2000). Young people have been particularly quick to adopt the mobile phone and the Internet into their lives: in fact, according to a study by Pori School of Technology and Economics, 60 percent of children aged nine to twelve own a mobile phone. Among thirteen to sixteen year olds, the figure is close to 90 percent. The phenomenon is by no means exclusively urban: regional differences in the distribution of mobile phones are relatively small in Finland.

Today, parents commonly acquire mobile phones for children aged ten to twelve. According to *City of Helsinki Urban Facts*, in 2000 every third ten year old in the Helsinki area owned a mobile phone. The relationship between chil-

Translated by Hanna Liikala

dren and mobile telephony generates a variety of questions concerning the suitable age to acquire a mobile handset, its effect on child rearing, the use of the mobile phone in schools, and the relationship between the child and the device, to mention but a few. A cultural negotiation conducted by the media, families, and professional educators is currently taking place around the phenomenon.

Mobile phone use expanded to younger age groups in 1997 as new, inexpensive mobile terminals entered the market, and mobile operators introduced more competitive prices for their services. The number of SMS messages sent during the first two months of 1998 was sevenfold greater than the preceding year. The same period saw the number of GSM subscriptions double (Kopomaa 2000, 56). The mobile phone quickly became an everyday appliance for Finnish teenagers.

The Information Society Research Centre at the University of Tampere has been studying the use of the mobile telephone by young Finns since 1997 in co-operation with mobile operator Sonera Mobile Operations and mobile phone manufacturer Nokia Mobile Phones. The National Technology Agency of Finland (Tekes) has been financing the project since 1998. The research project focuses on the mobile culture of under eighteen year olds in Finland.

In Finland, teenagers in particular adopted the mobile phone and developed their own communications culture, where it functions as a useful object in everyday life as well as a tool for constructing and maintaining social networks. The situation is very similar in other Nordic countries: Rich Ling (2001) has studied this aspect in the use of mobile telephony among Norwegian youth. The unreserved, everyday attitude of Finnish teenagers is visible in the fact that children do not refer to their phones as "mobile phones," but use the words *känny* or *kännykkä*, which can be interpreted as meaning "an extension of the hand."

> One of the Nokia owners in my class has now learned to carry the phone attached to his belt. The other is still constantly fiddling with it as if it were a body part, something that he can't detach from his hand. Perhaps it is a body part, at least an extension of a certain part of the body. (seventeen-year-old boy in 1999)

Pasi Mäenpää, who has studied the use of mobile telephones among Finns, points out that the word *kännykkä*, the most common term for mobile phone in current Finnish usage, is an affectionate term that signifies an extension of the hand. The hand is the most important part of the body, one that people use to manipulate their physical environment. The affectionate tone affords the word a sense of intimacy and closeness compared with the outside world (Mäenpää 2000, 147). It is interesting to consider this in relation to the usage in the United States, where the device is most commonly referred to as *cell phone*, a term that derives from call transmission technology and is, as such, much farther from the everyday lives of the users.

*Cultural Approach to Everyday Life and Technology*

Through the use of a methodology often termed as "media ethnography," we have aimed to explore the meanings attributed to mobile communication by children and teenagers. British scholars have used media ethnography to examine different media and communication devices in a socio-cultural context, often with a focus on domestic media environments (Morley 1986; Silverstone and Hirsch 1999). The method also focuses attention on the use of the communication device: it is by using the device in communication situations that the communication habits and meanings of mobile phone use are born. In addition to the user-oriented approach of usability research, the study of the use of mobile telephony in everyday interaction within the social and cultural environment of the user is also valuable.

The main emphasis is on hearing what the children and adolescents themselves have to say: the study is, for the most part, based on qualitative thematic interviews and observation. In the interviews, the researchers aim to gain an understanding of the everyday life and media environment of the participant, and the themes dealt with include matters such as mobile phone purchase and the use and meanings of the mobile phone in the lives of young people.

Since 1997, the researchers have conducted nearly 1,000 interviews for the study. The interviews reflect Finland as a whole, balancing the sample in such a way that the number of participants recruited from each area corresponds to the population of the area in question. The researchers included both rural and urban areas in the study, and the family backgrounds of the participants are socio-economically heterogeneous. The interviews lasted from one to four hours.

Aside from the interviews, various other types of qualitative material were collected: observation in youth events, photographs, text message material, observation diaries written by teens, evaluation of mobile portals and drawings of fantasy mobiles. Since 1998, the research group gathered a collection of 7,500 text messages.

In the years 2000 and 2001, more families enrolled for the research than the research group was able to include in the sample. The people who contacted the research group felt that the question regarding how children's use of mobile telephony touched the everyday lives of their families was important and wanted to reflect upon this matter in the context of their own family: "I saw an advertisement on your research and thought that this is for us."

## Reasons for "Mobile Parenting"

As in other Nordic countries, a high percentage of Finnish women participate in the work force. The number of stepfamilies and one-parent families in relation to nuclear families has increased, according to Statistics Finland. New domestic situations present families with needs connected with organizing everyday life: the mobile phone is, in part, an answer to the demands generated by new family and work cultures.

Parents frequently begin considering purchasing a mobile phone for a child when the child's living environment starts to broaden outside the home: the child begins school and hobbies, and friends become more important. Parents interested in new media and information technology are more likely to purchase a mobile phone for a child, and, having bought a mobile phone for their child, the parents may perceive themselves as pioneers in the use of technology. Parental worry for the child's safety, particularly in an urban environment, constitutes another significant factor in acquiring mobile phones for children, as does single parenthood: the significance of the mobile phone increases when the other parent is not present.

Teenagers' and parents' motivations for mobile phone purchase frequently differ. As parents see it, a young person's mobile handset is acquired for safety or security reasons or in order to improve the teen's accessibility to parents. Teens may use the accessibility argument themselves when negotiating the purchase with parents, though the actual reason for wanting a mobile handset is often the desire to keep in touch with friends. In the case of children, however, the purchase is in most cases initiated by the parents, and the child usually does not participate in the purchase decision.

Many factors influence children's adoption of mobile telephony. An important factor in this is the social network in regards to the family, as children mainly use the mobile phone to contact or to be contacted by their family. The child's degree of interest in the activities of child culture, such as playing and games out of doors and outside the home, also affects their interest in the use of the mobile phone. Parents also consider aspects connected with developmental psychology, such as the development of cognitive and motor skills, when purchasing a mobile phone for a child. Parents may explain the mobile phone purchase by attributing psychological maturity to the child. Generally speaking, the prevalent attitudes in society and the life situation of the parents affect the purchase.

Children frequently describe the mobile purchase as an event with an element of surprise in it. "Mom and dad just gave it to me" (eight-year-old girl). "It was a bit surprising really, dad just came in and said here's a mobile for you" (nine-year-old girl). Actual communication through the mobile phone between children and parents is not significant in quantity: the families value the connection afforded by mobile telephony:

> I really like being able to reach him, if at six o'clock I start to think, well, where is he? That's a really good thing. It makes me feel really insecure when I notice that the phone is lying on the kitchen table, and he's away for several hours. I get a feeling that the connection to that child has been cut somehow. How do I know where he is? Then I start calling his friends about if they've seen him. It does bring a certain sense of security. (Mother of eight-year-old boy in 2000)

After purchasing a mobile phone for their child, parents frequently view "mobile parenting" as a positive phenomenon and associate it with skills in organizing everyday life and caring for children. According to Timo Kopomaa (2000, 123–124), who has studied the Finns' use of mobile telephony, the mobile phone is often associated with efficiency in both time management and managing of social relationships, and it is used as a tool to maximize efficiency and utility. The mobile phone has contributed to the reorganization of work and leisure.

Some parents may also consider it their duty to raise their children to become "mobile citizens," as they believe that mastering the use of new communication technologies serves to spare their children from social exclusion and enhances their acceptance as full-fledged members of the information society.

## A Toy or an Article of Utility?

The wider the phenomenon has spread among Finnish teenagers, the more varied the attitudes to the device have become, and the more differentiated and specific the different user profiles have evolved. When in 1997 the mobile phone began its proliferation among Finnish teenagers, the mobile device still possessed some value as an indication of status. The make, model, and price of the handset mattered. Boys especially emphasized this aspect of the mobile phone, and it was important for them to carry the phone so that it was visible to others. Boys generally carried their phones attached to their waist with belt clips. It is worth noticing that girls usually carried their mobile phones in their bags or pockets. Girls also stressed in the interviews that for them, being aware of the phone was enough and that boys wanted to keep their phone where other people could see it. At the time, the mobile phone constituted a popular subject of discussion.

— Have you talked about mobiles in school?

— Among boys in general, it's probably the most talked about subject at the moment, the mobile. (Fifteen-year-old boy in 1997)

During the pilot study in 1997, teenagers' attitudes towards their mobile phones were respectful and cautious. They were careful to use their mobiles in the "correct" way. The object still retained the element of status: the mobile handset was a valued item in itself, enhancing the individuality of its owner without further personalization. Little by little, teens began to think of their mobile phones as consumer goods.

At the end of the first wave of proliferation between 1997 and 1998, parents began to acquire mobile phones for children under the age of twelve. The statements of the interviewees reflected appreciation of the mobile terminal: the parents found it necessary to clarify to their children that the mobile handset was not a toy but a real telephone, a device that was to be handled with responsibility.

— First I thought it was a toy, and then my mom told me it's not something to play with, it's a phone. I didn't understand that at first and I started to play with it. I imagined that it was a shark. That this one person came into the water, and it was a shark.

— How did you learn that it was not a toy?

— When Mom told me for the second time that it's not something to play with, that it's an ordinary phone. (Five-year-old girl in 1999)

— She would carry it round and play with it in the beginning, but then we came to an agreement that it's not a toy. So she understood completely that you're not to play with mobiles. (Mother in 1999; five-year-old Anna has had a mobile since 1998)

Particularly during the early years of the study, the teenaged informants made frequent comparisons between mobile phones and virtual pets, the tamagotchis. This can be seen as one example of the humanizing of the mobile phone that continues to take place among young people. Teenagers' perception of the mobile phone as a living thing is related to their tendency to see the mobile phone as symbolically representing the friends they contact through the device. The central position of the mobile phone in their lives is also connected with the animistic perception of the mobile. Humanizing the mobile phone was evident both in rhetoric and in emotional reactions directed towards the device.

The antenna of my mobile broke, and I freaked out completely and didn't know if I could do anything with it. I kept thinking: "Mobile, please forgive me!" The next day I just went out and got a new antenna. (Sixteen-year old girl)

In 2000, the mobile phone was no longer a new object in the everyday life of children: they had gotten used to the phones after seeing their parents and other people use them. Stressing the fact that mobile phones are not to be played with was no longer considered necessary in the families that had purchased mobile phones for children.

The incorporation of mobile phone use into the routines of teens' everyday life was evident in the interviews conducted in 2000. The common view of the teens taking the ubiquitous presence of their mobiles for granted was well illustrated in a statement where the mobile phone is compared to personal commodities that are carried everywhere without a second thought: "Your mobile is like your shoes." The unaffected attitude is evident in a citation where a seventeen-year old boy speaks of his typical day of mobile phone use:

You could say my mobile phone day starts in the evening as I set my phone's alarm to wake me at seven o'clock, usually. In the morning I wake up and turn off the alarm and check if I've got any messages. In school the sound is off. Sometimes I may have got some messages or calls from my parents or somewhere. I check them. And call them back. In the afternoon I have the sound on. That's when I get most of my calls and messages. For instance, someone may ask where I am at some point: if a friend's downtown, they may ask if I could see them. Then if Mom, Dad, or my sister needs to talk to me, they call and things like that. (Seventeen-year-old boy in 2000)

The many uses of the mobile phone were visible in the citation: the device functions as a useful object of everyday life as well as a versatile communication device. Teenagers' mobile communication centers on the maintenance of social networks and establishing of new relations.

## Defining Personal Space

The mobile phone is used to define borders and to open up new dimensions in relationships with parents and friends. As an object or being, the mobile phone reflects the self of the owner, its boundaries and how they are opened or closed from others (see Mäenpää 2000, 147). For the young, a significant function of the mobile phone lies in uniting circles of friends, but mobile phone use also affords a possibility to explore new relations. The definition of boundaries works both ways: both parents and children may establish rules on how to realize communications between family members. On the one hand, a teenaged boy may order his mother not to contact him in the evenings except via SMS, but on the other hand, parents may make it a rule that children should always answer their phone when "home" is calling. Teens have said that the mobile phone has increased freedom in their relationships with their parents, as after the purchase of the mobile phone, parents do not monitor their comings and goings as strictly as they may have before.

> The mobile's increased it [my freedom] a lot. After confirmation [age fifteen], they were asking quite a lot about where I was going and who with, but now when I leave home they don't ask anything, they just call if they want to know when I'm coming home. (Seventeen-year-old girl)

When spending time with friends, the young usually wish to limit parental contacts, whether for the purpose of controlling their actions or merely caring about them. They often find parental contacts irritating even though they understand the reasons behind them. However, being able to reach teens via the mobile phone also adds to parents' means to control their children.

Independent controlling of costs generated by mobile telephony may also enhance the independence of a teenager: paying one's own bill is considered a sign of independence, as it denies parents the right to interfere with the use of the device. In general, ownership of a mobile phone affords independence and freedom. Keeping the contents of the communication private is important for teens: a young person may be insulted if parents take the liberty of checking the messages in their mobile phone.

## Pragmatic vs. Expressive Relationship

In the winter of 1999, services connected with personalizing the device started to become increasingly common. First, it became possible to order logos for the screen of the mobile phone, and then ringing tones also became available. As the phones owned by teenagers increased in number, teenagers became large-scale consumers of services designed to personalize the phone. The appearance of the mobile phone served to express belonging to a certain group or to accentuate the individual style of the user. A metal fan ordered a logo with the name of the band Metallica, as well as selecting a song by her favorite group for her ringing tone. She also opted for a lightning motif for the cover of her mobile. A trend-conscious hiphopper made entirely different choices.

After several years of using their mobile phones, many have altered their attitudes to the device. The status symbol of the early days has become merely a tool for organizing everyday life, a natural part of life that teens no longer discuss with as much enthusiasm as when the mobile device still possessed the charm of novelty:

— What do you talk about when you talk about mobiles?

— Well, it used to be, when it was still a pretty new thing, it used to be quite a lot about different features. Now it's so common, everyone has one. People don't talk about them that much anymore. (Fifteen-year-old boy in 2000)

The attitude of some teenagers to their mobile phone is very practical. They stress the value of the mobile phone as a useful device for managing affairs. Personalizing the device or making it more aesthetic is of no interest to them. Offline use and all kinds of "tinkering" with the phone are equally rare: adolescents of this type are not really interested in mobile games. They emphasize the functional value, the quality, and durability of the mobile device and strive to minimize their bills. They consider the mobile purchase carefully after looking for information on different models and asking about friends' user experiences.

Some teens have what can be described as an expressive-affective relationship to the device. The role of the mobile phone is central in constructing and maintaining their social network. These young people may attribute human qualities to the device and even think of it as their friend: "We are like buddies" (seventeen-year-old boy). The mobile phone's appearance as part of the owner's style is highlighted with teenagers belonging to this group. They stress the aesthetic qualities of the devices: changing mobile covers and ordering logos and ringing tones are common with this type:

— You seem to take an interest in keeping your mobile phone in good shape. What do you think that's about most of all?

— It gives the message that it's important to me. That it's something dear to me and that I treat it like a flower. And also that it's like a tool, something that I work with, so I've invested some money in it. Maybe it's something like that. So everyone can see that it's important for me. (seventeen-year-old boy in 1999)

Another change in the teens' relationship to their mobile phones became evident in 2000. The young would no longer speak of the device itself, but instead focused their interest on logos, ringing tones, and the contents of text messages. Talking about mobiles has thus moved from comparing different models to discussing the various possibilities for personalizing the device. Moreover, Web talk has increased significantly and, to an extent, replaced mobile phone talk. Discussions frequently revolve around themes such as: Where have you got the coolest logo or ringing tone? What's your homepage like?

### Relationship to Technology

For young people, mastering the new communication technologies has become a norm. A seventeen-year-old high-school boy described the importance of remaining up-to-date with technology: "You have to keep up really, if you want to succeed in this world." The attitudes towards technology among teenagers remain gendered, however (see Brosnan and Davidson 1994, 73–78; Håpnes and Rasmussen 2000(a), 241-249, 2000b, p. 237-40; Oksman 1999, 173–186; Oksman and Rautiainen 2001).

Even teens who do not own a mobile phone nearly always know how to use one. They use the mobiles of their friends, parents or siblings. In 2001, resistance to mobile phones on account of moral reasons or on principle was rare among Finnish teenagers. As mobile phones have grown more common, teens have developed a general mobile literacy. Still, many teenagers show signs of technological determinism with regard to new technologies.

— How do you feel about the general development of technology?

— You can't help it; it just keeps on going forward. There are people, of course, older people, they don't have the need for them, they don't have a computer, just an old TV, and that's enough. They don't need it. They live in a different world; they don't live in an information society or where everything has to be shiny and as technological and expensive as possible. (Eighteen-year-old boy)

Though teenagers are accustomed to a deterministic way of thinking about technology, they speak for humane technology. For example, positioning systems and features developed to monitor other people's actions evoke suspicion and fear among teens: they see them as constituting deterministic "heavy" technology imposed from above. They see humane technology as serving the interaction of people and the spontaneous forming of friendships and communities.

Teens direct technology-related fears mainly to computers and the Internet. They perceive mobile communication devices as controllable technology, as consumer goods comparable to household appliances. Some teenagers think that new technologies alienate and isolate people:

It's no wonder about people becoming lazier and lazier when you may as well lie in bed with your mobile and key in all sorts of stuff, you don't have to move or think, just keep on pressing the buttons. (Seventeen-year-old girl)

According to a general view, teenagers are prepared to accept any new technologies as they have been so apt to adopt mobile telephones as an integral part of their lives. It should be remembered, however, that in the midst of the abundance of supply, they are very critical in their decisions as they rate new technologies and select the ones they want to use.

It is also commonly thought that young people follow trends and are automatically fascinated by anything new. Nonetheless, with mobile phones, some teens go for retro style: they appreciate old basic models they perceive as classics. In their opinion, the newest model is not necessarily the trendiest one. This can be seen to constitute a counter-technology of a kind, as the preference of older models stands in opposition to the latest phenomena. Retro teens regard the newest models as un-unique, sometimes even less fashionable than the "classic" ones. Teenagers favor the classic and the simplified, as they seem to contrast from a new consumer culture where commodities are disposable. Apart from the device, the teenagers may become attached to a certain feature in a handset or to a user interface. If radical differences existed between the models, some teenagers could even express dissatisfaction with a new user interface after acquiring a newer model by the same manufacturer. This conveys varying attitudes towards technology. The young have developed a new culture of mobile phone use that, instead of a passive acceptance of a commodity, is based on active selection and sometimes very critical utilization.

## Parents' Use Optimism

A cultural view according to which children are extremely interested in new technologies and become skilled users in a short space of time currently prevails in industrialized Western countries. Parents frequently exaggerate the ease with which children learn to use computers and mobile phones.

> I'm going to be calling kindergarten soon, when I have trouble with the computer, to ask if he could lend me a hand with it. The new generation is going to surpass us in this. (Mother of a six-year-old boy)

Parents often mistake manual dexterity in mobile games and general "tinkering" with the phone as actual communications skills. They frequently mention how their 8-year old is better at using the phone than they are. Leopoldina Fortunati made similar observations when studying the use of the fixed-line phone in Italian families. Parents had not always explained to children how to use the telephone. Children do, however, generally need help in learning to use the telephone (Fortunati 1995, 302).

According to the prevalent cultural view, the use of new technologies will increase in ever-younger age groups. In particular, the age at which the mobile phone is acquired is expected to fall. In 1997, young people generally received their mobiles for confirmation at the age of fifteen. In 2000, the parents anticipated that the age of mobile phone acquisition would go down to the school-starting age of seven. Parents also assumed that special reasons would no longer be necessary to purchase a mobile phone for a child, because they expected the culture to change in the direction that children's mobile phones would come to be seen as everyday appliances:

> In a few years nearly every child starting school at seven will have a mobile phone. Going lower than that makes no sense to me, since I at least am unable to think of any reason why a three-year-old should have a mobile phone when he's playing in the sandbox. (Father of a nine-year-old girl)

After acquiring a mobile phone for a child, parents expect the child to display sensible communication behavior. The child being able to use the mobile phone in a rational manner is a matter of honor to the parents. Parents perceive the smart use of the mobile phone as prudent and generating little cost. A typical description of child's mobile phone use characterizes the communication as economical and functional: "Niko is a very smart mobile user. He doesn't chatter. He says what he called to say and then it's bye-bye" (mother of an eight-year-old boy).

It often became clear in the interviews that children and parents make different interpretations and assessments regarding technology-related skills, their acquisition and the use of technology. The above citations speak of parents' sometimes unrealistic sense of pride deriving from an overly optimistic assessment of the child's skills in using technological appliances. Parents frequently idealize the child's unaffected and unprejudiced attitude to technology and, in general, refrain from commenting on any problems the child may have regarding the use of technology. Children themselves relate difficulties in the use of the new technology sometimes in a remarkably straightforward manner.

## Children's Relationship to the Mobile Phone

Children report occasional problems even in the use of functions that they are most familiar with. Contrary to the views of their parents, children also talk about spending a lot of time learning the functions of the phone:

> I still don't know how to use everything in it. But I've tried. I browsed it a lot, and it took me a couple of years to learn to send text messages and things like that. I just tried things out. (Eleven-year-old girl)

It is not rare for children to perceive the mobile phone games as the most interesting feature in the handset. From the child's perspective, the mobile phone may be seen primarily as a games machine. The communicative features, such as calls and text messages, may be secondary for small children. The relationship between small children and mobile communication is often rather distant, and small children are rarely active participants in the use of mobile telephony in the way teenagers are. Because of their overly optimistic views on children's skills in the use of mobile phones, parents may wonder about the child's communication being largely different to that of adults: "He can call about the most curious things, on the spur of the moment, things that he finds important. Like finding his keys." (Mother of a ten-year-old boy)

The communication of children is tied to the moment and requires immediate feedback. With children, the nonverbal side is also more important than with adults: besides facial expressions and gestures, children use their whole body to deliver their message (see Ling and Helmersen, 2000; Wood 1976, 181–206).

A five-to-ten-year-old child's relationship to the mobile phone may be practical, personifying or imaginative.

*Practical*

Children take an everyday attitude to the device: the existence of the phone is useful for them to be able to contact the parents and vice versa. The child does not have special nicknames for the mobile phone, but refers to it as *känny* or *kännykkä*. The device itself should, in the child's opinion, have the appearance of a telephone: a mobile phone resembling a teddy bear, for instance, would not be appropriate.

— What would you think if the mobile looked like a furry teddy bear?

— I wouldn't like it, it would feel stupid, a furry mobile (contemptuously). It should look like a phone. (Eight-year-old boy)

The child does not personalize or decorate the mobile phone, and the possible color covers, logos and ringing tones have been bought or ordered by the parents. The child's possible enthusiasm for mobile phones has died down quickly. In the everyday life of the child, the mobile phone does not hold the charm of novelty: mobile phones have existed in the child's environment for as long as they can remember. It is not uncommon for children with a pragmatic attitude to mobile phones to forget to take the phone along when visiting a friend, for example.

*Personifying*

The child may attribute a variety of different meanings to the device through pet names such as "Heart," "Cherry," or "Garfield." The child speaks of the mobile as if it were a living being with a body and vital functions. On a more general level, this kind of personifying attitude is referred to by the concept of animism in child psychology (see Hurlock 1978, 332; Piaget 1977, 147, 290–91). For example, the child may describe his or her father's technologically sophisticated handset as "real skinny, a lot more skinny than mine" or may perceive the extended battery of the phone as "a bump on its back." The child may also exhibit nurturing behavior towards the mobile phone, dress it in Barbie clothes or attribute qualities of living beings to it.

— This mobile has terrible hiccups.

— What did you say? Hiccups?

— Bad reception. I call it the hiccups. (Eleven-year-old girl)

In cases like this, the child is more interested in both mobile communication and mobile games than children on average. The child sees the functions of the mobile phone as easy and picks them up quickly.

*Imaginative*

I call it [the mobile] a ringing square sometimes. My friends said to me once: "Your mobile doesn't work." I just told them it doesn't matter; it's just a ringing square. (Eight-year-old girl)

Children may perceive the mobile telephone through their imaginary world, but the idea of mobile telephony may remain distant and the meaning of the device obscure. The child does not decorate or personalize the phone. For the child, the device in itself is too distant or peculiar to arouse an interest or to create an emotional bond. The child has the phone on when told, but does not understand why it should be on at all times. The child may perceive the phone as difficult to use and practicing the use of the device takes a lot of time.

Though children's use of the mobile contains variation, most of the interviewees have adopted a pragmatic attitude to mobile phones. According to Sherry Turkle, even though children nowadays view computers as "just machines," they "continue to attribute psychological properties to them . . . that were previously reserved for people." She goes on to state that "children often use the phrase 'sort of alive' to describe the computer's nature." Turkle points out that that electronic products are "significant actors for provoking a new discourse about aliveness" (Turkle 1998, 319-320).

## The Significance of the Mobile Phone at Different Ages

Discourse about aliveness and personifying the phone is visible particularly among teenagers, and it is connected with the mobile phone's more significant position in their life. Life is divided into periods before and after acquiring a mobile phone, and teens may speak of their "mobile life" denoting the period during which they have been in possession of a mobile handset. The organic nature of young peoples' relationship with the mobile phone is evident in the fact that after getting used to owning a mobile phone, it is very difficult for them to imagine living without one, and leaving the mobile phone at home creates a feeling of lacking some essential part of oneself. In one case, fourteen-year-old girls purchased a mobile phone for their friend after she had had to give hers up after a too large bill, as they considered the mobile phone as essential in their friend's life. In all, the speech of the young with regard to carrying the mobile phone paints a picture of a necessity that is almost organic:

— I've got hooked on it in a way; it would be impossible to give it up now.

— Sometimes when I've left the phone at home, I get this feeling I don't know what to do, I get all paranoid and positive that at that very moment someone's trying to reach me asking me to go someplace. (Seventeen-year old boys in 2000)

When small children were asked about their favorite things, toys surpassed the mobile phone in significance:

— What are your favorite things?

— First there is the Pokemon house and the Pokemon characters that live there. Then there are the Pokemon fluffy toys and third there's the Gameboy and the mobile's fourth. (Seven-year-old girl in 2000)

Hobbies and playing have a central role in the lives of small children. Children are not active subjects in the use of the mobile phone in the same way teenagers are. Around the age of starting school, children start to lose interest in playing with toys, and at the same time realistic thinking increases and animistic thinking decreases (Hurlock 1978, p. 298). Mobile telephones start to become interesting to children between the ages of ten and twelve, when the child's friendship circle expands, and they begin increasingly to take part in hobbies and activities outside the home. The age between 10 and 12 is a significant phase between childhood and teenage. Children of this age, who have also been called "tweenies," show signs of mobile phone fever, but they also start to get interested in online chats, music, popular culture, and fashion. Tweenies' culture of mobile phone use has its own cultural characteristics such as a teasing culture, which is maintained by sending empty text messages and developing new variations of "bomb call" games. A bomb call is made by letting the phone ring for a short time so the receiver does not have time to answer. As the number of the caller is stored in the phone's memory, the identity of the caller is revealed to the recipient. The number of calls made is shown on the screen of the mobile.

While with "tweenies," the use of the mobile phone increases, it still remains below the level of actual teenagers. According to *City of Helsinki Urban Facts*, girls in this age group have more mobile phones than boys. One possible reason for this is that girls develop more rapidly and are generally more sociable and talkative than boys. The mobile is also bought for girls for safety reasons more often than for boys.

**Table 22.1**
Relationship to Mobile Phone According to Age Group in 2000 Among Finnish
Children and Teenagers

| Age | Small child (under 7 yrs) | Child (7–10 yrs) | Pre-teen (10–12 yrs) | Teenager (13–15 yrs) | Pre-adult (16–18 yrs) |
|---|---|---|---|---|---|
| Relationship to the mobile phone | – Relationship is often either indifferent (imaginative) or personifying (animistic). <br> – The device may be interesting but important toys are more significant. <br> -Games as the most interesting feature. | – Attitudes begin to differentiate. The relationship is usually quite pragmatic. <br> – The mobile phone is seen as a games machine. | The age of "mobile fever": the mobile becomes an important appliance, the significance of toys has diminished and the importance of hobbies and friends increases. | – Attitudes to mobile phones differentiated: practical and instrumental for some and expressive and affective for others. <br> – Personalizing and making the device more aesthetic. | -Relationships where the practical and the instrumental side are highlighted become more common. <br> – Offline use decreases. |

## Conclusions

Children and teenagers of different ages attribute different meanings to the mobile phone. For teenagers and "tweenies," the mobile phone has become an important and natural part of everyday life, and the mobile phone functions as a tool in constructing social networks and defining one's space in relation to others (cf. Wynn and Katz 2001). The organic nature of the mobile phone's role in their lives manifests itself in how after acquiring a mobile phone, teenagers find it difficult to imagine life without a mobile handset, and they feel the mobile phone constitutes an important part of themselves. However, teenagers do not comprise a homogeneous user group: there is significant variation in the use of the mobile phone. When studying children's relationship to the mobile phone, one should take into account that children are not little adults or small teenagers but have their own styles of communication as well as their own specific needs and ways of thinking.

## References

Brosnan, M. J. and Davidson, M. J. 1994. *Computerphobia—Is It a Particularly Female Phenomenon?* The Psychologist, 2 (7): 73–78.

Fortunati, L. 1995. *Gli italiani al telefono: Collana di sosiologia.* Milano: Franco Angeli.

Hurlock, E. B. 1978. *Child Development* (6th ed.). New York: McGraw-Hill.

Håpnes, T. and Rasmussen, B. 2000a. New Technology Increasing Old Inequality? In *Women, Work and Computerization: Charting a Course to the Future,* eds. E. Balka and R. Smith, Boston, MA: Kluwer Academic Publishers.

Håpnes, T. and Rasmussen, B. 2000b. Young Girls on the Internet. In *Women, Work and Computerization: Charting a Course to the Future,* eds. E. Balka and R. Smith, Boston, MA: Kluwer.

Katz, James E. 1999. *Connections: Social and Cultural Studies of the Telephone in American Life.* New Brunswick, NJ: Transaction Publishers.

Katz, James E. 2001. The Telephone. *International Encyclopedia of Social Science* (2nd edition). Amsterdam: Elsevier. 2001. Vol. 23, pp. 15558-65.

Katz, James E. and M. Aakhus, eds. 2002. *Perpetual Contact: Mobile Communication, Private Talk, Public Performance.* Cambridge and New York: Cambridge University Press.

Kopomaa, T. 2000. *The City in Your Pocket: Birth of the Mobile Information Society.* Helsinki: Gaudeamus.

Ling, R. 2001. Fashion and the Domestication of the Mobile Telephone among Teens in Norway. (In press).

Ling, R. and Helmersen, P. 2000. "It Must be Necessary, It Has to Cover a Need": The Adoption of Mobile Telephony Among Pre-Adolescents and Adolescents. In *Sosiale konsekvenser av mobiltelefoni: Proceedings fra et seminar om samfunn, barn og mobiltelefoni,* eds. R. Ling and K. Thrane, Telenor FoU N 38.

*Morley, D. 1986.* Family Television: Cultural Power and Domestic Leisure. *London: Comedia Publishing Group.*

Mäenpää, P. 2000. Digitaalisen arjen ituja: Kännykkä ja urbaani elämäntapa (*Seeds of Digital Everyday Life: The Mobile Phone and The Urban Way of Life*). In 2000-luvun elämä: Sosiologisia teorioita vuosituhannen vaihteesta (*Life in the 2000s. Sociological Theories From the Turn of the Millennium*), eds. T. Hoikkala and J. P. Roos, Tampere: Gaudeamus.

*Nurmela, J., R. Heinonen, P. Ollila, and V. Virtanen. 2000.* Matkapuhelin ja tietokone suomalaisten arjessa (*The Mobile Phone and the Computer in the Everyday Life of the Finnish*). 2000/2 Statistics Finland.

Oksman, V. 1999. "Että ei niinku tykkää ollenkaan tietokoneista...on vähän niinku outsider." Tyttöjen tulkintoja tietotekniikasta (*"When You Don't Like Computers at All...It Kind of Makes you an Outsider." Girls' interpretations of ICTs*). In *Tietoyhteiskunta seisakkeella. Teknologia, strategiat ja paikalliset tulkinnat* (*Standpoints of information society. Technology, strategies and local interpretations*), eds. P. Eriksson and M. Vehviläinen, Jyväskylä: SoPhi.

Oksman, V. and P. Rautiainen. 2001. Extension of the Hand: Children's and Teenagers' Relationship with the Mobile Phone in Finland. (In press).

Piaget, J. 1977. *The Essential Piaget,* eds. H. E. Gruber and J. J. Vonéche. New York: Basic Books, Inc., Publishers.

Silverstone, R. and Hirsch, E. 1999. *Consuming Technologies: Media and Information in Domestic Spaces.* New York: Routledge.

Statistics Finland. 2001. World in Figures. http://tilastokeskus.fi/tk/tp/tasku/taskue_vaesto.html

Turkle S. 1998. *The Second Self: Computers and the Human Spirit.* New York: Simon and Schuster.

Turkle, S. 1999. Cyborg Babies And Cy-Dough-Plasm. Ideas about Self and Life in the Culture of Simulation. In *Cyborg Babies: From Techno-Sex to Techno-Tots,* ed. R. Davis-Floyd and J. Dumit, New York: Routledge.

Wood S. B. 1976. *Children and Communication: Verbal and Non-Verbal Language Development.* Englewood Cliffs, NJ: Prentice-Hall.

Wynn, Eleanor and James E. Katz. 2001. Teens on the Telephone. *Info,* vol. 2 (4): August 2000, 401-419.

# Coda

# 23

# Bodies, Machines, and Communication Contexts: What is to Become of Us?

*James E. Katz*

### The President's Theme is Missing

"The Great Society . . . is a place where leisure is a welcome chance to build and reflect, not a feared cause of boredom and restlessness."—*President Lyndon B. Johnson, May 22, 1964, speech outlining his Great Society program*

From the vantage point of today's "overworked American" (Schor 1992), it is difficult to imagine that any period of U.S. history might have been caught in the grip of hysteria over the prospect of excess leisure time. The idea seems farfetched, to say the least, that the President might have felt compelled to use a major national speech to reassure the citizenry that they need not worry about too much time in their schedules.

Today, of course, the concern is about not having enough time to relax. The prospect of leisure seems more distant than ever. Moreover, it is the case that many physicians now urge their patients to take a few minutes each day to simply relax, and professional medical associations have even urged this upon the country and said it should be adopted as a national goal. Books with titles such as *The Overworked American* (Schor, 1992), *Future Shock* (Toffler, 1970), *Faster: The Acceleration of Practically Everything* (Gleick 2000) and *Turn It Off!* (Gordon 2001) top the best-seller lists. So it is hard to imagine that the threat of some enforced leisure would strike fear into the heart of anyone. Rather, under contemporary conditions, the Great Society objective of easing the burden of excess leisure seems nothing less than risible.

Yet at one time the U.S. was abuzz over fears that automation would put everyone out of work. Robots and cybernetic machinery would empty lives of meaning just as surely as they have emptied warehouse and factory floors of people. With millions of IBM's dollars, Harvard University launched, in the 1960s, a massive program to study automation and help people and institutions with the means to deal with the inevitable fallout. Of course, what happened, as they say, is history. The enormous "job envy" that was expected never materialized. Few people face involuntary leisure or, through no choice of their own, sit with empty hours hanging about their shoulders. Rather, a great cottage industry thrives on the opposite: how to tackle efficiently the many tasks that lay before us (see the Caporael and Xie chapter, this volume). The cottage industry includes software tools and seminars, videos and gadgets. They attack not how to fill empty hours but how to empty overflowing "in-baskets" and squeeze maximum productivity out of each minute.

The great historical surprise and perhaps irony has been that the machine generically, and interpersonal communication technology specifically, has not been the ruination of mankind. Not in the narrow and not in the broad sense. Rather, at least insofar as we refer to the narrow or micro-level sense, ICTs have been closer to mankind's salvation than its destruction. In point of fact, unlike the suggestions of President Johnson, it took no massive government program to stave off the prospect of idleness. No, the very tools that were to have enforced idleness – the computer linked to the telephone — have instead led to the crowding out of leisure.

It is worth pausing a moment to inspect the two other major problems that President Johnson outlined in his "Great Society" speech. These two other problems are a necessary counterpoints, to understand some long-forgotten fears of 1960s Americans as they anticipated the problem of automation and excess leisure. "Too much leisure" was at that time a chilling prospect. We can support this claim is to show the magnitude and intractability of the other but by-no-means forgotten issues that that were linked in Johnson's speech.

On the eve of a still greater problem, namely the Vietnam War, President Johnson committed his administration to resolving three problems. One, as we have seen, was too much leisure time. But the other two remain as nettlesome today as they were when thePresident flung down the gauntlet. He said having a Great Society, to which the U.S. should aspire, "demands an end to poverty and racial injustice. He said that his administration was "totally committed" to this objective. He also committed the government to ensuring that all American children would have full and equal access to educational opportunity. These are, of course, hallmarks of good social policy, not only in the United States but everywhwere. Then the president listed a third challenge from which the nation must not shrink: free time!

Underlying President Johnson's concern was then widely held belief that people had no role in the future. This assessment was arrived at by some of the best scientific and engineering minds of the day. Fiction writers such as Ray Bradbury and Kurt Vonnegut, Jr. had delicious fun mocking this dehumanized future, where people's every whim is taken care of except that of a little human contact and social interaction. Yet, anticipated by Thorstein Veblen, a few foresaw a different world, one in which the ever-expanding taste for material goods and the theory of comparative advantage would keep all of us running as fast as we could on a giant squirrel wheel. Indeed, this scenario is the one that has been realized. More people are working longer hours, and feeling that they have less leisure time and more stress. As noted in the introductory chapter, "futurologists" of all stripes like to engage in extreme techno-fantasizing. A casual example may be found in the free-wheeling millennial predictions of scientist Ray Kurzweil. He writes,

> The freeing of the human mind from its severe physical limitations [is] a necessary next step in evolution.... Evolution moves toward greater complexity, elegance, intelligence, beauty, creativity and love. And God has been called all these things, only without any limitation, infinite.... Technological evolution... moves us inexorably closer to becoming like God. And the freeing of our thinking from the severe limitations of our biological form may be regarded as an essential spiritual quest." (Kurzweil 2000)

C. Wright Mills (1958) had a memorable phrase that he used in the context of Cold War theorists which can also be used to characterize the "robots will win" school of thought, which we will more precisely if cumbersomely describe as technologically deterministic ontologists. In the abstract, Mills argued that the mere fact that one could marshal arguments drawn from scientific and quantitative material did not mean that one was right, only that one could impress and silence others. He called this perspective "crackpot realism," and it would seem that the technological extremists might qualify for this moniker.

## Apparatgeist Theory

Crackpot realism, perhaps unsurprisingly given the description we have burdened it with, appears insufficient for the task of grasping the appropriate role of technology and likely directions of social change in the context of new powers of communication. While it is very well to criticize and discount other views, it is far more difficult to provide a serviceable alternative (Katz 1999). Yet in the context of the search for an understanding of the machines that become us, it certainly is worthwhile to look for one. The work of Katz and Aakhus (2002) in the context of mobile phones may offer a useful explanatory framework.

Katz and Aakhus coined the term "Apparatgeist" for their novel theory of the social uses of personal communication technology. They derived the term from apparatus (device; mechanical or social system to achieve human ends) and Geist (mind; consciousness; spirit). One purpose they had in building their theory was to capture the way people think about and describe their personal technology, especially communication devices. Katz and Aakhus use the term to characterize the interaction between social perceptions and folk theories, on the one hand, and social needs and their fit with technology, on the other. They believe this outlook (which they formally specify, in Katz and Aakhus 2002, chapter 19) gives both an interpretive and predictive framework to the changing social role of communication technology.

Clearly (at least to Katz and Aakhus) technology can possibly have any internal or inherent spirit or will. Its existence as an entity is limited to the human mind. Among the consequences of this view is that there cannot be technological determinism of social outcomes. (Still, they do underscore the important social consequences of human decisions about the use of technologies. Moreover, they also stress that limits of technological capabilities create boundaries to human behavior and potential social organizations [Katz 1999].) Yet they also see that human perception can lead to the feeling that the machines have a value, "mind," and separate evolution unto themselves. They seem to have a spirit that can be harnessed by and ultimately integrated with the physical capabilities of an individual, on the one hand, and on the other hand with the individual's social setting, namely the community of relationships, values, and interests.

The Apparatgeist theory emphasizes several dimensions since it seeks to explain the context of communication technology. These include folk theories of devices and mechanical systems as well as socially constructed opinions about mechanical operations and consequences. This theoretical approach, they claim, is a special and perhaps unique contribution to the development of discipline's formal understanding of communication theory. The work of Katz and Aakhus attempts to bridge the historical with the abstract, and the atomistic level of behavior with that of the social system.

The Apparatgeist perspective helps form the basis of what in this volume we have called the "Machines That Become Us" approach to understanding the social context of personal communication technology. Apparatgeist theory brings together diverse strands that can be used to assemble a crude model that in turn can be used to understand the social forces and nuances in the deployment and use of communication technology. As such, it can provide a base from which one can inspect the data and perspectives offered in this volume.

The Apparatgeist perspective directs attention to five areas, each with its own set of existing problems and questions that invite social scientific inspection. These are (1) function and social change; (2) values and sub-cultural norms of use and anti-use; (3) folk theories and life meanings; (4) social uses vs. functional needs; (5) public displays and norms. Although space constraints prohibit detailed elaboration, a brief expansion on the short-hand list may be provided. To wit, first, it helps us understand the functional uses of technological change and their social implications. Second, the Apparatgeist lens can explain why a technology that has certain performance characteristics will be embraced by one group and rejected by another. That is, we have found that people choose a communication technology not necessarily because of its performance characteristics but often because of the social significance of these characteristics. They also reject it for the same reasons. Third, the theory allows us to gain insight into the social meaning that people assign to the technologies which populate their social environment. Fourth, it enables a relative judging of technical versus social functions of a communication device. Finally, the lens can yield an evaluative schematic depiction of a device's social location. Hence, Apparatgeist can help give meaning and perspective on the issues that have been probed in this volume. Assuming acceptance of the Apparatgeist perspective, we can next turn to addressing the core theme explored in this volume.

## Do Machines Become Us?

Based on the human, historical, and actor-based perspective on the social context of technology, we can address central questions of this volume, laid out in the introductory chapter. The title of the book is, Machines That Become Us. We can put it differently and more problematically. Do machines become us? This question has several levels of meanings, as was pointed out in chapter 1: (1) technologies that enable one to be represented to other people or entities; (2) the physically integration of technology in the immediate social sphere and physical environment, even to the point of physical incorporation; and (3) machines as expressions of fashion and reflections of the self.

The phrase also is intentionally playful, partly as an antidote to the doleful tones and tomes of critics of technology and humanity. But, drawing on the essays in this volume, we can answer all three levels of the question as used here in the affirmative. The answer is yes: machines do indeed become us. This positive answer is based on the analysis of the contributors to this book. Yet, it must also be remembered that academics are professional critics. Every cloud, no matter how bright and cheery, it would seem, must for an academic cast a dark shadow and have a caliginous lining. Every positive comment must have a severe reservation or ironic twist. Otherwise we would not be doing our job. And so it is here, no chapter author presents an unalloyed positive view of the machine and human. But the weight of evidence and analysis is clear: people use and enjoy their machines, and find creative ways to advance their interests, social no less than material, through them. Even those who reject many forms of the communication technology find themselves embracing others. What is today's anathema is tomorrow's trustworthy standard. As suggested by the epigraphs in the book's preface, this was as true for Marcel Proust's little friend and as it was for Judy Garland. And so it is for the literally thousands of people observed, surveyed, interviewed, described and analyzed via the various studies in this book.

Let us inspect each of the affirmative answers for the three respective levels of meanings for the question of "do machines become us?"

At the level of the physical relationship between people and their gadgets, we see these devices proliferating in the social environment, among the accountreements, and on the surface and within the human body. The chapters in this volume amply demonstrate there has been enthusiastic uptake of personal communication technology in a variety of countries and groups. Chapter authors Aakhus, Haddon, de Gournay, Rice, Franzen, Vershinskaya, Beckers, Mante, and Rautiainen all provide persuasive evidence at levels ranging from national surveys to detailed observations of an individual's micro-behavior. This includes pre-teens in Finland and the elderly in The Netherlands. It ranges from the poorest classes in the United States to the struggling middle class of Russia. And the variety of devices which are being used in both traditional and novel ways range from the tiny to the tacky, and from outside environment and smart homes to the intimate crevices and crannies of the body. They also include the fabric of clothing and lacunae of backbacks. So, yes, the machine is becoming a physical and social part of us, though as has been made amply evident by studies from China, England, France, Norway, Switzerland, and the U.S., by no stretch can this integration be considered as proceeding in a way that subverts or suppresses the individual's selfhood or identity. (We will return to this theme.)

The second level is the way ICTs are used to represent people in social interaction, and even use machines to interact as their agents with other machines. This, of course, was suggested in the work of Falk and Bjork with the BubbleBadge, and Danese concerning fashion and fabric. In turn, Green, Johnsen, Ling, and Yu also pinpoint precisely some of the ways this process takes place via personal technology. They highlight the social and cultural importance of using technology as cultural representations of the self. Caporael and Xie show some intriguing ways that technology is also important in self-representation, "of the self to the self," as it were.

Finally, but no less importantly, it addresses, as well, their fashion and style aspects. Dominoni, Fortunati, and Grossi show in different domains the way that style and sense of self interpenetrates with communication technology. These include what is worn in the micro-gravity far above the earth's surface, in the most advanced electronic laboratories, and what is worn in the sub-basements of the grubbiest decayed warehouse. They also include the devices that are wired directly into the body as well as those that are embroidered on the clothing that covers it.

By looking at all three levels of the question of communication technology and the social context of users, we are able to gain more comprehensive understanding of the area. The temptation is, of course, to simply explore one level in depth. While this is absolutely valuable and necessary, it must also be complemented by a look across areas to understand their relationships and reciprocal impacts. That is what we have striven for in this inquiry. Further, we have tried to be methodologically broad. Rather than relying exclusively on literary deconstruction and decomposition, we have drawn in this volume on data gathered from thousands of users. Rather than rely exclusively on one country or one group within a culture, we have drawn from circumstances around the world, and widely varying groups within the global contexts of cultural possibilities. Further, we have drawn upon an unusually wide span of age categories, ranging from four year olds to octogenarians. Nor have we been restricted to a few technology enthusiasts, early adopters, or psychologically maladapted individuals. Of course, we certainly drew on these types of individuals. But we have also used random sampling and statistical controls to compensate for the inherent bias that researchers specifically and human generally have whenever they seek information. Significantly, too, we look not only at users, but nonusers, early adopters and late adopters. In something of a breakthrough, we look at dis-adopters, too. The dropout phenomenon which Katz, Aspden, and Rice discovered has gone from something that was attacked as not existing to something of a cause célèbre among anti-globalization cadres (Katz and Aspden 1998; Katz and Rice 2002).

This exploration is important on several levels. One has to do with what is perhaps the most compelling aspect of this inquiry—the evolutionary progress of technology and what it might mean for the teleology and ontology of humanity.

The destiny of the human race is one of our oldest questions. Most religions claim to have an answer, and so too do many social causes, political parties, and philosophical camps. Yet, despite millennia of arguments, ceaseless flows of text, acerbic debate, war, and fervent expressions of faith by untold billions, the answer, for the most part, is still not altogether clear.

Moving from the level of divine plans to silicone circuit drawings, a new perspective has been offered for humanity's ultimate fate. With rising pitch, these visionaries say the human race is ill equipped to keep up with computers and assorted machinery such as robots (e.g., Kurzweil 2000). Humans are destined not for heaven on earth, but history's trash heap. In their stead, behold the computer, *Ecce machina!* It has happened to others before: *Homo neanderthalensis* was supplanted by *Homo sapiens*. Many say that is our destiny too.

*Can you hear John Henry's hammer ring?*

> De cap'n he say, John Henry
> I'm gonna bring dat steam drill round
> I'm gonna bring dat steam drill out on da job
> I'm a gonna whup that steel on down
> John Henry he toll his cap'n
> Lord, a man ain't nothin' but a man
> But a'fore I'd let your steam drill beat me down
> I'm gonna die with a hammer in my hand
>
> — American folk song

The pessimistic view is rampant in the field of communication studies. There are even more dismal views offered by analysts in the fields of literary studies and long-term social forecasting. Yet the essays and data presented in this volume in general do not align with these negative views. The frustration that most people feel is not with their inability to keep up with the plethora of machines and what they might deliver. Nor is it that they will be pushed out of a meaningful job by a computer, although this does happen with sad consequences. (Significantly, though, as Schumpeter highlighted, the consequences for society are sadder still if this does not happen.) Rather, the frustration comes from the inability of the machinery to deliver what users want. Contrary to the great John Henry myth, nobody is a "natural born steel driving man." The "steam drill" in all its successive forms will always be pushing us out of whatever niche we occupy, and drive us into other, new ones.

However, the essays in this volume have tacitly demonstrated something else of great significance: first, there will always be more niches to occupy; second, these new niches often look pretty good. As impressive as the mythical John Henry was, and he and his ilk are certainly and justifiably enduring folk figures, steel driving is not something that all that many people wish to engage in these days. After all, few are nostalgic for, care about, or even perhaps have even heard of, a variety of tasks that once were a source of pride and self-esteem for those who engaged in them. This includes not only driving steel, but lifting 2,200 motors a day on a factory paint line, retrieving the corpses of eloped calves, or, under a sizzling summer sun, hacking volunteer corn out of soybean fields. (All these jobs, incidentally, I have spent part of my life doing. Nowadays my job seems to be complaining about computers, and I am pleased by the change.)

To draw several threads together, this volume has presented evidence on behalf of considering machines becoming us on three levels. They are (1) our representatives at a distance; (2) important parts and reference points in our self-concepts; and (3) meaningful accoutrements to our self-creation and symbolic interpersonal communication. Throughout, they serve both function and fashion purposes.

In sum, we see that there are some compelling points of convergence and divergence with traditional "deep thought" experiments concerning the relationship between people and their machines. Most future visions are that machines will supplant humans. The vision suggested here is that humans will never be vanquished by machines. Machines will always be the servants of humans, representing them in far-distant places, remote times and dangerous locations. They will be forever inside us, as much as the mechanical clock now lives inside our brains and guts. They will always move from external novelty to internal attribute, just as the crutch has become the implanted mechanical hip joint. And they will always be a part of who we are and what we communicate to others. This was true of the pencil tucked behind the ear of a clerk. It is true of mobile businessperson who slings electronic paraphernalia from belts and e-holsters. And it will be true of us in the future when our clothes double as computers and antennae, and that meaningful stare to a special someone across the room will be transferring data at two gigaflops per second. This book is about Machines That Become Us. But even after the many ways of "becoming" that have been explored here, it is, at the end of the road, still us. For some, it is a hopeful exercise that we could somehow shuck our mortal coil, and escape the heavy moral burden of living a life in a world of action. But though our technology can do many things, it cannot reasonably allow us to escape the moral dilemmas of existence. Putting aside the teasing, our machines might be able to save us from disaster, but they cannot save us from ourselves. They can only help us be our selves. Physical work may largely disappear. But the burden of the moral work in a world of choice and action will remain. Machines may become us, but we will never become machines.

## References

Gleick, James. 2000. *Faster: The Acceleration of Practically Everything.* New York: Pantheon.

Gordon, Gil. 2001. *Turn It Off!* New York: Random House.

Katz, James E. 1999. *Connections: Social and Cultural Studies of the Telephone in American Life.* New Brunswick, NJ: Transaction Publishers.

Katz, James E. and Philip Aspden. June 1998, Internet Dropouts: The Invisible Group. *Telecommunications Policy* 22, no. 4/5: 327–339.

Katz, James E. and Ronald E. Rice. 2002. *Social Consequences of Internet Use: Access, Involvement and Expression.* Cambridge, MA: The MIT Press.

Katz, James E. and Mark Aakhus. 2002. *Perpetual Contact: Mobile Communication, Private Talk, Public Performance.* Cambridge: Cambridge University Press.

Kurzweil, Ray. 2000. Live Forever: Uploading the Human Brain, *Psychology Today Online*, Jan. 26. Retrieved April 27, 2002.

Mills, C. Wright. 1958. *The Causes of World War Three.* New York: Simon and Schuster.

Schor, Juliet. 1992. *The Overworked American: The Unexpected Decline of Leisure.* New York: Basic Books.

Toffler, Alvin. 1970. *Future Shock.* New York: Random House.

# About the Editor

*James E. Katz* professor of communication at Rutgers University, is the author, co-author and co-editor of numerous books including *Social Consequences of Internet Use: Access, Involvement and Expression* (with Ronald E. Rice, 2002), *Perpetual Contact: Mobile Communication, Private Talk, Public Performance* (co-edited with Mark Aakhus, 2002), and *Connections: Social and Cultural Studies of the Telephone in American Life* (1999). He holds two patents for telecommunication technology related devices. Before joining the faculty at Rutgers, he was director of social science research at Bellcore. Prof. Katz is frequently interviewed by national and international news outlets about the impact of new communication technology.

# About the Contributors

*Mark A. Aakhus* is assistant professor of communication at Rutgers University. He investigates the design and implementation of new media, and communication formats, and their consequences for the quality of human activities such as learning, decision making, and conflict resolution. James Katz and he co-edited *Perpetual Contact: Mobile Communication, Private Talk, Public Performance*. His published works in international journals address communication, technology, discourse, and disputing processes. He is past co-chair of the National Communication Association's Human Communication and Technology Commission. He earned his PhD from the University of Arizona in communication, with a specialization in Management Information Systems.

*J.J. Beckers* is manager, Competence Centre, Maastricht McLuhan Institute. This is part of the European Centre for Digital Culture, Knowledge Organization and Learning Technology. His job is to focus on (co-)creating innovative, learning and knowledge applications that are specifically of interest to people who work in business. His central aim is to provide users with optimal experiences, and balance the various demands of design, usability, and social environment. Earlier, he worked at the Dutch Ministry of Housing and KPN Research.

*Staffan Bjork* received his Ph.D. in Informatics at Gothenburg University, Sweden in October 2000 for his work on information visualization techniques for small displays. He is the studio manager of the PLAY research studio at the Interactive Institute where also conducts research on interactive narratives, information visualization, and ubiquitous computing. His work has been presented at numerous international conferences, including CHI, UIST, AVI, HUC, ISWC, and InfoVis.

*Linnda Caporael* probes the social psychological and cultural relationships that link human evolutionary history and modern techno-scientific culture. As a scholar in Science and Technology Studies (STS) at Rensselaer Polytechnic Institute, her work has concerned topics such as computer use and social life, gender differences in hands-on tinkering, and evolutionary theory as myth and science.

*Elda Danese* teaches textile design at the Institute of Art in Venice. She has organized some exhibitions, including, in 1998, "Woven Jewels. Jewel Fabrics." She collaborates with the "Center for the Study of Textile and Costume" of Municipal Venetian Museums of Art and History, and in 2000 authored the catalogue of the exhibition "L'arte al telaio. L'arazzeria Scassa dal 1957 ad oggi," Allemandi, Torino - London 2000.

*Chantal deGournay* is a social scientist at the France Telecom R&D Center in Paris. Her department is Uses, Creativity and Ergonomy – UCE. Her academic training has been in sociology, political science and urban planning. Currently her work deals with information technology uses and the relationships between work and private life. Here she focuses on questions about social change in lifestyles. The sharing of tools in domestic space according to gender and age roles, and the regulation of public space are her main interests. Among the communication technologies that command her interest are the mobile phone, corded telephone, answering machine, fax, email, and television.

*Annalisa Dominoni* is an architect and industrial designer. She earned her PhD in Industrial Design at the Milano Polytechnic, where she is currently a lecturer of Industrial Design. She also serves as Head of Research Programs of SpaceLab, the research laboratory in space design at Milan Polytechnic, Italy.

*Jennica Falk* earned her M. Sc. in informatics at Gothenburg University, Sweden in 1999 for her work on a portable interface for awareness of presence. She is now pursuing a PhD degree, also in informatics. Her research interests are in the domain of human-computer interaction with a focus on interface design, particularly on interfaces that take computing beyond the desktop. She is currently residing at MediaLab Europe, Ireland, where she is pursuing ideas for new interfaces for computer games that are distributed into the physical world. Her work has been presented internationally at conferences including, CHI, HUC, ISWC, INTERACT and SIGGRAPH.

*Leopoldina Fortunati* teaches sociology of culture and sociology of organization at the Faculty of Sciences of the Education of the University of Udine. She
is vice-chairperson of COST 269 "User aspects of ICTs." She has conducted
many research projects in the field of gender studies, cultural processes and
communication technologies. Among her recent publications include *The Arcane of Reproduction* (1995), (ed.) *Gli Italiani al telefono* (1995), and (ed.)
*Mediating Bodies* (forthcoming) and (ed.) *Telecomunicando in Europa* (1995).

*Axel Franzen* is with the Institute for Sociology of Bern University, Switzerland. His main interests are the social consequences of new ICTs and the sociology of education. Her work has been based at the University ofSurrey.

*Nicola Green,* originally from New Zealand, now lives in Brixton outside of
London. This diverse and rugged neighborhood is an ideal proving ground for
her research ideas.

*Anna Maria Grossi* is an assistant to the alderman's office for fashion and events
for the City of Milan, Italy. She received her doctorate from the Politechnico
Institute of Milan, and writes frequently about fashion for popular outlets.

*Leslie G. Haddon* specializes in mobile communication technology research at
the London School of Economics. With a doctorate on the development of
home computing, he has for over a decade worked chiefly on the social shaping
and consumption of information and communication technologies (ICTs). EC
projects include the High Level Group of Experts report, telematics projects
and issues of social exclusion (ACTS-FAIR) and the role of users, especially the
disabled and elderly, within ICT development (TIDE).

*Jeroen Heres* is a member of COST working groups and participates in a variety
of EURESCOM projects. He is based in the Netherlands.

*Truls Erik Johnsen* is an ethnologist at the internet-consultancy Mind Norge
AS. His main focus has been on how groups of youngsters use cell-phones in
their daily lives and how this technology transforms the way they understand
their social networks.

*Christian Licoppe* is head of the social and cognitive sciences laboratory at the
France Télécom R&D center. His current interests involve the development of
the uses of mobile telephony and e-commerce from a social science perspective, and the history of science and technology.

*Richard S. Ling,* a sociologist at Telenor's reserarch institute located in Kjeller,
Norway, received his Ph.D. in sociology from the University of Colorado,

Boulder. For the past five years he has worked at Telenor and has been active in researching issues associated with new information technology and society.

*Enid Mante* a sociologist, directed for over a decade the social science analysis section at KPN Research in the Netherlands until 2002. She is now an associate professor at Utrecht University. There she lectures in the School of Governance on organizational change and ICTs.

*Virpi Oksman* studies the way youth use mobile phones in Finland. The research project she participates in is part of the National Technology Agency's technology program Telecommunications-Creating a Global Village (TLX), and it is carried out in cooperation with Sonera Mobile Telephone Services and Nokia Mobile Phones.

*Pirjo Rautiainen* is a project manger at The Information Society Research Centre of the University of Tampere. She has studied the mobile communication of under-eighteen-year-olds since 1997, and prior to that time she did research on American Indians in Wisconsin. Her research on Finnish children and mobiles has relied primarily on qualitative cultural research.

*Ronald E. Rice* is chair of the department of communication at Rutgers University. He has co-authored or co-edited several books, including *The Internet and Health Communication* (2001 with James E. Katz) and *Accessing and Browsing Information and Communication* (2001). His publications have won awards from the American Society for Information Science (ASIS), International Communication Association, and Academy of Management.

*Henk Schmidt* is a professor of psychology at Erasmus University, Rotterdam, the Netherlands, and founding dean of its problem-based psychology curriculum. His areas of interest are learning and memory, and he has published extensively on problem-based learning, memory, and the development of expertise in medicine.

*Zbigniew Smoreda* is a researcher at France Télécom R&D. He is the author of numerous studies, especially concerning sex and gender on the telephone. He is also a member of various COST actions, including 269.

*Tai Hou Tng* is a computer scientist with ethnological inclinations and publications in journals such as *International Journal of Human-Computer Interaction*. Based in Singapore, Tai Hou Tng is a member of Ericsson Cyberlab-Research, serving as Programme Manager, Chinese Applications & Terminals.

*Olga Vershinskaya* is a principal research scientist at ISESP, Russian Academy of Science. She received her Ph.D. in economics and has had advanced training in sociology. She has participated in various international projects, such as "Social protection of vulnerable groups" (TACIS, 1997-1999) and "Public electronic centers for disabled" with Manchester Metropolitan University (1996-1997), and "Family and Information technology" with Sussex University, UK and Berlin Technological University (1991-1992). She is currently participating in the "Programme of Moscow's Move to an Information Society" for the Moscow Duma.

*Bo Xie* is a graduate student in the Science and Technology Studies (STS) program at Rensselaer Polytechnic Institute.

*LiAnne Yu* has her doctorate in anthropology from the University of California, Berkeley and currently is an ethnographer for Point Forward, a San Francisco consultancy.

# Index